west-words

west-words

CELEBRATING WESTERN CANADIAN THEATRE AND PLAYWRITING

EDITED BY moira j. Day

University of Regina   CPRC PRESS

Printed and bound in Canada at Friesens.
The text of this book is printed on 100% post-consumer recycled paper with earth-friendly vegetable-based inks.

Cover and text design: Duncan Campbell, CPRC. Editor for the Press: Donna Grant, CPRC.

Library and Archives Canada Cataloguing in Publication

West-words : celebrating western Candian theatre and playwriting / edited by Moira J. Day.

(Canadian plains proceedings, 0317-6401 ; 39)
Includes bibliographical references and index.
ISBN 978-0-88977-235-9

1. Canadian Drama (English)—Prairie Provinces—History and criticism.
2. Canadian drama (English)—20th century—History and criticism.
3. Canadian drama (English)—21st century—History and criticism.
4. Theater—Prairie Provinces—History—20th century.
5. Theater—Prairie Provinces—History—21st century.
I. Day, Moira Jean, 1953– II. Series: Canadian plains proceedings ; 39

PS8177.5.W48W48 2011   C812'54099712   C2011-902698-8

10   9   8   7   6   5   4   3   2   1

CPRC PRESS

Canadian Plains Research Center Press, University of Regina
Regina, Saskatchewan, Canada, S4S 0A2
TEL: (306) 585-4758 FAX: (306) 585-4699
E-MAIL: canadian.plains@uregina.ca WEB: www.cprcpress.ca

The publication of this book was made possible through the generous support of:
• The University of Saskatchewan Publications Fund
• The Creative Industry Growth and Sustainability program, made possible through funding provided to the Saskatchewan Arts Board by the Government of Saskatchewan through the Ministry of Tourism, Parks, Culture, and Sport

We acknowledge the Government of Canada through the Canada Book Fund for our publishing activities.

Canadian Heritage
Patrimoine canadien

SASKATCHEWAN
ARTS BOARD

MIX
Paper from responsible sources
FSC® C016245
www.fsc.org

contents

MANITOBA

SASKATCHEWAN

ALBERTA

CROSSING REGIONAL BORDERS

Dedicated with love to my family, friends
and teachers, who first taught me the joy of words,
and Kathleen, Domini and Linnet,
who are now catching fire
and taking flight with their own.

Introduction

The relationship between the prairie provinces and the rest of Canada is a complex, ambiguous one, defined by a history of geographical isolation and evolving social, political, and economic tensions. Much of the early visual, performing, and literary art—painting, music, drama, poetry, and fiction—produced by European settlers on the prairies during the closing years of the nineteenth century and opening years of the twentieth tended to define itself strongly in reference to the values and forms of the "old country." Their country of origin, as a personally lived and remembered reality, may have loomed large in the consciousness of the many immigrants arriving in the West directly from Western and Eastern Europe, America, and the British Isles. However, the old country—as a cultural memory tenaciously preserved and handed down from generation to generation—also maintained a strong grip on the hearts and minds of many French- and English-Canadian settlers moving westwards from Québec, Ontario, or Atlantic Canada.

At worst, the new land was either excluded from artistic representation as an unknowable void threatening the familiar, or, if included, transposed so completely into the terms, expectations, and assumptions of the familiar as to become virtually unrecognizable. By contrast, those who valued the frontier precisely because it challenged the limitations of the familiar were more inclined to portray the territories as a utopian alternative to the old order: a place where human beings could shed the corruption, errors, and evils of the past—including a flawed or disappointing past self—in favour of working together to create happier, healthier forms of human community in a simpler, more natural environment. Rendered in sweeping terms of mythic or romantic grandeur, the Canadian Northwest expanded imaginatively to become one of the last great frontiers unspoiled by urbanization and industrialization—an image that often appealed as much to national and international audiences as it did to local boosters.

The paradoxical image of the West as threatening void and burgeoning utopia evolved into a more focused and consistent image—as tough, spare, and gritty—in the tumultuous period between 1914 and 1945. Scorched by two world wars and desiccated by drought and economic depression, this period saw the Prairies, now subdivided politically and geographically into provinces, begin to develop a consciousness of itself as a distinct culture with economic, social, and political parameters of its own. These years also saw the beginning of an indigenous playwriting tradition—largely for community, school, and radio audiences—intent on giving that emerging culture a distinct dramatic voice of its own. The first wave of feminism with its accompanying call for radical social, political, and economic reforms found expression in the early feminist agitation-propaganda plays of the suffrage movement; Marxist and socialist critiques of capitalism were further explored in the dramas of the Workers' Theatre. Still, given the comparatively large rural population of the provinces over those decades, the dominant "folk play" school of playwriting, especially as taught at the Banff School of Fine Arts (now the Banff Centre) between 1937 and 1945, continued to stress the relationship between the human being and the land—whether terrifying or inspirational—as being quintessential to the Western Canadian experience.

With the Depression and war years behind them, the Western provinces became more intent on producing a sophisticated, fully professional theatre to complement a booming urban and industrialized society. The founding of the first regional theatres in the West—the Manitoba Theatre Centre (1958) in Winnipeg, the Globe Theatre (1966) in Regina, Persephone Theatre (1974) in Saskatoon, the Citadel Theatre (1965) in Edmonton, and Theatre Calgary (1968)—represented the start of a dream come true for playwrights who had always hoped that they would one day be able to see their work professionally produced on a mainstage theatre in their own city. However, in the absence of other financial, educational, and institutional support systems for developing new work over the 1950s and 1960s, this promise of professional production implied by the building of these new theatres in the community was to remain for many Western Canadian writers (and, some would argue persuasively, still remains) a dream only partially and sporadically realized, and a hope too often deferred.

Between 1970 and 1990, influenced by both a rising tide of nationalism and regionalism as well as a strong government commitment to arts funding,

Western Canadian playwriting underwent a period of profound change and development that took it well beyond its early romantic, didactic, or folk play beginnings. This revolution tended to be driven by four distinct developments:

- the development of innovative playwriting programs and courses at the university level in Saskatchewan, Manitoba, and Alberta;

- the rapid expansion of professional associations dedicated to supporting and developing playwrights on an ongoing basis, most notably the Manitoba Association of Playwrights (MAP) (1979), the Saskatchewan Playwrights' Centre (SPC) (1982), and the Alberta Playwrights' Network (APN) (1985);

- the development of regional publishing houses in all three prairie provinces, including Coteau in Saskatchewan (1975), NeWest in Alberta (1977), and Blizzard (1988) and Scirocco (1993) in Manitoba, dedicated to bringing Western playwrights to a broader reading/production audience either as a primary mandate or as a significant part of a larger commitment to publish Western Canadian creative writing;

- the development of a Western alternative theatre system mandated to expose the work of Western playwrights to a broader live audience. Significant theatres in the network included Prairie Theatre Exchange (PTE) in Winnipeg (1973), 25th Street Theatre in Saskatoon (1972), Theatre Network (1975) in Edmonton, and Alberta Theatre Projects (ATP) (1972) in Calgary.

Going into the 1990s, the Western Canadian theatre scene experienced a period of severe financial retrenchment in arts and education funding that saw key playwriting programs, publishing houses, and alternative theatres either go under or severely cut back on their programming. Fifteen years later, the challenges of geographical isolation and deepening social, political, and economic tensions continue to exert pressure on Western Canadian playwrights who choose to remain on the Prairies.

At the same time, these have also been significant years of change, adaptation, and revitalization within the community. New theatres and theatre movements have emerged: the growing influence of the Fringe Festival movement, and other festivals for new work attached to established theatres and educational institutions, cannot be underestimated. Older institutions have reassessed and adapted their mandates: the Banff Centre, cradle of the Western Canadian folk play movement in the 1930s, has returned in recent decades to its original mandate for new play development, particularly in the area of musical theatre and opera. New partnerships between the private, government, educational, and professional sectors have been forged to keep production opportunities for new plays alive. In this regard, Calgary's Wagonstage Theatre enters the twenty-first century building not only on a close early-twentieth-century connection between school and community drama on the Prairies and the impressive blossoming of the secondary and post-secondary drama programs and professional Theatre for Young Audiences (TYA) movement of the 1960s and 1970s, but also on new international connections within the local theatre community.

The multiplicity of playwriting voices has also continued to expand. Older mythic, historical, literary, and folk traditions continue to be re-examined in new ways, even as new voices—feminist, gay, First Nations, ethnic—emerge from a Western Canadian society that is becoming progressively multiracial, multicultural and cosmopolitan. Many of the playwrights of the 1960s and 1970s continue to work alongside those of the 1980s and 1990s, as well as the rising generation of the new century, to create an ever deeper, richer, more multi-faceted theatre scene in response to the particular challenges of living and working in Western Canadian time and space.

This collection of essays had its beginnings in May 2007. That spring, the University of Saskatchewan Department of Drama, in conjunction with the Association for Canadian Theatre/Association de la recherche théâtrale au Canada (now the Canadian Association for Theatre Research/Association canadienne de la recherche théâtrale) hosted a national conference called "'West-words' into the 21st Century: Assessing Western Canadian Playwriting at the Millennium." Its intention was to celebrate Western Canadian playwriting—past, present, and future—going into the twenty-first century. Scholars and practitioners alike were invited to consider the meaning of "West-words" in a "multiplicity of meanings and contexts." This included possible explorations into:

- "the words" themselves—the growing body of scripts actually produced by playwrights working in Western Canada: the visions and realities the plays create within, for, and in reaction to their milieu;

- writing "the words"—the playwright—past, established and emerging—in the West: preserving and generating distinctive forms and visions;

- spreading "the words"—publishers, presses, distributors: bridging the gap between writer and reader within and outside of Western Canada;

- making "the words" flesh—dramaturges, directors, actors, and designers: negotiating the play from page to stage before a "live" critical and popular audience;

- assessing "the words"—critics, reviewers, men and women of letters: interpreting the play as written and performed text, social and aesthetic document, for the popular and scholarly audience;

- perpetuating "the words"—theatre companies, co-ops, festivals, play-writing centres, and school and university programs: creating continuity, canons, and traditions amidst the winds of change;

- contextualizing "the words"—Western time and space and beyond: assessing the larger social, economic, geographical, and political realities that shape and are shaped by the writing, performance, and production of "the words."

Twenty-four regional, national, and international scholars and practitioners active in the Western Canadian theatre responded, and read papers or performed work connected with the theme of the conference. (*See* www.ualberta.ca/~normang/WestWords_conf2007.html.) This anthology of eighteen essays represents the perspectives of twenty scholars, playwrights, directors, designers, actors, dramaturges, radio producers, and educators intimately and passionately involved in the Western Canadian theatre and the generation of meaning through the written and oral word.

Our journey begins with an overview of playwriting in Manitoba for the past twenty-five years by award-winning Winnipeg playwright, **Bruce Mc-Manus**. In an immediate sense, he suggests, indigenous playwriting, however brilliant the individual writer, relies strongly on material resources, spaces, and programming whose allocation is often beyond the direct control of the artist. Quoting playwright Alan Williams, he suggests that a city tends to produce the playwrights it feels it needs and deserves. By that measure, Winnipeg—for all its colourful nineteenth-century history as the first major professional theatre centre on the Canadian prairies and its critical twentieth-century importance as the cradle of the regional theatre movement in Canada—has remained remarkably timid and parsimonious in seeing the need to develop its own playwrights. Paradoxically, he suggests, the organizations with the greatest physical resources to support new playwriting are often the least reliable in their actual support of it, subjecting playwrights to frustrating cycles of boom and bust. Even after twenty-five years, he suggests, the main institutions responsible for consistently encouraging and developing new work tend to be artist-run dramaturgical centres, like the invaluable Manitoba Association of Playwrights (MAP), and smaller, alternative companies that have the least money and resources to fund it. The fact that there remains a grassroots desire and need for artists to give theatrical expression to the life and people of that particular place keeps local playwrights there and trying. However, the difficulty in translating that desire into sufficient fiscal and material support continues to make a life lived both in theatre and in Winnipeg a precarious existence.

Katherine Foster Grajewski, long-time resident of Winnipeg and now PhD candidate at the University of Toronto, explores the influence of physical space—and the human, social, and economic meanings attached to it—on theatre programming. When an alternative theatre—in this case Prairie Theatre Exchange (PTE)—moves into a shopping mall to be closer to the heart of the city, how much of its original mandate and operations are affected, for better and for worse, by the other human and commercial expectations associated with "the mall"? Sarasvàti Theatre's founder and artistic director, **Hope McIntyre**, further probes the paradox McManus expresses about the smallest companies often having the biggest commitment to facilitating the need of our communities—and their marginalized members in particular—to express themselves in new theatre while receiving only a fraction of the ongoing financial or physical resources required to develop emerging playwrights and theatre artists beyond a certain point. She also suggests that, even now, it is a paradox affected as much by gender as by geography, and that women playwrights and theatre artists in particular tend to remain on the margins. **Claire Borody**, scholar-practitioner at the University of Winnipeg, explores that paradox further in terms of alternative companies such as Primus, whose original work is more performance- than text-centred. Documenting the brief, but intensely creative, history of the Winnipeg-based collective (1989-1998), Borody discusses the particular challenges to survival faced by companies whose physical, multidisciplinary, collective work puts them at a disadvantage with funding agencies, theatre critics, and scholars still inclined to define theatre primarily as the art of delivering and interpreting the written word. **Glen Nichols** of Mount Allison University asks in his careful, detailed analysis of the plays of Carol Shields whether Shields's reputation as a novelist, combined with the marginalized place of women writers in the theatre, has led some literary critics to dismiss her plays as slighter versions of her novels instead of appreciating them for the complex, multilayered dramas they actually are in performance.

For an overview of Saskatchewan theatre, we turn to **Don Kerr**, who as an editor, publisher, teacher, scholar, and playwright has supported the development of new work in Saskatchewan specifically, and the Prairies in general. Kerr takes us from the early touring era through the development of an indigenous amateur and educational theatre during the 1920s–1940s and then to the flowering of the professional theatre and of playwriting in Saskatchewan—including his own—from the 1960s onward. He pinpoints Saskatchewan's chronic difficulties with funding and physical resources, which have prevented even its main regional theatres from developing into major production plants comparable with those of the Manitoba Theatre Centre (MTC) in Winnipeg, the Citadel Theatre in Edmonton, and Theatre Calgary and Alberta Theatre Projects in Calgary. On the other hand, he credits the distinctive fluidity, generosity, and self-reliance of Saskatchewan's arts and academic community for creating unusual alliances among the community, professional, and academic theatre that allow new work to flourish in a way it might not elsewhere. It is no coincidence that Saskatchewan was home to the first arts board in North America and the first degree-granting theatre department in the British Commonwealth. Kerr particularly highlights the role of drama departments and the Saskatchewan Playwrights Centre in encouraging the development of writers and theatre artists alike. He discusses the role that the regional theatres—the Globe in Regina and Persephone in Saskatoon—have played in producing the work of local playwrights, as well as focusing on the central role that 25th Street Theatre played in developing the lively theatre scene of the 1970s and early 1980s. While mourning the demise in the 1990s of 25th Street as an active production company, he also discusses the new generation of co-ops, rural-centered theatres, and francophone and aboriginal theatres that continue to revitalize theatre in Saskatchewan.

Pam Bustin, actor, teacher, playwright, and long-time affiliate of the Saskatchewan Playwrights Centre, charts the challenges and achievements of the Centre as an artist-run dramaturgical centre devoted to helping playwrights develop their scripts for production elsewhere, within and outside of Saskatchewan—and the particular role that its annual spring festival of new plays has played in accomplishing that. **Louise Forsyth**, professor emerita of the University of Saskatchewan, returns to the situation of the first strong waves of francophone settlers pushing into the western territories of Manitoba, Saskatchewan, and Alberta in the nineteenth and early twentieth centuries and their struggle to retain a separate cultural identity in the face of eroding language and educational rights and the growth of an increasingly large non-francophone population. She discusses the importance of theatre—with its ability to draw a community together to celebrate publicly a shared language, heritage, and history—in preserving both early-twentieth-century and contemporary French Canadian culture on the Prairies. She then focuses on the unique role that Saskatoon's La Troupe du Jour, Saskatchewan's only professional francophone theatre company, has played in keeping Fransaskois culture, language, and playwriting alive in the province. **Alan Long,** a recent graduate of the University of Saskatchewan's interdisciplinary master's program, further elaborates on the important role that the Saskatchewan Native Theatre Company (SNTC) and other experimental Saskatchewan companies such as 25th Street Theatre, Upisasik ("Little") Theatre and SUNTEP theatre have played in countering a dominantly Eurocentric understanding of theatre in Canada that has contributed to the marginalization and invisibility of Aboriginal artists in the past. His interviews with key members of the SNTC ensemble reflect their hopes that the Company will develop into a major training and production centre for Aboriginal artists and playwrights in Saskatchewan. Finally, **Wes Pearce,** stage designer and professor at the University of Regina, discusses the particular challenges of designing the absurdist Prairie Gothic world of Regina playwright Daniel Macdonald in a way that allows the "magic realism" of *MacGregor's Hard Ice Cream and Gas* to work onstage.

Mieko Ouchi, playwright, actor, and filmmaker, introduces us next to Alberta and a bustling, dynamic theatre scene dominated by its two largest cities—Edmonton in the north and Calgary to the south—and by the booms and busts of the oil industry. Surveying the provincial arts scene of the past thirty years, she reflects on how the theatre of the second oil boom of the late 1990s and the first decade of the twenty-first century differs from that of the 1970s. Can artists afford the exploding costs of living and soaring rent for rehearsal and production space? Why is it that, even now, women occupy so few positions of authority as artistic directors? Does Alberta playwriting adequately reflect the realities of a population that is becoming increasingly multicultural and multiracial?

Anne Nothof of NeWest Press in Edmonton and Athabasca University looks at the role that small regional presses can play in disseminating more culturally diverse work to a broader reading audience, while giving the plays of established and emerging regional artists alike a continuing life beyond production. **John Poulsen** of the University of Lethbridge and **Kathleen Foreman** of the University of Calgary look at the role that Wagonstage, Calgary's travelling summer theatre for children, has played in developing performers and playwrights for theatre in southern Alberta through forging a unique, long-term partnership between the University of Calgary, the City of Calgary Recreation Division, and the International Children's Festival. Finally, **Moira Day** of the University of Saskatchewan looks at the interface between life and art in Frank Moher's *Prairie Report,* a 1988 "comedy of ideas" examining the phenomenon of *Alberta Report* (1973–2003) and the rise and fall of a certain kind of populist regionalism that at its height blossomed into a nationalistic movement in its own right.

The volume closes with a final section exploring aspects of regionalism in prairie theatre that cross boundaries of physical and imagined time and space. **Arnd Bohm** of Carleton University explores the implicit feminism in the work of three women playwrights—Bicknell of Saskatchewan and Gowan and Ringwood of Alberta—intent on examining the family farm in crisis during the 1930s. He suggests that, far from being dated, the plays deserve to be examined anew in the context of more contemporary women's scripts—such as Katherine Koller's *The Seed Savers*—which see globalization and genetic engineering as the next significant challenge to the lives of women, men, and children living on the land. **Shelley Scott** of the University of Lethbridge examines Shoshana Sperling's *Finding Regina* as a drama that poignantly captures the ambiguous impact of small-town Alberta and Saskatchewan on the lives of young people and the ways in which "the self that was" continues to shape and influence "the self that is," even when the two are separated by time and distance. By contrast, **Martin Pšenička** of Charles University in the Czech Republic looks at the work of Brian Drader, Vern Thiessen, and Brad Fraser as being symptomatic of new cosmopolitan directions in Western Canadian playwriting that resist traditional definitions of regionalism based on a common experience and appreciation of land. Finally, **Allan Boss** of CBC Alberta and **Kelley Jo Burke** of CBC Saskatchewan discuss audio drama as a form of prairie theatre that dispenses with the boundaries of physical time and space altogether. They examine the ways in which rapidly changing technology has both exploded the traditional radio drama and its audience and opened up new possibilities for listeners and writers alike, possibilities undreamt of when CBC was founded in 1936. "I look forward," Burke concludes, "to its next phase of evolution."

The essays included in this collection suggest that her optimism is shared by Western Canada's writers, scholars, critics, publishers, directors, actors, designers, dramaturges, educators, students, readers, and audiences as Western Canadian theatre moves confidently "west-words" into the twenty-first century.

—Moira Day, University of Saskatchewan
April 2011

ACKNOWLEDGEMENTS

First of all, many thanks to the Canadian Plains Research Center Press. I don't think there is one of us in the collection who has not at some point expressed the deepest gratitude and appreciation for all the hours of work that Brian Mlazgar, the publications manager for CPRC, and editor Donna Grant have put into making this volume happen. Without their enormous patience, encouragement, vision and expertise, and that of others on the CPRC team, this book would never have seen the light of day.

I also owe a debt beyond repaying to the nineteen other writers in the collection who have been the best and bravest of companions throughout the long editing and writing process that began back in 2007: Bruce McManus,

Katherine Foster Grajewski, Hope McIntyre, Claire Borody, Glen Nichols, Don Kerr, Pam Bustin, Louise Forsyth, Alan Long, Wes Pearce, Mieko Ouchi, Anne Nothof, John Poulsen, Kathleen Foreman, Arnd Bohm, Shelley Scott, Martin Pšenička, Allan Boss and Kelley Jo Burke. Your brilliance is exceeded only by your dedication and perseverance.

My thanks as well, to everyone who participated in the original "'West-words' into the 21st Century: Assessing Western Canadian Playwriting at the Millennium" conference in 2007, and helped make it a success. To the sponsors of the event: The University of Saskatchewan Department of Drama and the Canadian Association for Theatre Research (CATR) for providing space, resources, help, and encouragement. To the Canada Council and University of Saskatchewan for additional speaker and conference funding. To the Saskatchewan Playwrights Centre who generously agreed to hold their annual spring festival of new Saskatchewan plays in conjunction with the conference, and to Jennifer Wynne Webber, Pam Bustin, Ben Henderson, and Michael Clark in particular for donating their expertise to panels, sessions and staged readings at the conference. To William Kerr for an insightful paper on the puppet theatre of Ronny Burkett. To playwright Ken Mitchell for donating a paper on cowboy poetry as well as a performance of his new play, *No Ordinary Cowboy*, about pioneering cowboy and rodeo icon Bill Gomersall. To Allan Boss for his reading of his one-act play, *Swimming with Goldfish*, as well as his paper on audiodrama with Kelley Jo Burke. To playwright Katherine Koller, who agreed to do the first public staged reading of her new play, *The Seedsavers*, at the Conference, and to Hope McIntyre, Bruce McManus, Don Kerr and Mieko Ouchi, who also shared public readings of their work as part of the conference. To the extent that this book grew out of that conference, and the CATR conference that followed, these people, too, have made an indelible mark on "the words" of the book.

Beyond that, the thanks of all of us to the many generations of writers, critics, publishers and practitioners—past, present and to come—who have managed to set the prairie to "words" and play them out in theatre performance, production, playwriting, and publishing, giving us indeed something to celebrate.

And last but not least, my never-ending gratitude and thanks to my family and friends for their continuing patience and support—and to Norman, Kathleen, Domini and Linnet, and my mother-in-law, Frances Gee in particular. Their love and generosity are also entwined into every word here.

MANITOBA

A Playwright's View of
Twenty-Five Years of Manitoba Theatre

BRUCE MCMANUS

I n general, art follows money. If you want your work exhibited, produced, and somehow paid for, it's likely you must gravitate to the great Canadian cities that have money. The artist seeks a congenial, cosmopolitan, stimulating environment that is inexpensive. Manitoba, and particularly Winnipeg, has enough of the former—many theatres, an opera, a ballet, a symphony, tens of galleries—and plenty of the latter: you can live cheaply, in any language, in your own home and, if you're lucky, your own home and cottage, for a tenth of the cost of Vancouver or Toronto. You can go to an opening, a launch, a concert, a performance every night of the year. Or stay home and work.

That is an advantage for artists in Manitoba and it is one of the reasons we have a small, but flourishing, theatre community.

I was asked to speak about Manitoba theatre, from the past through to the future. That is an impossibly big topic to deal with in ten minutes, so I will concentrate on what I know best: the history of the relationship between the institutions in theatre—mainly the producing bodies—and playwrights in Manitoba.

This is not a comprehensive survey. There are so many playwrights and theatre practitioners involved in the development of Manitoba theatre that I simply can't mention everybody, or even know the who, what, when, where, and why of my own theatre culture. For instance, I won't speak about Cercle Molière, a very important Manitoba theatre producing in French. I write in

3

English and I have no personal experience of the theatre.[1] I also cannot speak about Rainbow Stage, a venerable summer musical theatre. To my knowledge, they have never produced a new work. Further, I claim no objectivity in my presentation. I am an advocate for the playwright and for the Manitoba playwright. I have no critical observations of the work that has been done or that will be done. Instead, I offer a personal history of the development of English-speaking theatre in Manitoba from a playwright's perspective.

Looking at the past, I rely heavily on Rory Runnells, coordinator of the Manitoba Association of Playwrights (MAP); his introduction to *A Map of the Senses, Twenty Years of Manitoba Plays* (2000) is an excellent, comprehensive short history of Manitoba playwriting. The major institutional foundations of theatre in Manitoba include the Manitoba Theatre Centre (1958),[2] Manitoba Theatre for Young People (1965), and the Manitoba Theatre Workshop (1973), which became Prairie Theatre Exchange in 1981. They also include the drama departments at the University of Winnipeg (1966) and the University of Manitoba (1966), as well as the Manitoba Association of Playwrights (1979). These are the most significant and largest institutions in our environment. Two small theatres, Agassiz (1980) and Popular Theatre Alliance (1986), were critically important in the production of new work, but they are long gone. The last remaining small theatre, Theatre Projects Manitoba (1990), has survived to this day, contributing to the development of new work despite a precarious existence threatened with death every funding season.

Before these existing and deceased producing organizations were established, grew, and thrived, there was a vital theatre community in Winnipeg featuring

1   Editor's note regarding francophone theatres in the West: Manitoba's Le Cercle Molière (1925) is the "oldest permanent theatre company with uninterrupted programming in Canada" (*The Canadian Encyclopedia* online: www.thecanadianencyclopedia.com/index.cfm?PgNm=TCE&Params=A1ARTA0009120). As Rory Runnells points out in his introduction to *A Map of the Senses*, even as the Manitoba Association of Playwrights was being founded in 1979, Le Cercle Molière was already the centre of an active playwriting community in the province—in French. But, as Runnells further notes, the "two solitudes" were in existence then and have persisted, so that "what the bigger community could have taken from the energy of Le Cercle's home-grown playwriting never took place" (*Map of the Senses*, 9). In Alberta, L'Unithéâtre, the province's only professional francophone theatre company, was founded in Edmonton in 1992. For more information on La Troupe du Jour, Saskatchewan's only professional francophone theatre company, established in Saskatoon in 1985, see Louise Forsyth's "Creating Francophone Theatre in Saskatchewan" in this volume.

2   All dates in parentheses after theatres or institutions, unless otherwise designated, refer to their founding dates.

people that included John Hirsch and Tom Hendry and later, their creation, the Manitoba Theatre Centre (MTC). John and his colleagues all left Winnipeg, and for a long time MTC and the local community were forced to look outside the province's borders for theatre actors, designers, directors, and playwrights.

This barren period for local theatre creators extended through the sixties and most of the seventies. As a result, notes Rory Runnells quoting Doug Arrell of the University of Winnipeg, "we missed out on the wave of nationalist fervour and populist energy that transformed the theatre scene across the rest of the country" (2000, 10). With respect to that time, playwright Carol Bolt from Toronto once jokingly told me that if she could finish a play on Thursday there was a good chance they would start rehearsals the following Tuesday, Monday being a dark day. New Canadian work was considered exciting and important elsewhere in Canada, but not in Manitoba.

I was a latecomer to theatre and a relative latecomer to the Manitoba theatre scene. I didn't write a play until I was almost thirty, in about 1980, but I was early enough in the development of local Manitoba theatre to experience most of the significant events and developments in Manitoba playwriting.

At that time, our situation in Manitoba as writers for theatre seemed to be political and adversarial. Every play written, every production of new work mounted, seemed to arise from a struggle with a negligent, uninterested theatre establishment. We felt we weren't wanted, we weren't needed, and perhaps we weren't good enough. The last may have been true, but we wanted that assertion tested. No one was going to walk away without being on stage.

I seem to recall that, in the past, I was attending meetings twice a week to voice—belligerently, aggressively voice—my disapproval of arts funding policy, theatre policy, or some indignity to the playwriting community. I was in a near-perpetual state of readiness for some kind of struggle. This is a condition that is difficult to get rid of, and I am part of the generation of Manitoba playwrights who is vigilant, overly vigilant, to any slight to the Manitoba theatre community, or to the next development that will reduce the playwright's participation in Manitoba theatre.

We *did* miss that explosion of indigenous creation in the seventies. But then, in the eighties, Richard Ouzounian took over as artistic director at Manitoba Theatre Centre (serving from 1980 to 1984) and produced three plays by Winnipeg playwright Alf Silver.[3] Three in a row. Well, I was a novice, and I thought, *That's the way it happens: an artistic director likes your work and produces it—bang bang bang.* At the time, it was very encouraging to the few of

---

3   *Thimblerig* (1982), *Climate of the Times* (1983), and *Clearances* (1984).

us writing theatre in Winnipeg. However, after that binge, it was another ten or twelve years before MTC produced another Manitoba playwright.

Then Kim McCaw came to Prairie Theatre Exchange (PTE) in 1983, and he produced many Canadian plays and plays by Manitoba writers. That's what he wanted to do, what he was good at. He liked writers and he didn't treat us as though we were a necessary inconvenience on his personal road to becoming a theatrical legend. He was so good to me personally that I was disarmed in my subsequent dealings with other artistic directors, some of whom did not care for writers or new work, especially new work by new writers.

During those same years (the 1980s), Agassiz Theatre produced two or three Manitoba plays. The university theatre departments expanded and produced actors and directors, designers and writers. Things looked very promising. Not too long afterwards, Popular Theatre Alliance came along, doing mainly political plays and some new work. We had a little boom.

Then, in 1991, Kim McCaw left Prairie Theatre Exchange. There was a bit of a break in the participation of the producing bodies in developing and staging new plays. PTE still produced new work, and some very good work, under McCaw's successor, Michael Springate (1991–1995). For some reason, however, this did not work in terms of long-term playwright and play development; most importantly, it did not work as part of PTE's financial well-being. Audiences fell away.

Then Agassiz Theatre died in 1988. Popular Theatre Alliance remained active but, underfunded and starved, it, too, finally died in 1998. Prairie Theatre Exchange was undergoing change: new artistic directors came from away, and their seasons tended to focus more on international and Canadian plays. Manitoba Theatre Centre was absent in the development and production of new work. So we playwrights suffered another series of disappointments after the brief period of exhilaration and optimism in the eighties.

Through all of these stock market-like cycles of boom and bust, we had the Manitoba Association of Playwrights (MAP), a precarious but solid piece of debris in the oceanic turmoil of theatre. We playwrights clung to it. Without MAP there would be few, if any, writers for theatre in Manitoba. From my point of view, if you are a playwright, you can't count on theatres for sustenance or nurturing.

The Manitoba Association of Playwrights, our friend, is a well-established playwrights centre. Almost thirty years old, it has had only one coordinator, Rory Runnells, who came to the organization in 1983. He is a brilliant, dedicated writer, a loving man who is passionate and knowledgeable about theatre. Rory and MAP have kept playwriting alive in Winnipeg. Among other things, he recruited British playwright Alan Williams as a visiting playwright/dramaturge at MAP.[4]

---

4   Alan Williams, who was born in England and emigrated to Canada in 1983, contin-
     ues to work as an actor and playwright on both sides of the Atlantic. The author of

Alan was not only a produced playwright and an actor; he was also someone with sympathy for the development of the writer. He contributed significantly to theatre writing in Manitoba.

In preparing this piece, I wrote to Alan Williams, asking for his comments about these developing years, about his experience in Winnipeg, and about the development of plays and production. Of his own experience in England, he wrote:

> I'm from Manchester. And I was struck at that time by the way that in Liverpool, which is a town of the same size, about thirty-five miles away—essentially the same town, really—there were a number of playwrights writing in an avowedly local style who were doing exceptionally well—while in Manchester there was nothing, nobody. Such local playwrights as there might be—well, I guess I was one—had to leave to work.

Why the difference between the two towns? It didn't "make any sense to assume there was just some lack in the gene pool, some innate inability of local people to write plays." In fact, the dearth of playwriting in contemporary Manchester seemed all the more absurd to him, given the fact that "Manchester had been the site of a regional theatre boom in the early part of the twentieth century, when Miss Horniman had encouraged playwriting" by staging local work with her repertory company at the Gaiety Theatre in Manchester—Harold Brighouse's *Hobson's Choice* being the best-known play from the period. He concluded that perhaps the critical difference was that contemporary Liverpool now had theatres that were actively encouraging local playwriting, while Manchester did not:

> The difference seemed to me to originate from the theatre man-agements. [...] What had happened was that in Liverpool, the Everyman Theatre had, under, I think, the artistic directorship of Peter James, started to operate under the assumption that there would be worthwhile playwrights in the town, and that it was their job to find them—whereas the equivalent theatres in Manchester had taken the line that if there were any worthwhile playwrights in Manchester they would somehow naturally rise to the top

nine plays, he adapted his best-known work, *The Cockroach Trilogy*—*The Cockroach that Ate Cincinnati* (1979), *The Return of the Cockroach* (1981), and *The Cockroach Has Landed* (1981)—into a screenplay for film in 1996.

So, all in all, it seemed to me that any reasonable prediction theatres make about the availability of local playwrights will come true. If the local theatres think there won't be any, there won't be any. If the local theatre is convinced there will be a few writers, including one or two 'important' ones, then they'll be right about that too. (Williams, 2007)

I think Williams is right. So if the past offers expectations of the future, we in Manitoba can expect *anything* to happen—from the death of theatre to a Golden Age.

Currently in Manitoba there is a real interest in new work. Will this continue? Perhaps. We'll see. There is a healthy expectation that good work will be written and that it will be produced, if not by the established theatres, then by independent productions. This is good. I am, of course, still alert and apprehensive.

Let me close with a personal anecdote: Last winter, my neighbour's house was broken into. I thought I might have seen the man who did it and I called the police. That was at 3:00 P.M. At 3:00 A.M. a police officer, recruited in the days when they were required to be over six feet tall, knocked on my door, came in and filled my tiny kitchen. I know the routine and I started: "My name is Bruce McManus. At about three o'clock I saw a guy wandering the lane who was actively looking at all the houses. He was about thirty, bearded, wearing blue jeans and a down vest. I think he might have been the guy." The police officer said: "Bruce McManus? The playwright?" He sat down and complained about Canadian theatre for forty minutes.

There are many days when I am enthusiastic and hopeful about theatre in Manitoba.

Works Cited

"Alan Williams." *Canadian Theatre Encyclopedia*. Athabasca University, September 15, 2009. www.canadiantheatre.com/dict.pl?term=Williams%2C%20Alan (accessed March 9, 2011).

Gaboury-Diallo, Lise. "Cercle Molière, Le." *The Canadian Encyclopedia* online: www.thecanadianencyclopedia.com/index.cfm?PgNm=TCE&Params=A1ARTA0009120 (accessed March 9, 2011).

Runnells, Rory, ed. *Map of the Senses*. Winnipeg: Scirocco Drama, 2000.

Williams, Alan. Letter to Bruce McManus. May 7, 2007. Email.

The He(art) of the City:
Prairie Theatre Exchange at home in Portage Place

KATHERINE FOSTER GRAJEWSKI

I n 1989 the Prairie Theatre Exchange (PTE) moved from its original home in the old Grain Exchange Building in the Winnipeg Exchange District to a new $3.5-million facility in the Portage Place Mall in downtown Winnipeg. PTE's artistic director at the time, Kim McCaw, expressed an initial hesitation about the rehousing, considering Portage Place a "hostile environment" for PTE, since its strong reputation was based on a grassroots theatre style known for promoting local artists and producing a type of theatre that stood as an alternative to the Manitoba Theatre Centre by mirroring and drawing from the realities of Manitobans (Brask, 1991, 27). For many, including McCaw, a move into a glossy retail mall among fast-food shops and high turnover retail outlets threatened this reputation (Lacey, October 15, 1989, A15). However, McCaw's view changed with the persuasion of Professor David Arnason, who justified the move as "a matter of art seizing a position at the centre rather than willingly relegating [... itself] to a position at the periphery" (quoted in Brask, 1991, 27). Focusing on the relationship between the Portage Place Shopping Mall, which opened in 1987 as part of the North Portage Development Project, and PTE, which has made its home in this space for over fifteen years, I will examine the unique connection between the artistic space of the theatre and the consumer space of a shopping centre that was intended to be nothing less than the salvation of downtown Winnipeg and that has since become a struggling retail space. By doing so, I hope to explore how this relationship

9

has influenced PTE's sense of place within the Winnipeg arts community as it relates to the city's urban and civic ideology.

In *City Stages: Theatre and Urban Space in a Global City*, Michael McKinnie suggests "bringing the 'spatial turn' in theatre studies to bear on Canadian, and particularly urban, case studies" and exploring "issues arising from the intersection of theatrical and geographical inquiry" (14–5). According to urban theorists John Logan and Harvey Molotch, this type of intersection coincides with the process of "place patriotism," which, they argue, occurs when economic urban development is linked with cultural arts projects in order to build "sentiments of local well-being" (McKinnie, 2007, 30). I believe that the re-housing of PTE in relation to the North Portage development project creates just such an intersection between a local arts project and a city's urban economy and that the concept of "place patriotism" is, in fact, a fitting model for the relationship between Portage Place and PTE and how this relationship contributes to the greater project of downtown revitalization. However, my research into this relationship also revealed the ways in which this model is complicated by the unique circumstance of a theatre in a mall.

An examination of this circumstance must be foregrounded by recognizing the temporal and historical factors that are naturally imprinted upon any discussion of *space* and *place* (McKinnie, 2007, 5). While there is a lack of consensus in critical literature about the distinction between the two terms, it is necessary to define the conceptual relationship between space and place in the context of this project. Borrowing from McKinnie's distinctions between these terms, which he draws from the work of geographer David Harvey, I shall position my understanding of *space* as an entity that does not exist ahistorically, but is created through social practice over time, while *place* is a "certain manifestation of space in time," created through the "ideological constructions of physical space" (McKinnie, 2007, 4–5). Using the rehousing process of PTE as a point of departure, I will examine the changing place of PTE within Winnipeg's arts community as it relates to the changing place of the downtown core, in particular Portage Avenue and the Portage Place Shopping Centre, within Winnipeg's urban ideology.

For PTE, the issue of space has always played a shaping role in how the organization has been positioned within the arts community. PTE was established in 1973 as the Manitoba Theatre Workshop (MTW). Originally conceived as a theatre school in order to fill the gap created by the closure of the Manitoba Theatre Centre school in 1972, the Workshop had the support of past teachers and students of the Manitoba Theatre Centre (MTC); what they did not have was a theatre space. Charles Huband, chairman of the Workshop board of directors and former city councillor, approached the city with a request for space for the organization. The city offered the theatre an abandoned building at 160 Princess Street, the old Grain Exchange, on a five-year renewable lease for $1 a year, provided the organization renovated and maintained the building (Spencer, 1983, 17). The old Grain Exchange Building,[1] a four-storey Victorian commercial structure, was at the centre of Winnipeg's grain industry until the 1940s but had been left empty and deteriorating for ten years prior to PTE's move into the space. Because of the cost of renovations, the Workshop enlisted community volunteers to aid in the transformation of the Grain Exchange Building into a theatre, which made the process a community project. The influence of community involvement as well as the geographical location of the theatre contributed to MTW's reputation as accessible and unpretentious. The location in what was at the time a declining core area shaped the activities that the MTW pursued. The Workshop implemented the Classroom Arts Program in the nearby Victoria and Albert school, and designed an after-school club for children living in the core area. These programs were aimed at participants who might not otherwise have had opportunities to participate in theatre programs. The Manitoba Theatre Workshop thus consciously established itself as a community and education resource centre for the neighbourhood within the urban environment of Winnipeg's core area (Spencer, 1983, 29).

By taking up residence in the old Grain Exchange Building, MTW participated in Winnipeg's cultural renaissance of the 1960s and 1970s, at least in terms of building new facilities for various cultural organizations. The Centennial Project, which included the construction of the Centennial Concert Hall, the Manitoba Museum, and the Planetarium adjacent to City Hall, as well as the building of the new Manitoba Theatre Centre, was "intended to stimulate commercial and residential re-construction in the area, including the rehabilitation of older buildings" (Spencer, 1983, 153). The MTW participated in this rehabilitation by giving the historical Grain Exchange Building a new lease on life after having sat empty for ten years (154). The centennial project, the building of a new theatre centre to house Manitoba's flagship regional theatre, and MTW's rehabilitation of the old Grain Exchange Building all provide examples of Logan and Molotch's concept of place patriotism. The affiliation between these arts projects and the city of Winnipeg helped to create a sense of local well-being by injecting these urban spaces with the ontological notion of "downtown-ness," the perception of a thriving, populated urban community rich in both culture and economic capital (McKinnie, 2007, 31). McKinnie further states that although this practice is "relevant to [...] cultural institutions in downtown redevelopment in general [...] theatres are particularly useful from an urban planning and security perspective, since, unlike galleries and museums, they

---

1   See photograph of the Grain Exchange Building in the colour insert (photo 1).

[...] attract affluent citizens to an area at night" (31). By creating a theatre space in the historic Exchange District, the MTW not only contributed to the revitalization of the Exchange, but also to the area's growth into what has since become one of the major districts for arts and culture in Winnipeg.

As the MTW began to thrive in its Princess Street home, it shifted its focus from being solely a facility for theatre education to becoming an alternative professional theatre for Winnipeg. Along with this shift came another important change, the renaming of the organization as a way to distinguish itself from the other professional theatres in the city and the older regional theatre in particular. It was believed that the Manitoba Theatre Workshop (MTW) sounded too much like the Manitoba Theatre Centre (MTC), which was thought to confuse the general public and reduce the amount of public recognition (Spencer, 1983, 114). The MTW changed its name to Prairie Theatre Exchange (PTE) at the beginning of the 1981–82 season. The transition to PTE saw substantial developments within the organization and once again the issue of space came to the forefront. In looking towards the future, PTE was faced with the ironic situation that plagues many arts organizations: more of its budget ended up being assigned to overhead costs than to artistic costs (Spencer, 147). To remedy this situation the board suggested that there be either a reduction of space requirements and overhead costs for the entire organization or an increase in the size of the theatre to improve revenue potential (Spencer, 147–48). The most logical solution was a larger theatre. Once again, Charles Huband and artistic director Colin Jackson set out on a search for space, this time looking for a building in the core area to convert into a 400–500-seat theatre. Incidentally, this search coincided with several civic developments that had been implemented in the city, particularly Winnipeg's Core Area Initiative or CAI.

The CAI was established through the co-operation of the City of Winnipeg and the provincial and federal governments in response to the deteriorating social, economic, and physical condition of Winnipeg's core area (Douchant, Jopling, and Klos, 1987, xvi). PTE looked to the CAI as a possible resource for funding and support. In a letter to the Winnipeg Core Area Initiative, Charles Huband outlined a proposal to convert the Bank of Commerce Building on Main Street into a theatre space. Unfortunately, this proposal was denied. In May of 1981, the board of PTE authorized a committee to approach other arts groups to determine their needs and interests in the development of a cultural centre that would house PTE as well as other arts organizations. Although this cultural centre never became a realization, what this project established was PTE's recognition of the importance of maintaining a relationship with the other arts groups in the community, "if only to be aware of conflicting demands on the same sources of funding" (Spencer, 1983, 149).

PTE's lease was renewed at its Princess Street location in 1983; however, it continued to search out rehousing possibilities. In the same year a new development project was created to revitalize Winnipeg's downtown. The project, which was launched by the North Portage Development Corporation, resulted from the renewed interest in Portage Avenue following the Winnipeg Core Area Initiatives. Historically, Portage Avenue was known as the retail sector of Winnipeg's Central Business District. However, post-war suburban sprawl diffused retail activity to the suburbs. People moved away from the downtown, and the area suffered as a result. By the 1970s, Portage Avenue had ceased to be a major destination and had simply become another major thoroughfare (Gorluck, 2006, 267).

The North Portage Development Corporation was created in 1983 to manage and guide the development strategy to revitalize Portage Avenue. This strategy involved a combination of commercial, residential, educational, cultural, and entertainment facilities, and physical and environmental enhancements to the area. The key component of the development was the Portage Place retail complex and the skywalk system extending across Portage Avenue (Douchant, Jopling, and Klos, 1987, xxiii). The North Portage Development Corporation collaborated with real estate developers Cadillac Fairview to devise the Portage Place mixed-use retail complex. The developers and government officials were excited about the future of the shopping centre in the heart of the city, and saw the endeavour as an opportunity to bring new life to the city's downtown. It was believed that the project could consolidate retail activity and encourage people to visit the city centre (Fenton and Lyon, 1984, 1). After all, if shopping malls had drawn people away from downtown, it only made sense that a shopping mall would draw them back.

Portage Place opened in September 1987; the 500,000-square-foot, three-level, multipurpose centre included 153 shops, a food court, and three movie theatres, as well as the Imax theatre and two skywalks. However, on the third floor there was a space that was not yet operational. This space, located on the same floor as the Imax and movie theatres, had been reserved for "cultural not-for-profit public use" (Jackson quoted in Oswald, November 28, 1987, 23). The space was originally offered to the Royal Winnipeg Ballet, which declined the offer since it was too small to house the company. The North Portage Development Corporation then approached the Children's Museum, which initially agreed to inhabit the space, but backed out near the end of negotiations (Greenberg, n.d., 14). Left without a tenant and facing an impending deadline set by Cadillac Fairview to fill the space, the North Portage Development Corporation approached PTE.

PTE, which by this time had been looking to move out of its Princess Street theatre for ten years, felt it was in its best interest seriously to consider the offer from Portage Place. There was, however, a great deal of controversy surrounding its decision to move into a mall. In 1988, PTE commissioned a market research study to gather information to facilitate marketing efforts related to the theatre's move to Portage Place. What is most interesting about the results of this study is the level of apprehension and concern expressed by the participants, reflecting an acute awareness of the influence of space on theatre activity. The primary fear was that PTE would lose its distinguishing character and appeal by looking more like the Manitoba Theatre Centre, which, according to the research findings, was a "very disturbing concept for many" ("Market Research Study," 1988).

The study results note that much of the opposition to the move was attributed to a negative feeling about Portage Place in general. A 24 Hours newscast from June 1988, only nine months after Portage Place opened for business, reported that the shopping centre had failed to attract shoppers. The lack of customer traffic had caused many of the mall's retailers to complain to Cadillac Fairview regarding business hours and the cost of rent. Despite the launch of the "Alive After Five" campaign, people were not going downtown in the evenings to shop, especially since the downtown department stores, Eaton's and The Bay, were no longer open on Monday or Tuesday evenings due to the decline in retail activity (Rutherford, 1988). A major deterrent for both Portage Place shoppers and those interviewed by the PTE market research study was the issue of parking. Those visiting Portage Place to shop did not like having to pay for parking in the underground lot when they could park at no cost at the suburban malls. The patrons of PTE also echoed this sentiment, as they were used to the parking situation near the Princess Street building which, although less convenient, was free of charge.

Although many of the concerns voiced in the study dealt explicitly with practical issues such as parking, the concerns that had the most impact on the organization were those suggesting that the new space was incongruent with PTE's vision. Those who chose to attend PTE often did so because of its location, its old building, its small theatre, its stage design, and its comfortable atmosphere. These features had given the PTE a "down-home" or "grassroots" quality, which stood in opposition to what was viewed as the stuffy, pretentious atmosphere of the MTC. The move into a consumer space intended to be a high-class retail venue made many patrons uncomfortable. There was a general resistance to the concept of a theatre in a mall, as some believed that the consumer atmosphere would infiltrate the theatre space and change the essence of PTE. A number of participants in the study expressed concerns regarding the motives behind the organization's decision to relocate, feeling that the move to Portage Place was indicative of a decision to expand and become a profit-driven theatre. Underlying these concerns was the fear that a change of location would alter the type of work PTE produced.

PTE was known to promote Manitoban and Canadian playwrights, to employ local actors, and to take risks by presenting original, experimental, and innovative plays. The research study suggested that to encourage patrons to attend the Portage Place theatre, PTE would have to focus its marketing material on its intention to maintain these qualities in their programming, rather than concentrating solely on promoting the new space. Yet in almost every newspaper and magazine article written on PTE during the rehousing process, the issue of the new theatre space was the main focus. The emphasis placed on the physical space and the new location can be linked to the process of place patriotism; yet this marketing approach seemed to fly in the face of the recommendations put forward by the research study. This example points to the struggles faced by the organization in the process of repositioning itself in the heart of downtown and demonstrates how this struggle prevented Winnipeggers from associating the new space with feelings of locality.

During the rehousing phase, general manager Colin Jackson was continually positive about the move. He recognized that the opportunity presented by Portage Place would allow PTE to expand, which was something that had been impossible at the Princess Street location. As well, he was adamant that the new space would not affect elements of PTE that had established the theatre within the Winnipeg arts community. The design of the new theatre attempted to imitate the Princess Street space, maintaining the thrust stage, which was felt to account for the intimate atmosphere that the company's patrons saw as one of PTE's major strengths.

At the beginning, the sentiment within the organization concerning the move was not as positive as Jackson's. Kim McCaw, who had been hired as artistic director in 1983, was initially hesitant about the move, feeling, as many of those who had participated in the research study had, that Portage Place would be a "hostile environment" for the organization. However, McCaw also recognized PTE's need for a new theatre space. In a 2006 telephone interview, McCaw stated that he had been acutely aware of the rehousing issue even before he officially became the artistic director (McCaw, December 20, 2006). He also suggested that, in retrospect, there may have been other spaces in the city that would have been better choices for the organization, such as the Johnson Terminal space. McCaw explained the evolution of his views on the relocation as "a process of education in terms of what a centre like the one we now are part of was really trying to be" (Brask, 1991, 27). Influenced by David Arnason's view of the move as PTE "seizing a position at the centre," McCaw noted that there was a realization on his part, as well as on the part of the organization, that the move was an opportunity for PTE to be in the middle of things, like "The Bay and the Air Canada building," which would make them "more available to a lot more people than before" (Brask, 1991, 28).

As the artistic director, McCaw's main concern was how to create an artistic season for the new space.[2] McCaw's view is that, although PTE did not intend to alter the "kinds of philosophical and artistic impulses, desires and goals" of the organization, the new space forced a certain amount of change (Lacey, October 19, 1989, A15). One major change was in the kinds of shows PTE was able to produce in the new space in comparison to the old Princess Street location. Not surprisingly, the new technologies and larger space altered the nature of the work the company produced. In the first season in the new theatre McCaw designed a program "to work the kinks out of all the theatre's new knickknacks" (Crossley, May 11, 1989, 24), including John Lazarus's play *Village of Idiots* and American playwright Kevin Kling's *Lloyd's Prayer*, in which "an angel flies in from above," something that could not have been done in the old theatre (Lacey, October 19, 1989, A15).

Kevin Kling's *Lloyd's Prayer* was the first non-Canadian play produced by the PTE. McCaw, when asked if the decision to produce a non-Canadian play was in any way a reaction to the move, replied: "In a way, yes. I felt that we needed to continue to grow and to grow our audience, and in order to do that our programming needed to change" (McCaw, December 20, 2006). What McCaw was speaking to was the push to increase the audience demographic: "We had a core support group of patrons, subscribers and regulars, and we needed to increase the number of that group" (McCaw, 2006). By producing a play that shifted away from its old style, insofar as it wasn't Canadian, McCaw felt he was expanding what PTE was able to do: "We always had the option of doing non-Canadian work; we just hadn't up until that point" (McCaw, 2006). Although *Lloyd's Prayer* was moderately successful, McCaw felt that it confused the audience a little in terms of why it was being produced by a theatre company that had become known for producing Manitoban and Canadian work. After two seasons of programming for the new space and being dissatisfied with the results, McCaw resigned as artistic director. The main reasons for his resignation were that he felt "a more distinct change was needed to attract different people" and that he didn't know what the new programming had to be in order to create that necessary change (McCaw).

McCaw's statements regarding the difficulty in attracting new audiences to the theatre once again speak to the intersection between the place of PTE within the arts community and the shift of this place due to spatial influences. By making changes in the theatre's programming, McCaw was attempting to open up PTE's demographic in a way that would correspond with the theatre's new location. However, what this shift speaks to is certain assumptions about

2   See photograph of the new interior space of Prairie Theatre Exchange in the colour insert (photo 2).

the location itself. When PTE accepted the space in Portage Place, there was an assumption that Portage Place was going to be a vibrant cultural and commercial space. By the early nineties, however, it had become apparent that the mall in the heart of the city was not the destination it had promised to be, and this had an impact on PTE. Originally envisioned as an upscale downtown shopping centre, Portage Place soon realized that this vision did not fit with the mall's clientele. Portage Place failed to revitalize the downtown core and instead became like many other downtown locations in that it was alive with people on weekdays and quiet on evenings and weekends. The synergy between residential, commercial, and cultural space never came to fruition for the downtown mall, which forced PTE to reassess its position in hopes of finding a way to function successfully in its new location.

Having seized a physical position at the centre in an effort to become the most accessible theatre in Winnipeg, PTE had to face the fact that this centre was quickly becoming another periphery. In addition, having signed a seventy-five-year lease and invested $3.5 million in the building of the theatre, the organization was not about to move any time soon. The process of reassessment for the theatre was not easy, and it took a number of years for it to grow into its Portage Place home. PTE was no longer the small "grassroots" theatre on Princess Street where patrons attended partially for "the sense of adventure" the old theatre space provided (Greenberg, n.d., 15). The organization had recognized its need for expansion but struggled with the direction in which this expansion was leading it. In the period of struggle following McCaw's resignation in the early nineties subscriptions decreased to a record low of 2,000, the organization had a deficit, and there were major problems finding an audience. After three unsuccessful seasons, freelance director Allen MacInnis took over the role of artistic director in 1995. The critics were puzzled and shocked by MacInnis's first season, which included an adaptation of the novel *Crackpot* by noted Manitoba writer Adele Wiseman but also more eclectic fare like Ted Dykstra and Richard Greenblatt's *2 Pianos 4 Hands*, Scott McPherson's *Marvin's Room*, and Lerner and Loewe's *My Fair Lady*. This inaugural season seemed to be experimenting with more mainstream and commercial material than PTE had been known to produce in the past: Scott McPherson's *Marvin's Room*, based on McPherson's own experiences with AIDS in his family, had been recently adapted to film, while Lerner and Loewe's *My Fair Lady* was a well-known stage musical that had also enjoyed commercial success on the silver screen. However, the audiences responded, and what was referred to as "the subscription slide" was turned around; for the first time since the move to Portage Place, season ticket sales were on the rise (*Stages*, 1997, 18). MacInnis was able to widen PTE's demographic and steer the organization into a new era. Building on the PTE mandate of fostering "a creative community of interests in dramatic energy, committed to furthering theatre that reflects Prairie Roots," while "looking out the Prairie window to bring into the theatre a broader range of work," MacInnis was able to tap into the desires of Winnipeg audiences "without sacrificing the bite" that PTE had provided from the beginning (*Stages*, 1997, 18).

Some patrons, however, argued that PTE had, in fact, lost its "bite" and believed that PTE had sacrificed aspects of its programming, such as the development and production of works by Winnipeg and Manitoba playwrights, in favour of simply putting bums in seats. Yet despite these charges one could not deny that the organization was in a much better place than it had been during the previous three seasons. During MacInnis's term as artistic director, PTE developed its role as a community organization, becoming a resource centre for other Manitoba arts organizations such as Shakespeare in the Ruins, Theatre Projects Manitoba, Popular Theatre Alliance of Manitoba, and the Manitoba Opera. Additionally, the theatre school, which had always been central to the organization, experienced an increase in enrolment. By 2003, when Robert Metcalfe took over as artistic director, PTE was well on its way to re-establishing its place within the Winnipeg arts community. Since Metcalfe has come to the helm as artistic director, PTE has continued steadily to increase its subscription base, strengthen its role in the community through educational outreach and touring shows, and launch new and exciting programs such as the Carol Shields Festival of New Works and the Playwrights Unit, both of which celebrate local talent and promote new play development. This fostering of new local work was also reflected within the 2007/2008 season, as PTE produced its 132nd new play in January 2008: Winnipeg playwright Bruce McManus's *All Restaurant Fires Are Arson*, which received its first public reading at the Carol Shields Festival of New Works in 2005.

Although PTE has been able to achieve considerable success in its Portage Place theatre, the organization still feels that it is somewhat at odds with its location in a shopping mall. Robert Metcalfe indicated that the organization is still trying to figure out how to function within the Portage Place space in a way that is most suited to the theatre and its patrons. Numerous attempts have been made to figure out how to integrate the theatre-going experience at PTE with the experience of entering Portage Place. Metcalfe acknowledged that there is ongoing discussion within the organization about ways in which PTE can have a greater impact on an audience's experience from "the moment they take their ticket at the underground parkade to the moment they leave the parkade at the end of the night," suggesting that the issue of space will continue to influence PTE (Metcalfe, December 19, 2006).

As part of the project of downtown revitalization, the relationship between PTE and Portage Place seems to lend itself to Logan and Molotch's model of place patriotism; however, examining the rehousing process of PTE reveals the continuous struggle between the artistic space of the theatre and the consumer space of the shopping mall. Portage Place failed to become the heart of the city, and PTE's own struggles related to expansion prevented the smooth integration of the theatre into the multipurpose space of the mall. By the time PTE began to garner moderate success and re-establish its audience, Portage Place was reaching the low point of what was a steady decline. The relationship between PTE and Portage Place failed to create any sense of co-operation, and they have existed as curiously separate entities while sharing the same geographical location.

In 2007, Portage Place celebrated its twentieth year in operation with the *Winnipeg Free Press* headline: "Finding its Place: Downtown Mall Turns 20, Gains a Viable Identity" (Kives, September 16, 2007, A11). The article following the headline acknowledged the struggles that have led Portage Place finally to stop "trying to be a bastion of suburbia in the midst of the inner city," and instead be a downtown Winnipeg mall that "is OK being a downtown Winnipeg mall" (Kives, A11). The pressure on Portage Place to be something more than it is has finally seemed to subside, perhaps symbolically marked by the high-end clothing retailer Holt Renfrew vacating the mall in August 2007. Yet, while the mall is only now "Finding its Place" within Winnipeg's urban landscape, PTE has demonstrated over the last several years that it has re-established its place within Winnipeg's arts community, seeing itself as filling "a unique and important niche: producing works, often new, with a focus on Manitoban and Canadian artists, which speak to the 'non-arts' audience as strongly as to those who have always made theatre […] a part of their lives," while never forgetting "its roots as a provider of theatre education" (Prairie Theatre Exchange 2009). According to Kevin Longfield, of the some 220 plays and bills produced by the Workshop and PTE between 1974 and 2002, eighty-three were by Canadian playwrights outside of Manitoba and eighty-nine were works by Manitoban playwrights (Longfield, 2001, 232–5). By filling this niche, PTE has gained a local following, and although it may not be the same following as those who supported the theatre at its Princess Street location, the organization has embraced the changes that have led it to where it is today and that have proved its ability to generate the energy needed to grow beyond being simply a theatre space in the "hostile environment" of a mall.

Works Cited

Brask, Per. "Seizing the Centre: Per Brask Talks to Kim McCaw (Artistic Director of Prairie Theatre Exchange)." *Canadian Theatre Review* 66 (Spring 1991): 25–31.

Crossley, Karen. "Building future dream factories." *Winnipeg Sun,* May 11, 1989: 24.

Douchant, Christian, David Jopling, and Nancy Klos. *Winnipeg Insight: Compendium of Winnipeg Planning Literature.* Winnipeg: Institute of Urban Studies, University of Winnipeg, 1987.

Fenton, Robert, and D. M. Lyon. "Critique of the latest Winnipeg Core Project." CIP [Canadian Institute of Planners] *Forum* (May 1984): 1.

Gorluck, Russ. *Going Downtown: A History of Winnipeg's Portage Avenue.* Winnipeg: Great Plains Publications, 2006.

Greenberg, Annalee. "Theatre in the Mall," 14–5. Source and date unknown. Prairie Theatre Exchange files. Prairie Theatre Exchange.

Kives, Bartley. "Finding its Place: Downtown Mall Turns 20, Gains a Viable Identity." *Winnipeg Free Press,* September 16, 2007: A11.

Lacey, Liam. "Theatre overcomes its fear and takes its act into a mall." *Globe and Mail,* October 19, 1989: A15.

Longfield, Kevin. *From Fire to Flood: A History of the Theatre in Manitoba.* Winnipeg: Signature, 2001.

"Market Research Study Pertaining to the Relocation of Prairie Theatre Exchange," November 1988. Prairie Theatre Exchange Files. Prairie Theatre Exchange.

McCaw, Kim. Telephone Interview by Katherine Foster Grajewski. Typescript. December 20, 2006.

McKinnie, Michael. *City Stages: Theatre and Urban Space in a Global City.* Toronto: University of Toronto Press, 2007.

Metcalfe, Robert. Personal Interview by Katherine Foster Grajewski. Typescript. December 19, 2006.

Oswald, Brad. "PTE plans bigger, but no fancier quarters atop Portage Place mall." *Winnipeg Free Press,* November 28, 1987: 23.

Prairie Theatre Exchange. "About PTE." www.pte.mb.ca/about/about_pte.htm (accessed March 9, 2011).

Rutherford, Ross, reporter. "Portage Place has failed to attract shoppers." *24Hours.* Winnipeg, CBWT, June 1988. www.youtube.com/watch?v=_2Tko7LtREE&mode=related&search (accessed March 9, 2011).

Spencer, Peter J. "The History and Contribution of The Manitoba Theatre Workshop/Prairie Theatre Exchange." Diss. New York University, 1983.

Stages: Prairie Theatre Exchange Celebrates 25 Years. Winnipeg: Prairie Theatre Exchange, 1997.

Producing New Work in Winnipeg

HOPE MCINTYRE

I was asked to speak about my work and the particular rewards and challenges of creating and producing new Western Canadian work within Western Canada. I have spent most of my life in the Prairies, having grown up in Saskatoon and, after trying the bigger cities, relocating to Winnipeg in 2000. When I returned to Western Canada, numerous people asked why, as an artist, I would move from Toronto to Winnipeg. In particular, a lot of Winnipeggers asked that question. I think it was the prairie girl in me wanting to be closer to what felt like home—the horizon. I had also found in Toronto a very competitive and commercial industry that made it tricky to develop the type of theatre that I wanted to create—a theatre that serves the larger community and serves a social purpose. Of course there were also personal challenges living in a big city; I swear that my heart rate had increased, and I knew I could never buy a house in Toronto if I chose to stay in theatre. So, with the encouragement of a colleague in Winnipeg who spoke about its thriving cultural scene, I arrived in Winnipeg having lined up some teaching work. By the way, that colleague soon left for Vancouver.

Sarasvàti Productions had been functioning in Toronto for two years at that point, and the board of directors decided that the company should relocate with me. I've now been artistic director of Sarasvàti Productions for twelve years, ten of those in Winnipeg. Our namesake, Sarasvàti, is the goddess of inspiration and great change. Our mandate is to do work that promotes human understanding, to support emerging artists, and to explore the boundaries of the theatrical form. Our regular events include our annual festival of women

Lorraine James in *The Rats Are Waiting* by Leanna Brodie at International Women's Week Cabaret of Monologues 2008. PHOTO BY JANET SHUM.

Hope McIntyre in *Impact* by Hope McIntyre for International Women's Week Cabaret of Monologues 2008. PHOTO BY JANET SHUM.

playwrights, FemFest; a reading series for Manitoban playwrights entitled One Night Stand; and our International Women's Week Cabaret of Monologues.

While our mandate is not gender-specific, our goal to serve emerging artists and my own artistic interest fit ideally with a concentration on women's work. FemFest was founded in 2003 with the intention of showcasing women playwrights. In its first five years, fifty-two plays by women were performed or read at the festival and twenty workshops and panels were held. In 2004 we started to bring touring work from across Canada to expand the festival by also showcasing women theatre artists, and in 2006 we introduced an international artist-in-residence. In a similar vein, our International Women's Week Cabaret focuses on giving voice to women; it was started in 2004 with two casts, one performing in Brandon and one in Winnipeg. The Cabaret expanded in 2008 to include a tour to The Pas and community performances in a range of venues, including correctional centres.

Despite the importance of these activities, we do not focus on women's work exclusively. The One Night Stand series began with our move to Winnipeg in 2000, as it was a wonderful way to do outreach to Manitoba playwrights; by doing public readings of works in progress we were also able to find potential scripts for further development. In addition to our annual events, we've workshopped new plays and done occasional work at the Fringe Festival and for the Master Playwrights Festival in Winnipeg.

As a small independent company we have many challenges, most having to do with limited resources and lack of funding. But we continue doing the work because we believe in the need to support emerging artists and to use theatre to connect to our community. Over the years there have been many rewards, from working with community groups who feel their stories have finally been told to watching artists develop and move on to busy professional careers. Of course, this means that those whom we train and to whom we provide opportunities for growth ultimately move beyond us to the larger theatres and are no longer available to work with us. Ironically, it is generally the technicians, designers, and stage managers who move on, but the lack of work for actors and the lack of opportunities for playwrights in Manitoba means that we are able to form longer-term relationships with these artists. In particular, we've been able to work over the course of several projects with playwrights and watch as they develop their voices. We have found the key to benefiting both the

artists and ourselves as a company is to cultivate long-term relationships with playwrights, focusing on helping them to master their craft rather than just helping them to construct particular plays. By concentrating on developing the playwright rather than the script, we create mentorship relationships that ultimately lead to stronger scripts.

As I mentioned, our largest challenge is budgetary. Our struggle for funding is not unlike that of any other not-for-profit or arts organization in Canada. But working completely on project funding with no operating funds severely limits our ability to undertake larger-scale work or to grow as a company, since we cannot put the time into operational necessities such as development or ongoing marketing. So we do our best with very little and manage to provide opportunities to numerous artists. When I think about things from a regional perspective, there are similar challenges everywhere when it comes to new Canadian plays. The reality in Canadian theatre right now, which I have glimpsed through my role as the president of the Playwrights Guild of Canada, is that there are

Amanda Shimoji in *Giving It Up* by Hannah Moscovitch for International Women's Week Cabaret of Monologues 2008. PHOTO BY JANET SHUM.

Livia Dymond in *The Strawberry Monologues* by Talia Pura for International Women's Week Cabaret of Monologues 2008. PHOTO BY JANET SHUM.

many theatres willing to *develop* the work, but few that can afford to *produce* new works. The reality is that doing a workshop or reading a play is much cheaper and, as a result, carries less of a risk for the theatres than mounting a full production of an unknown work as part of a regular season. There is also specific money available for this work that can be used to top up a theatre's operating funds.

Manitoba, in particular, also has a few large theatres that receive the majority of operating funds, leaving smaller companies to struggle for project funding. Sarasvàti has yet to receive project funding from the Canada Council, and Manitoba as a whole doesn't seem to be well represented at the federal funding table. The province is not seen as a hub of theatre, and that perception, as much as the actual physical distances, isolates us from the theatrical hubs. While Winnipeg has a very vibrant arts and culture sector—much of it being far more grassroots than one might find in a larger city—we rarely see artists, artistic directors, or audiences travelling to Winnipeg to see theatre. This creates a sense of human and creative, as well as geographical, isolation. Another challenge is working under Canadian Actors' Equity Association (CAEA) contracts because of the cost and limitations for process-oriented work. Our mandate to support emerging theatre artists favours the use of both professional and pre-professional artists involved in a rehearsal period spread over an elongated period of time to allow for script rewrites. Even with the will to make it work on both sides, Equity agreements—which set a quota on the number of non-Equity artists a company is allowed to use on a project and tend to favour short, intense, regularly scheduled rehearsal periods with clearly defined products in mind—can present special challenges to a small, independent theatre company like ours. All of this means that, for a theatre, and particularly for an independent producer in Winnipeg, mounting the production of a new play is a huge investment with little payoff. It is even a challenge getting audiences in Winnipeg and fellow artists out to see new work.

Yet, in my experience, it is the smaller independent companies that are nonetheless taking many of the risks associated with developing new work. This is particularly true in the West, where there are fewer larger theatres, many of which do not often produce local work. To illustrate both the rewards and challenges we've experienced in recent years, I'll use the example of our process and relationship with new playwright Cairn Moore. Although she has written in the collective model for the Winnipeg Fringe Festival in the past, she is primarily trained as an actor and also teaches theatre. Our relationship with her as an artist began with her performance in the initial FemFest in 2003. I directed her in a production of Katherine Koller's *Cowboy Boots and a Corsage*. At the festival debriefing session she met playwright Alison McLean, whose work had been read at that FemFest. They immediately struck a chord, and Alison began working as a dramaturge for a piece Cairn had been contemplating. As we left the debriefing, Cairn was inspired and vowed she would be working on something for the next FemFest. In 2004 another piece of Alison's was read, and Cairn continued to labour away at this piece she kept mentioning to me.

Finally Cairn sent something in, and *Absolute Perfection*, originally titled *I'll Think About That Tomorrow,* was done as a reading at FemFest 2005. This was a very personal story for the playwright, as her brother had been diagnosed with cancer and the play dealt with the effects of this illness on two sisters. Her initial proposal was an outline with roughed-in scenes, but the potential for a powerful and funny piece was obvious. Once I committed to programming the reading, Cairn was forced to finish the piece, which led to several title changes. Drastic rewriting occurred before, after, and even during the rehearsal process for the reading. The core remained the story of two sisters, **Arlene** and **Darlene**. **Arlene** is a single mother, sportscaster, and free spirit who is diagnosed with lung cancer. **Darlene** appears to be the perfect Martha Stewart, with a doctor husband, homemade cakes, and a home in the suburbs. **Arlene's** diagnosis makes both sisters question their lives and their relationships. **Iggy**, the third character, is **Arlene**'s best friend, who runs away, unable to cope with her friend's illness. **Iggy** escapes through men, food, and drugs. Ultimately the journey takes them to a Montreal Canadiens game, where **Arlene** meets her idol, Saku Koivu. The reading was directed by Kayla Gordon and featured Barbara Green, Jessica Burleson, and Deborah Perry.

The reading gave Cairn the opportunity to see what did and did not work with the script. Many incarnations followed, as she submitted it for consideration as a full production. We then committed to produce it at FemFest

Lisa Lorteaux, Danielle Savage, and Jessica Burleson in *Absolute Perfection* by Cairn Moore at FemFest 2006.
PHOTO BY LYNNE KOLLER.

2006 and, as I was set to direct it, I became highly involved with its continued development. As part of a festival, the piece had to be kept minimal in terms of production demands, but we did our best to allow the playwright to see her vision realized. I gave her the props she asked for, and after opening we cut half of them. As part of the process, she learned she had written in both an extraneous number of props and impossible costume and set quick changes. Yet the heart of the piece remained very strong. The production featured Danielle Savage, Lisa Lorteaux, and Jessica Burleson and was made possible with extra support from the Manitoba Arts Council. Cairn's writing was also funded by the Winnipeg Arts Council.[1]

The response to the piece was extremely positive. Although it is difficult to get local media to review independent theatre when a show is performed only a few times, in the five years of the festival we have garnered reviews twice in the weekly *Uptown Magazine*. The review of *Absolute Perfection* was important in providing critical response for both Sarasvàti Productions' and the playwright's portfolio:

> From the play's opening moments, these characters become clearly defined and thoroughly enjoyable, and the actresses are aided by a fantastic script that tackles everything from motherhood to the Canadian health-care system, all in wonderfully funny fashion. (Burr, November 2, 2006, 23)

Cairn's entire family flew in to see the work, and it was an emotional evening with her brother in the audience and a post-performance talkback with representatives from Cancer Care Manitoba. They found the piece to be extremely authentic and were pleased to see lung cancer being dealt with on the stage. In fact, that very season, 2006–2007, two pieces next door at Prairie Theatre Exchange's mainstage also dealt with breast cancer (*Apple* by Vern Thiessen and *Mom's The Word 2: Unhinged* by the Mom's the Word 2 Collective: Jill Daum, Alison Kelly, Robin Nichol, Barbara Pollard, and Deborah Williams).

Although at certain stages in the process there was critical feedback about the amount of hockey and number of hockey references in a play by a woman and about women, it helped illustrate the point that women can write about a variety of topics. For us, the work truly fulfilled the mandate of the festival, showcasing a woman playwright and providing both development and promotional opportunities. In fact, some would argue that, at this stage, the limited production demands actually helped to focus on the script itself:

1 See additional photographs of the 2006 FemFest 2006 performance of *Absolute Perfection* in the colour insert (photos 3 and 4).

A scaled-down set allowed this talented cast to really shine without being masked by spectacle, and the crisp overlapping dialogue is presented in a way that, while splitting the audience'[s] focus, never leaves them confused as to what's going on. (Burr, 2006, 23)

Cairn then moved on to writing a new piece, and *Sex: The Ins and Outs* had an excerpt read at our One Night Stand at the 2007 Carol Shields Festival of New Works and was then read at FemFest 2007. Directed by Alix Sobler, this piece exploring women's sexuality featured a full female cast including: Jennifer Hupé, Nancy Drake, Tricia Cooper, Danielle Savage, Lisa Lorteaux, and Laura Lussier.[2] Cairn's work continues to show a stronger voice and greater understanding of the craft. Our audiences love her work and know to expect something heartfelt and funny, with a powerful emotional punch.

What is still missing is having her work picked up by a larger producer or theatres in other cities. Cairn is now working on an expanded version of *Absolute Perfection* and trying to find a producer. FemFest was the perfect test ground for her and allowed her to see how it worked. We are very limited, though, in what we can provide in terms of production demands, so the play would certainly benefit from a production with the ability to meet the heavy logistical demands of the piece. However, she has yet to get any interest from the bigger theatres even in Winnipeg.

I will close with a few additional observations I've had while working with the Playwrights Guild of Canada. We have far fewer members in the Prairie provinces than in Central Canada and British Columbia, but even fewer in the Atlantic provinces and Territories. Although it is difficult to get work produced in Canada, particularly in smaller cities, it is even harder getting second productions. In Manitoba, it is difficult to get the big houses to produce local playwrights. The past couple of years have shown improvement, with at least one local playwright per season at Prairie Theatre Exchange (PTE) and Manitoba Theatre Centre (MTC). Although we are hopeful that this programming is not an exception but a new trend, when we look at the 2008–2009 season, we see that Prairie Theatre Exchange had no local playwrights on its mainstage and that Manitoba Theatre Centre will have only one local playwright on its second stage. While this may not be a permanent setback, their track records are certainly uneven.[3]

---

2 Since presenting this paper a new version of this piece, *Love for Sale*, was workshopped at FemFest 2009.

3 In the year of publication, 2010/2011, there were no local playwrights in the MTC season, and PTE featured one local playwright, Sharon Bajer.

Yet, looking at the active membership of the Manitoba Association of Playwrights, it is clear that there are dozens of local playwrights developing work through the open door sessions, workshops, and dramaturgy that the organization offers. Overall, smaller companies seem to bear the burden of producing local playwrights and developing new work. Many playwrights form their own companies and this makes it harder to focus on the writing. Here I speak from experience.

Women playwrights continue to be highly under-represented across Canada, and Manitoba is no exception; our two regional theatres have produced few female playwrights over the last couple of seasons. In fact, in the season announced when this paper was presented, 2008-2009, Prairie Theatre Exchange had no work by female playwrights unless we include the adaptation of Munsch's children's stories by local playwright Debbie Patterson; Manitoba Theatre Centre had no female playwrights on its mainstage, although one piece was originally a novel by a female (*Pride and Prejudice* by Jane Austen) adapted for the stage by two male writers, and their warehouse season had one play written by a female (*Bad Dates* by American Theresa Rebeck) out of four plays that they produced.[4] As a result FemFest has filled an important void and continues to be necessary.

Over the past decade, through initiatives such as FemFest and the Cabaret, Sarasvàti Productions has managed to help several women gain valuable experience and thereby has honoured its mandate to serve emerging artists in need. Aside from our work for women, though, we have supported over thirty Manitoba playwrights in developing their work and introducing it to audiences. We have also provided opportunities to hundreds of artists as actors, directors, designers, and video artists.

Although we struggle to keep afloat due to funding limits for independent project-based companies and the inability to attract major corporate or private donors, who want bigger bang for their buck, the need to develop Western artists and theatrical work from local artists continues to drive the company. We are very proud of our ability to do so much with so little.

Works Cited

Burr, Grant. "Perfect? Damn near." *Uptown Magazine*. November 2, 2006: 23.

4   The 2010/2011 season looked a bit better with three out of seven shows at PTE by women, one local (Sharon Bajer). MTC's six-production mainstage season presented one work by a female writer: a stage adaptation of Noel Coward's 1946 screenplay, *Brief Encounter*. Of the four shows offered on its second stage, one featured a female playwright, while a second was developed by two female collaborators (in addition to a male collaborator). None were local.

Appendix.

Sarasvàti Productions' past shows include:

- *Hunger** by Hope McIntyre (1998), Toronto, Passe Muraille Theatre Backspace
- *Revisioning** by Hope McIntyre (1999), Toronto, Alumnae Theatre
- a reading series of new plays by various playwrights, Toronto, Alumnae Theatre
- *Missiah** by Hope McIntyre (2000), Toronto, Equity Showcase Theatre
- *Hunger* by Hope McIntyre (2000), Winnipeg, Colin Jackson Studio Theatre
- *Death of Love** by Hope McIntyre (Workshop, 2001), Winnipeg, Colin Jackson Studio Theatre
- *Fire Visions: Poems* by Bertolt Brecht (2002), Winnipeg and Sackville (NB)
- *One For The Road* by Harold Pinter (2003), Winnipeg and Sackville (NB)
- FemFest 2003, Winnipeg, Colin Jackson Studio Theatre
- International Women's Week Cabaret of Monologues (2004), Winnipeg and Brandon
- *You Whore** a collective creation (2003), Winnipeg, Fringe Theatre Festival
- *Jill's War* by Victoria Loa Hicks and Nancy Kruh (2004), Winnipeg, Fringe Theatre Festival
- FemFest 2004, Winnipeg, Colin Jackson Studio Theatre
- *Impromptu of Outremont* by Michel Tremblay (2005), Winnipeg, Forrest Nickerson Theatre
- International Women's Week Cabaret of Monologues (2005), Winnipeg, various venues
- readings of *Jesus' Penis in my Heart* by Jamie Lee Shebelski and *Ruth & Robert & Robert & Ruth* by Mary Humphrey Baldridge at the Carol Shields Festival of New Works 2005
- FemFest 2005, Winnipeg, Colin Jackson Studio Theatre
- International Women's Week Cabaret of Monologues (2006), Winnipeg, various venues

- FemFest 2006, Winnipeg, Colin Jackson Studio and The Contemporary Dancers Studio
- International Women's Week Cabaret of Monologues (2007), Winnipeg, various venues
- One Night Stand event at the Carol Shields Festival of New Works 2007
- FemFest 2007, Winnipeg, Colin Jackson Studio Theatre
- *Ripple Effect** by Hope McIntyre, workshop presentations in schools
- International Women's Week Cabaret of Monologues (2008), Manitoba tour, various venues
- FemFest 2008, Winnipeg, Colin Jackson Studio Theatre
- *Ripple Effect* Tour (2008), performances in Manitoba High Schools and community centres
- *Eden** by Hope McIntyre (2009), workshop presentation Winnipeg, Colin Jackson Studio Theatre
- *Bone Cage* by Catherine Banks (2009) reading, Winnipeg, Carol Shields Festival of New Works
- FemFest 2009, Winnipeg, Canwest Centre for Theatre and Film
- *Fen* by Caryl·Churchill (2010), Winnipeg, The Rachel Browne Theatre

In addition, Sarasvàti Productions has done readings of several scripts in development and eight One Night Stand Evenings of Plays by Manitoba Playwrights (providing opportunities to over thirty local playwrights to date).

*Indicates new plays. In addition to these, within each FemFest several new plays are developed and shown as readings, workshops or full productions.

Slow Dancing on Black Ice:
Primus Theatre and Navigating the Fringe

CLAIRE BORODY

I n July of 1989, Primus Theatre—five graduates of the National Theatre School (NTS) under the direction of Richard Fowler, an actor with the Odin Theatre in Denmark—premiered *Dog Day* at the Winnipeg Fringe Festival. The young company stunned casual Fringe-goers and critics alike with what CBC critic Robert Enright described not only as an "incredibly intense and incredibly well disciplined" performance, but also as "one of the most radical pieces" at the Fringe Festival (July 19, 1989). Jacquie Good of CBC Radio claimed that *Dog Day* "was a piece you understand emotionally, not intellectually [....] It resonates inside you long after the show is over" (July 19, 1989). Karen Crossley of the *Winnipeg Sun* described the performance as a "fascinating, beautifully acted piece to be felt rather than understood" and commented that "the impact of *Dog Day* is probably something you won't feel until after you leave the theatre" (July 20, 1989, 22).

This small selection of critical responses to *Dog Day* indicates several things about Primus's performance work: first, that the world the company had created was rendered in images that were not representative of daily experience. Furthermore, time and space were being explored and manipulated in ways that transgressed notions of form and structure associated with theatrical realism and the "real" world. This meant that without being able to refer to familiar literary structures more centred in conventional understandings of time and space, critics could not describe their reactions to the performance in traditional ways (using New Criticism or quasi-Romanticism). In general, further examination of the critical response to Primus Theatre's work indicates continuing visceral impressions, rather than the intellectual or empathetic reactions usually associated with reviewing literary plays.

Primus Theatre was originally organized as a temporary arrangement structured for the sole purpose of completing a work in progress begun by senior students at the National Theatre School (NTS). However, during the course of preparing to remount *Dog Day,* company members decided to forge a long-term association. This collaboration of the individuals known as Primus Theatre[1] was based in Winnipeg (Manitoba) for the duration of its operation, which would eventually span nine years (1989–1998). Over the course of the company's existence five major performance pieces were created and then toured in repertoire for extended periods of time across Canada and parts of the United States. Each piece was continuously fine-tuned until it was retired from the company's repertoire. This repertoire included: *Dog Day* (1989), *Alkoremmi* (1991–1996), *The Night Room* (1991–1997), *Scarabesque* (1993–1995), and *Far Away Home* (1995–1997). Primus members also collaborated with poet Patrick Friesen and the New Music ensemble Groundswell on the multidisciplinary piece *Madrugada* (1992 and 1995), wrote and performed a series of thirteen radio plays for CBC (1991–1994), and designed and facilitated two *Caravan of the Midnight Sun* New Year's Eve street parades (1991 and 1992) with the support and participation of hundreds of local volunteers. In the later years of operation, the company was instrumental in the organization

[1]   For most of its operating years the company consisted of permanent members Donald Kitt, Tannis Kowalchuk, Stephen Lawson, Karin Randoja, Ker Wells, and Artistic Director Richard Fowler. Two founding members of the company, Sean Dixon and Richard Clarkin, left the company in the spring and fall of 1990 respectively. Although he had not attended NTS, Kitt was considered a founding member and had trained with the company during the remaking of *Dog Day.* Kowalchuk was accepted into the company during the spring of 1990 and began her training that fall. For the first few years of the company's operation, many of the company members were contractually booked with commercial theatre companies in the city. The reason that the company continued to base its operations in the city of Winnipeg is not clear. It can be speculated that the low cost of living and the fact that two of the company members had family residing in the city might have contributed to this decision. Furthermore, establishing the presence of an "other than mainstream" theatre is difficult in most locations in Canada as considerable effort is required to educate and generate a spectatorship. The company had already devoted two years to audience development by the time it was decided that outside contract work would no longer be allowed during periods of performance construction. It can be further speculated that the company decided to remain in Winnipeg to build upon this pioneering work rather than to start from square one in another location.

and development of a series of community-based productions, *C'era una volta in montagna ...* [*Once upon a time in the mountains ...*] (1997, 1998, 1999), in Nocelle, Italy, under the organization of LA TOFA,[2] generated by Fowler and a group of local citizens. The development of these projects continued even after the company's demise.

Of key importance to Primus Theatre's company culture was the development of training and creative processes and a pedagogical practice. As a means of sustaining and transmitting their creative practices, company members planned and implemented an extensive series of workshops in centres across the country and in parts of the United States, often in the locations where they were performing. The company also organized three extended workshops/intensives in Winnipeg (1993, 1994, and 1997) that attracted participants from across the globe. In 1996, after an exhaustive two-part national tour, company members organized and facilitated the "Survivors of the Ice Age Festival and Symposium" as a vehicle to showcase original hybrid work and to create a network for companies engaged in such work. This venture was followed by the "Show Girls Festival" in 1997 directed at similar goals for the work of female performers.

During the spring of 1998, Richard Fowler received the M. Joan Chalmers National Award for Artistic Direction; ironically, it was at this time that the company ceased operation. The decision to disband in April 1998 reflected a collective decision to allow what company members regarded as the natural completion of a creative cycle. This coincided with the exit, for various reasons, of several company members and the artistic director. However, it can also be speculated that Primus Theatre's uneasy and, at times, highly difficult history with the national arts establishment had eventually taken its toll. After years of struggling to sustain their unique, highly original work on their own terms and conditions, the remaining members may have found the prospect of a continuation of that relationship, coupled with the anticipation of restructuring and rebuilding the company's foundational core—the artistic personnel—too overwhelming.

In many ways, the Winnipeg-based company played a strong leadership role in articulating the challenges that small experimental theatre companies were struggling to overcome in an increasingly chilly cultural, financial, and critical environment. In the spring of 1996 at Collège universitaire de Saint-

---

2   LA TOFA was a non-profit society created in 1997 by Fowler, scenographer Aniello Cinque, and four residents of Nocelle to provide an official status, administrative infrastructure, and a support system for the proposed project. LA TOFA was an umbrella organization run by a board of directors responsible for managing the official, regulatory, and financial aspects of the project.

Boniface (Winnipeg), Primus Theatre sponsored and organized the festival/ symposium "Survivors of the Ice Age," directed at addressing issues faced by small theatre companies creating original performance work and attempting to redefine established parameters of the art form in the aftermath of a major art funding freeze during the early 1990s. In the fall of 1996, *Canadian Theatre Review* (CTR) featured the event in an entire issue devoted to the discussion and demonstration of survival tactics by practitioners of what editor Ric Knowles described as "politically or aesthetically alternative or otherwise challenging art forms" (1996, 3). Even in the aftermath of the massive twenty percent reduction in federal arts funding that had occurred between 1993 and 1995, small arts organizations continued to struggle for survival (Taft, 1993, 10). However, as Knowles points out in his editorial, two years later, changes in arts funding practices were "less the result of local or provincial election results, bad economic times, temporary 'restraint' recessions or readjustments, than of major longer-term, and in many cases deliberately orchestrated shifts in the social, cultural and political climate" (1996, 3). In acknowledging that "high-culture forms seem secure, and commercial theatre is thriving like never before" (3), Knowles highlights the fact that a continued funding freeze was affecting only certain sectors of Canada's theatrical culture.

The gathering of that sector, along with counterparts in the United States and Europe, was the principal driving force behind Primus's organization of the symposium. In a summary of the symposium for the CTR special edition, Penny Farfan identified a series of commonalities that defined the work and work ethic of most of the companies involved in the "Survivors" event: a conscious decision to work as an ongoing collaborative; a clear delineation between actor and director in the process of creating a performance work, rather than the adoption of a collective decision-making process; the recognition of ensemble members as multi-faceted artists, not just as performers (or directors); the acknowledgment of training as a lifelong research venture; and an understanding of the necessity for evolution in the group dynamic (1996, 6–8). Farfan also identified Savannah Walling (artistic director of Vancouver Moving Theatre) and Richard Fowler (artistic director of Primus) as strong advocates for the redefinition of "the form, purpose and duration of training" (8). Through her observations, Farfan distinguished the collective practices of the companies involved in the symposium from those of the mainstream contract system and established a context from which to understand the origins of the resulting "alternative" performance aesthetic.

Farfan's profile also indicates that most of the companies represented at the "Survivors" symposium claimed "the politics of space"—the lack of, limitations of, trade-offs for, responsibility of, and the way in which the responsibility for space changed practice (8–9)—as a continuing site of contention, especially for companies trying to function on an ongoing, rather than single-project or occasional Fringe Festival, basis. In this way, the companies represented in Farfan's profile are further distinguished from mainstream practice, which is defined primarily by permanent architectural structures occupying clearly identified physical spaces. The building and its administrative infrastructure are often considered to be "the theatre." Personnel serves in a secondary function and fluctuates from project to project. In the theatre constructed by Primus and other Third Theatre companies represented at the symposium, the personnel, the processes employed, and the resulting interaction is "the theatre." Eugenio Barba of the Odin Theatre defines the Third Theatre as a social structure enabling the expression of "ideals, fears, multiple impulses which would otherwise remain more or less obscure" or invisible (1986, 194).[3] The Third Theatre is the identification of a particular kind of theatrical organization in which the development of the complex social relationships and artistic processes necessary in the creation of original performance work serve as the identifying core of the company's work. Barba describes the Third Theatre as "a social cell inside which intentions, aspirations and personal needs begin to be transformed into actions" (194).

While Farfan's collective profile of the work ethic and structural parameters utilized by "Survivors" participants clearly aligns the practice of these organizations and individuals with Third Theatre practice, this profile also positioned these practices outside of mainstream theatrical practice and therefore as "other" than the status quo. Savannah Walling's keynote address (also published in the CTR special edition) further distinguished the work of "Survivors" participants as "other" through the collective profiling of performance practices that extended beyond the realm of the literary theatre. Walling's assessment drew heavily from her then twelve years of experience with her interdisciplinary company, Vancouver Moving Theatre (VMT), and "twenty-five years of work and reflection in the performing arts in Canada" (1996, 17). Walling identified the label of social and political subversiveness as a critical factor in the assignment of an art form's marginal status and stated that "redefining the arts is a political move" (12). This stance is evident in her address, which reads in places as a manifesto for political insurgency and counterattack. She discusses "the act of naming of forces that devalue us and our work [... as a necessary] act of resistance and empowerment" (12). Military

---

3   Eugenio Barba's notion of the Third Theatre was first constituted as an internal address to participants at the "Encounters on Third Theatre" symposium in Belgrade in 1976. The content of this address was subsequently adopted as a kind of manifesto for Third Theatre practice.

strategy resonates further in her words as she encourages emotional detachment from everyday hardships in order to "focus on creative solutions and generate constructive action" (12). She talks of the importance of resisting the difficulties and of developing survival strategies. Her words are impassioned, somewhat foreboding, and highly cautionary.

The experiences of Walling and VMT during the early 1990s are representative of the treatment not only of Primus Theatre, the organizers of the event, but of most of the companies and individual artists attending the "Survivors" symposium and festival, as well as other companies not in attendance who had chosen to work outside of the parameters of mainstream theatre. Walling described VMT's performance work as original repertoire "informed by training practices, theatrical principles, and archetypal themes recurring in oral theatre traditions of many cultures" (12–13) and utilizing an inter-disciplinary array of performance form. The range of form and technique included music, mime, acrobatics, mask and clown work, stilt work, performer-produced musical scores, drum dancing, and elaborately detailed costumes and masks. Although the inspiration and informing principles varied from company to company, the range of technique and form utilized by VMT was highly representative of that utilized by symposium participants. Aware of the resulting hybridity of such a palette of form and technique, Walling stated:

> We know we are not creating dance. We know we are not creating theatre. We are creating what we call "moving theatre." The sum of what we do is not reducible to its parts. When any single element is removed from our work, the whole collapses, just as water, when reduced to its hydrogen and oxygen, disappears into air. (13)

According to Kier Elam, reflexivity occurs when "dramatic worlds [... are] revealed through the persons, actions and statements that make them up, and not through external commentary" (1980, 101). Dramatic worlds created in this way are revealed through the efforts of the artists that shape them rather than through a narrative of those worlds. Although members of VMT were entirely aware of this, their work was nevertheless a consistent subject of criticism and confusion for critics, analysts, and other performance artists.

In *Philosophical Investigations* (1953) Ludwig Wittgenstein argues that it is necessary to name things in order to talk about them. Conversely, without specific terminology it becomes difficult to discuss what "is." Subsequently, dialogue is constructed with existing terminology and generally becomes focused on what "is not." This issue is evident in the responses of numerous critics and analysts in their descriptions and discussions of experimental and hybrid work and contributes to the lack of critical dialogue about certain types of work. Even the expression of positive responses, such as the reactions to *Dog Day*, requires a language with the capacity accurately to represent the actuality of the performance in order to discuss the work with any degree of specificity. According to Walling, dancers criticized vmt's choreography and performance, and theatre practitioners criticized the narrative line (1996, 13). In dealing with these and other reactions, Walling and vmt discovered, almost accidentally, a host of prejudices growing out of rigidly held preconceptions and "rules" about what constituted the nature of theatre. Popular theatre, non-linear narratives, cultural forms from non-European sources, collective creation, performances designed for multiple interpretations, performances set in non-traditional spaces, and children's theatre (13–14) were all performance forms too often unduly dismissed in critical and fiscal contexts as "theatricals" and "spectacles" (13). They were also entirely representative of the range of performance work showcased at the "Survivors" event, including that of Primus Theatre.

Although phenomenologically vmt's work exhibited qualities of both theatre and dance, on paper it qualified as neither. What this meant—in practical and fiscal terms—for theatre artists engaged in the creation of these hybrid forms was that, without the benefit of solid, officially recognized parameters by which to define their art, they were subject to a bureaucratic funding slipstream—often with disastrous immediate and long-term results for the companies affected.

Arguably, the problem that Walling compellingly identified—that of small experimental companies failing to fit comfortably into the officially defined criteria of art required to secure critical institutional recognition and fund-ing—is symptomatic of a much deeper, chronic, and systematic bias against performance-based art forms that is as old as the contemporary English Ca-nadian theatre itself. Alan Filewod's (1998) account of the rise and fall of the Mummers Troupe in Newfoundland (1973–1982) exemplifies the bureaucratic nightmare encountered by companies unable to define their operations within funding agency criteria. The prejudice against collectively created work noted by Walling is substantiated in an excerpt from a Canada Council (cc) grant application assessment of the Mummers performance of *I.W.A.* (1976) found in the National Archives of Canada. In the opinion of arts officer Anna Stratton (nac A-75-1066), the Mummers show was "sketchy," and "suffered from the lack of depth and subtlety that most collectives do"; she credited any dramatic interest or depth to the work of playwright Rick Salutin (quoted in Filewod, 1998, 22). Although not a hybrid company, as defined by Walling, the Mummers Troupe similarly found that its political and dramaturgical parameters were constantly being called into question in funding application assessments. This left Filewod to conclude that "by its refusal to accept the Canada Council's terms of containment, the Mummers Troupe was the typifying expression of Canadian theatre in the 1970s" (1998, 31). That is, despite the now widely acknowledged vitality, originality, and long-term influence of the "alternative theatre" of the 1970s, the advancement of experimental work was being impeded by significant forms of bureaucratic marginalization, especially if, like the Mummers Troupe, it elected to remain "alternative" in its organization and approach to creating new work.

In *Producing Marginality* (1991) Robert Wallace further addresses the long-term implications of such early, definitive examples of marginalization within Canadian theatre through a comparative study of the emergence of indigenous theatre in English and French Canada. While specifically situated in the context of southern Ontario in the late 1980s, Wallace's argument is useful in determining the foundation from which English Canadian theatre developed and, subsequently, the cultural context of most Western Canadian theatre.

Via the content and context of Filewod's analysis in *Collective Encounters: Documentary Theatre in English Canada* (1987), Wallace establishes the postcolonial documentary quality of collectively created work in English Canada and the fact that "documentary theatre evolved parallel to, and in some cases as part of, an emerging dramatic literature" (Filewod, 1987, 182). Filewod points out that the stand taken by the "alternative" theatre movement was in opposition to the publicly supported regional theatre movement that supported foreign models, standards, and content (vii). He also notes that the development of English Canadian collective creation in the 1960s "coincided with a revival of nationalist (and by extension, regionalist) sentiment, and [that] it provided a generation of theatre workers with the artistic method to explore local themes in the absence of an appropriate dramatic literature" (182). In other words, collective creation projects served in the absence of text.

However, as Wallace notes, this parallel development was quickly displaced with the ascendancy of the indigenous playwright, the producer of concrete proof of a maturing national theatre, into a position of privilege and authority (1990, 177). This primacy, he notes (177), is exemplified in a 1961/62 Canada Council annual report stating that "living theatre demands living playwrights [...] the Canadian Theatre demands Canadian playwrights" (Canada Council, 1962, 33). In establishing this stand, the Canada Council not only placed literary text in a privileged position, but also effectively separated the playwright from the performance. Disturbingly, this early stand by Canada Council policymakers not only permeated the development of English Canadian theatre culture in the 1960s, but also continued, seemingly unchallenged, for the next three decades. As a result, the development of theatre in English Canada was very different from that in French Canada.

In contrast to the several dozen collective creations produced in English Canada as a means of jump-starting the development of indigenous dramatic literature, thousands of collectively created performance pieces were produced in Québec between 1958 and 1980. French Canadians testing their sense of self and culture had broken the mode of colonist complacency years before their English Canadian counterparts. By the early 1970s Québec had developed an active literary drama nurtured by Le centre d'essai des auteurs dramatique (CEAD), founded in 1965, and was producing a profusion of collectively created material through the efforts of the Association québécoise du jeune théâtre (AQJT). As the efforts of AQJT gained momentum, *jeune théâtre* became a movement in Québec and collective creation was acknowledged as a viable alternative to literary drama. Furthermore, AQJT was viewed as the centre of radical theatre, not as contributing to the establishment of an indigenous culture. By the 1980s, for Québec theatre artists "experimentation with theatrical structures and multi-disciplinary forms [...] had] replaced community research and development as the informing principle of group creation" (Wallace, 1990, 179–80).

While recessionary times in the 1990s created hardships for companies in both French and English Canada, the situation for small experimental companies in English Canada was particularly dire. Not only were they facing bleak economic times marked by diminishing arts funding, but they were continuing to deal with funding agencies with a historical bias against theatres that failed to "evolve" from their documentary or collective beginnings into "mature" producers and interpreters of an indigenous dramatic literature. It was a terrifying vise for small experimental companies already living on the margins to be caught in, and many of them, pressured beyond endurance, either disappeared or began a slow fade. Walling noted that the Canada Council discontinued funding to VMT because "the work had 'developed in such a way that it could no longer compete successfully with other funding priorities if situated exclusively in a dance context' (or alternatively, a theatre context)" (Walling, 1996, 14). In effect, the Canada Council was suggesting that VMT make an attempt to fit into a category in which they could be judged more easily, and in this statement essentially discouraged evolution and experimentation of form. While it is not difficult to position funding agencies and critics as disengaged saboteurs and spoilers of pioneering and experimental work, in reality this is only part of the issue. As Anne Wilson reveals in "A Jury of Her Peers" (1987, 8), artists are being judged by the paradoxical construction of a peer jury. This means that a select group of artists are given the power of authority to pass judgment on the work of other artists. Wallace further indicates that these individuals are "used to construct [...] the criteria that govern acts of evaluation and thereby to determine the means and manner in which other people create their work" (1990, 130). He concludes that "critics can only pass judgment once art is produced; teachers can only interpret art once it is available; artists, however, can dictate art's very existence" (129). Therefore, the resistance to the validation of evolving art forms can be seen as coming from other artists as well as from external forces.

However, for Fowler, Walling, Farfan, and other participants at the "Survivors" symposium, acceptance of the status quo was not an option, regardless of the safety and structure it offered. As Fowler stated:

> To me, the artist is the person in a culture who effects change. Our culture is mainly concerned with fixing things in place, making them predictable, reducing the unknown so that we can control it. I think that this is terribly dangerous—and boring. There is of course a necessary practical element to this. And it is good that some people concern themselves with it. But, god help us, if we are only a society of fixers and controllers, for our health and survival, there must also be those whose responsibility is to change our concept of reality, to break it open so that we can breathe inside it. (quoted in Brask, 1992, 88)

In the company's fall 1996 newsletter, which was published after the "Survivors" symposium, Fowler described the intense and hectic 1995–1996 season as the company's busiest and most successful season to date (Primus Theatre Newsletter, Fall 1996). Given the remarkably extensive body of work produced by the company in a relatively short period of time, it would be heartening to think that Primus Theatre's wide range of accomplishments was due to an increasingly supportive context in which to work. This, however, was not the case. Throughout its existence, company members continued to face the kinds of hurdles identified by Farfan and Walling in the context of the "Survivors" symposium/festival, and by Filewod and Wallace in reference to earlier hybrid or "alternative" work.

These adversarial conditions were often ignored, diminished, or remained undisclosed when the company was mentioned in prelude pieces or general arts community commentary in local periodicals. In an article in the *Winnipeg Free Press* revisiting Winnipeg theatre in the year 1996, entertainment writer Kevin Prokosh revealed a generally unacknowledged occurrence in the city: that there was very little support of any kind for small theatre companies. I suspect that Prokosh's point was unintentional, but it nevertheless supports Knowles's (1996) observations of the continued marginalization of certain types of theatre at a national level during this time period. Prokosh stated:

We may look back on 1996 as the year that Winnipeg companies finally split into the haves and have-nots. Large groups such as Manitoba Theatre Centre and Prairie Theatre Exchange, which boast stable financial support and resources, are as healthy as arts organizations can be in the '90s. PTE expanded its 1996-97 playbill in a bid for a larger audience, while MTC was able to dip into a rainy day fund to pay off a $165,000 deficit and remain the only Canadian regional theatre without an operating deficit. The news was not so good for small groups, such as Popular Theatre Alliance and Theatre Projects, neither of which staged productions this fall. [...] Signs of financial strain are also apparent in the Winnipeg Jewish Theatre. [...] By most standards, Winnipeg theatre is vibrant and supported by the most devoted fans in the country. It is cold reality that the better a company is doing the more people want to support it. The converse is also true: the worse you do, the less help is available. (December 30, 1996, C1)

On one level, the article is astute in acknowledging the presence of an entrenched systemic bias in favour of the "have" theatres with identifiable physical spaces and a recognized literary product. Yet ironically, in what he says and does not say about the companies that he feels do "worse" by that criteria, Prokosh simultaneously, and most likely less consciously, reveals a similar set of entrenched systemic biases in the critical establishment intent on reporting and supposedly analyzing the arts scene for the public.

As observed by Wallace, during the 1970s the English Canadian playwright increasingly assumed a central role in the theatrical creative process as the generator of a literary text that would be handed off to directors, actors, and a production and design team whose responsibility was "to 'realize' the playwright's work in a production that adheres to his or her demands, which are often contractually assured" (1990, 181). Subsequently, the main responsibility of critics and reviewers was "to determine a playwright's intentions in writing a script—a practice that perpetuates the separation of text from production" (181). Furthermore, if the premises suggested by Paul Leonard in his article "Critical Questioning" can be accepted, then it can be concluded that the critic in English Canada simply could not explain performance generated from "other" than a literary text. If one accepts Leonard's claim that the critic had been schooled to focus on the literary aspect of performance due to the tendency of learning institutions to classify theatre as literature (1988, 6–7); and if one accepts his deduction that as a result "the critic [...] considers the performance as simply a mediation between the audience and the script" (6–7), then an accurate assessment of a performance emerging from other than these presuppositions becomes highly improbable for the critic. When faced with a performance generated from other than a literary text, the critic all too often found the currency of communication unrecognizable. Unable to refer to a known entity, the form of a written text, the critic defined the difference as a deficit. The performance became suspect and was then either discussed and ultimately judged for what it was not, or, simply dismissed.

When a critic, assumed to be the mediator between a literary text and a potential audience member, cannot serve this function and lacks the vocabulary with which to offer an alternative analysis, but instead defaults to a discourse of perceived deficit or outright dismissal of the performance, a great injustice has been done to the experimental work in question. This is a serious matter in its own right, raising issues of public support for artistic innovation and of the critic's responsibility towards expanding audience awareness. However, such a course of action also has serious immediate ramifications. When a critic, such as Prokosh, uses fiscal standards in a public assessment of a the-atre company's "success" in a community in which s/he regularly reviews performance work, the result is an insidious reinforcement of the notion that the value of a performance is determined by box-office revenue. Given that Prokosh's article openly acknowledged slanted audience support for companies deemed to be "successful," he would have been aware of the effect that this information would have had on the theatre-going public in Winnipeg. Not only did Prokosh actively contribute to the construction of a hierarchical rank-ing of theatrical value in the city of Winnipeg, but in doing so he reinforced the parameters of marginalization and the perpetuation of the status quo for companies already leading a fringe existence. The "have-not" companies that Prokosh mentions—Popular Theatre Alliance, Theatre Projects (currently Theatre Projects Manitoba) and Winnipeg Jewish Theatre (wjt)—had been in existence for twelve, six and nine years respectively.[4] Yet Prokosh reduced the work of these companies to base monetary value instead of using the op-portunity to discuss the highly limited arts funding pool in Manitoba in which small companies were competing with large organizations such as MTC and PTE that were viewed as more financially viable investments.

Prokosh also completely ignores several small, established companies in his "have" and "have-not" stratification. At the time, Adhere and Deny[5] had

4   After years of struggling to make ends meet and several near collapses Theatre Projects (now Theatre Projects Manitoba) and Winnipeg Jewish Theatre have each reached a relatively stable position and have continued into the present (2011). Popular Theatre Alliance folded in 1998.

5   Adhere and Deny emerged from a company called Shared Stage that was founded in 1981. The company was renamed Adhere and Deny in 1987 and by 1998 had nar-rowed its focus to puppet and object-based theatre (www.adhereanddeny.com; Longfield, 2001, 171).

been in operation, in one form or another, for fifteen years during which time members of the company had attempted to redefine theatre and to appeal to an other-than-mainstream audience. Prokosh also failed to mention the then three-year-old Shakespeare in the Ruins, an initiative by local actors focused on the production of Shakespeare's plays using a promenade structure. In failing to mention these theatre companies, Prokosh unwittingly created the category of "are-not." In drawing attention to the financial struggle of some established companies without even acknowledging others, Prokosh inadvertently included the press in a kind of passive-aggressive exposure of the realities of Winnipeg's theatre culture. This kind of blindsiding of experimental and smaller scale theatrical operations is representative of the position taken by most reviewers in the city, which contributed to the "have" and "have-not" status defined by Prokosh.

Even when an "are-not" company was deemed worthy of mention in prelude pieces or general arts community commentary in local periodicals, the adversarial conditions impeding its success or progress were often ignored or diminished or remained undisclosed. In Prokosh's article, Primus Theatre was addressed in a single point-form comment, in which he makes claim to the company's well-being by noting "the continued success of the globe-trotting Primus Theatre Troupe" (December 30, 1996, C1). With this highly simplistic, and seemingly complimentary, statement, Prokosh has eliminated any notion of Primus Theatre's ongoing financial and cultural struggle. Yet he very blatantly stated these conditions with reference to other companies. He chose to ignore the fact that the company faced near extinction in early 1993, when the City of Winnipeg overestimated attendance for a New Year's Eve, First Night Celebration,[6] and was unable to pay performing artists whose services had been booked for the event. Primus was left with a $10,500 deficit: a staggering sum for a small theatre company. The seriousness of this shortfall was further compounded by the Winnipeg Arts Advisory Council (WAAC) decision to cut its funding to the arts by thirty percent and by the freezing of other government funding (Lett, June 3, 1993, A1). Prokosh also failed to explain, or perhaps was unaware of the fact, that the company's "globe-trotting" ventures

---

6   First Night 1992 was a financial disaster. Based on attendance numbers from the pilot First Night project in 1991, event planners expanded the format of the evening to include dozens more mini-events. New Year's Eve 1991 had been uncharacteristically mild. However, New Year's Eve 1992 was brutally cold and attendance was actually down from the year before. This resulted in financial disaster. Dozens of artists were not paid their fees as this was supposed to have come from collective box-office revenues. Low attendance meant that many artists and small companies were placed in devastating financial situations. For Primus this meant a ten thousand dollar deficit.

were actually company retreats to the tiny southern Italian village of Nocelle, Fowler's home away from Canada. During this time company members were training and developing new performance material and learning new skills from master instructors whom they would have been unable to access in Canada. Furthermore, living in southern Italy and bartering odd jobs for rehearsal space was actually a money-saving venture.

Instead, Prokosh's commentary alluded to an easy existence that was not only inaccurate but dismissive and disrespectful. Most specifically, this dismissal is evident in his failure properly to acknowledge the company's relationship to its cultural context. This is particularly disconcerting considering that Prokosh was a local theatre reviewer with first-hand access to support material for his article. This tunnel vision is resonant of a *Toronto Star* article, five years earlier, announcing Primus as Winnipeg's leading alternative theatre company ("Alternative," March 27, 1991, F7). While this was certainly a title that Primus Theatre made use of, this distinction detracts from the substantial pioneering ventures undertaken by the company in the advancement of an alternative theatre community.

In a 1991 article for the *Globe and Mail*, Stephen Godfrey noted the utter amazement expressed by auteur Robert Lepage towards what he viewed as the massive restrictions placed on English Canadian Theatre.[7] Well aware of these "restrictions," members of Primus Theatre were looking to make a difference and were working with the belief that theatre had the potential to "re-define inherited reality, be that reality political, physical, or psychological" and through that redefinition to create an "alternative model for human interaction" (Fowler, 1996, 54). It was this steadfast sense of artistic purpose combined with a concrete dramaturgical directive that fuelled company morale during difficult times of financial ebb and flow. Nevertheless, this did not mean that company members were immune to the hardships. In an undated journal entry summarizing company life in early February 1994, Stephen Lawson wrote:

> We have no money to pay ourselves these days. This is very hard on all of us. Ker and Don are working in Mary Dixon's warehouse, Karin is teaching, I am at Winnona's Café, Tannis doesn't have work (or is she doing some substitute teaching?) and Richard is trying to live off of a pitiful sum of money from a translation he did for Eugenio [Barba]. We are every day in the office though and I am proud to be working with such strong committed people. I despise poverty, and yet it is a cruel teacher,

7   Lepage was quoted as saying "we are making theatre here not shoes" (in Godfrey, October 12, 1991, C1).

exposing the excesses in my life, and the excesses in my society, my community. Give and Thou Shalt Receive, What Goes Around Comes Around, Money is the Root of All Evil—very small comfort these days. Slowly I chip away at everything that I think is valuable, trying to expose the necessities. (Primus Theatre Company Journal, February 1994)[8]

Although the early part of Lawson's summary indicates that plans are in motion for a Western Canadian tour, and that the company received notice from several granting agencies announcing forthcoming funding, the summary also indicates a continuing ebb and flow with regard to financial matters. Five years into a prolific and artistically sound company existence, Primus members were still scrambling for financial survival. A survey of archival materials serves to support this through the existence of dozens of files addressing various aspects of fundraising. Yet prelude pieces or general arts information in periodicals, local and otherwise, generally affirm Prokosh's pronunciation of Primus Theatre's "success." I surmise that this conclusion was drawn in part from a somewhat fundamental and automatic alignment of artistic and/or critical success with financial stability. Furthermore, as indicated by Prokosh's article, Winnipeg spectators generally tended to support theatres that were financially successful rather than those that were less so. Therefore, strategically, it would not have been in the company's best interest to draw attention to this fact. In light of this continual barrage of funding and audience development issues, Primus Theatre's achievements are even more remarkable.

When placed in the contexts provided by Filewod, Leonard, Prokosh, Wallace, and Wilson, the experiences of the Mummers Troupe, Vancouver Moving Theatre, Primus Theatre, and other participants of the "Survivors" symposium/festival reveal a three-decade span in which the work of theatre companies recognized as "creators of indigenous original art" or of "politically or aesthetically alternative" work (Farfan, Knowles, Leonard, Wallace, Walling) have not been fairly represented either qualitatively or quantitatively in critical or historical documentation. Critical material that does exist often subjugates these hybrid forms of theatre with a critical structure emerging from dramatic literature. Furthermore, the dearth of even skewed perspectives on this work can be seen as having a serious consequence for the accurate portrayal of the development of theatre in Canada, particularly in English Canada.

8   The entry is attached to the journal and appears after the entry for November 8–14, 1993. The next entry is dated October 4, 1994. The entry referred to is attached to a blank page between the two entries. The introduction reads "Journal entry for the period of . . . February?" The time period has been deduced mathematically.

As Filewod states in his examination of the Mummers Troupe experience, the most accurate representation of the development of English Canadian theatre can be found in the practical struggles of small companies in an effort to define or redefine the theatre that they were engaging in. Sadly, as indicated by Filewod and Prokosh, many of these struggles end in the demise of a theatre company. In the English Canadian theatre culture in which text was seemingly inextricably bound to the concept of theatre and in which collectively created work was utilized as a handmaiden for the development of an indigenous Canadian literary theatre, hybrid work was being punished by critical and funding structures simply for "failing" to serve this paradigm.

Worse yet, for those companies whose creative process and production structures do not serve to validate a literary text, it is an exclusion that also denies them a proper assessment in a historical record, which again is traditionally based on the survival of physical artifacts (like buildings) and written documentation. Without evidence transcribed or generated by scholars and informed critics, the work produced by these companies has not been represented in the landscape of Canadian theatre. Consequently the existing portrait of the Canadian theatrical landscape can be considered far from an accurate representation of the practical reality. As Shelley Scott notes in her study "Feminist Theory and Nightwood Theatre" (1997), "it is difficult to speculate how a project that was not realized might have altered the direction of history had it ever seen the light of day" (1996, 11).

Canadian theatre artists and their performance work are disappearing before our eyes, moving silently and ceaselessly beyond the grasp of public accessibility, both in live and historical contexts. Countless archives of small theatre companies and ensembles are already lost. Many more are in danger of extinction if action is not taken to articulate, preserve, and document the existing information. The absence of an ongoing administrative infrastructure, usually an issue related to funding, during the operational years of marginalized companies and solo ventures has contributed extensively to limitations in the quantity and quality of documented creative work and work processes. Furthermore, as indicated by Farfan, many fringe and marginalized theatre companies found themselves without a permanent space. As a result, the archive collections belonging to these companies were often stored in basements or attics or garages, both during and after the company's operation, rather than being housed in appropriate facilities. In addition to this loss of information due to a lack of appropriate storage space and/or due to limitations in the documentation itself, information referring to the creative activity of fringe and marginalized theatre companies occurring prior to the current and prevalent use of digital recording has been lost or overlooked in this shift from paper to digital modes of documentation.

The disappearance of information about theatrical activity in Canada is further compounded by factors that determine what information is most likely to be documented and collected. I refer to performance work condemned to obscurity in the carnage of shifting critical paradigms and terminology. At particular risk are theatrical forms that have not conformed to the dominant literary paradigm. I refer to work forged in geographically isolated places or in aesthetically isolated sectors of a larger demography. It is a simple fact that even marginalized performance work generated in large, financially thriving urban centres receives more attention than similar performance work in smaller and/or poorer sectors of the country. I refer to work created in a time not so far removed that has been kept alive only in recollections of those who lived it. It is shocking to realize how quickly phenomenology takes on the mantle of history and, without a tangible and publically accessible legacy, disappears almost as if it had not existed at all.

The term "black ice" is often used as a generic term to describe a highly treacherous and difficult-to-detect coating of thin ice that takes on the colour of the surface that it covers. In other words, the danger is essentially invisible until contact. It is a prairie winter-weather condition that is impossible to avoid if you are going to venture forth at all. What is required is a highly sensitive navigation of the condition that necessitates an ever-present readiness to negotiate the surface when the slippage occurs. Furthermore, this needs to be done with ease and grace in order to avoid falling. It is a kind of slow dance and exactly what Primus Theatre and other experimental fringe theatres did in order to survive.

Primus Theatre is described as "one of the most significant collectives in Canadian history" (Barton, 2008, xi) in the introduction to *Collective Creation, Collaboration and Devising,* a collection of articles focusing on the creation of original theatre in English Canada. Yet, beyond archival material, and a recently completed large-scale study of my own, print documentation of the company's work does not exist beyond a small collection of articles, minor chapter entries, and a series of performance reviews and prelude pieces. A new and evolving generation of devised and collectively constructed performance work is currently being produced by former Primus members and theatre artists influenced and inspired by the company's research and dramaturgical practices, and this new work has gained critical and scholarly attention. While these examinations and analyses refer to the former association or influence of Primus Theatre, they often default to the work of Eugenio Barba and the Odin Theatre by way of explaining the nature of the creative processes and the genealogy of this work.

I find it disturbing that a company whose work lives on in the origins of a second generation of performance work, and has been acknowledged as an important contribution to the development of Canadian theatre, has been largely ignored in the national critical discourse. I am also deeply concerned about the broader implications of this occurrence: the loss of an accurate discourse on Canadian theatre. How many other companies and individuals who dared to practice the art of slow dancing on black ice have been excluded from this discourse, and what is the cost of the absence of this knowledge?

Works Cited

Adhere and Deny. "Adhere and Deny: History." www.adhereanddeny.com (accessed December 27, 2009).

"Alternative Theatre Thrives in Winnipeg." *Toronto Star,* March 27, 1991: F7.

Barba, Eugenio. *Beyond the Floating Islands.* Trans. Judy Barba, Richard Fowler, Jerrold C. Rodesch, and Saul Shapiro. New York: PAJ Publications, 1986.

Barton, Bruce. *Collective Creation, Collaboration and Devising.* Toronto: Playwrights Canada Press, 2008.

Brask, Per. "The Anthropology of Performance: An Interview with Richard Fowler." *Canadian Theatre Review* 71 (Summer 1992): 81–88.

The Canada Council. *Annual Report.* Ottawa: 1961–62.

Crossley, Karen. "Around and About the Fringe Festival." *Winnipeg Sun,* July 20, 1989: 22.

Elam, Kier. *The Semiotics of Theatre and Drama.* London: Routledge, 1980.

Enright Robert. Review of *Dog Day. 24 Hours,* July 19, 1989. Typescript. Primus Theatre [company archives], Winnipeg, MB.

Farfan, Penny. "Survivors of the Ice Age Festival and Symposium." *Canadian Theatre Review* 88 (Fall 1996): 6–10.

Filewod, Alan. *Collective Encounters: Documentary Theatre in English Canada.* Toronto: University of Toronto Press, 1987.

———. "The Mummers Troupe, The Canada Council and the Production of Theatre History." *Theatre Research in Canada* 19:1 (Spring/Printemps 1998): 3–34.

Fowler, Richard. "Why Did We Do It?" *Canadian Theatre Review* 88 (Fall 1996): 54–55.

Godfrey, Stephen. "Practice, Practice, Pract. . . ." *Globe and Mail* [Toronto], October 12, 1991: C1.

Good, Jacquie. Review of *Dog Day.* CBC *Information Radio,* July 19, 1989. Typescript. Primus Theatre [company archives], Winnipeg, MB.

Knowles, Richard Paul. "Survivors of the Ice Age." *Canadian Theatre Review* 88 (Fall 1996): 3–4.

Leonard, Paul. "Critical Questioning." *Canadian Theatre Review* 57 (Winter 1988): 4–10.

Lett, Dan. "Cuts drop curtains on arts." *Winnipeg Free Press,* June 3, 1993: A1.

Longfield, Kevin. "And Now for Something Completely Different: From Theatre X to Primus." *From Fire to Flood: A History of Theatre in Manitoba.* Winnipeg: Signature Editions, 2001, 166–78.

NAC Canada Council Grants Applications. RG 63. A-75-1066, box 23.

Primus Theatre. Company Journal: Volume Four. September 7, 1993 to July 31/August 4, 1995. Primus Theatre [company archives], Winnipeg, MB.

——. Newsletter, Fall 1996. Primus Theatre [company archives], Winnipeg, MB.

Prokosh, Kevin. "Theatrical FareWel." *Winnipeg Free Press,* December 30, 1996: C1.

Scott, Shelley. "Feminist Theory and Nightwood Theatre." PhD diss., University of Toronto, 1997.

Taft, Beverly. "Hard Times: How Theatres are Surviving the Tough Economic Times." *Theatrum* 32 (February/March 1993): 10–16.

Wallace, Robert. *Producing Marginality: Theatre Criticism in Canada.* Saskatoon: Fifth House Publishers, 1990.

Walling, Savannah. "Survival Techniques: Forces on the Artists/Artists on the Forces." *Canadian Theatre Review* 88 (Fall 1996): 11–17.

Wilson, Anne. "A Jury of Her Peers." *Canadian Theatre Review* 51 (Summer 1987): 4–8.

Wittgenstein, Ludwig. *Philosophical Investigations.* Trans. G.E.M. Anscombie. 3rd ed. London: Blackwell Publishing, 2001.

Identity Performance in Carol Shields's Stage Plays

GLEN NICHOLS

[*The characters*] *fall silent again, while the clock ticks and a microwave dings. Everyone rises in one synchronized motion, grabs their books, bags and coats from hooks. Each pauses an instant to look in a mirror, pats their hair in a synchronized motion and then leaves. A clock ticks quickly; the lights darken outside; lamps go on inside. A door opens, the family rushes in one by one, and hangs their coats on hooks* [...]. (Fashion, Power, Guilt and the Charity of Families, 255)[1]

The three women gesture broadly at each other, shrugging, questioning. Nickelodeon music grows louder. They go again to the window and look out. One goes to the chart and turns to the next title: 'This is very mysterious.' One woman rushes offstage and returns with a tea tray; she mimes an offer of tea, but the others shake their heads. [...] *The young* CLARA *enters, running from stage left. The others embrace her and lead her to the table. They sit at the table, pick up their cards. A warm golden, steady light replaces the black and white film flicker; nickelodeon music fades to recorded music. The women freeze. Light slowly fades. Very gradual introduction of tape of women talking and laughing.* (Thirteen Hands, 416)

---

1   Unless otherwise noted, all page references refer to the 2002 reprint collection of Shields's plays.

I t may surprise some readers to learn that these theatrically heightened moments come from the plays of renowned novelist Carol Shields. While her fiction is the subject of considerable scholarly and critical interest, her theatrical contributions are relatively less well known. Although her plays have received many professional productions, their theatrical and thematic complexity has often been overlooked or misunderstood. Rather than being simplistic and clichéd, as is often charged, her plays provocatively explore the dynamics of identity formation in social space through the use of multi-faceted theatrical strategies.

There has been very little (and no recent) scholarly attention paid to her plays, and the critical reviews could be described as mixed. For example, Keith Garebian in *Quill and Quire* described her plays as "unfortunately neither experimental nor very good" (2002, 39). Jerry Wasserman commented that the sketches in *Departures and Arrivals* are "often clever but superficial" and exhibit the "gentle ironic humour of old TV variety show skits" (1991, 86). Dale Lakevold, damning with faint praise, considered *Anniversary* to be "modest and efficient" (1999, 177).

In fact, however, the less positive comments on her dramatic work come largely from literary reviews of the published plays, while reviews of the productions or, more accurately, reviews by critics with an understanding of the theatrical potential in the texts tend to be more positive about Shields's plays. For example, Wasserman, who is a stage and television actor as well as a renowned theatre researcher and critic, concluded his review in *University of Toronto Quarterly*, despite the lukewarm comments cited above, by connecting the play's "metatheatre and magic" to a recognition of Shields's "sense of real dramatic talent in the offing" (1991, 87). Chris Johnson, who came to Shields's plays first as a director, notes that "dense, emotionally complex, revealing [scenes] are found throughout" *Departures and Arrivals* ("Ordinary Pleasures," 1995, 162). Mira Friedlander wrote in *Variety* that she found the 1997 National Arts Centre production of *Thirteen Hands* "gracefully crafted" (1997, 94). Kathleen Flaherty, who would go on to direct *Thirteen Hands* at Prairie Theatre Exchange in 1993, reviewed the published text of *Departures and Arrivals* in 1991 as "absurdity at its best, delicate, slightly unreal dialogue spinning a web of incidents" (1991, 31). Flaherty's appreciation of theatricality is underscored by her comment that the "physical demands of the play are fairly onerous, [but] well worth solving" (32).

What these reviewers share, and what is clearly missing from the more negative literary reviews, is an understanding of the plays' diverse theatricalism. Instead, the latter seem to be expecting realistic representations of psychologically rounded characters in believable settings, etc., criteria that are inappropriate for Shields's plays.

For example, Garebian comments that the characters in *Departures and Arrivals* "inexplicably reveal things no air passengers ever would" (2002, 39), revealing his own expectations of realistic representation. An anonymous reviewer of *Fashion, Power, Guilt and the Charity of Families*, again in *Quill and Quire* in 1995, found that the "characters disturbingly, even embarrassingly burst into song which neither advances the play nor enriches the text" and critiqued the play for "purposely lacking in verisimilitude" (36). Further confusing a text intended for the stage with a text meant to be read, he or she noted, somewhat embarrassingly, that "[characters] spend 63 *pages* fretting and strutting" (36, emphasis added). This reviewer's resistance to seeing beyond the printed page or beyond the search for "verisimilitude" and linear and logical plot development prevented any recognition of the theatrical performance potential in the play. Finally, another anonymous reviewer in *Books in Canada* (1993), after spending most of the review of *Thirteen Hands* quibbling about punctuation misuse, is disappointed that Shields "achieves many of her effects by purely theatrical rather than literary means" (35). The reviewer seems surprised that such an accomplished novelist would fall so short by creating a play that was theatrical rather than literary; however, the observation is actually very revealing.

Not only did Shields write her plays for the theatre and not simply to be read, but she wrote plays that exploit the full potential of the modern theatrical medium. Reviewers applying criteria pertinent to the reading of her novels come up short when confronted with her plays, sometimes lacking even an appropriate vocabulary to discuss them.

It is worth noting that Shields's writing for the theatre spans the 1980s and 1990s, a period that saw English Canadian theatre move away from the dominance of kitchen-sink realism of earlier dramatists, such as David French and David Freeman, and towards a more "complex visual vocabulary" (Wasserman, 2001, 21). Shields was fascinated by the theatre of her time and, although her work has never been considered in light of contemporary Canadian playwrights, she was clearly influenced by modern Canadian staging ideas (2002, ix; and Bell, 1998, 5). However, Shields's plays cannot be dismissed as simply a series of showy tricks. Her theatrical sophistication is integral to the ideas the plays deal with: in particular, explorations of identity formation link Shields's skilled use of theatrical forms to contemporary social and community issues.

The interrogation of identity formation in these plays revolves around the enactment of a particular dynamic tension. On one hand, comments in the plays about "core of being" and "pretence" suggest a leaning towards essentialist identity formation; however, the plays also enact strategies that destabilize the essentialist view of identity. Indeed, the tension between identity as essential and static versus identity as contingent and performative develops a multidimensional resistance to the either/or binary throughout these plays. Furthermore, the plays do not simply depict this resistance, but rather use the theatrical medium itself to embody the performative tensions. Sherrill Grace calls this kind of dual performance "performing performativity" in her essay on auto/biographical representation in contemporary Canadian theatre (2005, 70). She endorses Jill Dolan's invitation to "locate ways in which live theatre performance can '*reveal* performativity'" (quoted in "Performing," 2005, 66). Although Grace is interested specifically in auto/biographical constructions of self on stage, her observation that "identities being performed live are inescapably embodied and performative" (2006, 16) points to the exploration of identity in Shields's plays. The conditions for this dynamic tension are also elaborated on by Marvin Carlson:

> [...]neither an essentialist performance of identity nor a materialist performance dealing with the process of identity construction is as common as some sort of negotiated space between these positions. Most modern politically oriented performance is flexible very much in the manner that [Elin] Diamond suggests, slipping back and forth between claiming an identity position and ironically questioning the cultural assumptions that legitimate it. The goal is not to deny identity but on the contrary to provide, through performance, alternate possibilities for identity positions outside those authenticated by conventional performance and representation. (2004, 194)

Although the object of Diamond's work is not strictly theatre, her observations can be useful here to understand how Shields's drama puts "performance" back into the "theatre," at the "ineluctable intersection of performativity and performance" (2000, 36):

> When performativity materializes as performance in that risky and dangerous negotiation between a doing (a reiteration of norms) and a thing done (discursive conventions that frame our interpretations) [...] we have access to cultural meanings and critique. ("*Introduction,*" 1996, 5)

This paper will explore how Carol Shields's four published plays—*Departures and Arrivals* (1990), *Thirteen Hands* (1993), *Fashion, Power, Guilt and the Charity of Families* (1995), and *Anniversary* (1998)[2]—set themselves up as

2   The dates indicate when the plays were first published, not first produced.

if based on the expectations of familiar forms, as if the characters are indeed representational truths, but then how the destabilization of scenic conventions negotiates a distancing between these "norms" of identity formation and the "discursive conventions" that frame them. The "norms" are indeed "reiterated" and the plays can be seen to respond to Diamond's search for a theatre that performs a "resignifying of performativity" (2000, 32). Her analysis looks to Samuel Beckett's *Waiting for Godot* which, "in performance, then, not only demonstrates performativity—the repetitive citing of the norms of meaning—it demonstrates what those norms dissimulate: the power relations and fantasies inhering in identification" (38). And I would suggest that such an approach is useful for understanding Shields's plays.

The argument will comprise three sections. The first will identify how each of the four plays does indeed destabilize traditional concepts of identity formation in social space by setting up expectations for essentialized characters and representational stage action only to undermine these expectations in performance. The second section will explore how the plays use metatheatrical scenic vocabulary to embody the tensions between essentialized and performative identity formations, suggesting alternate identity positions through a resignifying of reiterated norms and a "performance of performativity." Finally the third section will examine how the plays' resistance to closure gives rise to a kind of "playing between spaces" that enlarges upon the transformational potential of performative identity.

PART ONE: IDENTITY FORMATION AND SOCIAL SPACE

Carol Shields described how she hoped her earliest full-length play, *Departures and Arrivals* (1984), would "realize a fusion of the real and the unreal, the naturalistic and the fantastic. This is a comedy with edges" (2002, 2). First produced by The Black Hole Theatre at the University of Manitoba, the play, a loose collection of twenty-two, mostly unconnected, vignettes set in the departures and arrivals area of an airport, is significant for understanding Shields's approach to destabilizing putative concepts of identity.

One of the earliest scenes in the play depicts the arrival of an "important personage," **Miss Horton-Hollis**, who is met by a bevy of reporters. In the scrum, she describes her current therapy treatment as "Psychic reconstruction, unmasking the self so you can find the true core of being" (30). Asked to elaborate on this, she describes "core of being" as an "amalgam of the absence and presence. The intersection of innerness and outerness[, …] otherness and ethos, nature and anti-nature[, …] a question of arrivals and departures" (30–1). This important scene that alludes to the title of the play describes the self ("core of being") not as a stable, essential centre but rather as something in flux, an active relationship between the actions of a person and his/her contexts. There is the synthesis of representation and agency ("absence and presence"), the role of social space in the constituency of self ("otherness and ethos"), as well as the importance of "innerness and outerness." The scene plays on the tension between assumptions of identity as natural fact, something innate and knowable ("nature"), and the performative implications of the interaction with "anti-nature." The self is not constructed through one *or* the other of these binary positions, but rather is the interperformance of one *and* the other.

The key to reading the scene this way is the character named simply **Reporter Three**. He is introduced as the serious journalist in the scrum, who would have preferred to be covering the Agricultural Support Talks and who ridicules his colleagues for asking about **Horton-Hollis**'s romantic life: "This person is on a quest to the centre of being, and you slobs want to talk about some Tinseltown romance" (31). Ironically, however, it is he who is missing the point. **Horton-Hollis**'s performance of herself as the Tinseltown star through her manufactured romances ("**REPORTER ONE.** All I want to know is, is it on or off? **MISS HORTON-HOLLIS.** Off. But talk to me tomorrow." 31) is the centre of her being. The irony of the reporter vainly searching for some kind of essential truth ("Like… like… like life's kind of like, sort of, you know, a cycle… and the custom's officer sort of symbolizes, well, you know, he sort of represents—" 31) highlights by contrast the performative sense of identity being played out by **Horton-Hollis** herself.

In a second example, Shields continued to explore concepts of identity formation throughout the long evolution of the play that appears the most traditionally structured, *Anniversary*, first written as a Manitoba Playwrights Development Project in 1982 with Dave Williamson, a Winnipeg writer and educator. A one-act version called *Not Another Anniversary* was produced by Solar Stage in Toronto in October 1986. The full-length version, originally published in 1998, was produced at the Gas Station Theatre in Winnipeg in June 1996.

Anniversary, a play about "the nature of pretence" (127), is set in the living-dining room of a modern middle-class home in some disarray. The couple who used to live here have separated, but **Tom** has come over so he and **Dianne**, who still lives in the house with their two children, can begin to divide up their property. Shortly after **Tom** arrives, two old friends of the couple, **Shirley** and **Ben**, turn up unexpectedly, as does **Dianne**'s current lover, **Garth**. **Tom** and **Dianne** want to keep their breakup a secret from **Shirley** and **Ben**, and **Dianne** of course wants to keep **Garth**'s real purpose for being there under wraps. The result is a recipe for classic farce: unexpected arrivals and discoveries, the tension of near-revelations and misunderstandings, the titillation of illicit relations, witty language, and an apparently happy, restorative ending.

In keeping with the traditional formula for comedy, the play is structured around strict adherence to traditional Aristotelian conventions of time and place. There is a single setting for the entire play and after each act break the action picks up exactly where it left off before the intermission, effecting perfect unity of place and time. Ric Knowles, in his analysis of form in modern Canadian drama, makes the case for linking Aristotelian dramatic structures to "meanings and ideologies that [they] inscribe, fundamentally conservative and patriarchal" (1999, 31). However, while *Anniversary* never achieves what Knowles calls "dramaturgy of the perverse," that is, a form that revisions Aristotelian concepts of reversal and recognition (44), Shields does destabilize the conservative conventions she calls upon, both formal and thematic, including aspects of identity formation.

In the "Playwrights' Note" included with the published text, Shields and Williamson outline the various questions about friendship, marriage, and relationships they want the play to put before the audience. They conclude their list with these questions: "What is the nature of pretence and how damaging is it? And, finally, are we all, in some sense, pretenders?" (2002, 127). In traditional farce, pretence is often the object of ridicule, the social falseness the play exposes and ridicules. The playwrights' use of the term here seems to point to both conventional farce and conventional concepts of identity: stable and interior, something that can be hidden or dissimulated and thus the source of comic revelations leading to conservative restoration of social order. However, the play in fact turns both sets of conventions on their heads by suggesting, through upsetting the traditional farce expectations, that identity is actually a performative creation of self, a performance understood only within a social framework. Pretence is not the false mask hiding a true inner self, but rather the playful enactments that constitute the provisional "real" self.

When **Tom** and **Dianne** learn that their old friends are on their way over to the house, they must decide whether to reveal their separation or not. At first they figure they should be honest, but then they change their minds. In the past, the two couples, along with two other couples they used to visit, created a "Friendship Fund" and swore a pact that every couple who broke up would forfeit their portion of the fund. These are the last two couples still together, so, if **Tom** and **Dianne** admit they are breaking up, they must forfeit their portion of the fund; in fact, since two of the other couples had already split and forfeited their contribution, **Tom**, who was responsible for taking care of the money on behalf of everyone else, would have to hand over three couples' portions. However, **Tom** secretly spent all the money helping **Dianne** set up her new business, so they cannot pay and must therefore carry on the pretence of being in love. Meanwhile, **Shirley** and **Ben**, who have become celebrities for writing a variety of coffee-table books, pretend to be breaking up because it adds a bit of spark to their marriage. In effect, the members of each couple collaborate in constructing their mutual relationship as a "performance" for each other and for the other couple. At this point the play claims the traditional ground of comic dissimulating "pretence," but not for long.

As the layers of these pretences are variously exposed and reconstructed through the play, the four characters question the basis of their more complex foursome friendship, which itself is revealed to be constituted through performance. They each enumerate the various conventional acts of "friendship" they have or have not successfully performed for each other (or expected others to perform for them) in the recent past: asking about elderly relatives and children, calling the others when passing through town, sending meaningful letters. In the end, although they decide that the friendship is "finished," they will continue with the acts of sending Christmas cards and "keeping in touch." Admitting that the relationship is a mutually agreeable "performance" does not diminish its importance for the participants. Rather, it is through the performance itself that the power to create their identity as "friends" is embodied, and thus the value of the friendship to the individuals sustained:

> **GARTH.** Love. Friendship. It's awful—half the time it's hell—but at the same time it's full of noise, and we need that noise. It keeps us—
>
> **TOM.** —out of danger.
>
> **SHIRLEY.** Safe. Or pretending to be safe. (219)

At the end of the play, as the lights dim on **Tom** and **Dianne** dancing silently accompanied by the slideshow projection of random images from their life together, the surreal moment lifts the play out of its farcical conventions, both formal and thematic, creating resistance to the traditional comic resolution by suggesting that perhaps the pretences are not dissimulations after all; their "pretence" was not pretending in the traditional comic sense. Their enactments are not dissimulations, but rather performative of their relationship. The heightened theatricalism of the scene reinforces the self-conscious performance of the performativity of their relationship and of their identity as a couple: what they do is who they are.

In addition to foregrounding the tensions between stable identities claimed by traditional stage conventions and performative identities suggested by the destabilizing of the stage conventions, Shields's plays also explore more particularly another constituent of identity formation: the social space. In each of her plays, there is an overarching social structure that is transformed into

MANITOBA | Plays and Playwrights

the site of identity (and theatrical) performance: the airport, the family, the card game, friendships. These sites come loaded with arbitrary complexities of expectations, functions, promises, and dangers that the individuals Shields sets in motion there must negotiate in their performances of self. The result is a sense of identity that is performative, contingent, and arbitrary, both a construction of the individual's choices within a changing social formation and a constituent of that environment itself.

Written with the help of her daughter, Catherine Shields, *Fashion, Power, Guilt and the Charity of Families* (FPGCF) was first produced at the Prairie Theatre Exchange in Winnipeg in 1995. The family connection is fitting, since the play sets out "to interrogate the basic assumptions about the nuclear family by placing abstract commentary margin-to-margin with the ongoing life of a 'real' family, and bring music and drama edge-to-edge in order to open that question as far as it would allow" (2002, xi). The 2002 revision of the play further foregrounds the "family-as-theatre" idea with the rewriting of **Character Five**, "a woman actor who plays a number of roles and who provides the outsider's perception of the drama that every family sets up" (xi). The premise of this expressionistic play is that, in response to a growing problem with loneliness in the country, the government decides to experiment with the creation of a "new" social unit: the family. With prescribed numbers, carefully divided duties, and a well-managed environment (not to mention monthly checkups by the Fret & Worry Consultant just to keep track of how everyone is progressing!), a number of "prototypical family units" are set up to study the idea.

The play focuses on the performance (in the several senses of that word) of one of these "units" constructed of mother **Jane** (or more usually "Brian's wife"), father **Brian**, daughter **Sally**, and son **Michael**. The clichéd "perfection" of this unit, including (and perhaps because of) each individual's attempt to perform his or her identity role as prescribed, quickly succumbs to the messy fallout of living; as mother **Jane** says, "even prototypical nuclear families like us have their specific histories" (305).

So the family becomes a kind of double performance. First of all, the play depicts the performance of a family that has in turn been "constructed," literally, as an experiment in social control. The gender roles, familial relations, and identity behaviours are the "pretences" of assumed social order. Within that frame each family member constitutes his or her own identity "performances," which effectively decode the prescribed pretences and reveal identity, not in the expected roles of gender and age, but in the actions each character takes. In this way the play enacts an essentialist/performative tension similar to that examined in the plays above.

Secondly, the bureaucratic prescripts, an ironic wink at traditional stereotypes, matter less than the individual inscriptions of identity performance within the family structure. The identity roles for the family members are negotiated around and as a constituent of the social space, the relational space of the family. For example, mother **Jane** and father **Brian** shape their parental roles in relation to the death of their first child, who fell out of her bedroom window while unattended. Each blames the other, and they treat their surviving children with a particular protectiveness as a result ("We never open that window. [...] Never." 249). For their part, **Sally**'s and **Michael**'s roles in the family, and thus their senses of self, are shaken when they learn quite unexpectedly of the deceased older sibling. In their moment of insecurity **Michael** comes to his sister at night for comfort. She has to alter her "bickering sister" identity and encourage him to "touch that warm spot on the wall," a favourite childhood superstition that makes "the bad things go away" (297).

The impact of social space on identity formation was clearly an important aspect of *Departures and Arrivals* that Shields hoped would "contribute [...] to the human appreciation of the public place [...] as a venue for the theatrical sense that enlarges ordinary lives" (2). But this suggestion applies equally well to FPGCF. The space of the family is constituted by the identities performed within it and provides the contextual conditions for the constitution of those identities. **Michael** and **Sally** question: "Why don't we do things like other families? Hug, and kiss on both cheeks. And those feast days… all that Folklorama stuff" (298), just as the family at the end of *Departures and Arrivals* questions why "We never do it right, never. Other families can do it, but not us" (117). These characters attempt to reconstitute themselves in light of the particular social space around them.

The communal reconstitution of self within social space is also a key element in *Thirteen Hands*. Originally produced by Prairie Theatre Exchange in Winnipeg in 1993, the play depicts four generations of women who construct community and identity around their weekly bridge tables. As in *Departures and Arrivals*, the scenes are very episodic, with only a loose suggestion of overarching plot. Indeed, like FPGCF, which is an examination of the idea of family, this play is not really about a particular person or persons at all (although **Clara** is a main character and important aspects of the play are seen through her eyes and memory), but about an idea, in this case "to valorize [...] the lives of women, particularly those lives that have gone unrecorded, [...] a group who, for historical reasons mainly, were caught between movements" (Shields, 1993, "Playwright's Note," 9). In the Preface to the 2002 edition, Shields writes that she sees the conflict in the play occurring "between the differing social constructs that balance and assign the worth of a human life" (xii). In effect, the play seems to provide a response to Sue-Ellen Case's argument that "women do not have the cultural mechanisms of meaning to construct themselves as the subject rather than the object of performance" (quoted in Carlson, 185).The act of valorization here is read as a self-conscious process of "creating" the lives, both from the point of view of the author and but also from that of the subjects themselves. By building the play on the game of bridge as a metaphor for the women's performance of self, again a kind of double playfulness is created: the play enacts the game, which is itself the site where these women, ironically perhaps, were able to play out their identities as subjects, not objects, of their own performances.

In the final scene of the play, **Clara** is accused of "Running away from reality" (413) by the daughter of a former bridge player who was an alcoholic. The daughter feels her mother's friends should have done something, not turned a blind eye to the fact that the only day of the week she wasn't drunk was the day of her bridge games. Her ultimate, but revelatory, accusation comes in the following exchange:

> **SCARF.** You just let her be. Just let her (*pause*) be.
>
> **CLARA.** (*Softly*) That's what we did. Yes.
>
> **SCARF.** You let her be. (*Her voice breaks. The two women take each other's hands, a sudden open embrace of understanding.*) (414)

The daughter realizes that by letting her "be," the space opened by the women around the bridge table allowed her to play herself as subject in a way her familial and social obligations didn't. The daughter recognizes both the multiplicity and performativeness of her mother's identity and sense of self. The daughter's mother was not the woman her bridge partners knew, nor the one her daughter knew, and yet all of these "selves" were part of the complex performance that was her mother.

From the tensions between essentialist identity stability and materialist identity construction to the implications of social space in the constitution of identity, each of Carol Shields's four plays contributes to a collective interrogation of traditional concepts of identity and representation. In each case there are apparent claims to essentially stable characters or character representations that in various ways are then destabilized within a particular social space, thus ironically questioning the cultural discourse that legitimates received assumptions about identity. It is the tension and interaction between these two positions that create the dramatic energy of the dramas. *Departures and Arrivals* and *Anniversary* both deal with "pretence," first driven by the traditional comic conventions of dissimulation, but then playing out identity to reveal that the dissimulatory pretences are in fact the performatives of self, not the disguises that prevent the self from appearing. In *Fashion, Power, Guilt and the Charity of Families* and *Thirteen Hands,* Shields opens the thematic lens more broadly to interrogate the roles of family and gender implicit in identity formation within conventionalized social space.

PART TWO: METATHEATRICAL PERFORMANCE

This section will explore how the plays use metatheatricality to induce the sense of "performance of performativity." Shields's vision of identity performativity, the tensions between essentialized and constructed identity formation within social spaces, is embodied by her complex scenic vocabulary and sophisticated dramaturgical models. By heightening and disrupting the traditional, stable modes of theatrical representation, the plays perform more fluid and contingent concepts of identity formation.

Metatheatricalized stage performances go beyond simply disrupting and questioning the creative process. More dynamic theatrical strategies embody reiterative aspects of performative identity formation, reconfiguring conventions of both representation and identity. Picking up on Herbert Blau's position, Elin Diamond, as noted above, argues that "the resignifying of performativity *needs* a performance, an embodiment (2000, 32, emphasis added). While challenging Judith Butler's "shunning" of the link between theatre and performativity,[3] she builds her argument on Butler's observation that "in reiterating or 'citing' these conventions we may also resignify (somehow alter or displace) them" (31). Although Butler refers below specifically to gender identity, I would read the argument in this context to have relevance to broader issues of identity formation:

> The possibilities of gender transformation are to be found precisely in the arbitrary relation between such [reiterative] acts, in the possibility of a failure to repeat, a de-formity, or a parodic repetition that exposes the phantasmatic effect of abiding identity as a politically tenuous construction. (1999, 179)

Besides various formal strategies including the mixing of multiple theatrical modes, complex actor/character doubling, and the incorporation of music and songs, a significant aspect of performative playfulness (playful performativeness?) is Shields's metatheatrical reconfiguration of the audience/stage relationship. Of course the multi-faceted theatricalism of her plays means

---

3   For example, in *Gender Trouble*, Butler is fastidious in separating the "expressive" from the "performative": "The distinction between expression and performativeness is crucial. If gender attributes and acts [...] are performative, then there is no preexisting identity by which an act or attribute might be measured" (1999, 180).

that the audience is never allowed simply to slip into the comfortable zone of suspended disbelief; rather, it is constantly confronted with the foregrounding of performance as performance. However, Shields also incorporates particular strategies to intensify this experience for the audience. For example in the opening scene of FPGCF the amorphous **Character Five** greets the audience directly, teases them with a couple of direct questions, outlines the plot in the style of a classical prologue, and concludes with the following invitation to "play" with the actors in the creation of the play:

> We'll do some role-playing tonight. See a few dramatic examples… Of course there'll be some song and dance. And there will be time for a Q & A session at the end. […] Now, let us begin. It just so happens that I will be participating in our first vignette. Here we go. (235)

The actor-character-audience configuration here becomes a multi-layered *mise en abîme* because, while **Character Five** is a "character," a figure being performed by an actor, the character constitutes herself in a kind of liminal state capable of performing subsequent roles. She is neither fully a "character" nor fully an actor but some kind of in-between figure that constitutes a number of functions: "narrator and chairwoman, and instructor and interpreter" (234). So where does representation end or begin?

In addition, this line between audience and stage is blurred in a second direction. Not only does the actor/character cross the footlights by speaking directly to the audience in the guise of a character who describes how she will portray other characters, but the house also hears itself in facsimile from the stage through taped applause and laughter played from a portable machine that **Character Five** carries in with her: *"shushing and a couple of coughs and low murmurs as the canned audience prepares for the theatre to begin"* (235). The convention of the stage as immutable representation reflecting back to an equally stable audience is undermined by this performance configuration. Audience and stage worlds are foregrounded as constructs of each other, transformable and contingent.

The performance of identity formation that is contingent and transformable continues later in FPGCF as **Sally** explicitly complains about "playing" the role of ditzy teen in response to her reading of her family's expectations of their daughter and sister:

> I worry because I have this hideous affliction. I'm forced to do this impersonation all the time of this vacuous person who worries about like zits and boyfriends and how my hair looks, and

the truth is I'm worried about God and peace and humankind
and the future of women in the national workforce. (270)

It is similar for the other characters. **Jane** is the nameless mother constructed
by others through her service to the family. Likewise, the father's and **Michael**'s
"roles" are conditioned by the perspective of the others in the social construct,
not based on any essential "beingness." As **Brian** says,

> But it's strictly arbitrary. How did I become a husband and fa-
> ther? It was just something that happened to me […]. It struck
> me across the eyes one day, the person I could be, husband,
> father, and ever since, I've been walking around, sort of… sort
> of blinking. (252)

The metatheatrical strategies in the play undercut the representational stage
performance of the family unit and in turn undermine the conventional assumptions about "family" and the formation of individual identities within that
space. The relational social space becomes the site of performative performance
through the characters who constitute it and whose performance as stage embodi-
ments is also foregrounded. The enactment of character as a creative process is
highlighted and the characters in turn make explicit how they "personify" the
norms constructed by the traditional representation of the family; however, the
undermining of that representation and the reiteration of the prescribed identities reveal these roles as "arbitrary" and ultimately dysfunctional.

Thirteen Hands also reconfigures the audience/stage relation, but in ways
that foreground the gender issues motivating Shields's writing here. As the lights
come up, the audience sees the actors helping each other with bits of costume.
As the characters move downstage they note the audience—"Everyone… (*she
surveys the audience*) is assembled" (327)—and discuss whether they should
"begin at once"; however, remarks to the audience at several points, comments
about "conventions," self-reflections like "what we're here for," and the gener-
ality of their discussion (cards are never mentioned) open a rich ambiguity
in what is beginning to be played out. They are not only actors preparing to
play the game of theatre and characters played by actors preparing to play a
game of bridge, but they are also figures created by Shields playing out the
valorization of a generation of women:

> **SOUTH.** Is it really necessary—posing these kinds of questions?
>
> **EAST.** There are those… who may not…
>
> **WEST.** —comprehend who we are—

NORTH. —who doubt our… seriousness, our—

EAST. —our essential value, to put it baldly. (329–30)

Thirteen Hands further reinforces the fluid stage-audience configuration when Shields suggests that the "action" move into the public space of the lobby at intermission. These various formal metatheatrical strategies invite the audience to confront their own participation in the creative/performative process: in the construction of their own identity as "audience," just as the actors are foregrounding their creative processes as characters and actors.

Part of the reason Shields wrote the play was to revision the "differing social constructs that balance and assign the worth of a human life" (xii), in particular of this group of women "overlooked" (2002, xi; and Ross, April 29, 1995, C17) by husbands, children (and maybe even themselves). Perhaps the clearest example of Shields's interrogation of identity formation through metatheatrical scene construction is the scene near the middle of the play depicting a group of women in the 1950s meeting to play bridge for the first time. Shields uses an interesting approach here, having the characters address the audience directly, revealing their interior thoughts in parallel to the general dialogue continuing between the women. The women have been encouraged to meet "the other company wives": "Do it for me," **Woman One**'s husband told her (359). **Woman Two** is "not cut out to be the boss's wife. Charming, sweet, thoughtful. Arghhhh" (359). And **Woman Four** has to hurry home because "Jonathan likes me to be there when he comes in the door. He likes dinner waiting, likes to walk in and smell dinner cooking" (362).

But it is not only their husbands' views that shape their identities and behaviour; they are also aware of how the other women view them. **Woman One** is horrified by what she fears the others will think of her when she breaks one of the hostess's sherry glasses. She also turns down another glass because she fears the others will think she is drinking too much (357). Others worry about whether they are overdressed or underdressed or talk too much.

But then, at a certain point, they begin to discuss their mothers, and the discovery of a common language triggers a change in the way they perform themselves. Instead of acting in the ways prescribed to them by others, they begin to enact identities that are contingent on mutual understanding. The interior monologues cease, implying that what is being shared openly is no longer in contrast with their inner thoughts. They begin to finish each others' sentences, implying they both understand the other women and have found ways to enact their inner selves mutually (363). As the social space is transformed by a rereading of its meaning to the women, so too are their identities transformed in the ways they perform individually and with each other.

Even *Anniversary* undermines its apparent claims of representational conventions of space, time, and character identity through a sort of metatheatrical reiteration: the four characters of *Anniversary* re-enact a canoeing accident they had many years before by miming it on the living room floor. Through this scene they both question the roles the others played and re-perform what they said at the time in order to clarify their positions within the group structure and reconstruct their social identities as "leader," "problem-solver," "object of desire," and so on. However, there is no consensus on the original events. They each remember and replay their roles differently from the way the others perceived them. The impossibility of affirming stable identities, in the present or in the past, suggests that the outcomes of this re-enactment are no less "real" than those of the original accident, that their identities are the results of individual performances within the social context. The re-performance temporarily redefines their identities and thus repositions their significance within the social group, reconfiguring that social group itself in the process.

The performativeness of identity here is underscored by the metatheatrical structure of the scene. The sudden scene-within-a-scene, contrasting the realism dominating most of this play, forces the audience's perspective to shift from simply accepting the representationalism of the characters and their "reality" to seeing the performance as a performance, thus destabilizing the reliability of unified character identity formation. The contrast between these two readings performs the tension between expectations of essentialized and stable character identity and suggestions of socially performed identity.

Another particularly striking example of this sort of metatheatrical reiteration is the penultimate scene of *Departures and Arrivals,* which is overtly metatheatrical on several levels as the family replays their airport reunion several times until they "get it right." The scene begins with the stage directions: "*She speaks in a loud stagey voice <u>as though</u> reading a script.* [...] *As though reading lines*" (116; emphasis added). Since the characters are not actually reading their lines, this vocal heightening of the scene would appear at first to jar with the apparently realistic conventions. However immediately after the **Father** appears and the family is reunited, they begin to self-analyze their "performance": "We never do it right, never. Other families can do it, but not us. [...] Is it that we lack style? Panache?" (117) and they begin to repeat the scene. A **Director** and **Assistant Director** appear, and the visual vocabulary and dialogue recall a movie set ("Ready for the retake, everyone? One, two, three, roll" etc.). However, the stage directions are explicit that "*This is not a 'real' filming*"; rather, the approach suggests a new perspective on the relationship between social space and identity construction: "*an extension of the characters' self-consciousness as* *they indulge in the self-conscious drama of an airport reunion"* (117). Over the next several repetitions the scene becomes more and more outlandish until the final "take": "*FATHER enters, searches the crowd with a madman's eyes, runs and embraces his wildly heaving wife and hysterical children*" (121).

The metatheatrical structure of this scene (the film within a play) foregrounds the performativeness of the family members' relationships with each other and, by extension, of their individual identities within the social space of the family. A reader of the play knows this is Shields's intent from the stage directions, but the effect is also signalled for the viewing audience through the vocal and visual cues and through the absurdity of the scene's over-playing. Because the metatheatrical aspects are gradually layered onto a scene that appears realistic at first, the moment enacts the identity tensions (essential versus performative) discussed earlier. In addition, because the allusion to filming is clearly intended to be played very broadly and not to be confused with a literal film scene, the theatrical performance is heightened, thus amplifying the performativeness of the characters.

Departures and Arrivals is also interesting in the way it plays out the role of social space and the transformation of identity through metatheatrical performance. The airport setting creates the context of public "nothingness," an active neutrality full of expectations signifying nothing, which allows the characters who appear there to construct identities and be observed in the act of self-creation. As one of the characters says of the space:

> "It's the crossroads of a million private lives; a gigantic stage on which are played a thousand dramas daily." [...] People coming. People going. Departures. Arrivals. Get it? It's an equation of the absurd. Going cancels out coming, see? And that means ... no one's going anywhere. (67)

The loose structure of ever-flowing bits and pieces of scenes imitates the fragmentary images identity uses to constitute its sense of self and of others. The episodic structure of the play is so loose, in fact, that Shields suggests directors should feel free to omit scenes or reshuffle the elements as they see fit. With the exception of one couple that appears four times over the course of the play, each of the vignettes is completely unrelated to the others; this randomness forces the audience to become aware of their own role in the creation of sense and coherence.

The variety of forms, styles, and characters and the explicit metatheatricalism of the play disrupt the closed order of traditional realistic representation, theatricalizing the performance of the public place (the airport) so that it can be read as a site of constructed expectations where identity is particularly vulnerable and thus more easily interrogated. For example, the third sequence of the play depicts two middle-aged women, **Rachel** and **Janice**, who meet at the life-insurance counter, having just seen their husbands depart for business trips. The anonymity of the public space allows the women a kind of confessional space in which they admit things to each other they may not even admit to themselves. Each fantasizes to the other what her life could be like *if*, heaven forbid, her husband were killed in an air crash and she collected on the insurance she is purchasing. Built entirely around an ironic make-believe "if," the women perform new and freer lives for themselves, identities that are provisional and contingent on the social space in which they are enacted.

Each of the characters the audience meets is in effect performing his or her identity within the expectations (or absence of expectations) of the public space of the airport. And the number of cases in which this performance is heightened through audience addresses, voice-overs, transformations, and so on leads the audience to question the "pretence" of them (us?) all. It is not the quality of the characters themselves in particular that is of interest: their problems and solutions remain largely clichéd and simplistic, as demonstrated by the father's advice to his daughter to "Be happy. Be kind to each other" (55). Rather, it is the act itself of constructing identity that matters here, as the characters negotiate their way through the conflicting expectations of self and others.

The highly episodic form and the airport setting recall Robert Lepage's 2000–2002 spectacle, *Zulu Time*, and it is useful in helping to read Shields's play. "Zulu" refers to the letter "Z" in the international alphabet language used in communications and aeronautics. The twenty-six scenes of *Zulu Time* echo the twenty-six letters of the international alphabet code. The term "Zulu time" refers to standardized "universal" international time based on the Greenwich Mean, or as the PA announces in *Departures and Arrivals* the "Zero hour call." Shields's play predates that of Lepage by several years and it is doubtful that Lepage was influenced by or even knew of Shields's work, but they seem to be posing similar questions. As Lepage notes:

> Airports are a common space found at cross-roads. An area of *métissage*, an intersection that should bring us together. Para-doxically, airports create a great deal of loneliness. (quoted in Koustas, 2003, 11. Translation: GN)[4]

In both Lepage's description and in that by Shields noted above, there is coming and going, but no one connects; the value is not in the result but in the process. The goal is not the destination but the process of getting there. The

---

4   "Les aéroports sont un lieu commun qui se trouve à la croisée de chemins. Une aire de métissage, un Carrefour qui devrait faire nous rencontrer. Paradoxalement, les aéroports génèrent beaucoup de solitude."

play queries a traditional sense of identity, enacting character as performative within a fluid social space that

> attempts to go beyond all notions of dominant/subordinate culture, language, theatre practice or geographical space to a linguistically, culturally, temporally, geographically generic zone beyond and between traditional boundaries. (Koustas, 9)

PART THREE: PLAYING BETWEEN SPACES AND RESISTANCE TO CLOSURE

While these various metatheatrical devices help to perform the interplay between essential and performative concepts of identity formation, Shields's plays offer a further dimension to explore the role of social space in the constitution of identity. Enlarging upon the transformational potential of performative identity, an openness to alternate or multiple identity relations, her plays resist essentialized, stable identity formation by resisting dramaturgical or representational closure or resolution and thereby opening up spaces between the binaries of essentialism and performativeness where the characters realize their potential.

A similar tension between essential representation and performative identity is described by Jennifer Harvie in her analysis of Judith Thompson's play *Lion in the Streets*. This play, where character, time, and place are depicted at first as fairly representational, frequently slides into surreal and indefinable moments. Harvie's analysis of characterization, imagery, and language shows how "the apparently real and the real problematized [... m]ay be seen as compatible if we consider a concept of an essential reality as perhaps necessary but only ever provisional, in other words as a fiction of an essential reality" (48). The destabilizing image of the "dead" **Isobel** running through the streets of her city, the slippery memories of **Father Hayes** and young **David**, or the fantasy dance sequence of **Scarlet** who suffers from advanced cerebral palsy, enact the same kind of dynamic tension between stable representation and performative provisional "reality" that Shields's plays reveal.

The plays' resistance to closure performs this provisionality of identity so important to Shields's interrogation of traditional identity formation; in the end, nothing is closed off or finally determined, with the result being an open-ended, unresolved sense of possibilities. This paper began with the simple observation that Shields's construction of identity in her plays appears to be a fluid relationship between identity as essential and identity as performative. But, in fact, this basic fluidity and instability is more than just "appearance" or representation; fluidity and instability are what the plays do, how they enact themselves, reinforced by the lack of closure or final resolution of either plot or characterization.

Although *Anniversary* appears to depict closure in accordance with its claims to the conventions of farce, it is actually much more ambiguous. In the end are **Ben** and **Shirley** really breaking up? Are **Tom** and **Dianne** really staying together? Is the foursome friendship really over? All of these ideas are suggested but also put into doubt by contradictory actions or dialogue. The characters exist in a state of in-betweenness, open to possibilities and further constructions.

Just as there is a tendency to dismiss the characters of Shields's *Thirteen Hands* as "LOLs" ("Little Old Ladies," as they are called in *Departures and Arrivals*, 62ff), or the "'blue-rinse set,' 'the white glove brigade,' 'the bridge club biddies,'" as Shields rehearses in her preface (2002, xi), boxing them into preconceived categories, so there is also a risk here of treating the play as if it intends a tidy conclusion, a maudlin and nostalgic reminiscence. Certainly more than one reviewer followed this line of thinking. Longfield called it "an apology for middle-class complacency" (1993, 42), and Moser noted that, despite the "remarkable fluidity to the play," it is "ultimately forgiving and humanistic." She calls *Thirteen Hands* "a lovely memory play, sentimental and respectful of generations dismissed and ignored" (1994, 163–4). These descriptions overlook the power of these women to claim their own subjective space in contrast to the roles assigned for them by others (husbands, relatives, etc.) or themselves. The card game as theatrical metaphor is double played; the staging performs the performative space of these women's subjectification. Their identities, like the play as a whole, are not resolved or bordered by a final closure; rather, they perform multiple and fluid subject positions in a changing social space.

In the episodic *Departures and Arrivals* the parade of characters means that the majority are seen only in snippets. Whether it's the **People-Watcher** who yearns to be like the others she imagines around her (6–9), the son who calls his mother, who is only interested in hearing about the caller's brother (33–4), the **Young Man** and **Young Woman** who flirt in the ticket lineup (71–87), or any of the many other cameos the play presents, the moments pass and no resolution to the problems encountered in the scene is achieved. The characters live in the moment; their identities are not the representation of a sustained essence, but a fleeting enactment within the open-ended social space of the airport.

The only characters in this play that have continuity are the **Pilot** and **Flight Attendant** who appear in a series of four scenes that follow their relationship. And while the sequence does appear to have a happy resolution, it is clearly made ironic by the use of soap-opera allusions. The exaggerated style underscores the moment as a performance and thus disrupts the apparent closure of the ending. In addition, the moment is intercut by the pathos of a monologue, or more accurately one side of a telephone conversation, spoken by a caller to a woman he met once and who now wants nothing to do with him. This monologue is delivered in a series of highly realistic sections that contrast with the melodramatic scene that alternates with it: the performance of an apparently happy ending is undercut by the metatheatrical overplaying of the dialogue scene and by the slice-of-real-life monologue that is left unresolved and unhappy.

And finally, of course, the very last image of the play assures resistance to any closure the soap-opera scene might suggest:

> [A] tiny **FAIRY** appears spotlighted at the top of the Arrivals stairs. She is carrying a lighted wand. She dances lightly down the stairs in a dainty ballet step, pauses, surveys the dark and empty airport, spies the silver bag rotating on the luggage platform, takes it, then points her wand at the automatic doors, which open to the sound of tinkling music. She exits. (124)

This fantasy moment, reminiscent of childhood fairy tales, is left unexplained, an unresolved enigma. In the crossroads that is the airport anything can happen, any identity can be constituted.

Like *Thirteen Hands*, FPGCF is not ultimately about the characters but rather about an idea, in this case the idea of family. In the expressionistic mode, the characters are only figures in the performance of "family," so no resolution is expected or achieved. Their identities are shaped by performance and, while they experience some tension over their individual inclinations towards a kind of essential interiority, their actions are, ultimately, who they are. But more significantly, it is the idea of family itself that is left unresolved; indeed, the concept of family itself is forced open through the intensely ironic nature of the play, something not all reviewers perceive. Doug Arrell, for example, was "disappointed" by the "resolute shallowness of this play" (1995, 177, 178) because

> Although there is brief lip-service paid to alternative living arrangements—gay couples, people who prefer to live alone […] the play in fact becomes a glorification of the mythical '50s family, and the "typical" family turns out to be essentially that of Ozzie and Harriet. (177)

True, on the surface certain aspects feel sexist: the preciousness of creating the word "family" by melding "female" and "male" into "Fe-male-ie" (239); the division of tasks within the family (males take on hunting, provisioning, and protection while females are assigned child-rearing, cleaning, and hospitality; for example 240–2); the token mentions of gay or alternate family constructs; and, of course, the "experimental" family as a clichéd, so-called traditional heteronormative unit. However, the play's performance makes it apparent that these must be seen ironically. The house, after being presented to the audience with flashing stage lighting, is described by **Character Five** (playing **Real Estate Agent**) as "a highly charged metaphor for the family as we idealize it" (246). The intended irony is underscored by the father, who immediately afterwards tries to contradict the idea of house as metaphor, ending with "What I mean is, real estate is real, not a flimsy stage setting" (246), contradicting what the audience sees. Likewise, the nuclear family itself, which Shields explicitly wishes to interrogate through this play (2002, xi and 234), is an "invented" family (244), a "putative" family (245), emphasizing that the assumed idea of the traditional family, like the stage set, is a construction, not something real, essential, and stable.

In the end the family is described as a place of healing and protection (319); there "doesn't seem to be any formula" (322). Rather a "family's whatever you want it to be" (318), "a crucible of … hmmm… whatever" (319); it is the people constituting and being constituted by the family who "just carry on and sort of see what happens" (322). The family is not a defined, essential structure, but a doing, a performance of the people who constitute it. The play does not resolve what a family should be; rather it is the "carrying on" that is the family, not its appearance; it is the fashion, the power, the guilt, and the charity that is the family, not a particular predetermined structure. The experimental artifice of the traditional family as ironically established in the play is unmasked as exactly that—an artifice—the apparent essentialism of that structure is the disguise for the performative family which indeed can have any structure. And it is the performed and embodied space of the theatrical action here, deformed and multiplied and left unresolved through various metatheatrical devices that perform the performative nature of identity within the social space of the family.

CONCLUSION

Perhaps Carol Shields's four plays offer an unresolved enigma altogether. Some reviewers may find justification for their less positive critiques in the sometimes clichéd sentiments, often mundane situations, frequently nonlinear and fragmented structures, and apparent silliness of the musical interventions which pepper these plays. Her work is written off or ignored in discussions of contemporary Canadian dramatists. Yet her plays are theatrically challenging and in the hands of visionary directors reveal complex layers of original work in performance. Shields, appropriately, never nails down what her vision of identity formation is in any absolute way. Rather the texts play out a complex, variable, and fluid exploration of personal, spatial, and social dynamics, using the stage performance itself to enlarge and embody the questions she raises. Perhaps it is this indeterminacy that defies her critics, who are lulled into expecting tidier answers because of the apparent superficiality of the plays' subject matter. Or perhaps it is Shields's renown as a novelist that simply overshadows her dramatic work, which at four full-length stage plays and numerous radio scripts is nevertheless not insignificant. Whatever the reason, these plays offer a wealth of intriguing puzzles that have not been fully appreciated; they are superb stage plays and deserve more critical and theatrical attention.

Works Cited

Anonyomous. "[Review of] *Thirteen Hands.*" *Books in Canada* 22.6 (1993): 34–35.

Anonymous. "[Review of] *Fashion, Power, Guilt & the Charity of Families.*" *Quill & Quire* 61.11 (1995): 36.

Anonymous. "All in the family." *Maclean's* 108.12 (1995): 59.

Arrell, Doug. "[Review of] *Thirteen Hands.*" *Prairie Fire* 16.4 (1995): 108–9.

———. "[Review of] *Fashion, Power, Guilt & the Charity of Families.*" by Carol Shields, dir. Micheline Chevrier. Produced at Prairie Theatre Exchange, Winnipeg, MB. March 9–25 1995. *Prairie Fire* 16.1 (1995): 177–78.

Bell, Karen. "Carol Shields: All these years later, still digging." *Performing Arts and Entertainment in Canada* 31.3 (1998): 4–6.

Brecht, Bertholt. *Brecht on Theatre: The Development of an Aesthetic.* Ed. and trans. John Willet. London: Methuen, 1964.

Buccholz, Garth. "[Review of] *Thirteen Hands.*" *Theatrum* 35 (1993): 15–16.

Buss, Helen. "Abducting Mary and Carol: Reading Carol Shields's *Swann* and the Representation of the Writer Through Theories of Biographical Recognition." *English Studies in Canada* 23.4 (1997): 427–41.

Butler, Judith. *Gender Trouble: Feminism and the Subversion of Identity.* 2nd ed. New York: Routledge, 1999.

Carlson, Marvin. *Performance: A Critical Introduction.* 2nd ed. New York and London: Routledge, 2004.

Case, Sue-Ellen. *Performance and Theatre.* New York: Methuen, 1988.

Currie, Rod. "[Summer theatre in Ontario 50 years old and flourishing]." *Canadian Press NewsWire* (1998): n.p.

Diamond, Elin. "Re: Blau, Butler, Beckett, and the Politics of Seeming." *The Drama Review* 44.4 (Winter 2000): 31–43.

———. "Introduction." *Performance and Cultural Reader.* Ed. Elin Diamond. New York & London: Routledge, 1996, 1–12.

Dolan, Jill. "Geographies of Learning: Theatre Studies, Performance, and the 'Performative.'" *Theatre Journal* 45.4 (1993): 417–41.

Dvorak, Marta. "Carol Shields and the Poetics of the Quotidian." *Journal of the Short Story in English* 38 (2002): 57–71.

Flaherty, Kathleen. "[Review of] *Departures and Arrivals*." *Theatrum* 22 (1991): 31–32.

Friedlander, Mira. "[Review of] *Thirteen Hands*." by Carol Shields, dir. Marti Maraden. Co-produced by NAC and Canadian Stage Company, Ottawa/Toronto, ON. January 23–March 22 1997. *Variety* 366.6 (10–16 March 1997): 94.

Garebian, Keith. "*Thirteen Hands* and Other Plays." *Quill & Quire* 68.11 (2002): 39.

Grace, Sherrill. "Performing the Auto/biographical Pact: Towards a Theory of Identity in Performance." *Tracing the Autobiographical*. Ed. M.Kadar, L.Warley, J.Perreault, and S. Egan. Waterloo: Wilfrid Laurier University Press, 2005, 65–79.

———. "Theatre and the AutoBiographical Pact: An Introduction." *Theatre and Auto-Biography: Writing and Performing Lives in Theory and Practice*. Ed. S. Grace and J. Wasserman. Vancouver: Talonbooks, 2006, 13–29.

Hammill, Faye. "Carol Shields: An Annotated Bibliography." *Carol Shields, Narrative Hunger, and the Possibilities of Fiction*. Ed. E. Eden. Toronto: University of Toronto Press, 2003, 285–309.

Hansen-Pauly, Marie-Anne. "Carol Shields: A (De)Constructivist Approach to Identity in Auto/Biography Writing." *Latitude 63° North: Proceedings of the 8th International Region and Nation Literature Conference, Ostersund, Sweden 2–6 August 2000*. Ed. D. Bell. Östersund, Sweden: Mid-Sweden University College, 2002, 295–315.

Harvie, Jennifer. "Constructing Fictions of an Essential Reality, or, 'This Pickshur is Niiiice': Judith Thompson's Lion in the Streets." Ed. Ric Knowles. *Judith Thompson: Critical Perspectives on Canadian Theatre in English*. Vol. I. Toronto: Playwrights Canada Press, 2005, 47–57.

Hollenberg, Donna Krolik. "An Interview with Carol Shields." *Contemporary Literature* 39.3 (1998): 339–355.

Johnson, Chris. "Beyond rhetorical nationalism: Michael Springate at the Prairie Theatre Exchange." *Canadian Theatre Review* 76 (Fall 1993): 18.

———. "Ordinary Pleasures (and Terrors): The Plays of Carol Shields." *Prairie Fire* 16 (Spring 1995): 161–67.

Keller, Wolfram R. "'At Home behind the Screen of Each Other's Face': Theorising Postmodern Reflexivity and Narrative Identity in Carol Shields's Short Story 'Mirrors.'" *Postcolonial Subjects: Canadian and Australian Perspectives*. Ed. M. Buchholtz. Torun, Poland: Wydawnictwo Uniwersytetu Mikolaja Kopernika, 2004, 29–58.

Knowles, Ric. *The Theatre of Form and the Production of Meaning: Contemporary Canadian Dramaturgies*. Toronto: ECW, 1999.

Koustas, Jane. "Zulu Time: Theatre Beyond Translation." *Theatre Research in Canada/ Recherches théâtrales au Canada* 24.1–2 (2003): 1–20.

Lakevold, Dale. "[Review of] *Anniversary*." *Prairie Fire* 20.1 (1999): 177.

Longfield, Kevin. "[Review of] *Thirteen Hands.*" by Carol Shields, dir. Micheline Chevrier. Produced at Prairie Theatre Exchange,Winnipeg, MB. January 28–February 14, 1993. *Theatrum* 33 (1993): 42.

Martel, Denise. "Zulu Time, une fresque signée Robert Lepage." *Le Journal de Québec* 14 April 2000: 40.

Mellor, Winifred M. "'The Simple Container of our Existence': Narrative Ambiguity in Carol Shields's *The Stone Diaries.*" *Studies in Canadian Literature* 20.2 (1995): 96–110.

Moser, Marlene. "[Review of] *Thirteen Hands.*" *Canadian Theatre Review* 79/80 (Summer/Fall 1994): 163–64.

Niederhoff, Burkhard. "How to Do Things with History: Researching Lives in Carol Shields's *Swann* and Margaret Atwood's *Alias Grace.*" *Journal of Commonwealth Literature* 35.2 (2000): 71–85.

Portman, Jamie. "[Review of] Carol Shields's play *Thirteen Hands.*" Dir. Marti Maraden. Co-produced by NAC and Canadian Stage Company, Ottawa/Toronto, ON. January 23–March 22, 1997. *CanWest News* (1997): n.p.

———. "[The Blyth Festival may be located in...]." *CanWest News* (1998): 1.

Prokosh, Kevin. "Women build bridges of support." Review of *Thirteen Hands* by Carol Shields, dir. Micheline Chevrier. Produced at Prairie Theatre Exchange, Winnipeg, MB. January 28– February 14, 1993. *Winnipeg Free Press* January 28, 1993: C6.

Rosborough, Linda. "Great talkers: mother-daughter chat spawned play." Review of *Fashion, Power, Guilt & the Charity of Families* by Carol Shields and Catherine Shields, dir. Kathleen Flaherty. Produced at Prairie Theatre Exchange, Winnipeg, MB. March 9–25, 1995. *Winnipeg Free Press* March 4, 1995: B1.

Ross, Val. "Unsung lives of girls, women Carol Shields's strong suit." *Globe and Mail* [Toronto], April 29, 1995: C17.

Shields, Carol. "Anniversary." *Thirteen Hands and Other Plays.* 125–231.

———. "Departures and Arrivals." *Thirteen Hands and Other Plays.* 1–124.

———. "Fashion, Power, Guilt, and the Charity of Families." *Thirteen Hands and Other Plays.* 233–323.

———. *Thirteen Hands.* Winnipeg: Blizzard: 1993.

———. *Thirteen Hands and Other Plays.* Toronto: Vintage, 2002.

———. "Thirteen Hands." *Thirteen Hands and Other Plays.* 325–416.

Slethaug, Gordon E. "The Coded Dots of Life: Carol Shields's Diaries and Stones." *Canadian Literature* 156 (Spring 1998): 59–81.

Wasserman, Jerry, ed. *Modern Canadian Plays.* Vol. II. 4th Ed. Vancouver: Talonbooks, 2001.

———. "[Review of] *Departures and Arrivals.*" *University of Toronto Quarterly* 61.1 (1991): 86–87.

saskatchewan

Saskatchewan Theatre—Plain Talk

DON KERR

I'm a kind of gentleman playwright, like a gentleman farmer. I've made my living in the English Department at the University of Saskatchewan teaching stories for a living, as I've told people who ask what I do. My main courses have been Modern Drama, Canadian Drama, and Introduction to Film. I also co-wrote *Saskatoon: The First Half-Century* (1982), largely from newspaper sources. It comes naturally to me as a historian, teacher, and story-teller, then, to start my story at the beginning and move forward from there.

Theatre began modestly in Saskatchewan's two main cities in the late nineteenth century. In Regina, there was an early battle of the minstrel shows between the RCMP and the town group. Ken Mitchell's *Davin the Politician* (1979) gives a sense of Regina's raucous early culture. The first permanent theatres, the Regina Theatre in Regina and the Empire Theatre in Saskatoon, both opened by 1910, and both seated over 800 people. Those early theatres were part of prairie tours of stock companies in stock plays, plays ranging from Shakespeare to vaudeville, opera to circus acts. Such history is more extensive in larger prairie cities. John Orrell's *Fallen Empires, Lost Theatres of Edmonton (1881–1914)* tells the story of that city.

Amateur theatre has had long innings in both cities—and began later in much of the province. The Regina Little Theatre, begun in 1926 and still going, is the winner. It performed in Darke Hall at Regina College for years, before building its own theatre in 1981. Among its luminaries was Mary Ellen Burgess, who in 1944 became Saskatchewan's first government employee in "dramatic activities" (Stuart, 1984, 184, 121), travelling across the province as many as 260 days a year in some years, until 1964. Florence James, appointed in 1953 as the first drama consultant for the Saskatchewan Arts Board (1948), continued on as the heart of amateur theatre across the province until 1968. Coteau Books has named its line of drama books the Florence Bean James series in her honour. Saskatoon's Little Theatre was established in 1922. As was to be the case for too many other Saskatoon theatre companies over the years, it laboured under the disadvantage of never possessing a permanent theatre facility; it finally gave up the struggle and disbanded in 1949.

There was a second incarnation of Saskatoon amateur theatre from 1952 to 1956, followed by the establishment of the Gateway Players in 1965. Unfortunately, after performing full seasons annually for over forty years, Gateway had to cancel its 2010-11 season because of sharply rising rental, storage, and transportation expenses; its future remains uncertain. Unlike the later, professional 25th Street Theatre and Persephone Theatre, which, for many years, were to be peregrinating theatres moving from one makeshift place to the next, Gateway for many years did have a home, in the new Castle Theatre completed at Aden Bowman Collegiate in 1966. Based on Canada's Stratford Theatre, it was designed by high school drama teacher Bob Hinitt, who had attended performances at the Stratford Festival from its first year. His theatre, which has recently been renamed the Robert Hinitt Castle Theatre in his honour, had an apron stage, trap doors, a cyclorama, and ramps to the stage for speed—now lost to stairways. The theatre opened with *A Midsummer Night's Dream* featuring three student actors, Peter Roberts, Jaquie Presley, and Irene Blum. All three went on to the Greystone Theatre at the University of Saskatchewan, with two travelling onwards to professional careers (Brenna, "Fifty-six," 2008, n.p.).

Doubtless, the Department of Drama at the University of Saskatchewan played an important role here, as it has with many other students over the years, in boosting its graduates on to consider careers in the professional theatre. A truly Saskatchewan innovation that was crucial in fuelling the transition between the amateur and professional theatre in the province, the department had its beginnings in 1946 when Emrys Jones was hired to teach drama at the University of Saskatchewan and Regina College. He was the first professor of drama in Canada, and the department offered "the first degree-granting program in the British Commonwealth" (Brenna, *Emrys*, 2007, 9). In time, the department occupied an air force hangar with a mainstage theatre called the Greystone Theatre. The first Greystone production was *Candida* in 1946 with Alice Turner (who was to become Chief Librarian at the Saskatoon Public Library) as **Candida** and Frances Hyland as **Prossie**. Hyland became the department's star graduate. Two other graduates, among many, are Kim Coates, who is currently pursuing a successful career in Hollywood, and Jim Guedo, an eminent Canadian director, who is currently head of the department.

I remember the fifties and sixties as a dynamic time of transitions between the various theatre periods I have mentioned. During these years, I made my own personal acquaintance with at least one of the original 1910 theatre houses. As a teenager in the early 1950s, I saw a magic show at the old Empire, which had become primarily a double-feature cheap cinema. A friend and I attended every Friday night, first buying vinegar-laden chips from Ye Olde Fish and Chip Shop and then entering the movie house uncontested to see the Bowery Boys, followed by battles between a giant dinosaur and a giant ape while our dishevelled hero and heroine escaped.

Fortunately, the rising professional theatre in Canada and abroad soon provided me with more substantial viewing experiences and food for thought, at least as a potential playwright. Three plays in particular were to serve as models for my own kind of historical and non-psychological plays. The first I saw was Brecht's *The Caucasian Chalk Circle*, brought to Saskatoon about 1960 by the Canadian Players. It was for me, a neophyte playgoer, amazing, and I thought theatre could do anything. I taught the play twice a year for all the years I taught. The second play was Joan Littlewood and Company's *Oh What a Lovely War*, which I loved so much that I saw it four times in London in 1963. It's a tragic, comic, musical, documentary account of World War I, featuring the songs of that era. The third play, seen in Saskatoon again, was *The West Show* presented by Paul Thompson and Theatre Passe Muraille in 1975. It's an eight-episode version of Saskatchewan history, a collective creation that supports Saskatchewan's co-operative or collective tradition. I watched it being created, my first experience of the brilliance of actors. It's the Canadian model of the episodic, externalized history play.

All these sources use history, though more mythically than I do. All are episodic, and anything goes. They're the kind of plays I found most congenial—although over the many years I have spent in London I've seen half a dozen great productions of Chekhov and at least that many of Ibsen. I've admired those plays—they've fed my imaginative life—but only the history plays have fed my ballpoint pen.

In the meantime, the professional theatre in the province had also started to come into its own, providing new possibilities for playwriting and production within the province. As is generally known, Regina's Globe Theatre, which now has a fine home in a refitted Regina Post Office, was the first professional theatre in Saskatchewan. Begun in 1966 by Ken and Sue Kramer as a theatre for children, it expanded to a full adult season in 1969 and toured both children's and mainstage plays. The funding from the Saskatchewan Arts Board and Canada Council were fundamental to the Globe's success and that of subsequent professional companies. Rex Deverell was writer-in-residence for fifteen years, and we enjoyed his topical satire *Mandarin Oranges*; during the

Ken Kramer years we made a pilgrimage to Regina for a play a year and were never disappointed. Kramer's forte was political theatre. I'd been at an NDP convention in the late sixties, early seventies. The debate in those days was left vs. right, or radical vs. conservative. After one convention, I attended a play at the Globe, Slavomir Mrozek's *Police*. In Act 1 the police are worried. There are no criminals (in this communist nirvana) and they're afraid they'll lose their jobs. So they choose by lot one of their members to be the criminal. The great speech in Act 1 is on the joys of conformity. The great speech in Act 2 is on being an outsider, a radical. Thus art mirrored, with comedy and distance, the convention I'd just attended.

The Globe's equivalent in Saskatoon, Persephone Theatre, was founded in 1974 by the Wright sisters, Susan and Janet, and Janet's then-husband, Brian Richmond. They hit a bonanza in year one with *Cruel Tears*, the country opera based on *Othello* written by Ken Mitchell with music by a great bluegrass band, Humphrey and the Dumptrucks. I saw it with pleasure in the basement of the Mendel Art Gallery, an intimate space adding to the excitement.

From the ferment of all these experiences emerged my own first play. While researching the history of Saskatoon, I had come across some splendid materials on World War I, with none of the censorship that marked World War II. I decided as a teacher of plays to write a play, called *The Great War*, about four men—two of whom had written books about their experiences—who enlisted in Saskatoon. The play covered the period between 1914 and 1921 in about two and a half hours—and seemed to take an eon finally to move from the page to the stage.

The Saskatchewan Playwrights Centre (SPC) was founded in 1982 with the specific intention of helping Saskatchewan playwrights through that difficult transition from writing for the page to writing for the stage, and *The Great War* was one of the scripts chosen to be workshopped at the second Spring Festival of New Plays in 1984 at Regina. It was not a happy experience. The dramaturge kept no control of the ensuing discussion, which was mostly painful. An actor said *how can we believe in this play, there are no trenches.* So much for theatrical illusion. Another person was angry because religious ministers were under attack, though every minister's speech was copied from newspapers and almost all favoured the war.

Fortunately for the script, and my future as a playwright, 25th Street Theatre, which had been founded over 1972–73 and had become professional in 1975, was actively looking for new Saskatchewan scripts. Just as encouraging, it had already had a singular success with exactly the kind of epic, historical storytelling that interested me. Under Andras Tahn, the collective *Paper Wheat* became its most famous production, and I saw it in all its iterations. I didn't see, but read about, opening night, March 18, 1977, in Sintaluta (home of famous farm leader Ed Partridge, a central figure in Act 2). An hour before the play, the actors were arguing about the finale. With the audience entering, the backdrop arrived from Saskatoon. There was a list of scenes taped up backstage so the actors knew what came next. They'd never had a complete run-through. Some scenes never made it to night two. Layne Coleman, a member of the company, hid in the cloakroom for the most embarrassing scenes. For Andras Tahn, the low point was actor Michael Fahey saying, "Look at the wheat growing out of my hair." The play didn't end until eleven, with what was always to remain its last line: "I'd give it all to be young again and feel that I could change the world." Well, the audience cheered and gave the play the first of many standing ovations. I saw that first version in Saskatoon two weeks later, and it had such energy and joy. The play, as revised, was performed over two hundred times.

It was a good omen, and my first play was indeed accepted for production at 25th Street Theatre. In fact, it was accepted *three* times at that theatre: first by Gordon McCall, who was briefly general manager at 25th, then by Andras Tahn, who returned as caretaker for the summer, then by Tom Bentley-Fisher as one of his first productions. The necessary changes, which had not materialized during the initial SPC workshop, began to happen as I worked with Tom. In August, before the season began, we drove to Edmonton and talked of the play—Tom said *start it with music* and I added, "if you were the only boy in the world . . . ." We stayed at Diane Bessai's and visited the Edmonton Fringe, which was the seed that led Tom to create the Saskatoon Fringe four years later. Two decades later, the Saskatoon festival is still going strong.

The Great War went into rehearsal and I discovered two things. I liked the process of creation as much as the product, and I was delighted with the skill of the actors. I learned, too, that the central difference between myself and Tom, or later directors, is this—I write in time, in sequence, while Tom had a spatial vision. They're opposite ways of perception. On the Sunday morning before a Thursday preview, Tom said *will you or I take 40 minutes out of Act 2*. I said I would and did, three episodes disappearing forever. It is possible to do that in an episodic play, with the audience not knowing anything is missing. There was a big finale to Act 1. I asked *where did that come from? I didn't write that*. But there was a typo and Tom ran with it. The Epilogue, where the dead rise to talk of the war, I borrowed from the only good scene in Shaw's *St. Joan*.

The play did have one other outcome. I taught my drama class at the university in a new way. I had taught plays as structures of meaning in time. Now I asked students to read passages aloud or I asked *how would you stage this scene*. The classes were better because there was more participation, and for those students who had difficulty reading plays, reading them aloud helped.

I made $1000 for a sold-out ten days and spent most of it on an opening night party. Clearly a gentleman dramatist. If I made my living as a writer, primarily a poet as well a playwright, I'd be begging on street corners.

A person who had to make a living in theatre would write some two- and four-handers that might travel. All my plays have casts of eight. In history plays, even eight performers have to double roles, which is fun for actors. To give two other examples of my eight-handers: *Talking Back, The Birth of the CCF* covers 1932 to 1938; *Lanc*, about two air raids over Germany, covers 1939 to 1945. All are episodic, serious or tragic, with comedy and some songs—and eight actors.

Between 1985 and 1997, Tom Bentley-Fisher produced thirty original Saskatchewan plays, concluding in the 1990s with a series of Indian and Métis plays (such plays are also produced by Ruth Smillie at the Globe). 25th Street was a theatre that wanted new plays, and professionally produced three of mine: *The Great War* (1985), *Talking Back* (1989), and *Talking West* (1992). Had 25th Street Theatre not existed I wouldn't have become a playwright. While the company still facilitates the production of new work through its annual Fringe Festival, its decision to cease active production in 1999 is still regarded with sadness and regret by many of us whose work was first developed and premiered there.

Of the remaining theatres in Saskatchewan, most, regardless of their formal categorization, usually try in some way to include new Canadian and specifically Saskatchewan work in their seasons. In this regard, Saskatoon's La Troupe du Jour, founded in 1985, has ably served Saskatchewan's francophone community; it has offered full seasons since 1986, including new work by local Fransaskois writers. Another small company, Tant per Tant, was founded in 1997 to promote the translation, exchange and production of Canadian and Catalan plays. Shakespeare on the Saskatchewan, which was founded by Gordon McCall in 1985 as a celebration of the Bard, is an exception, but even here it could be argued that some of its more striking interpretations of the classics have both reflected and influenced a more flowing style of local playwriting. Its most famous early production was a bilingual *Romeo & Juliette* (1989–90), co-produced with Robert Lepage and his Quebec actors. Henry Woolf's years as artistic director (1991–2001) included a great *Merchant of Venice* with Tom Rooney in the lead role. The Globe (Regina) and Persephone (Saskatoon) also have a notable track record of original plays, translations, and adaptations by Saskatchewan playwrights. Tibor Feheregyhazi, who remained artistic director of Persephone Theatre from 1982 until his death in 2007, lived long enough to see the foundations laid for the theatre's great new home on the riverbank, which opened in winter 2007. He also lived long enough to schedule the premiere of a new play about the last woman to be hanged in Canada, *At the End of Her Rope* by Saskatoon playwright Cheryl Jack as part of the new theatre's inaugural 2007–08 season. Del Surjik is the new artistic director.

Heading into the twenty-first century, the newest wave of professional theatres—represented by co-ops, rural, and aboriginal theatre—continues to demonstrate the power of good storytelling in relatively intimate, small, found spaces. There is a new co-operative-based theatre in Saskatoon, Live Five, which performs as many as seven plays a year by the companies that make up the co-op. It is the best example of the importance of the university drama department to the city. Performers are almost all graduates, and some plays are directed by members of the department. The Regina equivalent is Curtain Razors, begun in 1989 with Michele Sereda as artistic director; they perform plays as well as works with other disciplines.

The Saskatchewan Native Theatre Company (SNTC) began in 1999, with Kennetch Charlette as artistic director. One of its most recent plays, *Kihew* (2007), which examines the cost and horror of residential schools, is a good example of how SNTC works. The writer, Curtis Peeteetuce, composed the play with the help of the cast after they had participated for eight months in a Circle of Voices, learning their own culture and techniques. The actors, who were from First Nations reserves at Beardy and Okemasis, Muskoday, Mistawasis, Cote, Montreal Lake, and Onion Lake, were all performing for the first time on stage.

Finally, it is worth mentioning two professional companies in smaller centres. The Stations Arts Centre in Rosthern offers a play each summer. Its home is a revitalized railroad station and it offers meals as well as performances. Dancing Sky Theatre at Meacham is housed in a renovated Ukrainian Hall and it, too, offers meals. It performs on average three plays a year including new Saskatchewan and Canadian plays. Among its successes are James O'Shea's *Dogbarked* and the Christmas pantomimes. I attended the first pantomime when my friend Dwayne Brenna invited me as well as a Czech exchange student. The theatre is a converted Ukrainian Hall in almost original condition. The chairs are as heterogeneous as a good audience. The Czech student said with delight, "There hasn't been a theatre like this in Europe in two centuries."

In concluding, it is perhaps a measure of the openness of Saskatchewan companies to new work that my most recent plays have been premiered in a variety of professional, university, and community contexts. Ironically, my experience with the large professional regional theatre was the least satisfying in terms of the overall creative process. If I have had the joy of watching my plays being created on stage, imagine my frustration when my last play, *Tune Town, the Saskatoon Musical* (music by Angie Tysseland) was performed at Persephone in 2006. Tibor Feheregyhazi refused my participation, as if a playwright were the enemy. While the play was generally very well done, and some scenes perfectly, there was one scene so stupid and insulting that I shut my eyes, and other small moments that I could have helped make better. Not to be.

I had a happier experience with *Lanc*, a play about a Lancaster bombing raid over Germany, which was staged at Greystone Theatre in 1996. I'd written *The Great War* and wanted to write a play on World War II. My original plan was a sex comedy based on the Commonwealth Air Training Plan in Saskatoon, but there was no material to assist me, so I chose *Lanc*, perhaps because as a child I'd listened to a CBC radio show, *L is for Lanky*. I composed the play by interviewing Bomber Command veterans, sixty-three of them. The trick was verbally to take off a bomber and then land it. No books gave any of that precise knowledge. I met a man in Twwassen, Al Avant, who'd stayed in the air force after the war and had a marvelous memory. So I put the Lanc in the air. When I needed to land it at night, others told me how radio signals worked. So I brought the aircraft home. Did it all over in Act 2 when three men of the crew of seven were killed (fifty percent of men in Bomber Command died). It's the only play I've written where I got it right the first time. When Henry Woolf directed it as the Greystone Theatre's fiftieth-anniversary play, he was directing my play and his own world. As a boy, Henry had been moved out of London's East End to East Anglia because of German bombing, the sky filled with aircraft. Henry became an airplane spotter, so he did my play and his play.

A recent drama, *Two Gun Cohen* (2005), presented as a community play at a wonderfully refurbished Roxy Cinema, had not eight but twenty actors, with one person playing twenty roles. The production was also unique in bringing together members of the Jewish and Chinese performing arts communities in the city, including musicians and dancers, to play out the extraordinary true story of an East End London Jewish boy who after amazing adventures in Western Canada, some of them centred in the very neighborhood where the Roxy is located, travelled abroad to become bodyguard to Sun Yat Sen for a time and stayed in China for thirty years. If *Lanc* was the play I had most control over, *Two Gun Cohen*, set in Chinese history, was the most intractable and difficult. But it happened, directed by Henry Woolf, and was a success in the end. After one performance a delightful three-year-old shook my hand and said, "Don, that was wonderful." My best review.

We can't predict how our plays will be received. I imagine my own plays as populist, performed in lively ways and accessible to a wide audience, like the models—Brecht, Littlewood, and Theatre Passe Muraille—that inspired my plays. Perhaps, as with *Paper Wheat*, the essence of being a playwright in Saskatchewan is to be able to return perennially to that last line "I'd give it all to be young again and feel that I could change the world"—and go back the next day and try again.

Works Cited

Brenna, Dwayne. *Emrys' Dream, Greystone Theatre in Photographs and Words*. Saskatoon: Thistledown Press, 2007.

———. "Fifty-Six Years at Stratford and Still Going Strong: An Interview with Robert Hinitt." *Saskatoon History Review* 22 (2008), special issue on "Celebrating the Arts in Saskatoon." n.p.

Orrell, John. *Fallen Empires, Lost Theatres of Edmonton, 1881–1914*. Edmonton: NeWest Press, 1981; Landmark Edition, 2007.

Stuart, E. Ross. *The History of Prairie Theatre, 1833–1982*. Toronto: Simon & Pierre Publishing Co., 1984.

The Encyclopedia of Saskatchewan. Regina: Canadian Plains Research Center, 2005.

Twenty-fifth Street House Theatre. *Paper Wheat: The Book/Created by 25th Street Theatre*. Saskatoon: Western Producer Prairie Books, 1982.

Theatres, Theatre Companies and Dramaturgical Centres

Between the Bottles and the Knives:
Celebrating Twenty-Five Years
with the Saskatchewan Playwrights Centre

PAM BUSTIN

> *Some things only start to make sense around a kitchen table. A funeral. A new baby born. A marriage gone ripe. You start to figure it out here. Over coffee. Over beer. Over over-proof Jamaican Rum, you talk it over right here.*
>
> *Whatever happens, blood on the rock face, your kid's first hockey game, you bring it all back here and you lay it out between the ashtrays and the needles and you work on it. Right here.*
>
> *Between the bottles and the knives.*

Mansel Robinson (Spitting Slag)

INTRODUCTION

In 1982, on a dark and stormy night (according to Rex Deverell) (Deverell, 2006, 2), a bunch of playwrights sat around a table in a basement rec room and hammered out an idea. They wanted to create a place to work on their plays and find people to support and participate in that work. The playwrights were: Lorraine Blashill, Steven Michael Berzensky (AKA Mick Burrs), Janice Dales (AKA Kim Morrissey), Rex Deverell, Doug Hicton, Marie Powell Mendenhall, Ken Mitchell, Greg Morley, Roy Morrissey, Susan Martin (AKA Susan Pavelick), Barbara Sapergia, Eugene Stickland, and Geoffrey Ursell. Most of them were already members of the Saskatchewan Writers' Guild (SWG) (founded in 1969), but they wanted to create a place of their own—*to foster the development of Saskatchewan plays in a risk-friendly environment; to develop but not to produce plays* (Saskatchewan Playwrights Centre, "About Us," 2009). Their main development strategy was to provide an annual series of professional workshops of new Saskatchewan plays including a public event that showcased plays in development. They called this event the Spring Festival of New Plays—and it and the Saskatchewan Playwrights Centre (SPC) have been going strong ever since.

As we explore Western Canadian playwriting going into the twenty-first century, I'd like to give you a glimpse into the work that has been going on in Saskatchewan for the last twenty-five years: the work that started around that table in 1982 with the formation of a playwright-run organization called the Saskatchewan Playwrights Centre. The body of this article is a revised version of a show I pulled together to celebrate the twenty-fifth anniversary of the SPC's Spring Festival of New Plays. I'll use the introduction to give you a quick rundown of how and why the SPC has become one of the best places in the country to develop new work.

Our founders came up with two principles that remain the prime directives of the SPC: that the playwrights are "in charge" and that we develop plays but do not produce them. The first is self-explanatory—it's our organization and we need to put the work in on the Board and committees to keep it strong and vital. We need to be in charge, at least within this organization, of our own destinies. The second directive often raises questions. Why doesn't the SPC *produce* plays? Isn't *production* the point? In the end—of course it is. We all want our plays produced, but that's not what the SPC does. What we do, and have been doing very well for over twenty-five years, is to develop the stories our members bring to the table—whether or not these stories ever make it to the stage. We develop plays. We are also developing dramaturges, directors, actors, an audience that is excited about new work and, most importantly, Saskatchewan playwrights. Our wise foremothers and forefathers saw fit to ensure that we do this work away from the pressures and seductions of the marketplace. On a personal note, as a playwright and longtime member of the SPC, I can't applaud them enough.

Here's the thing. *Of course* we all want our plays to be produced—but first we need to … get the story right. Find out what it is we are actually trying to say and make sure we say it in the strongest, clearest, most entertaining way possible. Some of the stories we want (or need) to tell may not, let us say, appeal to theatres that are constantly searching for the next big hit to fill their seats. Not in the *beginning*, anyhow.

I'll cut to the chase with a case in point: the play quoted above is Mansel Robinson's *Spitting Slag*. The development of this play hit a roadblock at a major Canadian theatre due to its political content. *Spitting Slag* is the story of a miner hunting for justice—or revenge—after the death of his son. Development was stopped and Mansel was, to put it politely, released from his contract. He came back to Saskatchewan and carried on developing the play with the SPC. The play has since gone on to successful productions (in both English and French) across the country and has been published (along with Robinson's *Ghost Trains*) in both English (Thistledown Press) and French (Éditions Prise de parole). Joanne Paulson of the *Saskatoon Star Phoenix* had this to say about the Theatre With a Crooked Grin fringe production (2000) of *Spitting Slag*:

> *Spitting Slag* is a gripping, intelligent, fierce and moving tale, beautifully performed (Robert Benz) and eloquently written— and one of the best pieces of theatre ever to hit the fringe. *Ever.* An amazing journey from hate to love, punctuated by sex and bad jokes and all the terrible mistakes made in every stratum of society. (Paulson, D3)

I venture to say, and I'm pretty sure Mansel would back me up, that *Spitting Slag* would not have become the play it is without the development support of the SPC. If we were dependant solely on theatres (or producers whose main interest is finding the next big hit and whose foremost fear is offending their subscriber base and/or their sponsors) to develop our plays, **Floyd**'s story never would have seen the light of day and the hundreds of people who have stood to salute him would've missed a great ride. *Spitting Slag* is a bloody GREAT play—a great bloody play—however you want to say it. I've seen it more than once, and it breaks my heart every time.

So, the adventure (or misadventure) of *Spitting Slag* serves as a very specific example of why the SPC does not produce plays. A more general, and dare I say insidious, reason is that once our brains (playwrights' included) slip into production mode, there is a tendency to halt exploration of sections, scenes, and even moments in a play that … don't really work. We shift our focus from "what the playwright is trying to say" to "how does it play for the audience." The shift is natural and necessary once we've moved into production mode, but it can cripple a play in an early stage of development. I've also seen it do some serious damage to a play that is *almost ready to go*. Why? Because production panic can push us towards the easiest route out of a *problem*, "If it doesn't work, cut it!" And if we do that, we may be cutting out the heart of the play. In my experience, the juiciest stuff, the most powerful truths, are found in the moments that the playwright has to grapple the hardest with. The easiest answer isn't always the best.

So, how does the SPC develop new plays, and what steps do we take to help our members find theatres that will produce them? We start where the telling and sorting out of all good stories start—at the kitchen table or, if you prefer a more exact location, the workshop table. Script development is provided according to members' needs—from one-on-one dramaturgy and cold reading of scripts, through more intensive workshops with professional actors, directors, and dramaturges, to the Spring Festival of New Plays—a week of workshops and public staged readings of new plays by our members.

Because of the size and public nature of the event, the Spring Festival of New Plays is the highlight of the SPC's year. The deadline for submissions to Spring Festival is, traditionally, October 31 each year. All members are welcome to send in submissions. It is a blind competition, meaning the playwright's name doesn't appear on the script. The scripts are then sent to the Outside Reader—a professional dramaturge—who reads the plays and ranks them according to *interest*, choosing the plays that intrigue, excite, and challenge him or her. To ensure fairness and variety, our Outside Reader, traditionally, serves no more than two years in a row. The Reader also serves as the Festival Dramaturge. He or she attends the Spring Festival as a sort of uber-dramaturge along with the SPC Dramaturge. The Reader acts as: a troubleshooter if a workshop gets off track, animateur if a director gets stuck, provocateur if the work seems to need it, confidante (for the playwright, director, actors), supporter, and cheerleader. Once the plays are chosen, we invite directors from across the country to come to Saskatchewan and work on the plays. In the last few years, there's been a slight change in the policy of choosing directors for the Festival plays. Originally, we only invited artistic directors of theatres that produced new Canadian plays, the idea being, of course, to interest them in the work of our members. We noticed, over the years, that more and more of our work was being championed by directors (and actors) who weren't necessarily "in charge" of theatres, so the Board opened up our stable of directors to include freelancers we really wanted to work with. As you can see in the Appendix, which lists the production histories of plays that have appeared at Spring Festival, our work continues to get picked up for production.

One of the truly unique aspects of the SPC Spring Festival is its "retreat" nature, that is, a group of artists living and working together in community for a short and intensive period of time. As mentioned earlier, we bring in directors and dramaturges from across the country to work with our playwrights and actors in workshops that range from two to six days and culminate in a staged public reading. We also invite artistic directors from across the country to attend the readings and, if they want (and the playwright is okay with it), to attend the workshops in progress. We stay in residence at either the University of Regina or the University of Saskatchewan (Saskatoon), and participants are urged to attend all of the public readings and to participate in the after-hours events where much of the informal creative work is done.

The staged readings are open to the public and give the playwrights opportunities to see and hear their work *with* an audience and to ask that audience a few questions about what they've seen. After the presentation, discussions usually continue at the bar (an integral part of any theatre festival). The public readings are not an "end product"—they are simply another part of the development process. They feature the play in a way that will allow the audience to respond to it most clearly. Whatever seems right, given the work that has been done during the workshop time, is perfectly acceptable. This could mean reading at lecterns or music stands, some minimal staging, full staging with a detailed ground plan, or a play that is half-staged/half-read.

The focus of Spring Festival is on serving the play and the playwright. We are not there to "fix the play"—we are there to explore what is on the page and bring it to the playwright (and the audience) clearly.

After Festival, the playwright returns to work on the play, integrating what she or he has learned from the workshop, the public presentation, and the discussions at the bar.

I attended my first Spring Festival in 1986 as an actor—playing **Blanche** in Connie Gault's *Sky*. Shortly after that, I ran off to the big city (Toronto) to become an actor. In 1993, I returned to Saskatchewan as a playwright. My first play, *Saddles in the Rain*, was part of Festival in 1994, and I've been at almost every Festival since—as a playwright, an actor, a coordinator, or simply as an avid fan of new Saskatchewan work. The Spring Festival of New Plays is a time of inspiration. It's a time to meet people who are busy working on new stories and new ways to tell stories. It's a time to see what's cooking with the playwrights of the province and to meet theatre professionals from across the country. It's a time to pull out my own stories and lay them on the table to hash them out with people I respect and trust.

There are a lot of writers in Saskatchewan. Some blame this on the long, cold winters. I blame the high proportion of *playwrights* in the province on the ongoing support and camaraderie of the SPC. An impressive list of some of this country's foremost playwrights hail from Saskatchewan and have been active members of SPC. These include: Kit Brennan, Rex Deverell, Connie Gault, Don Kerr, Daniel MacDonald, Ken Mitchell, Kim Morrissey, Greg Nelson, Barbara Sapergia, Eugene Stickland, Vern Thiessen, Geoffrey Ursell, Dianne Warren, Kenneth T. Williams, and, of course, Mansel Robinson. Works by these playwrights, developed with the support of the SPC, have gone on to productions and awards both nationally and internationally.[1] Some of these writers have moved away—from Saskatchewan, or from writing plays. We want them to know that if they ever want to come home, we'll be there, at the kitchen table, ready to listen to their stories and to help them hammer out the rough spots.

As Festival Coordinator in 2007, and long-time SPC member, I pulled together the *25th Anniversary Clip Show*, from member submissions, to celebrate our past, honour those who'd come before us, and encourage those who are just gaining the courage to put pen to paper.

The original show ran just over an hour and included excerpts from:

- *Dora: A Case of Hysteria* by Kim Morrissey
- *Back Fence* by Rex Deverell
- *Some Assembly Required* by Eugene Stickland
- *Saddles in the Rain* by Pam Bustin
- *Comfort and Joy* by Kelley Jo Burke
- *Blowfish* by Vern Thiessen
- *Spitting Slag* by Mansel Robinson
- *Double Blind* by Ian Nelson and Kevin Power
- *Hope and Fury* by Will Brooks
- *Out in the Cold* by Cheryl Jack
- *Bite the Hand* by Mansel Robinson
- *Peaches and Cream* by Jennifer Wynne Webber
- *Burning In* by Natalie Meisner
- *The Passage of Georgia O'Keeffe* by Pam Bustin

The show was directed by Ben Henderson and presented on May 20, 2007, at the University of Saskatchewan, featuring:

Robert Benz—as himself, **Freud**, **Charlie**, **Gordon**, **Jake**, and **Floyd**
Will Brooks—as himself, **Edward**, **Walter**, **Lumiere**, and **Mrs. Kisby**
Pam Bustin—as herself, **Margaret**, **Fury**, **Josie**, and **Georgia**
Jamie Lee Shebelski—as herself, **Kat**, **Hope**, and **Lois**

The following version of the show has been edited substantially for publication and includes only excerpts from plays that have been previously published. These excerpts are included with the playwrights' permission.

---

1 See Appendix: Saskatchewan Playwrights Centre Spring Festival Plays and Participants, 1983–2007 for production histories of plays that have been through the SPC's Spring Festival of New Plays. Production histories of other members' plays can be obtained from the SPC ("Play Catalogue" www.saskplaywrights.ca).

For information on any plays or playwrights mentioned, please contact The Saskatchewan Playwrights Centre, Box 3092, Saskatoon, SK, S7K 3S9, email us at sk.playwrights@sasktel.net, or check out our Catalogue of Plays at www.saskplaywrights.ca. You will also find links to other provincial play development centres on our site.

If you are interested in more historical information on the SPC, please refer to *The Playwright's Path: An Analysis of the Canadian Play Development Process as Practiced by the Saskatchewan Playwrights Centre, 1982–2000,* written by one of our founding members, Marie Elaine Powell Mendenhall. You can also contact the office and ask for a copy of our newsletter, *Playworks* 6.3 (Fall 2006) (The SPC 25th Anniversary Edition). It contains pieces by Dan Macdonald, Rex Deverell, Connie Gault, and Ben Henderson.

For now, here's a quick look at Spring Festivals past and a wee taste of the work that has been developed by the SPC.

Enjoy the show.

The SPC 25th Anniversary Clip Show

Setting: Onstage, opening night of the SPC's 25th Annual Spring Festival of New Plays.

Four music stands, four chairs, four actors.

Will: Hey everyone, thanks for coming out tonight. I'm Will Brooks, President of the SPC, and I'd like to welcome you all to our 25th Anniversary Party. We've pulled together a little "clip show" for you tonight, featuring some scenes from Festivals past. We'd like to give a nod to Last Exit's recent production of Yann Martel's show *The Facts Behind the Helsinki Roccamatios.*[2] You'll see why in a minute.

Jamie: **1982.** Premier Grant Devine appoints Saskatchewan's first female cabinet ministers, Joan Duncan and Patricia Smith.

Pam: Grant Devine is a/

Robert: Don't start.

Will: Thirteen people, including playwrights Rex Deverell, Connie Gault, Eugene Stickland, and Ken Mitchell, attended the founding meeting of the Saskatchewan Playwrights Centre.

Pam: Thirteen. Nice.

Robert: *(rolls his eyes at Pam)* **1983.** Henry Taube, born in Neudorf, Saskatchewan, wins the Nobel Prize in chemistry.

Jamie: Saskatchewan's population tops one million for the first time.

Will: The SPC holds the first Spring Festival of New Plays featuring work by: Cheri Lynn Cooke, Rex Deverell, Ken Mitchell,

Jamie: Barbara Sapergia, and Dianne Warren.

---

2   *The Facts Behind the Helsinki Roccamatios,* originally a short story by Yann Martel, revolves around a man who invents stories about a family of Italian immigrants living in Helsinki, Finland, to help pass the time with a friend who is dying of AIDS. In order to guide the plot of their strange attempt at fiction they use *Encyclopedia Britannica* extracts from each year starting from 1901 until present (1986) metaphorically to write each chapter. That story won the Canadian Journey Prize in 1991. Last Exit Theatre produced Martel's stage adaptation of the story in March 2006.

Robert: 1984. Prud'homme native Jeanne Sauvé is appointed the first female Governor General of Canada.

Pam: The government changes the "Crow Rate"—to the *benefit* of prairie farmers.

Will: Festival features work by Mick Burrs, Alexina Dalgetty, Don Kerr, and Ken Mitchell.

Jamie: 1985. The debit card, the first in North America, is tested at the Swift Current Pioneer Co-op. Evil is foist upon the world.

Will: Ken Gass[3] is our "playwright-in-residence" and leads the charge on new work by Sharon Butala, James Misfeldt, Jeff Park,

Jamie: Barbara Sapergia, and Dianne Warren.

Pam: And we get the first look at *Dora, a Case of Hysteria* by Kim Morrissey: "a satirical feminist play debunking Sigmund Freud's theories about hysteria. In the famous case, Dora is sent to Dr. Freud by her father, who feels she is suffering from neurosis. Despite her claims that her father's friend has been sexually harassing her, Freud believed her to be exhibiting symptoms of hysteria caused by... repressed sexual desire."[4]

Robert and *Jamie* play scene.

FREUD. Look at me, Dora: You did not notice his Member?

DORA. His what?

FREUD. His Member ... his John Thomas ... his Man Below Stairs. [*DORA looks blank*] His Flagpole, his Wiener, his Schlong ... his Penis ... His Peter, His Prick, His Cock. You did not notice?

DORA. Well ... no.

FREUD. No?

DORA. No.

3   Ken Gass was the founder of Factory Theatre Lab—the first theatre to announce, in 1970, that it would produce exclusively Canadian plays.

4   Synopsis of *Dora* by Kim Morrissey from Nick Hern Books website (www. nickhernbooks.co.uk). The site also contains information on cast size and ordering information.

FREUD.   But you know now, don't you. You know what a man's Member is, don't you?

DORA.   Yes.

FREUD.   And you felt it, did you ... when he pressed you .... when he pressed you by the staircase ... when he pressed you by The Lake?

DORA.   No! I didn't! I swear I didn't!

FREUD.   You didn't feel it when he pressed you here ... or here ... or here ...

DORA.   [*breaking away*] No I didn't. I didn't! I couldn't! I— Oh dear—Excuse me. May I use your [*embarrassed*] ... your ....

FREUD.   You mean the ...? Ah. Of course, of course!

   DORA exits.

FREUD.   Note that from the very beginning I used the greatest care not to introduce the patient to any new information in the area of sexual knowledge.

End of scene.

Pam: **1986**. Saskatchewan builds a spectacular glass grain elevator for Expo 86 in Vancouver.

Will: Festival features work by Jeanne Heal, Tim McCashin, Geoffrey Ursell, Kim Morrissey, and James Misfeldt,

Robert: *Tommy* by Ken Mitchell,

Pam: *Sky* by Connie Gault.

Jamie: **1987**. The University of Saskatchewan begins offering distance education by satellite television.

Will: We see new work from Rod MacIntyre, Kay Nouch, Gail Robinson, Harry Rintoul,

Jamie: And *Round Up* by Barbara Sapergia.

Pam: **1988**. Sylvia Fedoruk is appointed Saskatchewan's first female Lieutenant-Governor.

Will: Michael Springate[5] directs *Exile* by Archie Crail.

Robert: About time you mentioned a director.

Will: We don't have all night.

Robert: Right. *A Killing Frost* by Sharon Butala, *Nice Guy* by Rod MacIntyre. *Fortinbras in Denmark* by Rod Macpherson.

Jamie: *The Soft Eclipse* by Connie Gault.

Pam: *Club Chernobyl* by Dianne Warren,

Will: And Springate's *Dog and Crow*.[6]

Jamie: **1989.** Cellular phone service is introduced in Saskatchewan. More evil foisting!

Will: Don Kerr, Greg Nelson, Dianne Warren, and Ken Mitchell.

Jamie: **1990.** Ray Hnatyshyn is appointed Canada's Governor General. He is the first person of Ukrainian descent to hold the office and I got the day off school!

Will: New works leap forth from Mel Melymick, Greg Nelson, Judy Smith, and Henry Woolf.

Jamie: **1991.** The Kramer IMAX Theatre, the first of its kind in the province, opens at the Saskatchewan Science Centre in Regina.

Robert: When do we get more scenes?

Will: Soon.

1991. DD Kugler[7] makes his first appearance as Festival Dramaturge.

5   Springate acted as Festival Dramaturge. He is a playwright/director who began his career in Montreal, Québec, as founding artistic director of the alternative and experimental theatre, The Painted Bird, in 1974. Springate has served as artistic director of Playwrights' Workshop and, from 1995 to 1996, as artistic director of Factory Theatre in Toronto.

6   As noted in the Appendix: I am not sure if Springate was a resident of Saskatchewan at this time, and therefore eligible to be an SPC member and submit to Festival, or if inclusion of his play was a special event.

7   As you'll see in the Appendix, DD Kugler has been a mainstay of Spring Festival for years. Kugler was artistic director of Edmonton's Northern Light Theatre (1993–98) and production dramaturge with Toronto's Necessary Angel (1985–93). A long-time member of Literary Managers and Dramaturgs of the Americas, Kugler served a two-year term as LMDA's first Canadian President (2000–2002). Kugler's work as a freelance dramaturge and director has appeared on stages across Canada. He is currently an associate professor in the Theatre Area of School for the Contemporary

All: Huzzah!

Will: The plays are *Goddessness, Learning the Rhumba, Fuse, Castrato, Girl from God's Country* and *Windchill.*

Pam: Hey, isn't that the year the brouhaha broke out at the talkback?

Will: No.

Pam: You sure?

Jamie: (cutting in) **1992.** Wanuskewin Heritage Park opens near Saskatoon!

Robert: Why are you so excited by that?

Jamie: I like Wanuskewin.

Robert: Move it along.

Pam: Spring Festival 1992 showcased *Mazo and Caroline* by Joan Givner, *The Bottom Line* by Mary Love, and *Back Fence* by Rex Deverell.

Jamie: **1993.** The government gambles with the introduction of video lottery terminals. Definitely more foisted evil.

Will: spc gambles with *Collateral Damage* by Mansel Robinson.

Robert: *Baggage* by Kit Brennan.

Pam: *Playing the Game* by Kelley Jo Burke, and Eugene Stickland's *Some Assembly Required.*

"Mom and Dad aren't going to have Christmas this year, or so they think. When their three grown-up children unexpectedly return home Christmas Eve—and hide out down in the basement with the barbed-wire, Barbies, and a BB gun—it seems that Christmas might just happen after all."[8] Here's a little peek into Stickland's twisted Yuletide cheer.

Will and ***Robert*** play scene.

Arts at Simon Fraser University in Vancouver, British Columbia, where he teaches directing, dramaturgy, playmaking, and his version of theatre history.

8 Synopsis of *Some Assembly Required* by Eugene Stickland from www.playdatabase. com. The site also contains information on cast size and ordering information.

GORDON *and* WALTER *are in the basement, drinking eggnog. We hear a bit of* **Carmen** *by Georges Bizet.*

GORDON. ... It's one big giant oxymoron.

WALTER. Like jumbo shrimp.

GORDON. Exactly.

WALTER. Like military intelligence.

GORDON. Yes. I jusss....

WALTER. Like *Little Big Man*.

GORDON. Right...

WALTER. Like Richie Rich, Poor Little Rich Boy.

GORDON. Looks like you've got the oxymoron thing pretty well covered there, Walter.

WALTER. Figures of speech have always been a favourite of mine.

GORDON. I don't think I knew that about you.

WALTER. Oh yes. Metaphor... simile... conceit... I know them all. But oxymoron holds a special place in my heart.

GORDON. Is this something that comes up a lot in the insurance business? Figures of speech?

WALTER. People expect a lot of their adjustor. I make it my business to know how things work, and I include language in that. Anyway... *(Pause)* So... what's going on, Gordon?

GORDON. What do you mean?

WALTER. You're holed up down in the folks' basement. You're armed.

GORDON. I don't want to talk about it.

WALTER. Where's Carla?

GORDON. *Carlene.*

WALTER. Carlene. Sorry.

GORDON. I don't want to talk about it.

WALTER. OK. That's OK. We don't have to talk about it.

GORDON. Good, 'cause I don't want to.

WALTER. No problem. We can just sit here and listen to *Carmen.*

Long pause.

GORDON. She took off. Up north. With a bush pilot.

WALTER. Wow!

GORDON. I don't know what it is now, Walter. But I don't feel comfortable out there. Everybody's talking about it.

WALTER. About what?

GORDON. You know. Carlene, the bush pilot... me.

WALTER. Who's talking about it?

GORDON. The people in the malls. In restaurants. I can hear them, sometimes. They stop talking when I get in range.

WALTER. If they stop talking when you get in range, how do you know they're talking about you?

GORDON. I can tell by the way they look at me. I know they know. They take one look at me and they know. Even Kenny knows.

WALTER. What?

GORDON. That I blew it. Despite all my potential, no one will have me.

WALTER. I think you're being a little hard on yourself there, Gordon.

GORDON. You just don't know what it's like. I envy you for that.

WALTER. For what?

GORDON. You're kind of an old-fashioned man, Walter.

WALTER. What's that supposed to mean?

GORDON. Well, you've got a job. You put on a tie and drive to work. You come home and have a martini, I'd imagine. Taffy has supper ready. After supper you watch TV. Or read. You're not sitting in your shorts staring at the clock, wondering where your wife is. She's right there beside you. Or out in the kitchen, ironing. You go to bed, get up the next morning, do it all again.

WALTER. In fact—Never mind. This *(referring to his drink)* isn't so bad, once you get on to it.

GORDON. You want another? One.

WALTER. Why not? We can drink some milk later.

> GORDON *cracks three eggs into the crystal bowl and pours in half a bottle of rum. Fade to black as he prepares to stir this with a contraption he has constructed by fitting a few loops of barbed wire into a three-speed cordless rechargeable reversible Makita hand drill.*

End of scene.

Pam: 1994. SGI [Saskatchewan Government Insurance] introduces "no-fault" insurance.

Will: Kate Lushington[9] is our outside reader, Patti Shedden is our dramaturge and we see new plays by Rachel van Fossen and Darrel Wildcat, Greg Nelson, Geoff Ursell and *[looks at Pam]* you, right?

Pam: Yep. My first play, *Saddles in the Rain*. I needed a gentle hand and Patti brought in Mr. Ben Henderson[10] to direct. I call it my Canadian Kitchen Sink Family Trauma Drama. There are things in every family that break our hearts; things that shame us; and things that make us so proud we could burst. I'd say that *Saddles* is the story of a family that splintered into darkness and the strength of the daughters who are determined to pull themselves back into the light.

Will: It's also been called "… a vivid and disturbing narrative of family violence interwoven with surprising moments of compassion and comic lightness" (Johnston, 2006, 128).

Pam: Nice.

---

9   Kate Lushington was artistic director of Nightwood Theatre for six seasons, engaged in developing and promoting new Canadian women's voices.

10 Ben Henderson is another mainstay at Spring Festival. He came as a director (see Appendix), dramaturge and audience member for years. Ben was the founding artistic director of Nexus Theatre and the artistic director of Theatre Network, both in Edmonton. We were blessed to have Ben as our own SPC Dramaturge from 2000 to 2007.

Jamie and *Robert* play scene.

JAKE.	Yer mom asleep?
KAT.	Yep.
JAKE.	What're ya doin'?
KAT.	Beading.
JAKE.	Yeah? Had a friend who did that.
KAT.	Eddie.
JAKE.	Yeah, Lil Eddie. Told you about him, huh? Full blood Cree—crazy as a wild dog—but he sure could do carvin' and beadin'. I lived with him and his ole man.
KAT.	I know.
JAKE.	Yep. After I left home. Went down to Little Eddie's and he and his ole man took me in. Dad took a fit when he found out I was livin' on the Rez. Come down and tried to drag me home. Got the shit beat outta him for once. I was what... about...
KAT.	Ten.
JAKE.	Yeah, ten years old... Just couldn't stay there no more. Ole man had me locked up in the back room for days. No food. Dried blood on my face from the fight we'd had.

Crazy bastard wouldn't even let me out to take a shit. Had a spot in the corner. Christ.

He got called in to work and Mom came in to bring me some food 'n' clean me up. She was wailin' and "Oh Holy Motherin'" and I couldn't stand it. I left.

He waits for a response. **KAT** *keeps beading.*

She got in trouble for that—lettin' me out while he was gone.

Yep, she got in trouble all right. Sonny told me she was in the hospital for a week on accounta me. Ole Dad never took shit from nobody.

Sonny wanted me to come home, but I just stayed with
Little Eddie. He was more my brother than Sonny ever was.

Me 'n' Eddie rode with the Angels y'know.

KAT rolls her eyes in disbelief. Keeps beading.

KAT.   Uh huh.

JAKE.   Hey, Kat.

KAT.   What.

JAKE.   You ever meet Eddie?

KAT.   No.

JAKE.   Nope.

He's dead, eh.

KAT.   I know.

JAKE.   You'da liked him, y'know? He was fun.

KAT.   Uh huh.

Silence except for the television.

JAKE.   We were runnin' like mad for the bikes. The pavement
was wet. I remember.

He reached his first, kicked it into gear and started off.

I was just jumpin' on mine when the bullet hit him. Pulled
him right off the bike—sideways—and the bike kept on
goin'. Went a hundred yards, tipped, and kept sliding along
the pavement like a fuckin' movie bike in slow mo.

Christ.

We were only sixteen.

Cops still coming and Eddie screaming "Go. GO!" So I went
and left him. Just left him in a fuckin' rainy parkin' lot.

Silence except for the television.

You don't understand.

KAT.   Understand what.

End of scene.

Pam: Thanks guys. That was great.

Robert: Oh no thank you.

Pam: Oh no thank/

Will: And we're moving on. **1995**.

Pam: The government abolishes the Crow and the Wheat Board goes public.

All.   BOOO!

Jamie: *Otherwise Bob* by Connie Gault!

All: Yay!

Will: *The Christmas-all-year-round Room* by Kelley Jo Burke, *The Last Journey of Captain Harte* by Dianne Warren, and *Lanc* by Don Kerr.

Pam: **1996**. Canada's last federally operated Indian residential school, located on the Gordon Reserve north of Fort Qu'Appelle, closes.

Will: John Murrell[11] and Bob White[12] come to town.[13]

---

11   Murrell's plays have been translated into fifteen different languages and performed in more than thirty countries around the world. He has worked as playwright-in-residence at both Theatre Calgary and Alberta Theatre Projects, as associate director of the Stratford Festival of Canada, as head of the Banff Playwrights Colony (1986–1989), as head of the Theatre Section of the Canada Council for The Arts (1988–1992), and as artistic director/executive producer of Theatre Arts at The Banff Centre (1999 to 2007).

12   Bob White was the first artistic director of Playwrights' Workshop (1975–78) and served as artistic director at Factory Theatre (1979–87). He was the artistic director of Alberta Theatre Projects from 1999 to 2009.

13   See Appendix.

Jamie: *The Heart as it Lived* by Mansel Robinson, *Blue Zone* by Rod MacIntyre, *Waking up Demons* by Donald B. Campbell—featuring Bongo Ben Henderson on the plastic bucket.

Robert: And *Blowfish* by Vern Thiessen, directed by Micheline Chevrier.[14]

Pam: "What do food, funerals, the Edmonton tornado and Mila Mulroney have in common? Let's join the elegant and debonair caterer Lumiere as he serves you up a whole new eating experience."[15]

Will plays scene.

LUMIERE. Hello.

And thank you for coming.

My name is Lumiere. I am a caterer, and what I have for you tonight is a fete, a special event. I've requested your presence here this evening—and you have been so good as to oblige—for a variety of reasons. Number one: To Eat. As much as you like. We have victuals to meet your every dining desire; we have foodstuffs to tantalize your discerning palate; we have edibles that will nourish your mind, as well as your soul; we have it all. Number two: To listen. To me. Tell a few stories, nothing too dull or overly long I promise. Just a few anecdotes to help you digest and hopefully, in the process, entertain and... enlighten you. Number three: To observe, to witness, to...

But more on that later. Until then, rest, relax, and be assured that throughout this evening's event, I am here to serve you: my esteemed guests.

Let me tell you a story:

14   Micheline Chevrier has worked across the country, as a director, in French and English. She's been the associate artistic director at Theatre New Brunswick, associate dramaturge at Playwrights' Workshop, and artistic director of the Great Canadian Theatre Company.

15   "*Blowfish*" by Vern Thiessen (synopsis). Playwrights Canada Press (www.playwrightscanada.com). The site also contains information on cast size and ordering information.

Thunder threatens in the distance.

The brand new 1979 Ford barrels down Highway 3 and turns off onto a dirt road. Gravel and dust fly.

The driver is not speeding.

He is 16 years old and this is his first day driving by himself after acquiring his Alberta driver's licence.

He is not stoned.

He is not drunk.

He is not careless.

His parents are loving and encouraging, but do not spoil him. He makes his own lunches. He does his own homework. Occasionally he masturbates. But he always cleans up afterwards, and is fully cognizant of its moral implications and biological purpose. He mows the lawn Saturdays. He plays ball with his... brother.

He goes for his driver's licence as soon as he turns 16. And—like most teenagers—as soon as he receives it, he goes to his father and asks him for the keys, who, after a number of questions and warnings, gives the keys to his son, who happily—but not deliriously—starts the engine.

A taste of freedom. The brink of adulthood. His whole life before him.

The brand new 1979 Ford barrels down Highway 3 and turns off onto a dirt road. Gravel and dust fly.

Thunder threatens.

The clouds brew all day long in the western sky. Now, in the early evening, a swirling storm boils onto the dirt and gravel road. Hail splatters the windshield of the 1979 Ford, making the teen's visibility less than desirable. A cold coil of wind sends the brand new Ford twisting and turning on the wet road.

The teen does not panic. He brakes normally.

Cold rain. Loose gravel. A deep ditch. Metal and fibreglass fly.

A piece of the Ford's frame,

Through the windshield,

Through the nose,

To the brain.

Pause.

The teen never speaks intelligibly again. He can not communicate, he can not walk unaided, and his nose runs endlessly. The family wonders who is responsible for this:

God? or Fate? or Ford?

Later, the teen's brother and the teen's parents send him to an institution, where everyone who visits the teen (now a man) takes him to be defective from birth, or crazy, or both.

He will...die.

Eventually.

Would anyone like some more?

End of scene.

Pam: **1997.** Former members of the Progressive Conservative and Liberal parties found the Saskatchewan Party.

Will: Our outside reader is Urjo Kareda,[16] and Peter Smith[17] is our Festival dramaturge.

---

16   Urjo Kareda served as the literary manager for the Stratford Festival (1975-80) and artistic director for the Tarragon Theatre (1982–2001).

17   Peter Smith has also worked on play development at the Banff Centre for The Arts playwrights colony, Prairie Theatre Exchange, Blyth Festival, Alberta Theatre Projects, and as artistic director for Playwrights' Workshop.

Jamie: *Bim and Bub* by Henry Woolf, CANADA ENDING *and other wars of 1812* by Robert Bartel, *Taproot* by Mary Love.

Robert: *The Girl From God's Country* by Barbara Sapergia.

Pam: Ah ha! *That's* the year the brouhaha broke out.[18]

Will: Shut up.

Pam: Censor.

Jamie: **1998.** The Sandra Schmirler rink and Catriona LeMay Doan win gold at the Nagano Olympics!

Will: *Chasing the Wind* by James Misfeldt, *Deer Bring the Sun* by Geoffrey Ursell, *Oh I Go* by Connie Gault, and *Spitting Slag*—Mansel Robinson's story of a miner hunting for justice—or revenge—after the death of his son.

Robert plays scene.

FLOYD. Day six I hallucinate.

Great whacking slabs of hallucinations.

Some woman, she's about three hundred pounds. Shaved head and rubber boots. No teeth. And we're doing it. In an upper berth on *The Canadian*. The train's rocking, she's on top, three hundred pounds of railroad Jello. Then she starts to laugh. She laughs and laughs. What's so funny, I say. Your dick, she says. What's so funny about my dick, I say. It tickles, she says. It tickles. My dick gets even smaller, gets littler and littler, she's laughing harder and harder. Then we're pulling into the station. There's a marching band. I get off the train. I'm wearing her rubber boots. My head is shaved. I got no teeth. And I got no dick. And when the train pulls out of the yard, that woman is driving.

My withered dick. No hallucination.

---

18 There was indeed some excitement that year during the talkback, but let's just say, "What happens at Festival, stays at Festival." Unless, of course, you'd like to find a playwright who was there that year and buy him or her a drink. Never know what tales could slip out.

Day seven.

I'm thinking about bones in the slag.

Blaine Alrich. Falls into a debarker, some mill near Kapuskasing.

Johnny Hill. Out on the mainline. Lousy track.

Larry Wallace. Out on the mainline. China White.

Kelly McWatch. Log truck hits his train near Cartier.

Jimmy Scott. Some greener kills em both scaling.

Doug McNab. Drunk on the job.

Almost everybody I know.

Auntie Bev. Black ice and a rock cut. That'll teach her to drive sober.

Gerry Koski. Sun-stroke on the Gulf of Thailand. Hey buddy! Wear a hat!

Tim Dube. His brother shoots him. Accident. Or that's what we tell the cops.

Tommy Beulieu. No. He's in jail. Kills his wife's boyfriend.

Sam Mah. Falls out of his boat duck hunting. Goof.

Bob Wilson. Found dead in bed with the sheets full of porno. Guess which kind?

Sarah Thomson. Roof. Thought she had wings. Now she does.

Kenny Righetti. .22 long in the head. Took him two days to die.

I wouldn't use a .22 to kill myself. 12 gauge.

Brain-pan stuccoed to the kitchen ceiling.

Gonna do a job, make sure you do it right.

Protestant work ethic.

I'm thinking: this town is cursed.

I'm thinking: no surprise.

We're on an Indian graveyard.

First shaft of the mine. Sunk her right through the bones. Ribs in the slag.

Mostly, I am thinking about my son.

I'm thinking I wish he was in school somewhere, being a teacher a lawyer, an accountant. Something. Anything. Even a double-gut brakeman. Doing anything anywhere but down here. I'm wondering if he made it out.

I'm praying.

End of scene.

Pam: **1999.** The McArthur River Mine in northern Saskatchewan begins to extract ore from the world's largest, known high-grade uranium deposit.

Will: Paula Danckert[19] serves as outside reader and Festival Dramaturge.

Robert: *Red Lips* by Connie Gault, *White River Junction* by Rod MacIntyre

Jamie: *Patriots Divided* by Dennis Hunt, and *Just Julie* by Janice Salkeld.

Will: **2000.**

Robert: The Redberry Pelican Project near Hafford is designated by UNESCO as a World Biosphere Reserve.

Will: *Prairie Tomten* by Mary Love, *Andy and Annie* by Don Kerr, *Hunter Memorial* by Ken Mitchell.

Robert: *Scorched Ice* by Mansel Robinson.

19 Paula Danckert was the artistic director of Playwrights' Workshop Montréal (1998 to 2007). She has also been the programme dramaturge for the PlayRites Colony at the Banff Centre.

Jamie: *Pauline In Concert* by Les Hurlburt, a special presentation of *Hangin' around the Berri Station with My Uncle Marcel,* translation by Deborah Cottreau.

Pam: And my play, *Dancing with the Magpie* directed by Stephen Heatley.[20]

Will: Was that Stephen's first time at Festival?

Pam: Think so.

Will: You sure get the good guys.

Pam: I do.

Robert: I thought you got Ben the first time.

All: Oooooh.

Will: 2001.

Jamie: Saskatchewan takes a lead in providing high-speed Internet service to almost 400 communities spread across the province through CommunityNet.

Will: We bring in a designer, Bretta Gerecke.[21]

Robert: *Alexander the Great, Pageant, Saint Jimmy, Ghost Trains, Street Zone, Life's Like That,* and *Comfort and Joy.*

Jamie: That was the one with all the Christmas lights, right?

Robert: Yep. And we got coal and creosote for *Ghost Trains.*

Jamie: Right. What happened to all that coal?

Robert: I think Ben took it home.

Jamie: Ah, the perks...

Will: 2002.

Pam: Saskatchewan is plagued by drought and a shortage of cattle feed. The Hay West campaign brings hay from eastern Canada to hungry western cattle.

....

20   Stephen Heatley was the artistic director of Theatre Network in Edmonton (1981 to 1992) and director of the theatre school and associate artistic director of Citadel Theatre (1994 to 1999). He is currently a faculty member in the Theatre Program at the University of British Columbia.

21   We decided to try something new and bring in a designer to respond to the plays visually and give the playwrights a look at how a designer might see the world of their play. Bretta Gerecke has been the resident designer of Catalyst Theatre since 1996.

Jamie: Catriona LeMay Doan wins gold again at the Olympics in Salt Lake City!

Will: Stephen Heatley mans the helm as Festival Dramaturge *(All HUZZAH!)* and Wes Pearce[22] designs work by Leanne Griffin, Madeleine Dahlem, Robin Mueller, Kelley Jo Burke, Marie-Pierre Maingon, Lloyd Deshaye, Scott Douglas, and Byrna Barclay.

Pam: 2003. A case of mad cow disease causes a crisis in the cattle industry when the American border is closed to Canadian livestock imports.

They give her a look.

Stephen and Wes are back at Festival.

Jamie: *Angels Are Us* by Byrna Barclay and *The Captive* by Will Brooks,

Will: *[Takes a wee bow] Random Acts* by Sean Hoy, *Dancing Backwards* by Donald B. Campbell, *MacGregor's Hard Ice Cream and Gas* by Daniel Macdonald, and *Double Blind* by Ian Nelson and Kevin Power.

Robert: 2004. In a CBC television competition, Canadians choose Tommy Douglas, former Saskatchewan premier and father of medicare, as the Greatest Canadian.

Jamie: The Canadian Light Source Synchrotron opens in Saskatoon!

Robert: *The Passage of Georgia O'Keeffe, Things Missed,*

Pam: *Picking Up Chekhov, Give 'Er Snoose, Out in the Cold* and ...

Will: My play, *Hope and Fury.*

Robert: 2005. Saskatchewan celebrates 100 years as a province!

Will: *Prelude to Munich* by James Trettwer, *Evil Among Us* by James Misfeldt, *Bite the Hand* by Mansel Robinson, *Wanton* by Rob van Meenen and Cherise Arneson, *Valentine's Day at Bathurst Station* by Trenna Keating

Robert: And *Peaches and Cream* by Jennifer Wynne Webber.

Pam: 2006. The Saskatchewan government issues a syphilis alert.

---

22 Wes Pearce's set and costume designs have appeared at: Globe Theatre, Persephone Theatre, Alberta Theatre Projects, Western Canada Theatre, and Prairie Theatre Exchange among others. He was head of the Theatre Department at the University of Regina from 2006–2009.

Robert: They did not.

Pam: Did so—There were over five times as many syphilises reported in Saskatchewan in 2006 than there were in previous years.

Will: Syphilises?

Pam: Syphili?

Robert: Syphilum.

Will: **2006.** Spring Festival is dedicated to actor Ian Black,[23] and Yvette Nolan[24] joins our merry gang as Festival Dramaturge.

All: Huzzah!

Pam: *The Selkie Wife* by Kelley Jo Burke, *The Last Shall Be First* by Cheryl Jack.

Jamie: *Velocity* by Daniel Macdonald, *Whistling at the Northern Lights* by Jennifer Wynne Webber, *Broken Bones* by Damon Badger Heit, *Burning In* by Natalie Meisner, and a special presentation of *At Grandma's House* by Natasha MacLellan—visiting us all the way from Nova Scotia thanks to the Playwrights Atlantic Resource Centre.

Will: And here we are in **2007.** You'll have to come back to see what Catherine, Tim, Marushka, Brent, Ken, and Mansel have in store for you. As we look forward to more work from Saskatchewan playwrights, we'll close with some words of wisdom from Pam's play *The Passage of Georgia O'Keeffe.*[25]

Robert: You can't do that!

Pam: Why not?

Robert: Isn't it a little… self-promotey?

23 Ian Black was a leader in the Saskatchewan arts community. He performed in theatres from Vancouver to Toronto. He also acted in film, television, and radio, and played **Jake** in the first professional production of Bustin's *Saddles in the Rain.* We were blessed to have Ian as one of our Spring Festival actors almost every year. He taught us a lot and he is greatly missed. Ian died on Monday, December 19, 2005 after a heroic battle with cancer.

24 Yvette Nolan has worked across Canada as a dramaturge. She was president of PUC (now Playwrights Guild of Canada) from 1998 to 2001. In 2003, she was appointed managing artistic director of Native Earth Performing Arts in Toronto.

25 Pam Bustin's *The Passage of Georgia O'Keeffe* has appeared at the Her-icane Festival of Women's Art and the London, Ontario, Fringe Festival (2003). It is not yet published.

Pam: I can do whatever I want. I'm the writer.

Jamie: And so, we give you... Georgia O'Keeffe.

Pam plays scene.

> **GEORGIA.** I did what I came here to do.
>
> I lived. I paid attention. I chased my vision and I offered it up and said, "Look."
>
> Do the work—and get the work out there—even if it makes you take to your bed—even if it makes you feel ILL.
>
> Create for yourself—and make the buggers take notice! Let them write what they will—knowing you did what you must.
>
> We work. We must work. It is why we're here. To search. To explore our world—the land—the spirit—the beauty... and to bring it to others—as clear as we can.
>
> Do not let the fear stop you. You mustn't let them stop you from marking your passage.

End of scene.

Robert: *(Bit of a mocking stage whisper)* What she means is: "Get the hell out of here and write something!"

> *Blackout.*
> *End of Play.*[26]

---

26   My biggest regret, in the writing and performing of *The Clip Show*, is that, due to time constraints, I was not able to squeeze in a fitting tribute to the amazing people who have worked with us as staff members of the SPC, or the brilliant actors who continue to work with us at Festival and throughout the year. I've included their names in the Appendix. The playwrights of Saskatchewan have been blessed to work with the best and the brightest. On behalf of all of us, I salute you!

Works Cited

PRIMARY SOURCES

Bustin, Pam. *Saddles in the Rain*. In *The West of All Possible Worlds: Six Contemporary Canadian Plays*. Ed. Moira Day. Toronto: Playwrights Canada Press, 2005, 151–236.

Morrissey, Kim. *Dora: A Case of Hysteria*. London: Nick Hern Books, 1995.

Robinson, Mansel. *Rock 'n Rail: Spitting Slag and Ghost Trains*. Saskatoon: Thistledown Press, 2001.

Stickland, Eugene. *Some Assembly Required*. Peterborough, ON: Broadview Press, 2002.

Theissen, Vern. *Blowfish*. Toronto: Playwrights Canada Press, 1998.

SECONDARY SOURCES

"*Blowfish*" by Vern Thiessen (synopsis). Playwrights' Canada Press. www.playwrights-canada.com (accessed November 10, 2009).

Deverell, Rex. SPC—*the Early Years: Playworks* 6.3 (Fall 2006) (The SPC 25th Anniversary Edition): 2.

"*Dora*" by Kim Morrisey (synopsis). Nick Hern Books. www.nickhernbooks.co.uk (accessed November 10, 2009).

Johnston, Kirsty. "Play Gathering: Western Imaginaries and Toronto Snappy Shorts." *Canadian Literature: A Quarterly of Criticism and Review* 188 (Spring 2006):127–30.

Mendenhall, Marie Elaine Powell. *The Playwright's Path: an Analysis of the Canadian Play Development Process as Practiced by the Saskatchewan Playwrights Centre, 1982-2000*. Ottawa: National Library of Canada, 2002.

Paulson, Joanne. Review of *Spitting Slag* by Mansel Robinson. *Theatre With a Crooked Grin*. Saskatoon Fringe Festival, SK. *Saskatoon Star-Phoenix*, August 8, 2000: D3.

Saskatchewan Playwrights Centre. "About Us: Who We are and What We Do." www.saskplaywrights.ca/about.htm (accessed November 10, 2009).

——. "Play Catalogue." www.saskplaywrights.ca (accessed November 10, 2009).

"*Some Assembly Required*" by Eugene Stickland (synopsis). Playdatabase.com. www.playdatabase.com (accessed November 10, 2009).

Appendix.

SASKATCHEWAN PLAYWRIGHTS CENTRE
SPRING FESTIVAL PLAYS AND PARTICIPANTS, 1983–2007

2007
Outside Reader: Yvette Nolan
Festival dramaturge: Yvette Nolan

- *The River Valley Sanatorium Ghost Tour* by Catherine Harrison, directed by Michael Clark

- *The Man from Nantucket* by Brent McFarlane, directed by Glenda Stirling (Manitoba Association of Playwrights [MAP] Playwright's Colony Selection 2008)

- *Beside the Apple Tree* by Timothy Boechler, directed by Johanne Deleeuw

- *No Shame in Loving (The Belated Love Story of Abelard and Heloise)* by Marushka, directed by Stephen Heatley

- *A Box for Bones* by Kenneth T. Williams, directed by Vinetta Strombergs (Now titled *Three Little Birds*. World Premiere: Workshop West, Edmonton 2008)

- *Trigger Happy* by Mansel Robinson, directed by Roy Surette (Trans-Canada Reading Series at Factory Theatre, Toronto 2007. Ten Days of Madness Theatre Festival at the University of Alberta, Edmonton 2008)

2006
Outside Reader: Yvette Nolan
Festival dramaturge: Yvette Nolan

- *The Selkie Wife* by Kelley Jo Burke, directed by Sarah Stanley (World Premiere: Dancing Sky Theatre, Meacham SK 2008)

- *The Last Shall Be First* by Cheryl Jack, directed by Stephen Heatley (Now titled *At the End of her Rope*. World Premiere: Persephone Theatre, Saskatoon 2008)

- *Velocity* by Dan Macdonald, directed by Jennifer Tarver (Lark Play Development Center's Playwrights Week, New York, USA 2007. Rattlestick Playwrights Theater, Dirty Works, New York, USA 2008. World Premiere: Persephone Theatre, Saskatoon 2011)

- *Whistling at the Northern Lights* by Jennifer Wynne Webber, directed by Susan Ferley

- *Burning In* by Natalie Meisner, directed by Sarah Stanley

- *Broken Bones* by Damon Badger Heit, directed by Jennifer Tarver

- Special Guest Playwright from Cape Breton: *At Grandma's House* by Natasha MacLellan, directed by Stephen Heatley (Natasha's visit to Spring Festival was sponsored as a Playwright Exchange with Playwrights Atlantic Resource Centre)

2005
Outside Reader: DD Kugler
Festival dramaturge: DD Kugler

- *Peaches and Cream* by Jennifer Wynne Webber, directed by Rachel Ditor

- *Prelude to Munich* by James Trettwer, directed by Stephen Heatley

- *Evil Among Us* by James Misfeldt, directed by Yvette Nolan

- *Biting the Hand* by Mansel Robinson, directed by Bill Lane (Now titled *Bite the Hand*. World Premiere: Persephone Theatre, Saskatoon 2008. Published by Scirocco, 2009)

- *Wanton* by Rob van Meenen and Cherise Arneson, directed by Bill Lane

- *Valentine's Day at Bathurst Station* by Trenna Keating, directed by Stephen Heatley

2004
Outside Reader: Stephen Heatley
Festival dramaturge: Stephen Heatley

- *The Passage of Georgia O'Keeffe* by Pam Bustin, directed by DD Kugler (Earlier draft was presented at the Her-icane Festival of Women's Art, Saskatoon and the London ON Fringe 2003)

- *Things Missed* by Larry Parsons, directed by Trevor Schmidt

- *Hope and Fury* by Will Brooks, directed by Johanne Deleeuw (World Premiere: Flux Theatre, Saskatoon 2004. Lunchbox Theatre, Calgary 2004)

- *Give 'Er Snoose* by Leeann Minogue, directed by Bob Metcalfe (Now titled: *Dry Streak*. World Premiere: Persephone Theatre, Saskatoon 2006.

Produced in Lacadena, Saskatchewan under the title *Give 'Er Snoose*. Station Arts Center, Rosthern SK 2006. Presented by the Saskatchewan communities of Cabri and Mortlach, and the Weyburn Agricultural Society. Published by Scirocco Drama, 2006)

- *Out in the Cold* by Cheryl Jack, directed by Johanne Deleeuw (Aired on CBC Radio 2007)

- *Picking Up Chekhov* by Mansel Robinson, directed by DD Kugler (National Arts Centre [NAC] On the Verge Festival, Ottawa 2005. World Premiere: Alberta Theatre Projects [ATP], Calgary 2006. Published by Scirocco Drama, 2007)

2003
Outside Reader: Stephen Heatley
Festival dramaturge: Stephen Heatley
Designer: Wes D. Pearce

- *Angels Are Us* by Byrna Barclay, directed by Kathryn Bracht.
- *Double Blind* by Ian Nelson and Kevin Power, directed by Joey Tremblay
- *The Captive* by Will Brooks, directed by Rob Moffat (University of Saskatchewan, Saskatoon Student Production 2005)
- *Random Acts* by Sean Hoy, directed by Trevor Schmidt (Aired on CBC Radio 2004. World Premiere: Dancing Sky Theatre, Meacham SK 2006)
- *Dancing Backwards* by Donald B. Campbell, directed by Rob Moffat
- *MacGregor's Hard Ice Cream and Gas*, by Dan Macdonald directed by Maxine Kern (On the Verge Festival, Ottawa 2004. World Premiere: Persephone Theatre, Saskatoon Winter 2005. Prairie Theatre Exchange, Winnipeg 2007. Ship's Company Theatre, Parsboro NS 2007. Shadow Theatre, Edmonton 2008. Published by Playwrights Canada Press, 2008)

2002
Outside Reader: Stephen Heatley
Festival dramaturge: Stephen Heatley
Designer: Wes D. Pearce

- *Serpent's Tooth* by Leanne Griffin, directed by DD Kugler
- *Almost Home* by Madeleine Dahlem, directed by Linda Moore

- *Just a Cup of Tea* by Robin Mueller, directed by Rachel Ditor

- *Jane's Thumb* by Kelley Jo Burke, directed by Kathryn Bracht (Queen's University, Kingston ON 2007. Published by Signature Editions in anthology: *Two Hands Clapping,* 2006)

- *The Mermaid* by Marie-Pierre Maingon, directed by Rachel Ditor

- *Walt* by Lloyd Deshaye, directed by Kathryn Bracht

- *2K* by Scott Douglas, directed by DD Kugler (Retitled: *Undiscover'd Country.* Fresh Ink Festival, Alberta Playwrights' Network [APN], Calgary 2002. World Premiere: Undiscover'd Country Collective, Edmonton 2005)

- *The Room With Five Walls* by Byrna Barclay, directed by Linda Moore (World Premiere: Curtain Razors, Regina 2004. Published by NeWest Press 2004. Winner of the Regina Book of the Year 2004)

2001
Outside Reader: DD Kugler
Festival dramaturge: DD Kugler
Designer: Bretta Gerecke

- *Comfort and Joy* by Kelley Jo Burke, directed by Mary Vingoe

- *Alexander the Great* by Dolores Ewen, directed by Philip Adams

- *Pageant* by Dan Macdonald, directed by Stephen Heatley (Playrites ATP, Calgary 2003. Hyde Park Theatre, Austin Texas USA 2005. Keyano Theatre, Fort McMurray AB 2006. Last Exit Theatre, Saskatoon 2008. Published by Playwrights Canada Press, 2008)

- *Saint Jimmy* by James Misfeldt, directed by Vanessa Porteous

- *Ghost Trains* by Mansel Robinson, directed by Philip Adams (International Fringe Festivals Fringe in Winnipeg, Saskatoon and Edmonton 2001. CBC Radio 2001. Last Exit Theatre, Saskatoon 2002. The CD, *Ghost Trains: All of the Songs and Some of the Story,* was released by Stewart MacDougall, 2003. Translated into French [*Le train fantôme*] by Laurier Gareau and produced by La Troupe du Jour, Saskatoon 2003. Translated into French [*Trains fantômes*] by Jean Marc Dalpé 2007. *Trains fantômes* Théâtre Triangle Vital, Montreal, New Brunswick 2007. Published by Thistledown Press [*Rock 'n Rail*] 2002 and Éditions Prise de parole [*Roc & Rail*] 2008. Translation nominated for a Governor-General's award 2008)

- *Street Zone* by Janice Salkeld, directed by Stephen Heatley (FemFest, Winnipeg 2005)
- *Life's Like That* by David Sealy, directed by Vanessa Porteous

2000

Outside Reader: DD Kugler
Festival dramaturge: DD Kugler

- *Dancing with the Magpie* by Pam Bustin, directed by Stephen Heatley
- *Prairie Tomten* by Mary Love, directed by Rob Moffatt
- *Andy and Annie* by Don Kerr, directed by Ben Henderson
- *The Hunter Memorial* by Ken Mitchell, directed by Angus Ferguson
- *Scorched Ice* by Mansel Robinson, directed by Ben Henderson (received John V. Hicks Award for long manuscript, Fall 2002. Last Exit Theatre, Saskatoon 2005)
- *Pauline in Concert* by Les Hurlburt, directed by Stephen Heatley
- Pre-Festival Special Event: *Hangin' around the Berri Station with My Uncle Marcel,* a special translation adjunct to Festival. Original by Gilbert Dupuis. Translation by Deborah Cottreau, directed by Rob Moffatt (This play was not a part of the competition for Festival as translations are not considered new plays and are therefore not eligible)

1999

Outside Reader: Paula Danckert
Festival dramaturge: Paula Danckert

- *Red Lips* by Connie Gault, directed by DD Kugler (PlayRites ATP, Calgary 2001. Above the Line, Chicago USA 2001. Kitchener ON 2002)
- *Patriots Divided* by Dennis Hunt, directed by Henry Woolf
- *White River Junction* by Rod MacIntyre, directed by Bob White
- *Just Julie* by Janice Salkeld, directed by Vanessa Porteous

1998
Outside reader: Peter Smith
Festival dramaturge: Peter Smith

- *Chasing the Wind* by James Misfeldt, directed by Ruth Smillie
- *Deer Bring the Sun* by Geoffrey Ursell, directed by Wayne Strongman
- *Oh I Go* by Connie Gault, directed by Marina Endicott (Gallery, CBC Radio 1998)
- *Spitting Slag* by Mansel Robinson, directed by Angus Ferguson (World Premiere: Dancing Sky Theatre, Meacham SK 1998. Nominated for Saskatchewan Writers' Guild Award 1998. Globe Theatre, Regina 2000. Winnipeg and Saskatoon International Fringe Festivals 2000. Winner of Audience Choice Award, Saskatoon. Translated into French [*Slague, L'histoire d'un Mineur*] by Jean Marc Dalpé, 2007. Slague Productions: Théâtre du Nouvel-Ontario, Montréal, Longueuil, Joliet, Ottawa, Caraquet, Moncton, Le Bic, Baie-Comeau, Sept-Iles, Québec City, Rouyn-Noranda, and Sudbury 2007/2008. Published by Thistledown Press, 2002 [*Rock 'n Rail: Ghost Trains and Spitting Slag*], 2002 and Éditions Prise de parole [*Roc & Rail*], 2008. Translation nominated for a Governor-General's award 2008)

1997
Outside reader: Urjo Kareda
Festival dramaturge: Peter Smith

- *Bim and Bub* by Henry Woolf, directed by Beata Van Berkom (25th Street Theatre, Saskatoon 1997)
- CANADA ENDING *and other wars of 1812* by Robert Bartel, directed by DD Kugler (Saskatoon and Winnipeg Fringe Festivals 1997)
- *Taproot* by Mary Love, directed by Sharon Pollock (Now titled: *Holdfast. Afternoon Edition*, CBC Radio)
- *The Girl from God's Country* by Barbara Sapergia, directed by Ben Henderson (Featured at Women in the Arts conference, Saskatoon 1995)

1996

Outside reader: John Murrell

Festival dramaturge: Bob White

- *The Heart as it Lived* by Mansel Robinson, directed by Janet Amos (Play-Rites ATP, Calgary 1997. Theatre Network, Edmonton 1998. Kitchener, ON, March 2000; Prince Albert SK, April 2000. Persephone Theatre, Saskatoon 2003)
- *Blue Zone* by Rod MacIntyre, directed by Tom Bentley-Fisher (25th Street Theatre, Saskatoon 1997)
- *Waking up Demons* by Donald B. Campbell, directed by Ben Henderson
- *Blowfish* by Vern Thiessen, directed by Micheline Chevrier (World Premiere: National Arts Centre, Ottawa and Northern Light Theatre, Edmonton, 1996. Published by Playwrights Canada Press, 1998. Sage Theatre, Calgary 2005. Raleigh Ensemble Players, Raleigh NC, USA 2006)

1995

Outside reader: DD Kugler

Festival dramaturge: DD Kugler

- *Otherwise Bob* by Connie Gault, directed by Bob White (world premiere at Northern Light Theatre, Edmonton 1997. Published by Scirocco and nominated for Saskatchewan Book Award 2001. Globe Theatre, Regina 2001)
- *The Christmas-all-year-round Room* by Kelley Jo Burke, directed by Susan Ferley
- *The Last Journey of Captain Harte* by Dianne Warren, directed by Kathleen Flaherty (25th Street Theatre, Saskatoon 1997. Published by Nuage Editions and nominated for Saskatchewan Book Award 2001)
- *Lanc* by Don Kerr, directed by Tom Bentley-Fisher (Greystone Theatre, University of Saskatchewan, Saskatoon 1997)

1994

Outside reader: Kate Lushington
Festival dramaturge: Patti Shedden

- *Welcome to Main Street* by Rachel van Fossen and Darrel Wildcat, directed by Roy Surette

- *Spirit Wrestler* by Greg Nelson, directed by Tom Bentley-Fisher (25th Street Theatre, Saskatoon 1995. Published by Blizzard 1997. Station Arts Centre, Rosthern SK 1998. Nominated for Saskatchewan Writers' Guild Award 1998)

- *Windchill* by Geoffrey Ursell, directed by Kate Lushington

- *Saddles in the Rain* by Pam Bustin, directed by Ben Henderson (Excerpt published by Playwrights Canada Press in *Taking the Stage,* 1994. World Premiere: 25th Street Theatre/Realife Productions, Saskatoon 1994. Received John V. Hicks Award for long manuscript, Fall 2002. Published by Playwrights Canada Press in *The West of All Possible Worlds: Six Contemporary Canadian Plays,* 2004)

1993

Outside reader: DD Kugler
Festival dramaturge: DD Kugler

- *Collateral Damage* by Mansel Robinson, directed by Sharon Bakker (Won a Saskatchewan Writers' Guild Literary Award for drama 1993. Theatre Network, Edmonton 1994. Nominated for a Sterling Award, Edmonton as the best new play 1994. Summer Works Festival, Toronto 1994. Published by Blizzard Press 1994. Globe Theatre's Satellite Series, Regina 1995. McMaster University, Hamilton ON 1996)

- *Baggage* by Kit Brennan, directed by Sharon Dalgleish

- *No Moving Parts* by Eugene Stickland, directed by Bob White (Now Titled: *Some Assembly Required.* playRites ATP, Calgary 1994. Northern Light Theatre, Edmonton 1994. Published by Coteau Books 1995. Nominated for a Governor-General's award and a Writers Guild of Alberta prize for drama 1995. ATP, Calgary 1996)

- *Playing the Game* by Kelley Jo Burke, directed by Roy Surette

1992

Outside reader: Kim McCaw
Festival dramaturge: Rex Deverell

- *Mazo and Caroline* by Joan Givner, directed by Marina Endicott (Excerpt published by Playwrights Canada Press in *Taking the Stage* 1994)
- *Back Fence* by Rex Deverell, directed by Rex Deverell
- *The Bottom Line* by Mary Love, directed by Pamela Haig Bartley
- *A Retrospective Evening*, directed by Marina Endicott and Patti Shedden

1991

Festival dramaturge: DD Kugler

- *Goddessness* by Kelley Jo Burke (text workshop) (Fringes in Winnipeg, Edmonton and Saskatoon 1990)
- *Learning the Rhumba* by Jeanne Heal (text workshop)
- *Fuse* by Doris Hillis (text workshop)
- *Castrato* by Greg Nelson, directed by Patti Shedden (Wins Theatre BC's national playwriting competition, Theatre Network, Edmonton 1993. Wins the Sterling Award, Edmonton for outstanding new play 1993. Published by Blizzard 1993. Wins the Alberta Book Award for Drama 1993. Globe Theatre's Satellite Series, Regina 1995. CBC's *Monday Night Playhouse* 1997)
- *The Girl from God's Country* by Barbara Sapergia, directed by Allen MacInnis
- *Windchill* by Geoffrey Ursell, directed by Bob White

1990

Festival dramaturge: Judith Rudakoff

- *Street* by Mel Melymick, directed by Steven Gregg
- *Sidney* by Greg Nelson, directed by Marina Endicott (25th Street Theatre, Saskatoon 1993)
- *Moths to a Flame* by Judy Smith, directed by Tom Bentley-Fisher
- *Out There* by Henry Woolf, directed by Eileen Sproule

1989

Festival dramaturge: Michael Springate

- *A Kingdom of My Own* by Don Kerr, directed by Ken Kramer
- *Save the Pigs* by Ken Mitchell, directed by Gerald Lenton-Young (featured in ATP's Nova playRites, Calgary and produced by Nakai Theatre Ensemble, Whitehorse YT 1990)
- *Slow Zoom* by Greg Nelson, directed by Pamela Haig (Theatre Eleven, Saskatoon 1990. Winnipeg and Edmonton Fringe Festivals 1990)

1988

Festival dramaturge: Michael Springate

- *A Killing Frost* by Sharon Butala, directed by Ken Mitchell (Vancouver Fringe Festival 1988)
- *Exile* by Archie Crail, directed by Michael Springate (Saskatchewan Writers' Guild major award for drama 1989. Published by Blizzard and produced at 25th Street Theatre, Saskatoon 1990. South African Arts Festival, Oudtshoorn South Africa 1993)
- *The Soft Eclipse* by Connie Gault, directed by Marina Endicott (Globe Theatre, Regina 1989. Published by Blizzard and produced at 25th Street Theatre, Saskatoon 1990. Prairie Theatre Exchange, Winnipeg 1993. Subject of a documentary film about the staging of the play, 1993)
- *Nice Guy* by Rod MacIntyre, directed by Gordon McCall (25th Street Theatre, Saskatoon 1990)
- *Fortinbras in Denmark* by Rod Macpherson, directed by Gabe Prendergast
- *Dog and Crow* by Michael Springate, directed by Henry Woolf (Note: I am not sure if Springate was a resident of SK at this time, and therefore eligible to be an SPC member and submit to Festival, or if inclusion of his play was a special event)
- *Club Chernobyl* by Dianne Warren, directed by Kathy Allison (25th Street Theatre, Saskatoon 1993. Published by Coteau Books 1995. Wins the City of Regina prize in the Saskatchewan Book Awards 1995)

1987

Festival dramaturge: Frank Moher

- *St. Genesius* by Rod MacIntyre, directed by Steven Gregg
- *The Vinegar Jug* by Kay Nouch, directed by Kate Gregg
- *Joy Bag* by Gail Robinson, directed by Tom Bentley-Fisher
- *Round Up* by Barbara Sapergia, directed by Tom Bentley-Fisher (Saskatchewan Writers' Guild major award for drama 1989. 25th Street Theatre, Saskatoon 1991. Published by Coteau Books 1993)
- *refugees* by Harry Rintoul, directed by Marina Endicott (Winnipeg Fringe Festival 1988)

1986

Playwright-in-Residence: Per Brask

- *Sky* by Connie Gault (25th Street Theatre, Saskatoon 1989. Tours in Edmonton as part of the Carlton Trail Festival 1989. Published by Blizzard 1989. Simon Fraser University 1991. CBC and BBC Radio 1993)
- *September Crocuses* by Jeanne Heal (Dinner theatre performance in Claydon, SK 1993)
- *Painting the Roses Red* by Tim McCashin
- *Tommy* by Ken Mitchell (produced and widely toured by Wheatland Theatre, Regina 1986)
- *St. Tommy* by Kim Morrissey
- *King Arthur* by James Misfeldt
- *Secret Life of Railroaders* by Geoffrey Ursell
- *Bush League Boys* by Geoffrey Ursell/Stephen Scriver

1985

Playwright-in-Residence: Ken Gass

- *Natural Disasters* by Sharon Butala, directed by Kim McCaw (Co-winner of the Saskatchewan Writers' Guild [SWG] major award in drama 1985)
- *Dora: A Case of Hysteria* by Kim Morrissey, directed by Steven Gregg (BBC Radio 1991. Islingston, England 1993. Published by Nick Hern Books 1994)

- *Unfinished Business* by James Misfeldt, directed by Ian Paul
- *Broken Glass* by Jeff Park, directed by Susan Pavelick (Co-winner of the Saskatchewan Writers' Guild [SWG] major award in drama 1985)
- *The Great Orlando* by Barbara Sapergia, directed by Steven Gregg (Persephone Theatre, Saskatoon 1985)
- *Angel Claire* by Dianne Warren, directed by Greg Morley

1984

- *The Playwright's Discourse* by Mick Burrs
- *Beached* by Alexina Dalgetty
- *The Great War* by Don Kerr (25th Street Theatre, Saskatoon 1985)
- *The Hunter Memorial* by Ken Mitchell

1983
Playwright-in-Residence: Michael Cook

- *Madame Capet* by Cheri Lynn Cooke
- *Righteousness* by Rex Deverell
- *Gone the Burning Sun* by Ken Mitchell (Wins the national Canadian Authors Association award for drama 1985. Also produced at the Guelph Spring Festival and Magnus Theatre in Thunder Bay. Published by Playwrights Canada Press and nominated for the Governor-General's award 1985. Tours China 1987. Globe Theatre, Regina 1989)
- *The Unicorn* by Barbara Sapergia
- *The Red Triangle* by Dianne Warren (University of Saskatchewan, Saskatoon 1990)

SPC SPRING FESTIVAL ACTORS HAVE INCLUDED:
Kent Allen, Wendy Anderson, Sharon Bakker, Julianna Barclay, Joshua Beaudry, Robert Benz, Darla Biccum, Ian Black, Katie Bowes, Kathryn Bracht, Skye Brandon, Alan Bratt, Dwayne Brenna, Will Brooks, Matt Burgess, Pam Bustin, Clifford Cardinal, Tantoo Cardinal, Angela Christie, Paula Costain, Cavan Cunningham, Emma Davison-Roy, Mark Dieter, Patricia Drake, Lorne Duquette, Cynthia Dyck, Louisa Ferguson, Kristi Friday, Sheryl Gardner,

Alphonse Gaudet, Blayne George, Brad Grass, Jade Groat, Pamela Haig Bartley, Melissa Hande, Kelly Handerek, Heather Hill, Tim Hopfner, Sean Hoy, Bill Hugli, John Huston, Cheryl Jack, Shannon Jardine, Trenna Keating, Erroll Kinistino, Heidi Little, Alan Long, Brad Loucks, Christine MacInnis, Rod MacIntyre, Amy Matisio, Bruce McKay, Elizabeth McRobbie, Andrea Menard, Clare Middleton, Joseph Naytowhow, Greg Odig, Tom O'Hara, James O'Shea, Eden Phelps, Rodrigo Pino Hellman, Mitchell Poundmaker, Tom Rooney, Rob Roy, Jodi Sadowsky, Michele Sereda, Munish Sharma, Jamie Lee Shebclski, Li-pin Tan, Joey Tremblay, Beata Van Berkom, Rob van Meenen, Lee Ward, Lou Wetherall, Alison Whelan, and Jennifer Wynne Webber.

SPC STAFF:

Kate and Stephen Gregg—coordinated Spring Festivals in the mid '80s

Marina Endicott—our first Dramaturge/Administrator (1987–1991) and returned for a short stint in 1996 between Patti and Angus (1996–1997)

Rod Macpherson—our first Administrator when we divided the staff duties (1991–1996)

Patti Shedden—Dramaturge (1991–1996)

Margaret Kyle—Administrator (1996–2004)

Angus Ferguson—Dramaturge (1997–2000)

Ben Henderson—Dramaturge (2000–2007)

Sheila Angelstad—Administrator (2004–present)

Heather Inglis—Dramaturge (2007–2011)

Jennifer Wynne Webber (2011–present

Theatres, Theatre Companies and Dramaturgical Centres

Creating Francophone Theatre in Saskatchewan

LOUISE H. FORSYTH

french-speaking people have been in the area we now call Saskatchewan for centuries. They came in the beginning to find adventure and employment in the fur trade. Many whose explorations took them deeply into the territory belonging to the First Nations counted on the aboriginal peoples to teach them survival skills. They learned Cree and the other languages of the plains. Often, they stayed for the rest of their lives, thereby founding the people and the unique culture called Métis and creating a new language called *métchif*. The impact of vast migratory movements during the nineteenth and early twentieth centuries was significant in Saskatchewan. French-speaking people came with the purpose of settling on the land. They established their small rural communities throughout the territory that became the province. While some came from Europe or transited through the United States, most of the francophone immigrants to Saskatchewan came from Québec. Population growth and the resulting shortage of arable land at that time in rural Québec led the Catholic clergy to encourage young families to head west and to take with them the precious cultural heritage of their language and their Catholic faith. This migration to open new agricultural communities was generally considered preferable to the massive emigration to the factories of New England that was occurring out of Québec as a result of the same population explosion.[1]

---

1   Sociologists and demographers have estimated that more than one million people
    from Québec moved to the industrial heartland of the northern United States in
    the final decades of the nineteenth century in search of employment. Work in the
    factories was, of course, done in English. Following Québec socio-cultural traditions

From the start, families in these small francophone communities organized social and cultural evenings that highlighted traditional and improvisational music, dance, recitations, and dramatic scenes or skits. These evenings
provided entertainment and opportunities to enjoy family and neighbours.
They were also proud affirmations of shared identity, language, and traditions.
There was widespread and strong commitment among these early settlers
in Saskatchewan to preserve the French language, even when, in the early
twentieth century, the provincial government closed French schools and
forbade the teaching of French in public schools. Making theatre together,
often inventing skits and scripts (unfortunately never published), was an
important way to share this collective commitment. There was a close association between the very real fear of linguistic and cultural assimilation
in these minority communities and the determination to affirm the beauty
and significance of their shared history and culture. These dramatic events
were staged in parish halls and people's homes.

As Lise Gaboury-Diallo has shown, themes of celebrating the shared identity of francophones *de souche*, speaking their language collectively and telling
their stories on stage, has remained compelling into the twenty-first century:

> *Ainsi, dans la dramaturgie contemporaine de l'Ouest, les sujets traités*
> *reflètent les préoccupations premières des minorités francophones.*
> *Les thèmes liés aux problèmes d'identité, d'altérité, d'assimilation*
> *ou de lutte pour la survie linguistique et culturelle sont développés*
> *à des fins cathartiques.* (2003, 207)[2]

---

the families of these emigrants continued to be large, even in narrow and insalubrious
urban conditions. It was most often men who found factory work. Married women
were strongly encouraged by the Catholic clergy who accompanied the emigrants
to remain in their homes, and, as part of their child-rearing responsibilities, to
prepare the children for First Communion and to speak only French to them. At
the same time, these women were discouraged from learning English because of
the fear of assimilation and influence of American cultural values. There was a
tenacious although illusory belief that the economic need to emigrate in order to
find jobs was temporary and that the families would be able to return to Québec
within no more than one generation. Women were deemed to be guardians of the
traditions of language, faith, and culture, which had to be preserved in order to
ensure reinsertion into francophone Québec society.

2   Gaboury-Diallo, 207. "And so, the subjects treated in plays written today in Western
     Canada reflect the primary preoccupations of francophone minorities. Themes
     that are developed and linked to problems of identity, alterity, assimilation, or the
     struggle for cultural and linguistic survival serve cathartic purposes." (All transla-
     tions in this article are by Louise Forsyth.)

In recent decades, plays on this theme have been performed in theatres, schools, and parish and community halls around the province. An excellent example of this determination to see their own history reflected on stage is shown in the well-constructed *De blé d'Inde et de pissenlits* by Lorraine Archambault (first produced by La Troupe du Jour in 1994), which tells the moving story of the daily life over the first half of the twentieth century of two tenacious families who settled in Saskatchewan, one from Québec and one from Europe, as well as in the sardonic title and drama of André Roy's *Il était une fois Delmas, Sask... mais pas deux fois!* These plays were published in *Le théâtre fransaskois. Recueil de pièces de théâtre. Tome 1.* The first play of the 2009-2010 season of La Troupe du Jour, *Bonneau et la Bellehumeur* by Raoul Granger, provides evidence of the sustained interest within francophone Saskatchewan communities in all that pertains to the Louis Riel story, including the moral dilemmas it continues to raise.

It is true in Saskatchewan, as it is throughout Western Canada, that francophones represent a small minority of the population. The distribution in Saskatchewan is unique, however. The francophone population is scattered in small communities throughout the province, with no major city having a concentration of French-speaking citizens. This dispersion has been a significant challenge for those wishing to create and produce francophone theatre. Theatrical events must attract audiences that are sufficiently large to support their productions. An additional challenge has been the diversification of the francophone population of Saskatchewan. The descendants of the original settlers are no longer the only significant group. Migration patterns over the past decades have brought people from many countries to the province. Their religious and cultural traditions and collective memory, their shared sense of identity, are not the same as those whose families have been here for a century or more.

This diversity has brought with it additional challenges with regard to the French language. The words, expressions, accents, structures, and symbolic significance surrounding language vary widely among various groups. This diversity represents challenges in both communicating with audiences and in casting. As well, francophones have married in significant numbers with non-francophones. In a majority of such couples, English becomes the language of communication. A further challenge to creating theatre that reflects the experiences of the audience and satisfies their aesthetic expectations and entertainment wishes is the growing number of francophiles in the province. Those who have completed programs in French immersion and enjoyed the francophone universe this opened to them often now wish to retain their knowledge of French through an enjoyable evening in the theatre. However, they may have little or no experience living in a French-speaking community and have greater knowledge of French classical theatre than contemporary Canadian theatre. Another demand on francophone theatre practice in Saskatchewan comes from French and French immersion programs in the schools throughout the province, where theatre for young audiences is recognized as an excellent complement to learning that occurs in classrooms. Theatre for young audiences has had to be an integral part of the aim of theatre companies.

Unlike large francophone cities where a range of theatres can choose to specialize and offer seasons of plays that respond to the tastes and expectations of a particular segment of the population, Saskatchewan's cities do not offer the opportunity for specialization, nor do they even offer theatre buildings that could be permanent homes for francophone companies. Thus, there are huge challenges—artistic; linguistic, social, educational, administrative, financial—in trying to be all things to all people, while also maintaining the aesthetic standards and the opportunities for innovation and experimentation that serious creation in theatre demands. These are daunting challenges to which a number of individuals have risen with amazing success. The presence of francophone theatre is focussed around Saskatoon's La Troupe du Jour, the only francophone professional theatre company in the province.

There is now a body of exciting and high-quality dramaturgy in Saskatchewan. It began to emerge in the 1980s thanks to the talent, vision, determination, and leadership of many people. The Regina historian, playwright, actor, director, journalist, educator, translator, public intellectual, and cultural activist Laurier Gareau is recognized throughout the province as the pioneer in this exciting development. Gareau, who holds an MFA in Playwriting from the University of Alberta, is the author of more than fifty plays for adult and young audiences. Many of these plays have been published and performed on stage by professional companies as well as school and community groups. Gareau was born and grew up in St. Isidore de Bellevue, a town near the middle of Saskatchewan where fransaskois history and culture have been remarkably preserved and nurtured. Many members of the Gareau family played important roles in this commitment to cultural tradition. As a result, Laurier Gareau enjoyed the mentoring and encouragement of many gifted artists in his formative years. The play for which he is best known, published in both French and English versions and produced on stage through several revisions, is *La trahison/The Betrayal*, a depiction of a fictional encounter between Gabriel Dumont, at the end of his life, and Father Julien Moulin, priest at Batoche at the time of the Métis Resistance in 1885. In the play, **Dumont** accuses **Moulin** of having betrayed all the members of the Métis community by preaching appeasement and so having been the direct cause of Métis defeat and humiliation. While *La trahison* demonstrates Gareau's talent for dramatizing aspects of the history of francophones in Saskatchewan and even incorporating elements of *métchif* in the play, his work for theatre reveals the vast horizons of his passionate commitment to hold up a dramatic mirror to broad and diverse Saskatchewan audiences reflecting a range of subjects of contemporary relevance. Gareau has been an extraordinarily generous writer and man of theatre, not only creating for the first time in Saskatchewan an admirable dramatic *oeuvre*, but also regularly visiting schools for storytelling, serving as a mentor to young writers, actors, and directors, encouraging journalistic and critical notice of francophone theatre, playing a central role in the creation in Regina of the community company Théâtre Oskana, and, above all, collaborating energetically with all those everywhere in the province who are making theatre in French. Gareau has been a close and regular collaborator with La Troupe du Jour, never hesitating to commute between Regina and Saskatoon and the other centres visited by La Troupe's touring casts.[3]

During the same decade when Gareau began to write for the stage, a group of young people in Saskatoon, smitten with theatre and determined to dramatize stories of themselves and their community in French on Saskatchewan stages, created La Troupe du Jour as a semi-professional/community company (1985). These founders of what would quickly become a professional theatre company that is now entering its twenty-fourth season were particularly inspired by their earlier experiences in theatre at the University of Saskatchewan. In 1969 Ian Nelson—librarian, actor, director, author, and translator—and a group of students created a theatre company, Unithéâtre. Unithéâtre's initial purpose was not to create original plays, but rather to stage plays from the classical and contemporary French and Québec repertory. However, it did produce one collective creation and one authored play: *C'est ben l'fun* (1976) and *Visions* by Madeleine Costa and Éveline Hamon. This latter show was presented at the fourth Festival fransaskois in 1982, thereby attracting attention to its existence as part of the francophone cultural scene.

From the beginning of La Troupe du Jour, the young company gave priority to new plays, in the form of cultural evenings, collective creations, and authored plays. The importance of supporting fresh dramaturgical initiative in order to produce authentically fransaskois theatre was stated in the brochure for the 1987-88 season:

> La Troupe du Jour [...] regroupe des jeunes comédiens de [Saskatoon] dont le rêve est de faire du théâtre francophone, communautaire et professionnel, du théâtre qui reflète la réalité fransaskoise, par l'entremise de spectacles et d'animation théâtrale. C'est par la création et des

---

3   Laurier Gareau's important contribution to Canadian theatre was recognized in 2007 by the award of Honorary Member by the Canadian Association for Theatre Research.

représentations de textes fransaskois que La Troupe espère développer
un nouveau sens théâtral dans la communauté francophone.[4]

Since that time, and particularly since the arrival in 1989 of the present artistic
director, Denis Rouleau, La Troupe has focussed on its commitment to new play
creation and the entire range of activities necessary to support such creation. It
is a *poor* theatre in the sense that Grotowski used the epithet, but it has always
provided a rich haven for those working in every phase of theatrical creativity.
La Troupe's mission highlights this commitment *to "offrir un soutien à la création"*
["support for creativity"]. In this regard, one can say that the obstacles making the creation of original plays in French difficult have been overcome with
such vigour at La Troupe du Jour that it is easy to see that the challenges have
been transformed into opportunities. The program of La Troupe's 2006 Gala
celebrating twenty seasons of fine theatre highlighted once again the sustained
commitment to new plays and showed that members of the company have am-
bition for creating good theatre well beyond the boundaries of Saskatchewan.
Their objective was and continues to be the creation and production of plays
and shows worthy of showing in other provinces and everywhere in Canada:
"Lors de sa récente session de planification, La Troupe du Jour s'est donné la mission
de devenir le centre de création théâtrale dans l'Ouest canadien" (3).[5]

It has been largely due to the talent, ingenuity, and determination of Rouleau
that an active and gifted professional and volunteer community of francophone
and francophile talent has formed at La Troupe du Jour. Thanks to their hard
work and commitment, both as participants in production and as apprecia-
tive audience members, the company has succeeded not only in surviving
but in thriving. It has become a fertile site for the creation and production of
theatre and dramatic texts in French, not only in Saskatoon but throughout
the province. Rouleau recognized that the minority situation of French in
Saskatchewan and the diversity of origins among French speakers made it
absolutely necessary to devise new strategies in order to preserve the magic
that only live theatre can produce. In an interview (January 2001), Rouleau
explained that there is simply no model to be found elsewhere that could serve
to guide those creating professional theatre in French in Saskatchewan. While

---

4   "La Troupe du Jour brings together young Saskatoon actors whose dream it is to make
     francophone theatre—community and professional—theatre in which francophone
     reality in Saskatchewan is reflected through shows and theatrical development. The
     company is hoping to nurture a new theatrical sense in the francophone community
     through the creation and production of Saskatchewan texts."
5   "At the time of its recent planning session, La Troupe du Jour adopted the mission
     of becoming the centre for original theatre in Western Canada" (3).

the people and the stories to be told are unique, the audience's knowledge and competence in French vary widely. These factors can never be overlooked as insignificant, even when financial and other material circumstances might suggest the need for facile, yet artistically unsatisfactory, solutions.

La Troupe du Jour has faced these challenges with remarkable ingenuity and creativity, particularly in the many ways in which it encourages the writing, trial, and production of original works. It has become a sort of laboratory for theatrical experimentation in ways that are technical, linguistic, thematic, and philosophical. Rather than viewing Canada's bilingualism as a threat, its members have found many theatrical ways to turn it to their creative advantage. Several of its shows have played magically with bilingual dialogue. The most recent initiative to address the challenge of making theatre in French in a minority situation has been the introduction of Surtitling for some of its performances. In recognition of the artistic originality and integrity of the work done by La Troupe du Jour, it became the first theatre company to be inducted into Saskatchewan's Margaret Woodward Memorial Theatre Hall of Fame (2004). One year later it received the Prize "Hommage aux arts et industries culturelles" from the Fédération culturelle canadienne-française.

The fact that almost one of every two La Troupe shows has been a new play is not the result of chance or mere good fortune. It is the fruit of considerable energy, vision, ingenuity, artistic integrity, and a number of ancillary activities: playwrights-in-residence, courses and workshops in playwriting, le Cercle des écrivains, new play festivals in collaboration with other francophone theatre companies of the western provinces and elsewhere in Canada, translations, playwright exchanges, dramatic readings, publication of theatre texts and mainstage productions. Unfortunately, because they have remained unpublished, many of the earlier scripts are no longer available for study and remounts. Early in the twenty-first century, members of La Troupe du Jour recognized the urgent need to preserve their dramaturgical work through publication. A number of them took the necessary steps to collaborate in the preparation of the first anthology of fransaskois theatrical texts: L'R libre. The volume contains six one-act plays that were staged during the 2002–2003 season.

Subjects drawn from history and based on local cultural traditions have been a significant component of francophone dramaturgy in Saskatchewan. It is now normal, however, to situate plays evoking collective experiences derived from the past in a contemporary context so as to highlight their evolution over time and, therefore, their relevance. This fresh perspective is found in Granger's Le mariage d'la fille Gareau[6] and Blais-Dahlem's Foyer. Even further,

---

6   See photograph of the 2005 production of Le mariage d'la fille Gareau in the colour insert (photo 7).

Saskatchewan playwrights are demonstrating a remarkable ability to open the range of subjects that interests them and to see their particular experiences and sense of identity in horizons that are worldwide and universal in terms of the human experiences they dramatize.

Although seemingly threatened by the surrounding anglophone language and culture, La Troupe du Jour has benefited from collaboration with other small theatre companies, both anglophone and francophone, and has drawn positive results from the creative and collaborative opportunities offered by translation. Beginning in the 1980s, it was not unusual for the regular theatre season to include a translation of a new Canadian play, as the following examples illustrate: *L'homme à tout faire* (1991), translation and adaptation by Laurier Gareau and Simone Verville of Frank Moher's *Odd Jobs*; *La belle fille de l'aurore* (1991), translation of Daniel David Moses's *The Dream Beauty*; *Les reines de la réserve* (1996), translation by Jocelyne Beaulieu of Tomson Highway's *The Rez Sisters*; *Le train fantôme* (2003), translation by Laurier Gareau of Mansel Robinson's *Ghost Trains*; *Cette fille-là* (2005), translation by Olivier Choinière of Joan MacLeod's *The Shape of a Girl*. This latter translation, in co-production with La Catapulte of Ottawa and La Seizième Vancouver is one indication among many of La Troupe du Jour's fruitful collaboration with other francophone theatre companies across Canada. Always seeking new challenges to resolve creatively, the company has also produced its own new plays in English and French versions on alternating evenings, with different directors but the same cast. A successful example of this was the simultaneous production in 2000 of David Baudemont's new play *Le six* and its adaptation in English done by Ian Nelson, *Five, Six, Pick Up Sticks*. The same actors played in both languages. The show, directed by Denis Rouleau in French and Angus Ferguson in English, was offered on alternating evenings with such success that many spectators, fascinated by the opportunity to see and compare different directorial choices, returned to see the play in the second language and were particularly impressed. As well, new anglophone plays with bilingual potential have been presented with the French part of the dialogue enlarged, for example: David Fennario's *Balconville* (1990) and Rick Salutin's *Les Canadiens* (1993).

Denis Rouleau, the actors, directors, and technical people, along with the playwrights, stay on top of what is happening elsewhere in theatre: new plays and new approaches. They are in regular contact with francophone colleagues across the country. This allows them to work in horizons more vast than those that would initially appear to be available to professional francophone theatre in Saskatchewan. These contacts, exchanges, and conversations are necessary for the nurturing of their own creative energy. Gaboury-Diallo recognized in her study of Western dramaturgy in French the incredible power of renewal demonstrated by francophone companies: "*La diversité des troupes, leurs choix de répertoire et leurs créations indique[nt] à quel point la francophonie s'enrichit* (2003, 207)."[7]

Playwrights such as Raoul Granger, Madeleine Blais-Dahlem, and David Baudemont, who have each had more than one full-length play extensively workshopped and mounted in a full production on the main stage of La Troupe du Jour insist particularly on the importance of the *Cercle des écrivains*, which Ian Nelson created and in which he continues his central role as *conseiller dramaturgique*. It would be impossible to overestimate the generous, vital, and critical role played by Ian Nelson for the past four decades in encouraging the creative vitality of francophone theatre in Saskatchewan. The members of the *Cercle*, which is open to all—students, actors, directors, aspiring writers in the community—meet twice monthly to share ideas, read their texts, and comment on them. Nelson is not only the leader of *Le Cercle des écrivains*. He also organizes a regular season of dramatic readings of plays in development on the Troupe's second stage.

Strong commitment to new play development and all the activities and collaborations hold the promise of continuing into the future, since a new generation of talented writers and actors is already active. La Troupe has well-developed plans for building its own theatrical and administrative spaces. In Spring 2008 La Troupe offered Saskatchewan audiences a dramatic reading of Gerard Vàsquez's ironic comedy *Ouuuh!*, in collaboration with the Tant per Tant collective,[8] as well as a reading of four scripts by young fransaskois: *Les mots d'ados*. This same evening, honed and perfected, was presented on the mainstage in December 2008. The second new play for 2009, which is the result of La Troupe's collective commitment to new dramatic creations and

---

7   "The diversity of the companies, their repertory choices, and their new plays provide evidence of the rich renewal occurring in francophone communities" (207).

8   Tant per Tant was founded in 1997 by Elisabet Ràfols. Here is what it says about itself as of October, 2009: "Tant per Tant is a non-profit cultural collective whose goal is to contribute to a dialog between Catalan and Canadian [French and English] cultures by translating and producing Catalan and Canadian plays." Its main activities include the "translation of Canadian plays into Catalan and production of these plays in Catalonia, in order to provide Catalan audiences with an opportunity to better appreciate the cultural diversity of Canada" and the translation "of Catalan plays into French or English and production of these plays in Canada, in order to give Canadian audiences an opportunity to become familiar with Catalan culture." It also offers translation workshops and staged readings. ("Tant per Tant" www.tantpertant.ca/english.html.) Elisabet Ràfols lives half of each year in Saskatoon and the other half in Barcelona. The Vàsquez production is an example of her translation from Catalan and her collaboration with La Troupe du Jour on a production in French. For current projects and activities as of 2009/10 see www.tantpertant.ca/index.html.)

Gilles Poulin-Denis and David Granger in *Deux Frères* by David Baudemont (2007). PHOTO BY YVAN LEBEL.

new artists, is Gilles Poulin-Denis's *Rearview*,[9] already highly lauded throughout the province and invited to tour in Québec. Poulin-Denis was one of the main actors in the creation by La Troupe of David Baudemont's magnificent *Deux frères* (2007). Poulin-Denis also benefited from a ten-day workshop at Emma Lake under the direction of Alain Jean from the *Centre des auteurs dramatiques* of Montréal. This highly talented young man of theatre, having benefited from work with La Troupe, was invited by the renowned Québec playwright Wajdi Mouawad, director of the French sector of the National Arts Centre in Ottawa, to be *artiste associé* at the Centre during the 2008–2009 season, with a commission for a new play.

The four shows of the 2008–2009 season at La Troupe du Jour were all plays written by Canadians in the twenty-first century. The choices for the season demonstrate once again La Troupe's commitment to new play development and to the encouragement of this country's writers and theatre artists. In addition to the two shows mentioned in the previous paragraph, the season was completed by productions of Évelyne de la Chenelière's *Au bout du fil Bashir Lazhar* and a translation of Kevin Kerr's *Unity (1918)* [*Unity Mil neuf cent dix-huit*]. Similarly, the entire 2009–2010 season was made up of new Canadian plays. As well, La Troupe du Jour now has its own permanent administrative offices and is moving forward aggressively with building plans for its own permanent theatre space.

9   See photograph of the 2009 production of *Rearview* in the colour insert (photo 6).

Josiane Roberge, Réjean Denis and Lauren Allen in *Unity (1918)* by Kevin Kerr; translated by Paul Lefebvre, 2008. PHOTO BY YVAN LEBEL.

The challenges for its very survival faced over the past almost three decades by La Troupe du Jour have been enormous and never-ending. Its artistic director, playwrights, actors, advisors and dramaturges, board members, and all others contributing to the team have faced these challenges with artistic integrity, incredible energy, and the will to work together. The total package of theatrical activity that it has maintained—from early professional training of actors and directors; support for playwrights through the *Cercle des écrivains*, writers-in-residence, dramaturgical festivals, workshops and retreats, dramatic readings and full productions; collaboration with other theatre companies for the cultivation of its diverse publics—has allowed it to thrive and to publish what is now a unique and varied dramaturgical repertory of high quality.[10]

10   Over the 2010-2011 season, La Troupe du Jour premiered a new work by Madeleine Blais-Dahlem, *La Maculée (sTain)*, a bilingual play with French and English surtitles, that focuses on a young fransaskois woman in 1920s Saskatchewan who retreats into the hospital for the mentally ill at North Battleford to preserve her culture and language after her husband decides to assimilate the family into the dominant English-Protestant community. While set in the past, *La Maculée* addresses current issues of domestic violence, poverty, abuse of authority, and greed in consumer society. The company also moved into the new theatre production centre on 20th Street that they currently share with Tant per Tant and The Saskatchewan Native Theatre Company. In addition, La Troupe du Jour co-sponsored, with the Department of Languages and Linguistics and Saint Thomas More College at the University of Saskatchewan, a conference in March 2011: « *On célèbre le théâtre de chez nous : le théâtre de l'Ouest canadien, ses défis, ses enjeux identitaires et son action évolutive.* » ("Celebrating our theatre: theatre of the Canadian West, its challenges, issues for identity and adaptability.")

Works Cited

Archambault, Lorraine. *De blé d'Inde et de pissenlits.* In *Le théâtre fransaskois. Recueil de pièces de théâtre.* Tome 1. Regina: Éditions de la Nouvelle Plume, 2006, 1–58.

Baudemont, David. *5 ans.* In *Le théâtre fransaskois. Recueil de pièces de théâtre.* Tome 2. Regina: Éditions de la Nouvelle Plume, 2007, 1–76.

———. *Le Six.* Unpublished manuscript. 1999-2000. La Troupe du Jour [company archives], Saskatoon, SK.

———. *Deux Frères.* Unpublished manuscript. 2006–2007. In possession of author.

Blais-Dahlem, Madeleine. *Foyer.* In *Le théâtre fransaskois. Recueil de pièces de théâtre.* Tome 2. Regina: Éditions de la Nouvelle Plume, 2007, 121–67.

Collective. *L'R libre. Théâtre et contes urbain.* Saint-Boniface: Éditions des Plaines, 2002.

Forsyth, Louise H. "Les enjeux d'une pratique théâtrale et dramaturgique francophone à Saskatoon. Notes pour un historique d'*Unithéâtre* et de *La Troupe du Jour.*" *Revue historique* 11.1 (October, 2000): 1–11.

———. "*La Troupe du Jour* de Saskatoon: une compagnie-laboratoire." *Les théâtres professionnels du Canada francophone. Entre mémoire et rupture.* Eds. Hélène Beauchamp and Joël Beddows. Ottawa: Le Nordir, 2001, 135–50.

Gaboury-Diallo, Lise. "Théâtre et dramaturgie en français dans l'Ouest canadien." In Beauchamp, Hélène et David, Gilbert (dirs.) *Théâtres québécois et canadiens-français au XXe siècle.* Sainte-Foy: Les Presses de l'Université du Québec, 2003, 197–219.

Gareau, Laurier. *La trahison/The Betrayal.* Bilingual Ed. Regina: Éditions de la Nouvelle Plume, 2004.

Granger, Raoul. *Le mariage d'la fille Gareau.* In *Le théâtre fransaskois. Recueil de pièces de théâtre.* Tome 1. Regina: Éditions de la Nouvelle Plume, 2006, 59–133.

———. "Mot du président." Au fil du temps, La Troupe a 20 ans. Soirée gala vingtième anniversaire de la Troupe du Jour. 2006, 2–3.

———. *Le costume.* In *Le théâtre fransaskois. Recueil de pièces de théâtre.* Tome 2. Regina: Éditions de la Nouvelle Plume, 2007, 77–118.

Michaud, Guy. *Mis à part.* In *Le théâtre fransaskois. Recueil de pièces de théâtre.* Tome 2. Regina: Éditions de la Nouvelle Plume, 2007, 169–203.

Poulin-Denis, Gilles. *Rearview.* Montréal: Dramaturges Éditeurs, 2009.

Rouleau, Denis. Interview by Louise Forsyth. Typescript. January 16, 2001.

Roy, André. "Il était une fois Delmas, Sask ... mais pas deux fois!" In *Le théâtre fransaskois. Recueil de pièces de théâtre.* Tome 1. Regina: Éditions de la Nouvelle Plume, 2006, 135–50.

"Tant per Tant." www.tantpertant.ca/english.html (accessed October 7, 2009).

———. www.tantpertant.ca/index.html (accessed December 29, 2009).

La Troupe du Jour. Season Brochure 1987-1988. *La Troupe du Jour* [company archive], Saskatoon, SK.

Saskatchewan's Aboriginal Theatre: Growing Pains and New Hope

ALAN LONG

T he earliest plays found on Canadian stages about Aboriginal people and issues (1950s and 1960s) were written by non-Aboriginal "white liberals"[1] eager to educate a mainstream Canadian audience about the plight of Aboriginal people. Beyond the formal theatre structures, original Aboriginal theatre also existed in those early years, and Maria Campbell was one artist who used theatre in her community activism work beginning in the 1960s (Campbell, January 10, 2008). Tomson Highway's *Rez Sisters* is often considered the first nationally recognized piece of original Aboriginal theatre (1986), with the efforts of those staging community productions often being overlooked.[2] While mainstream Canadian theatres were growing in the mid-

----

1   The term "white liberal" is broadly used in North America to describe those in the dominant Caucasian community who are concerned about the plight of people of colour, or racial minorities. Despite the efforts of these writers to re-envision our history, in Canada there is still very little "white liberal guilt" associated with our country's treatment of Aboriginal people. See George Elliot Clarke, "White Like Canada," *Transition* 73 (1997): 98–109. Only a few of the plays written by non-Aboriginal men about Aboriginal people were produced in Saskatchewan in the 1970s. See Appendix One.

2   For example, see Charlebois, "History of Canadian Theatre," *Canadian Theatre Encyclopedia*, Athabasca University, April 6, 2009, www.canadiantheatre.com/dict. pl?term=History%20of%20Canadian%20Theatre (accessed November 7, 2009).

twentieth century, Aboriginal theatre continued to languish in obscurity well into the 1980s. E. Ross Stuart's *The History of Prairie Theatre* does not mention a single Aboriginal play or playwright, even though he discusses 25th Street Theatre in Saskatoon, where Maria Campbell's nationally successful play *Jessica* was produced in 1983 (Stuart, 1984, 22). The bias in Stuart's work seems to be linked to the common misconception that theatre developed only when civilization was brought to the prairies, and that the pioneers of professional theatre must necessarily follow a British model (17–78). Even important non-Aboriginal Canadian works such as *Paper Wheat* and *If You're so Good, Why Are You in Saskatoon?* are frequently referred to as "experimental," because they were developed collectively and do not adhere to traditional linear storylines. It continues to be problematic that many define theatre as primarily a literary art constructed and professionally produced in accordance with high-culture European models. By doing so, the official funding and theatre structures unnecessarily exclude a large contingent of theatrical work and audiences, and Canadian theatre histories often fail properly to acknowledge community and collective works and their influence on social and cultural change.[3]

Aboriginal people and their cultural expression have historically lived on the margins of Canada and have only recently begun to enter the consciousness of the dominant, non-Aboriginal Canadian society. After intermittent appearances in the 1980s, original Aboriginal theatre finally began regularly to appear as part of the repertoire of established Saskatchewan theatre companies in the 1990s. However, only 25th Street Theatre produced a significant number of these plays, while others included one play per season, usually from an established, nationally known Aboriginal playwright. What has been lacking until recently is a distinctively Saskatchewan Aboriginal company with its own venue and a focus on developing and producing original Aboriginal work grounded in our community.[4] Saskatchewan Native Theatre Company

---

3   The legacy of the British model was firmly established in the Canadian Regional Theatre system, developed after the Massey Report in 1951. These theatres featured mainly British, American, and Irish plays on their mainstages, and relegated Canadian works to their second stages. Even the National Arts Centre, built in Ottawa in 1969, imported much of its season from abroad. See Brian Kennedy, *The Baron Bold and the Beauteous Maid: A Compact History of Canadian Theatre* (Toronto: Playwrights Canada Press, 2004), 185.

4   Since 1972, Persephone Theatre and 25th Street Theatre in Saskatoon, and Globe Theatre in Regina have hosted a handful of Aboriginal plays, and only a small portion of those were homegrown in Saskatchewan. Since 1999, when Saskatchewan Native Theatre Company (SNTC) was founded, the number of professional and community theatre plays created by Aboriginal people has increased significantly. See Appendix One. Many of these plays have also reached more Aboriginal people through SNTC's outreach programming.

(SNTC) has brought significant change to the Saskatoon and Saskatchewan theatre scene and is filling a desperate need to give a voice to Saskatchewan's poorest and most marginalized population. The presence of SNTC has resulted in a significant increase in the number of original Aboriginal plays produced in Saskatchewan over the last nine years, as their company continues to create an educational environment where new work can grow from the community level.

Located on 20th Street, or as some youth refer to it, in "the hood,"[5] SNTC has placed itself in the heart of the rapidly growing urban Aboriginal population. Saskatoon's west side has historically been the home to the less affluent immigrant and Aboriginal population in the city, particularly the latter in recent years.[6] The source of the company's success has been an ability to engage Aboriginal youth and provide them with a means to tell their stories. Through guidance from elders, SNTC's innovative programs often lay bare the issues that lie beneath the problems that face Aboriginal people, while simultaneously teaching the youth and the audience about traditional Aboriginal stories. These programs are also successful because they occur in the nurturing atmosphere of a uniquely Aboriginal theatre space that allows the voices of these often vulnerable youth to come out.

It is important here to put the significance of SNTC into a Canadian theatre context. While mainstream Canadian theatre creators saw significant increases in the resources available to them in the 1950s and 1960s, Aboriginal theatre received little or no support. Although Stuart contended he was documenting the rise of "Indigenous Canadian Theatre" in his book, he primarily recognized the theatre of the colonizers. Perhaps this bias is a reflection of the way that the mainly non-Aboriginal, patriarchal Canadian government, the primary source of funding for Canadian theatre, also understood theatre arts in the 1980s. Professional theatre arts funding and training have been primarily the property of non-Aboriginal Canadians, and it is only recently that Aboriginal theatrical training has been recognized as worthy of separate funding. In 1974, James Buller started a Native theatre training program through the Association

5   Curtis Peeteetuce, interview by Alan Long, January 18, 2008. 20th Street in Saskatoon is also associated with prostitution or called "the stroll." Many community groups in the Riversdale area of Saskatoon are working hard to change this image. For example, see Station 20 West Community Enterprise Centre, www.station20west.com.

6   Between 1996 and 2001, the Aboriginal population of Saskatoon had twice the growth rate of the overall city population. More than eighty percent of Saskatchewan Aboriginal peoples (Canada's largest per capita Aboriginal population) now live in its urban centres. Saskatoon is located in the heart of the province's reserves and is designated a natural "catchment area." Alan B. Anderson, "Socio-Demographic Study of Aboriginal Population in Saskatoon: The Bridges and Foundations Project on Urban Aboriginal Housing" (Saskatoon: Community-University Research Alliances (CURA) Project, University of Saskatchewan), 13, 14.

for Native Development in the Performing and Visual Arts (ANDPAVA)—now called the Centre for Indigenous Theatre (CIT)—but this eight-week summer program was a long way from Saskatchewan and not nearly as well supported as the National Theatre School (NTS).[7] Until the arrival of SNTC, Saskatchewan Aboriginal theatre artists had limited access to theatrical training and struggled to have their work produced. SNTC has long been the dream of Aboriginal artists like Maria Campbell, who have not been able to express their authentic voices in Saskatchewan's primarily non Aboriginal theatrical environment.

What Campbell and many other Aboriginal artists have always known is that Aboriginal theatrical expression comes from a very old tradition. If only western classical theatre is used as a benchmark, then Native theatrical expression has a relatively short history. However, as Aboriginal communities in Canada slowly rebuild after years of segregation, racism, and substandard living conditions, important components of their recovery have been storytelling and dance, their own unique theatrical traditions that come from their language and culture.[8] In a 2008 interview, Marrie Mumford, a long-time Canadian Aboriginal theatre artist, educator, and activist, likened the roots of the Aboriginal theatrical tradition to that giving rise to the first Greek plays, the same tradition that Western theatre claims as its precursor. She argues that Greek and Aboriginal cultural expression grew from tribal societies strong in music, physical expression, and the spoken word. To Mumford, it is not the lack of Aboriginal education or ignorance of theatrical tradition that has kept Aboriginal people off the stage, but the barriers put in place by a limited view of what theatre is. She argues that in spite of many Aboriginal students having university degrees in dramatic arts, only two have graduated from NTS.[9] Only very recently, in 1991, did a task force recognize the importance of separate funding for Aboriginal theatre groups because of their cultural differences and importance to the artistic fabric of Canada as its first peoples.[10] This long fight for recognition finally culminated in 1999 when Heritage Minister Sheila Copps

....

7   Marrie Mumford, personal interview by Alan Long, July 9, 2008. See also The Centre for Indigenous Theatre (CIT) website, www.indigenoustheatre.com/.

8   For a discussion of the circular philosophy of Native culture versus the linear model of the Western world as it relates to Native Canadian theatre, see Kennedy, 221–55.

9   August Schellenburg and Alanis King are the only two Aboriginal graduates known to Mumford and Alanis King. Alan Long in conversation with Alanis King, September 4, 2008.

10   Marrie Mumford, personal interview by Alan Long, July 7, 2008. Mumford was a major part of these discussions with then Heritage Minister Sheila Copps. The task force was called the Task Force on Professional Training for the Cultural Sector of Canada. Meeting (Toronto, 1991). Verbatim transcripts are available from Library and Archives Canada, 395 Wellington Street, Ottawa, Ontario.

made culturally specific funding a reality, resulting in the formation of several new Aboriginal theatre companies.[11] Mumford named six of these companies as examples of important regional theatre educators of primarily Aboriginal students and as representing the many different languages and traditions from coast to coast to coast.[12] Mumford was particularly proud of the work of SNTC and their commitment to Saskatchewan Native artists and the Aboriginal cultures of the prairie region. SNTC's most recent artistic director was CIT/ NTS graduate Alanis King, and the company was the brainchild of important, nationally known theatre artists Kennetch Charlette (CIT graduate), Gordon Tootoosis, and Tantoo Cardinal.

The spark for this paper happened during Congress 2007 at the University of Saskatchewan, when Maria Campbell and Kenneth Williams were invited to lead a panel discussion on Aboriginal theatre in Saskatchewan. SNTC general manager Donna Heimbecker and three young Aboriginal artists were also invited to a separate session to discuss the work of their company, and how it was changing the theatre landscape of Saskatoon. This chapter is an effort to expand on those discussions with a focus on how SNTC has affected the work of Saskatchewan Aboriginal artists. As I have mentioned, SNTC is recognized across Canada as one of several new Native theatre companies leading a groundswell of original Canadian Aboriginal work. However, since Tomson Highway's *The Rez Sisters* garnered national attention in 1986, Aboriginal theatre has made only intermittent appearances in the Canadian mainstream, as not all regional theatres have fully embraced original Aboriginal work as a regular part of their programming.[13] This article focuses on how Aboriginal theatre began in Saskatchewan and how SNTC can keep this theatre vital and help Native theatre artists bring their work to the national theatre scene. I have focused on a small number of artists who are leading the way in nurturing and

11 According to Mumford, this funding was available under the National Arts Train-
     ing Contribution Program that began under Sheila Copps in 1999. Mumford, July
     7, 2008.

12 Mumford, July 7, 2008. These companies include SNTC, Saskatoon, Saskatchewan;
     Full Circle First Nations Performance, Vancouver, BC; De-ba-jeh-mu-jig Theatre,
     Wikwemikong, Ontario; Centre for Indigenous Theatre, Toronto, Ontario; En'owkin
     Centre, Indigenous Fine Arts Program, Penticton, BC; Qaggiq Theatre Company,
     Iqaluit, Nunavut.

13 In a January 2007 article in *This Magazine*, Drew Hayden Taylor talks about his work
     and the work of others who have broken into the Canadian Regional Theatre scene.
     He laments that for the most part Native playwrights have failed to break through,
     perhaps because of cultural tendencies to shy away from shameless self-promotion.
     SNTC is helping Native playwrights to work collectively with other like-minded
     Native artists and to gain confidence about their work.

creating original Native theatre, and any omissions of Saskatchewan artists and plays are unintentional.

Maria Campbell has been in the thick of the Saskatchewan and Canadian Aboriginal theatre scene since before such a thing existed in the minds of mainstream Canadian theatre artists. In the 1960s in Saskatchewan, as in many parts of Canada, there were movements afoot to change the fortunes of many disadvantaged Aboriginal peoples. By the 1970s, when the rapid urbanization of Aboriginal people in Saskatchewan was well under way,[14] Campbell was struggling to create theatre as a catalyst for change, work she began in the 1960s through her political endeavours. She was one of many creative Aboriginal people who were desperate to find new ways to inspire and organize their people, and eager to create broader social change. An integral part of this pursuit was her compelling autobiography, *Half-breed* (1973), which brought nationwide attention to the plight of Saskatchewan Métis people. This frank and unapologetic work revealed to Canada an articulate and driven Métis woman who, at present, continues to seek new artistic avenues that speak to the needs of her community. "My reason for doing anything, is that it's for my community. I am a community worker, the [theatre] work has to be useful to the community, has to be healing" (Griffiths and Campbell, 1989, 69). Campbell's journey from this early work to her involvement in the establishment of SNTC is a major component in the advancement of Aboriginal theatre in Saskatchewan and Canada, as it outlines the difficulties of crossing cultural barriers in our colonial country.

In her early years as an activist she worked in Edmonton, Alberta, with a small group of mainly non-status, female, urban Aboriginal activists who found that people did not always respond to speeches and often could not relate to political rhetoric. In an attempt to connect more effectively with their audience, her group began to experiment with play-acting and performed short plays with their messages built into them. They would get together, write their "skits," as they called them, and then find whatever space they could to perform their work. As Campbell related to me, the formula worked, and soon their community theatre grew to the point where "by the late sixties we would do those performances outside because we didn't have a space [large enough] to work in" (Campbell, January 10, 2008). Seeing how their plays worked inspired Campbell and her colleagues to envision taking their theatre to a wider audience that included more non-Aboriginal people. She went to the local library and began to read books on theatre and tried to learn how

---

14   "The urban proportion within [Saskatchewan's Aboriginal population] increased from 5.5% in 1961, to 21.7% in 1971. Most of this change was in Saskatoon and Regina," Anderson 2005, 13.

to write better plays. However, without a space suitable to do theatre work and with little knowledge of the world of professional theatre, the group was unsure how to pursue their dream.

Inspiration came after Campbell saw *The West Show*, a production devised by the Toronto theatre company Theatre Passe Muraille (TPM) in collaboration with 25th Street Theatre in Saskatoon and led by TPM's legendary artistic director, Paul Thompson. The vitality of Thompson and his company's work, and their unique approach to collective community creation, was new and exciting. Campbell soon developed a relationship with Thompson, and they discussed her desire to bring the stories of the Aboriginal community to a professional theatre stage and to a wider Canadian audience. Campbell's optimism was high, as she found Thompson's energy "incredible"—"it made my head work and I felt like I was flying, like there was no such thing as impossible" (Griffiths and Campbell, 1989, 16). However, the cultural gap between Campbell and the theatre troupe from Toronto soon proved to be a huge obstacle to their success. The eventual result of their collaboration with actor Linda Griffiths in the lead role was the play *Jessica*, the product of a long and difficult process that had many highs and lows. As described in a memoir of their experiences called *The Book of Jessica*, Campbell had immense difficulties coming to terms with how Griffiths, a non-Aboriginal woman, interpreted her story. Griffiths was inspired by Campbell's connection to her community and the Native spiritual world she inhabited. However, when they travelled to Campbell's Northern Saskatchewan community, Griffiths became racked with guilt as she listened to Campbell's stories and witnessed the poverty of the Saskatchewan Métis people first-hand. The more she became immersed in the culture, the more awkward she felt as she began to comprehend the gap between their upbringings and communities.

While they recognized each other's talents, each woman faced her own internal struggle over how to portray sensitive cultural material with the right type of emotion. Although Campbell knew Griffiths made a very sincere effort, watching her perform the spiritual component of their work was uncomfortable for Campbell (Griffiths and Campbell, 20–30). They pressed on despite their own difficulties and the outside obstacles,[15] and found several moments of joy and play throughout the process. However, the complexity of the emotional and cultural gap between them was not

15   There was outrage in the white liberal community that a white woman would play an Aboriginal woman on stage when Aboriginal actresses were available. Despite her own struggles with this, Campbell argued that she was part white and therefore either race should be able to play the role. Griffiths and Campbell, *Jessica*, 44, 45.

easily reconciled, especially leading up to the first Saskatoon performance of *Jessica*. After successful workshops in Toronto, all of Campbell's initial fears returned because of her anxiety about offending people in her home community. After this difficult run in Saskatoon, Thompson and Campbell met to discuss future productions of *Jessica*, something they unfortunately could not agree on. Campbell had hoped her last meeting with Thompson would be an opportunity to discuss and better understand the extensive improvisational process they had used to develop *Jessica*, but instead she left their last meeting feeling angry and frustrated.

As they outline in *The Book of Jessica*, it took Campbell and Griffiths five years before they were able to talk through the process, and what had happened in Saskatoon, and come to an agreement about further productions of the show. In this conversation, the pair owned up to their faults and misconceptions about each other, and also attempted to understand the flaws in Thompson's process for them and for the Native community. Campbell felt that Thompson's work took away too much from her community and that Griffiths did not give enough back in the presentation of the show. For Campbell, good art "walks off with all your stuff, but then gives it back to you and heals you, empowers you, and it's beautiful" (Griffiths and Campbell 83, 84). Griffiths wanted *Jessica* to do this, but admitted that Thompson had not recognized the emotional life of Griffiths in relation to the character she was trying to play and how to reconcile these differences before she could tackle such a challenging role. She felt that "ignoring the emotional lives of his actors became an Achilles' heel of his work" (87). Campbell and Griffiths also discussed the divergent histories of Canadians versus Aboriginal people as perhaps the largest obstacle that prevents the two communities from producing "healing" work in a theatrical setting. They argued quite strongly that, as immigrants who had come from oppressive backgrounds and did not recognize their past beyond a few generations in Canada, many non-Aboriginal Canadians did not understand their history. As a result they could not identify with the oppression they perpetrated upon their Aboriginal neighbours. Campbell felt that many low-income non-Aboriginal Canadians are actually more oppressed than Aboriginal people because they vote for governments that continue policies that keep both groups at a disadvantage. She told Griffiths that elders in her community often describe white people as ghosts trying to find their clothes. As a Canadian historian of British heritage who has recently written and researched his family history, and sought several family members' interpretations of our past, this author has to agree that this phenomenon still exists. I recently sought to understand my ancestor's past as an Indian agent and in the process experienced many of the emotions felt by Griffiths as I tried to reconcile this history with the current state of Aboriginal people in Canada.[16]

After *Jessica*, Campbell was determined to continue her quest to have a strong Aboriginal voice heard on professional Canadian stages. She wrote many plays, but had little success having them performed professionally.[17] She has always felt that the two divergent world views of western and Aboriginal people could exist in the same theatre space and worked hard to reconcile this in her work with Griffiths. However, she has continued to find it difficult to work in theatres where mainly non-Aboriginal people had the final say in how her work was produced. Although she is grateful for forward-thinking artistic directors like Persephone Theatre's late great Tibor Feheregyhazi who hired her as the first Aboriginal writer-in-residence for the 1983–84 season, her work was never produced on their mainstage.[18] Although other Aboriginal artists like Drew Hayden Taylor and Tomson Highway have since had more success in Canadian regional theatres,[19] Campbell abandoned this pursuit and began to think about creating an Aboriginal professional theatre space, operated by Aboriginal people. It was, after all, an Aboriginal theatre company (Native Earth in Toronto) that first produced Tomson Highway's *The Rez Sisters*. It has become important to Campbell that the Native community has its own theatre where Aboriginal designers, managers, technicians, and actors support original Aboriginal theatre work. She feels that this is essential for any meaningful growth in Aboriginal playwriting to occur, and she believes the recent work of SNTC speaks for itself: "for me it's really important because the amount of plays that SNTC has produced over the last eight years, nine

---

16 Alan Long, *George Mann was not a Cowboy: Rationalizing Western versus Aboriginal Perspectives of Life and Death 'Dramatic' History* (MA Thesis, University of Saskatchewan, 2007). Indian agents were government employees charged with overseeing the "civilization" of Indians on reserves. Because they are often vilified for their role in the oppression of Aboriginal people, I focused on a humanistic approach and explored his family's relationships with Aboriginal people. In this work I identify very strongly with the historical knowledge gap between Aboriginal and non-Aboriginal people as outlined in Elizabeth Furniss, *The Burden of History: Colonialism and the Frontier Myth in a Rural Canadian Community* (Vancouver: UBC Press, 1999), 3–27.

17 See Appendix One.

18 Saskatoon's 25th Street Theatre helped bring Aboriginal work forward in Saskatchewan in the 1990s under artistic director Tom Bentley-Fisher, but since his departure in 1997 the theatre has not produced Aboriginal work. Cam Fuller, "Bentley-Fisher Bidding Farewell," *Saskatoon Star Phoenix*, April 23, 1997: C1. Since 1999 Saskatchewan's regional theatres (Globe, Regina and Persephone, Saskatoon) have produced fewer and fewer Aboriginal plays. See Appendix One.

19 See Appendix One.

years—that would not be possible without the theatre here. Especially in Saskatoon. We had *Jessica* and then about ten years later I was able to produce another play. That was a long space, so now we have a place of our own. That's really important" (Campbell, January 10, 2008).

In the years after *Jessica*, Campbell did her best to keep Aboriginal theatre alive in Saskatoon by sharing the skills she had learned with Thompson at the newly founded Saskatoon Native Survival School that later became Joe Duquette High School, and now is named Oskayak High School (Oskayak is the Cree word for youth). *Uptown Circles* was the name of Campbell's first play with these youth, a play that was developed through improvisation, with Campbell taking Thompson's place as dramaturge and director. Oskayak still has a large contingent of Aboriginal students and a drama program now led by the first Aboriginal student to receive a provincial acting award, Maureen Belanger (Bouvier, 1997, 20).

Belanger was part of an earlier and highly successful drama program that began at Rossignol School in Ile-a-la-Crosse, Saskatchewan, in 1976. There, an ambitious teacher named Lon Borgerson developed a high-school drama program unlike any other in Saskatchewan at the time. Without a curriculum guide to start from, he and his students created Upisasik ("Little") Theatre, and developed their own style of collective creation through improvisation. Their first play, *Sakitawak Kayas*, was developed to celebrate the 1976 bicentenary of one of Saskatchewan's oldest communities. Sakitawak is the Cree name for "meeting place," which is what the Cree-Métis community called Ile-a-la-Crosse when it was established over 250 years ago (Borgerson, 1998, 48). All of the plays they created—and there were many in the late 1970s and early 1980s—were developed without scripts.[20] They only committed their work to paper after each play was fully developed and, on many occasions, had completed a tour of other northern communities. Aboriginal and Métis students participating in Borgerson's drama class generated the plays, which involved grades 7 to 12 (Borgerson, 2001, 25–27). Although their achievements were numerous, two significant events were Miss Belanger's acting award in 1983 and the production of *Gabrielle* in 1985 on the one hundredth anniversary of the 1885 Northwest Resistance.[21]

Borgerson continued his theatre work after he moved to Prince Albert in the late 1980s, where he was an instructor with the Saskatchewan Urban Native Teacher Education Program (SUNTEP). He continued to use the same style of collective creation with these university students and founded SUNTEP theatre,

---

20   See Appendix Two.

21   *Gabrielle* was published in *The Land Called Morning: Three Plays*, Caroline Heath ed., introduction by Vye Bouvier (Saskatoon: Fifth House, 1986).

which created at least six plays between 1989 and 1996.[22] Two of their plays, *The Great Canadian Golf Crisis* and *A Thousand Supperless Babes,* were performed at the World Indigenous Peoples Education Conference, the former in New Zealand and the latter in Albuquerque, New Mexico.

The "ripple effect" created by Borgerson's students is still a large part of Aboriginal theatre in Saskatchewan and spawned the careers of notable artists such as Belanger, Duane Favel, Bruce Sinclair, Ida Johnson, Elaine Johnson, and Muriel Gardiner (Borgerson, 2001, 27). Some of these students again joined with Borgerson in 2000 to form The Batoche Theatre Company, which created "The Batoche Musical" in 2001. It has been performed several times since at the annual summer Batoche Days in Batoche, as well as at the Saskatoon International Fringe Festival in the summer of 2003. This theatre movement, in which Maria Campbell and many Métis people were heavily involved, paved the way for the formation of SNTC, which began its programming in 1999 based on the same notion that Aboriginal theatre must first reach out to the youth as a way of engaging them in their culture and stories. From this, SNTC began slowly to add professional productions to its season as the youth of its program returned to the theatre and as more interest in Aboriginal theatre developed in the community.

As can be seen in Appendix One, Aboriginal theatre in Saskatchewan has indeed experienced revitalization in recent years thanks to SNTC. The most important component in the creation of new work at their theatre continues to be their innovative theatre training programs. Right from the establishment of the theatre in 1999, artistic education was the focus of Kennetch Charlette, Tantoo Cardinal, Gordon Tootoosis, and others, who knew the power of theatre to engage and motivate young people (Heimbecker, January 18, 2008). What began as a program for youth has evolved into a successful professional Saskatchewan theatre company that is widely recognized for high-quality, engaging work. Although they now have professional Equity productions as a regular part of their season, and a new two-year Red Spirit Arts intensive training program, the foundation of their company continues to be the introductory seven-month Circle of Voices (COV) program, in which they foster unique relationships between established Aboriginal and non-Aboriginal artists and inner city Aboriginal youth, a process that has produced a number of provocative and compelling plays since the first COV production in 1999.

As an audience member of many COV productions, I agree strongly with Campbell that the work of these youth is key to the future success of SNTC. Virtually every COV production has engaging theatrical moments and edgy writing that is intimately connected to the often difficult issues that face Saskatchewan's

22   See Appendix Two.

most disadvantaged population.[23] These urban youth have an uncanny ability to face the sensitive issues head-on and to find clarity and humour where others have failed. The playwrights that have collaborated with them talk of inspiration, creative energy, and the magic that happens when, as artists, they are required to help these young people distill their often harrowing tales into an essential truth accessible to a wide audience. The COV collective process has developed vital grassroots Aboriginal theatre that has inspired many artists in Saskatoon, with energy perhaps similar to that of the exciting and important collaborative work that Theatre Passe Muraille (TPM) brought to Saskatoon in the 1970s. More significantly, the plays and process of the COV program have changed the Aboriginal theatrical landscape of Saskatoon, the same way Thompson's collective process at TPM inspired a generation of Canadian theatre creators.[24] The urban Aboriginal youth of Saskatchewan have helped create a base of work that has become a source of ongoing productions at SNTC, and there is potential to develop these works as future professional productions.

The seven-month intensive COV program involves all aspects of theatre training (acting, voice, movement, technical stagecraft, stage management, etc.), but the two most important aspects are (1) a strong spiritual and healing component, guided by a resident Aboriginal elder, and (2) an opportunity to express their creative ideas in a self-produced show, aided by an experienced Aboriginal playwright, director, and design and technical staff. As the students reconnect with their heritage with the help of an elder, and become involved in a regular theatre practice, their stories and experiences begin to pour out. Early on in the COV program, each group of students shares their ideas for stories and characters with the resident Aboriginal playwright who has been given the opportunity to work with them. Collaboratively they build a one-hour production that the COV students will tour as a company in the final two months of their program. These productions have focused the playwrights on the important issues in the Aboriginal community. The collective environment creates opportunities for these artists to learn from the students and together they create an atmosphere of healing with the Saskatoon inner-city community and the many reserve communities visited by the COV students. Their past shows—*Truth Hurts, Love Songs from a War Drum, The Alley, AWOL, Indian Time, Where Spirits Walk, Crystal Clear,* and *Kihew*—dealt in innova-

23 For example see Wendy MacDermott, *Child Poverty in Canada, Saskatchewan and Saskatoon: A Literature Review and Voices of the People* (Saskatoon: Community-University Institute for Social Research, University of Saskatchewan, 2003), 1. In 2003 the urban Aboriginal poverty rate in Saskatoon was an alarming sixty-five percent.

24 For more explanation of Thompson's work and process, see Kennedy, 189–97.

tive ways with difficult issues such as suicide, youth gangs, alcohol and drug abuse, and residential schools. The magic in these plays often comes from a spiritual component that emerges as the students begin to better understand their identity and traditional stories through guidance from the resident elder. These blended narratives have, quite unwittingly, helped significantly change a fledgling Saskatchewan Aboriginal theatre scene.

In 2002, Campbell worked with the COV participants on their show called *The Alley*, which featured mature characters alongside young ones, a challenge that was successively tackled in this and other COV productions. According to Campbell (who has served as SNTC's cultural advisor until recently), twenty-five to thirty-five years ago the majority of young Aboriginal people in inner-city Saskatoon had not grown up there. They came from rural, often remote, reserve communities, hoping to find new opportunities in the city, only to face incredible hardship as they tried to adjust to a foreign way of life. Today, the majority of the urban Aboriginal youth that come to SNTC have grown up in the city. Campbell feels these youth have an uncanny ability to play a wide range of characters, and to disarm the sensitive issues that face the greater Aboriginal community. "[A]ll of those [COV] plays have incredible humour, [which] is something that a lot of older writers have to work at. It happens automatically for them because this is their place and this is what they are writing about. And the experience might be horrific but people are surviving and there is a great deal of love and warmth in that survival and the way that the work [COV plays] comes out" (Campbell, January 10, 2008). The correct mixture of emotional truth and sharp wit is what Campbell has been looking for ever since she felt like she was floating on air watching TPM do their collaborative work. SNTC has lit a fire in Campbell's spirit again through its unique creative collaboration with Aboriginal youth, which has become a foundation for vital Native theatre in Saskatoon. The program has created a community of Aboriginal artists, and several COV alumni continue to work with SNTC as actors, directors, writers, and administrative staff.

One SNTC success story is Curtis Peeteetuce, who joined the COV program in 2001 and who was part of the second COV show, *Love Songs from a War Drum*, a Romeo and Juliet style piece that focused on the issue of youth gangs in Saskatoon. Mark Dieter was commissioned by SNTC to be the writer of this COV program production where, under the guidance of Kennetch Charlette, he wrote a play based on the experiences and improvisations of the young people in the program. After this collaboration experience with the COV, and the resounding success of *Love Songs from a War Drum* in Saskatoon, Peeteetuce was hooked on theatre, and his dedication to SNTC eventually led him to a leadership role with the company. His own start as a "lead writer" on an SNTC project began later that year, when Kennetch Charlette and Donna Heimbecker asked him to write a "Native Christmas Carol" with a young company of actors who had graduated with him from the COV program. As they had done with Dieter, the young people worked collectively, with Peeteetuce taking the lead role in devising a coherent story. Again, they brainstormed ideas and developed characters based on family members and scene work based on their own experience. Seven years and six plays later, the *Rez Christmas Story* series has developed into SNTC's yearly bestselling show.[25]

I asked Curtis if he took over the writing of the *Rez Christmas Story* shows on his own after that first somewhat collaborative effort. Although Peeteetuce has developed his solitary writing skills, he always gives credit to the actors as much as himself as the inspiration for his storylines and characters. This modest, co-operative attitude has become a sort of signature approach at SNTC, where young and old work together in a family-like environment. After writing several Christmas shows and acting in several SNTC productions, including an outstanding portrayal of "The Warrior that never Sleeps" in their Equity production of Drew Hayden Taylor's *Buz' Gem Blues* in 2004, Peeteetuce was asked by the Saskatoon Public Library Board to sit as their writer-in-residence for nine months from September 2006 to May 2007. Following this successful contract, Peeteetuce's time at SNTC came full circle, as he returned there to act as the lead writer for their latest COV show, *Kihew*, based on the timely issue of residential school compensation payments. In the summer of 2007, the Canadian government ended many court battles by agreeing to pay each former student an amount based on the time he or she spent in the institution.[26] Payments in Saskatchewan were just beginning to be received by claimants when the youth began to write their play with Peeteetuce. The move from comedy to a more serious subject was handled well by Peeteetuce, who, with the help of the COV students and SNTC's resident cultural elder, blended humour and touching moments into a compelling piece of theatre.

Like the COV plays before it, *Kihew* was poignant, moving, and thought provoking, and put a human face on a very complex and emotional issue in the Aboriginal and greater Canadian communities. I was fortunate enough to attend opening night, which, given the relative freshness of this issue, was surprisingly a moving experience for many of us in the audience. Perhaps the

25 See photograph of the 2008 performance in the *Rez Christmas Story* series in the colour insert (photo 8).

26 The residential school payment process was initiated by a class action lawsuit launched by the Merchant Law Group in Saskatchewan on behalf of residential school claimants. The basic claim agreed to by the Federal Government was $10,000 for one year of school plus $3,000 for each additional year. For more information go to Merchant Law Group LLP (www.residentialschools.ca).

most emotional line of the play came from the character **Patricia**, an elder conflicted about either taking the cash payment offered by the Government of Canada or opting out completely. She tells stories to an imaginary lawyer about the large payments some have received and how this money is destroying their lives. As she went on to describe her own experience, it seemed logical that her dialogue would eventually reveal the physical and emotional abuse so many suffered in those institutions. However, when she unveiled her greatest fear at residential school to the lawyer, the simplicity of it was touching and surprising. "You know the worst thing about being in a residential school? It's not about getting strapped...it's not even about getting abused...it's the fear of never getting out and seeing your family again" (Peeteetuce et al., 2008). This simple line put a complex issue into a context that everyone in the audience, Aboriginal or not, could immediately relate to. As she delivered her monologue, a young Aboriginal actress brought a palpable emotional depth to the role of a grandmother and residential school survivor, quite possibly by drawing upon difficulties she had faced in her own life. As in other COV productions, the play cleverly counters this sadness with humour and featured the antics of three young men trying to shoot an amateur documentary film inside an abandoned residential school. They discover a ghost at the school whose identity is revealed to them later in the play by **Patricia**'s story of a sister she had lost there. As is the case in all of SNTC's COV productions, primarily Aboriginal theatre professionals, elders, and young people came together to formulate strategies to deal with a complex problem with emotional honesty and humour.

Long-time Aboriginal playwright Kenneth Williams has also recognized the vitality of this work and, like Campbell and Peeteetuce, has had some of his most inspired moments writing with the COV program. Williams' show with the COV was called *AWOL* (Aboriginals Without Official Leave), which was written and produced in 2003. It took the residential school experience and likened it to a military prison camp. For Williams it was the intensity of the experience that was most memorable. In reflecting on being bombarded by all the great storylines and characters that came from the improvisations with the COV students and then trying to compress it all into an hour-long show, Williams explains: "it is kind of like the [Saskatchewan Playwrights Centre] 24-hour playwriting competition; I really like the parameters [...] because [the pressure] really makes you creative—you have to come up with some really good ideas" (Williams, January 19, 2008).

Williams has also had some past success in having his own work, separate from the COV, supported and produced at SNTC. His play *Thunderstick* premiered at SNTC in 2001 and was well received by Saskatoon audiences. Williams has travelled across Canada doing all kinds of jobs, including TV journalism for the Aboriginal Peoples Television Network (APTN). However, Williams always finds that he ends up in Saskatoon, and for the last three or more years he has made it his permanent home. At the time that this article was written, *Thunderstick* and a new sequel, *Bannock Republic*, were slated to be part of the 2009/2010 season at Persephone Theatre in Saskatoon. Another new work, *Gordon Winter*, has been added to Persephone's 2010/2011 season. Despite the recent success of SNTC and the COV program in producing new Aboriginal work, Williams agrees with Campbell that the next step has to be developing more professional productions. For Williams this means spending even more time developing Aboriginal playwrights because "Theatre is still a very, very small part of Aboriginal people's lives. But I witness the response that Aboriginal people have to it, [and] they are really responding positively to it. They are a huge audience that needs stories, and right now there is only one theatre company (SNTC) that is giving them their stories, and that is not enough. They are a hungry, hungry audience here" (Williams, 2008). SNTC has a vision for the future to have a more modern, but still modest, theatre on 20th Street in Saskatoon. After moving around from space to space for its first two years and essentially doing theatre where the rent was the cheapest, it has made 220 20th Street West its home since October 2001. Its current plan is to remodel its modest 150-seat black box theatre to a modern facility that will seat 250 people. Although it wants to continue being an essential voice of Aboriginal people, Donna Heimbecker feels the new theatre can expand its role as a unique educational voice for the non-Native population. Using **Patricia's** line from *Kihew* as an example, Heimbecker related to me that it is these emotional moments that help others truly understand the issues facing Aboriginal people in Saskatchewan and across Canada. She hopes that they can continue to reach out to all people, bridging gaps between Aboriginal people and the greater Canadian community one play at a time.

> Well, most of our work [was] written because of the intergen-
> erational impacts of the residential school experience. They
> (non-Aboriginal people) weren't taught that in school, but
> they can learn about that at SNTC. [For example, they] didn't
> know about the scoop up of Métis and First Nations babies in
> the 50s and 60s. [The play] *400 kilometres* directly dealt with
> that issue in a very respectful and meaningful way. So they walk
> away having gained some insight, and a new found respect, if
> you will, or understanding, of who we are. So that is all part of
> that community development through the arts. (Heimbecker,
> January 10, 2008).

Colonization (and its effects) remains an extremely sensitive issue in Saskatchewan, and there is a need for young Aboriginal artists to have an environment where they can learn their culture and use that empowerment to share the stories of growing up Aboriginal in Canada. There is still a need for an atmosphere where Native people can understand their situation on their own terms and from there develop theatre for a wider audience.

That said, SNTC is by no means an exclusively Aboriginal environment. Its focus on generating spiritual healing and creative theatre that avoids simplistic victim-oppressor constructions has allowed the company to attract not just audience members from all backgrounds, but also non-Aboriginal artists, including myself, who have taught, acted, directed, and collaborated with SNTC. The difference is that the work occurs in an Aboriginal theatre space with uniquely Aboriginal mandates and philosophies. A stronger voice is therefore created and legitimized that can become part of our national multicultural society. The filter through which their voices pass must be a contemporary Aboriginal one that understands the colonial situation from their point of view.

The success of SNTC is the result of the hard work of many individuals and organizations with a vision of strengthening Aboriginal cultural identity through the arts. The innovative and grassroots Aboriginal approach to their COV program continues to empower Aboriginal youth and create a foundation for engaging theatrical work. The COV plays need to continue to disturb and delight theatre audiences, humanizing the plight of some of the most disadvantaged people of inner-city Saskatoon. Their compelling stories have universal appeal and explore broad truths that SNTC hopes local writers and dramaturges will help them further develop into full-length professional shows. They invite theatre people from all backgrounds to enter their space and share their knowledge with the COV students as these youth enter a world of expression previously unknown to them. They take these skills and their own experience and travel out into Saskatchewan reserve communities and show their own people a way to understand the issues that face them and their communities.

Prior to the establishment of SNTC in 1999, Aboriginal theatre received only intermittent attention from the Saskatchewan theatre community and Saskatchewan audiences. As Appendix One shows, other than 25th Street Theatre's 1990s productions, the two main professional Saskatchewan stages (Persephone and Globe Theatres) have typically had one Aboriginal production per season, but not in every season. The historical gap between the communities, and the barriers to Aboriginal theatre artists in mainstream theatrical circles, has contributed to this under-representation. SNTC was established in 1999 when a wider recognition of Aboriginal issues began to take hold in our province and across Canada.[27] SNTC has tapped into a new generation of Aboriginal artists who now have a home where they can create theatre and community together. At the centre of this search for truth is the troubling history of segregation, residential schools, and attempted cultural annihilation, complex issues that SNTC helps the average Canadian address without ascribing blame or resorting to political rhetoric. The work of SNTC must continue to face these issues and share them with a diverse audience if they wish to continue to be a vital theatre company in Canada. Their voices emanate from one of Canada's most poverty-stricken core neighbourhoods, where SNTC has become a source of pride for that community.[28] As Curtis Peeteetuce stated, "I think having an Aboriginal theatre company on 20th Street, especially right in 'the hood,' is so beneficial to the community because, as one of the young people said in the [COV] program(s) [...] I'm actually on 20th Street and I can be proud to hold my head up high and say I work on 20th."[29]

27   Besides the Oka crisis, the freezing deaths of three Aboriginal men in Saskatoon, and the alleged involvement of the Saskatoon Police, also garnered national attention in the mid to late 1990s. For example, see David H. Wright, "Report on the Commission of Inquiry into Matters Relating to the Death of Neil Stonechild" (Regina: Saskatchewan Justice, 1984). Also see Susanne Reber and Rob Renaud, *Starlight Tour: The Last Lonely Night of Neil Stonechild* (Toronto: Random House Canada, 2005).

28   Unfortunately, shortly after this article was completed, SNTC revealed it was in financial trouble. They have since temporarily closed their doors while they restructure their organization. In the meantime Alanis King and Kennetch Charlette have formed an Aboriginal artistic collective called Askiy ("mother earth" in Cree) Productions. They plan to create professional productions based on Aboriginal stories and legends. Their premiere performance, *Born Buffalo*, occurred in the summer of 2010 at Wanuskewin Heritage Park, Saskatoon, Saskatchewan.

29   Curtis Peeteetuce, interview by Alan Long, January 18, 2008. In Saskatoon, "working on 20th" is often associated with prostitution.

Works Cited

Anderson, Alan B. "Socio-Demographic Study of Aboriginal Population in Saskatoon: The Bridges and Foundations Project on Urban Aboriginal Housing." Saskatoon: Community-University Research Alliances (CURA) Project, University of Saskatchewan, 2005.

Borgerson, Lon. "Ile-a-la-Crosse: Upisasik Theatre in Our Schools." *Canadian Theatre Review* 65 (Winter 1990): 48–51.

———. "Storytelling in Play: Upisasik Theatre Revisited." Masters of Education Thesis, University of Saskatchewan, 1993.

———. "Upisasik Theatre Kayas." *New Breed Magazine.* Saskatoon: Saskatchewan Native Communications Corp., May/June 2001: 25–27.

Bouvier, Vye. "Behind the Scenes with Upisasik Theatre." *Awasis* 4.2 (Fall 1985): 23–24.

———. "Upisasik Theatre Wows Dillon." *Northern Pride,* June 3, 1997: 20.

Campbell, Maria. *Half-Breed.* Toronto: McClelland & Stewart Limited, 1973.

———. Personal interview by Alan Long. Audio recording and typescript in possession of the author. January 10, 2008.

Charlebois, Gaëtan (with Anne Nothof). "History of Canadian Theatre." *Canadian Theatre Encyclopedia.* Athabasca University, April 6, 2009. www.canadiantheatre.com/dict.pl?term=History%20of%20Canadian%20Theatre (accessed November 7, 2009).

Centre for Indigenous Theatre (CIT). "Welcome to the Centre for Indigenous Theatre." www.indigenoustheatre.com/ (accessed November 7, 2009).

Clarke, George Elliot. "White Like Canada." *Transition* 73 (1997): 98–109.

Fuller, Cam. "Bentley-Fisher bidding farewell." *Saskatoon Star Phoenix,* April 23, 1997: C1.

Furniss, Elizabeth. *The Burden of History: Colonialism and the Frontier Myth in a Rural Canadian Community.* Vancouver: UBC Press, 1999.

Griffiths, Linda, and Maria Campbell. *The Book of Jessica: A Theatrical Transformation.* Toronto: Coach House Press, 1989.

Heath, Caroline, ed. *The Land Called Morning: Three Plays.* Introduction by Vye Bouvier. Saskatoon: Fifth House, 1986.

Heimbecker, Donna. Personal interview by Alan Long. Audio recording and typescript in possession of the author. January 18, 2008.

Huntley, Bente, "SUNTEP Theatre." *New Breed Magazine.* Saskatoon: Saskatchewan Native Communications Corp., May/June, 2001: 13.

Kennedy, Brian. *The Baron Bold and the Beauteous Maid: A Compact History of Canadian Theatre.* Toronto: Playwrights Canada Press, 2004.

Long, Alan. *George Mann was not a Cowboy: Rationalizing Western versus Aboriginal Perspectives of Life and Death 'Dramatic' History.* MA Thesis, University of Saskatchewan, 2007.

MacDermott, Wendy. *Child Poverty in Canada, Saskatchewan and Saskatoon: A Literature Review and Voices of the People.* Saskatoon: Community-University Institute for Social Research, University of Saskatchewan, 2003.

Merchant Law Group LLP. "Residential Schools Class Action: Compensation Settlement Information." www.residentialschools.ca/residentialschools.html (accessed November 7, 2009).

Mumford, Marie. Personal interview by Alan Long. Audio recording and typescript in possession of the author. July 7, 2008.

———. Personal interview by Alan Long. Audio recording and typescript in possession of the author. July 9, 2008.

Peeteetuce, Curtis. Personal interview by Alan Long. Audio recording and typescript in possession of the author. January 18, 2008.

——— et al. *Kihew.* (Unpublished manuscript) 19. 2008. Copy on file at Saskatchewan Native Theatre Company, Saskatoon, Saskatchewan.

Reber, Susanne, and Rob Renaud. *Starlight Tour: The Last Lonely Night of Neil Stonechild.* Toronto: Random House Canada, 2005.

Station 20 West Community Enterprise Centre. "The Engine for Urban Renewal: Capital Campaign." www.station20west.com (accessed November 7, 2009).

Stuart, E. Ross. *The History of Prairie Theatre: The Development of Theatre in Alberta, Manitoba and Saskatchewan, 1833–1982.* Toronto: Simon & Pierre Publishing Co., 1984.

Taylor, Drew Hayden. "Native Theatre's Curtain Call? Twenty years later, the medium is set for a new stage." *This Magazine,* January/February 2007. Copyright 2008, Red Maple Foundation. www.thismagazine.ca/issues/2007/01/nativetheatre.php (accessed January 6, 2010).

Williams, Kenneth. Personal interview by Alan Long. Audio recording and typescript in possession of the author. January 19, 2008.

Wright, David H. "Report on the Commission of Inquiry into Matters Relating to the Death of Neil Stonechild." Regina: Saskatchewan Justice, 1984.

Appendix One.

**PROFESSIONAL PRODUCTIONS OF ABORIGINAL PLAYS
IN SASKATCHEWAN SINCE 1972[30]**

PLAY	PLAYWRIGHT	THEATRE	SEASON
The Ecstasy of Rita Joe	George Ryga*	Globe	1973/74
The Great Hunger	Leonard Peterson*	Globe	1975/76
Canadian Gothic/American Modern	Joanna M. Glass*	Persephone	1975/76
Jessica	Maria Campbell & Linda Griffiths*	25th Street	1982/83
The Rez Sisters	Tomson Highway	Globe	1987/88
The Grey Owl Masquerade	Rex Deverell*	Globe	1988/89
Blind Girl Last Night	Greg Daniels	25th Street	1991/92
Dreamkeepers	Bruce Sinclair	25th Street	1991/92
The Path with no Moccasins	Shirley Cheechoo	Globe	1992/93
Toronto at Dreamer's Rock	Drew Hayden Taylor	Globe	1993/94
The Harrowing	Scott Douglas*	25th Street	1994/95
One More Time	Maria Campbell & Harry W. Daniels	Globe	1995/96
One More Time	Maria Campbell & Harry W. Daniels	25th Street	1995/96
Percy's Edge	Greg Daniels	25th Street	1995/96
Someday	Drew Hayden Taylor	Globe	1996/97
Sacred Places	Joe Welsh	25th Street	1997/98
Lady of Silences	Floyd Favel Starr	Globe	1998/99
Four Horses	Greg Daniels	25th Street	1998/99
Truth Hurts	Floyd Favel Starr & COV	SNTC	1999/00
Governor of the Dew	Floyd Favel Starr	Globe	1999/00
The Rez Sisters	Tomson Highway	Persephone	2001/02
Love Songs from a War Drum	Mark Dieter & COV	SNTC	2001/02
Thunderstick	Kenneth Williams	SNTC	2001/02
The Alley	M. Campbell & COV	SNTC	2002/03
Only Drunks and Children Tell the Truth	Drew Hayden Taylor	Persephone	2002/03

30 This list is derived from each theatre company's website and discussions with current general managers. The Globe is located in Regina; SNTC, 25th Street Theatre, and Persephone are in Saskatoon.

PLAY	PLAYWRIGHT	THEATRE	SEASON
Ms. Purdy Parsimonious	C. Peeteetuce & Youth Ensemble	SNTC	2002/03
Wawatay	Penny Gummerson	SNTC	2002/03
AWOL	K. Williams & COV	SNTC	2003/04
Askiy- 'The Land'	M. Dieter & Youth Ensemble	SNTC	2003/04
Velvet Devil	Andrea Menard	SNTC	2003/04
How the Chief Stole Xmas	C. Peeteetuce & Youth Ensemble	SNTC	2003/04
400 Kilometres	Drew Hayden Taylor	SNTC	2003/04
The Sleeping Land	Floyd Favel Starr	Globe	2003/04
Indian Time	D. H. Taylor & COV	SNTC	2004/05
Miracle on 20th Street	C. Peeteetuce & Youth Ensemble	SNTC	2004/05
The Buz' Gem Blues	Drew Hayden Taylor	SNTC	2004/05
Where Spirits Walk	Mark Dieter & COV	SNTC	2004/05
RRAP	Mark Dieter	SNTC	2004/05
In a World Created by a Drunken God	Drew Hayden Taylor	Persephone	2004/05
Annabelle	Mark Dieter	SNTC	June 2005
A Rez Christmas Story IV	C. Peeteetuce & Youth Ensemble	SNTC	2005/06
*Caribou Song***	Tomson Highway	SNTC	2006/07
Vegas Vacation	C. Peeteetuce & Youth Ensemble	SNTC	2006/07
Crystal Clear	Dawn Dumont & COV	SNTC	2006/07
Louis Riel Celebration	M. Campbell	SNTC	2006/07
Kihew	C. Peeteetuce & COV	SNTC	2007/08
Luff Actually	C. Peeteetuce & Youth Ensemble	SNTC	2007/08
Pe mo kit a kin	M. Campbell	SNTC	2007/08
Berlin Blues	Drew Hayden Taylor	Persephone	2007/08
Are We There Yet?	Jane Heather* & Kenneth Williams	SNTC	2007/08
Annie Mae's Movement	Yvette Nolan	SNTC	2007/08

*Non-Aboriginal playwright (sometimes referred to as a "white liberal")

**Highway's story was adapted for stage by Kennetch Charlette.

Appendix Two.

**COMMUNITY/COLLECTIVE PLAY CREATIONS
OF LON BORGERSON AND HIS STUDENTS:**

**ILE-A-LA-CROSSE, SK: 1978–1985
PRINCE ALBERT, SK: 1989–1996**

Community/Collective play creations of Lon Borgerson and his students at Rossignol School in Ile-a-la-Crosse, Saskatchewan, 1978 to 1985, and of his students in the Saskatchewan Urban Native Teacher Education Program in Prince Albert, Saskatchewan, 1989 to 1996. This list and description of plays was obtained directly from Mr. Borgerson's personal files. According to his notes: "Both theatre collectives have drawn on the oral traditions of Métis and First Nations people in the telling of these stories [...] in the making of these plays."

**UPISASIK (LITTLE) THEATRE, ROSSIGNOL SCHOOL,
ILE-A-LA-CROSSE, SASKATCHEWAN**

1978   *Sakitawak Kayas*—A bicenntenial project that celebrated the history of the northern Métis Community of Ile-a-la-Crosse, Saskatchewan.

1979   *Napew*—A young Métis man from across the lake moves with his family into the community and comes into conflict with southern institutions.

1980   *The Pin*—A "Celebrate Saskatchewan" project that highlighted the unique history of the North and of Ile-a-la-Crosse.

1981   *Scrip Van Winkle*—A young man accepts scrip in 1906, falls into a deep sleep, and wakes up seventy-five years later with land title to valuable property: "Kitsiwanis Park" and the "Burroughbess" Hotel in downtown Saskatoon.

1983   *Come Tomorrow Come*—Three young women graduate from high school and are confronted with racism and sexism as they try to make careers for themselves.

1983   *It's My Life*—A young man's choice: school or money? Education or the promise of money and employment at a uranium mine?

1984   *Me No Indian*—A young woman attempts to reject her heritage, as represented by her kohkom (grandmother), in her attempt to "make it" in mainstream society.

1984   *Oops*—Upisasik's response to a series of radioactive spills at the Key Lake uranium mine in Northern Saskatchewan.

1984/85   *Another Home*—A television soap series that chronicled the misadventures of the "Whitefish" family and friends. The series was videotaped in and around Ile-a-la-Crosse, and then broadcast by the local television station every Friday night.

1985   *Gabrielle*—The events of 1885 as they might happen in 1985, in Ile-a-la-Crosse instead of Batoche, with a woman leader who has visions of Riel—just as Riel had visions of God. Published in *The Land Called Morning* (See Heath, Caroline in the reference list).

SUNTEP THEATRE, PRINCE ALBERT, SASKATCHEWAN

1989   *Martha*—A play with nine Marthas, the story of a woman's journey through SUNTEP.

1990   *The Great Canadian Golf Crisis*—Prime Minister Macarooni decides to turn every reserve in the country into a lush, green golf course. His plan is thwarted when Aboriginal peoples across Canada join to "blockade the whole damn country," with a little help from the Cree trickster, Wesakechak. It was performed at the World Peoples' Education Conference in New Zealand.

1992   *Wheel of Justice*—SUNTEP Theatre's irreverent response to the 500th anniversary celebrations: Christopher Columbus on trial, with "Voices from the Past" that testify to the 500 years of genocide that he set loose on this continent. Published in *Eureka!: Seven One-Act Plays for Secondary Schools*. Regina: Coteau Books, 1994.

1993   *Silent Voices*—A video drama that was created at the request of the Prince Albert Mayor's Committee on Family Violence. The format is a panel discussion interspersed with scene flashbacks, as four women present personal stories of spousal abuse.

1994   *Family Feudalism*—A satirical look at men's attitudes towards women. The format is a game show, with women in the role of stereotypical males like Harley Davidson, Biff Jerky, and Puck Enright. During commercials they step out of these comic roles and speak candidly as women. Performed at the 1994 Saskatoon Fringe Festival.

1996   *A Thousand Supperless Babes*—A multimedia production that celebrates the story of the Métis people. To create the play, the actors researched Métis history, archival material and, more importantly, the stories and photographs of their own families and communities. It was performed at the World Indigenous Education Conference in Albuquerque, New Mexico, in 1996.

"... like magic, which always works best on cold, prairie nights": Elements of Prairie Gothic in Daniel Macdonald's *MacGregor's Hard Ice Cream and Gas.*

WES D. PEARCE

W hen Daniel Macdonald's[1] play *MacGregor's Hard Ice Cream and Gas* opened at Persephone Theatre in 2005, the reviewer for the *Saskatoon Star Phoenix* referred to the play as "part Prairie

---

1   Daniel Macdonald is a well known Saskatchewan actor, teacher, director, and writer who makes his home in Regina. For the last decade he has been establishing himself as one of the sharp and acute new dramatic voices in Saskatchewan. *Pageant* was featured as part of the National Arts Centre's On the Verge festival in 2002 and premiered as a part of Alberta Theatre Projects playRites 2003 festival and in 2005 had its American premiere in Austin, Texas. *MacGregor's Hard Ice Cream and Gas* was part of the On the Verge festival in 2004, premiered at Persephone Theatre in March 2005 and was programmed as part of Prairie Theatre Exchange's 2006/07 season. It was then produced at Ship's Company Theatre (Parsboro, NS) in the summer of 2007 and by Shadow Theatre (Edmonton) during the 2007/08 season and was published by Playwrights Canada Press in 2008. See photographs from the 2005 performance at Persephone Theatre in the colour insert (photos 9 to 14).

His play *Velocity* won the New Works of Merit playwriting competition in New York City, was part of the 2006 Saskatchewan Playwrights Centre's (SPC) Spring Festival of New Plays, and in 2011 was featured as part of Persephone Theatre's season. In 2007 he was commissioned to write a new play for the University of Regina; this commission eventually became *Radiant Boy,* which was produced in

Gothic and part absurdist comedy" (Fuller, March 7, 2005, B2). The preview article in the *Winnipeg Free Press* that preceded Prairie Theatre Exchange's 2007 production concluded that the play was "prairie gothic with a sense of humour" (Prokosh, January 27, 2007, D3). A year later, Liz Nicholls of the *Edmonton Journal* headlined her review of Shadow Theatre's 2008 production as "Absurdist Comedy Embraces the Frozen Prairie Gothic" (Nicholls, January 27, 2008, B5). Little wonder, then, that playwright Dan Macdonald observed in the *Winnipeg Free Press* that "Whenever people talk about *MacGregor's*, they also call it prairie gothic, but prairie gothic re-written because it's so damn funny" (Prokosh, January 25, 2007, D3). Despite the varying responses and reviews that various productions have generated there does seem to be some general consensus about the play's genre.

Macdonald's play is set in a small, dying, and unnamed town in west-central Saskatchewan and focuses on the somewhat dysfunctional MacGregor family. **John MacGregor,** patriarch of the family, has recently died, but it is February in Saskatchewan. Naturally, it's really, really cold; naturally, the ground is frozen solid, with the result that it's impossible to bury him. Macdonald comments, "the land, the climate and our own sense of place at times makes us do strange things"(Mathieson, 2007), and the play seems to bear witness to this statement. Because of the aforementioned weather conditions, **Jack** (the youngest son) has kidnapped the coffin from the parlour and is keeping it cool by filling the casket with buckets of flavourful, homemade ice cream. **Fred,** the humourless middle child, is trying to get his father's body back downstairs for the second day of the wake, but in the meantime he kills time trying to "fix" the broken "Hard Ice Cream & Gas" sign, the broken house, and the broken town.[2] While this literal tug of war with the coffin is going on in **Jack's** attic bedroom, their mother, **Marlene**, exercises

2009. *Johnny Zed! The Musical!* (co-written with Sheldon Davis and Henry Piovesan) was workshopped as part of the 2008 SPC Spring Festival and in 2010 *History of Breathing* was part of the SPC Spring Festival.

    In the summer of 2005 he co-conceived, co-developed, and directed the actor-driven series *Redemption, SK* (a quirky and original dramatic event) for SCN (Saskatchewan Communications Network) and has directed *Mr. Marmalade* and *Pageant* for Regina's Hot House Theatre. He has appeared in a number of movies and television series and has twice received the SIMPIA Showcase award for acting. He has won the Regina Writer's Award, is past president of the Saskatchewan Playwrights Centre, and is currently pursuing an MFA in directing from the University of Regina.

2   **Fred** is at once the most pragmatic of the three children and yet at the same time is the most illogical, as **Jack** comments, "**Fred**, how come you come up here and board up all of our houses but you keep on trying to fix the sign for our store?" (18). It should be noted that the store has been closed for years.

in the basement by pacing in circles and angrily counting off the steps she should have taken to escape the family when she was still young (Mathieson, 2007). Into this "frozen landscape and frozen family" (Mathieson, 2007) enters (or re-enters) **Missy**. **Missy**, the oldest child and only daughter, was seventeen when she left home; when she reappears, not only is she unaware of her father's death, but, more importantly, she's ten and a half months pregnant and convinced she has to return to her past in order to give birth. The play is also haunted by a trio of unseen characters; the body of **John MacGregor** (or at least the coffin holding his body), the vivid ghost of John's best friend (and the district accordion champion), **Allabaster Tuckus**, and the landscape, which "is as much a character as the MacGregors and their dead accordion-playing neighbour" (Nemetz).

For the three years that I was working with the play I also referred to it and its style as "Prairie Gothic" (or, as Macdonald suggests, prairie gothic comedy) without necessarily really knowing what that meant. For some time, literary critics have been bemoaning the difficulty of "speak[ing] of 'the Gothic' with any assurance" (Botting, 2001, 1), in part because "this multi-generic and malleable mode of writing" (Hogle, 2001, 153) has, possibly, become *too* multi-generic and malleable. Regardless of this uncertainty, "the Gothic" can still, at least according to Botting, be defined as a genre completely "conscious of itself," with an emphasis on "mysterious supernatural energies, immense natural forces, and deep, dark human fears" (1). Further, critics such as Judie Newman argue that "[i]n Canada, Gothic is almost the norm" (85) and Faye Hammill notes the "centrality of Gothic in the Canadian canon," adding that

> [t]he vast, sparsely-populated forests of Labrador, Quebec and Ontario, or the frozen areas further north, are the classic setting for Canadian Gothic texts, although some authors have substituted different regional landscapes. For example, sub-genres such as Southern Ontario Gothic and Prairie Gothic suggest, as Susanne Becker puts it, "the confining terrors of small towns in a bleak landscape." (47)

In his discussion surrounding the "gothic legacy" of Jacques Derrida, Jodey Castricano argues that

> learning to "talk with ghosts" is complicated by the understanding that "the word *with* produces a sense of simultaneity and doubleness" [… and] this undertaking has proven precarious because it involves rethinking what Derrida refers to as "the sharp distinc-

tion between the real and the unreal, the actual and the inactual, the living and the non-living, being and not being [...] in the opposition between what is present and what is not." (2006, 801)

This duality is central to the world Macdonald creates, allowing for a world that is at once so seemingly recognizable (almost "normal") and yet at the same time is a world in which interaction with the supernatural (as hypothesized by Derrida) seems (almost) as natural as breathing. It can be further argued that the development of Prairie Gothic parallels some aspects of Southern Gothic insofar as the "warped rural communities and small towns of the modern South, [and] the comic antics of the characters [... central to both gothic forms] become the often farcical attempts of a lost individual to find redemption" (Boyd, 1994, 42). I'm not sure one can argue that *MacGregor's* finds its literary ancestors in the works of Tennessee Williams, but the connection between these regional gothic literatures is seen in the combining of "isolated rural settings with [...] elements of dark humour and the grotesque" (Boyd, 43). Derrida's discussion of doubleness further echoes the works of Southern Gothic writers who, as Lewis Simpson argues, create "a vision of life that blends realism and grotesquery in a manner that we readily grasp" (xiv).

This essay focuses first on a general discussion of the Gothic elements of Macdonald's play and then, in the second part, addresses the scenographic realization of these Gothic elements in various productions of the play. In particular, this paper explores the tensions in the text that seemingly argue for two oppositional ways of staging the fantastical/Gothic. Much of the discussion around the scenographic solutions to the text emerges from my work on this play: first, as the visual dramaturge at the 2004 Saskatchewan Playwrights Centre (SPC) Spring Festival of New Plays[3] and later, as the costume and set designer for Persephone Theatre's premiere production in March 2005. This production was directed by Ben Henderson, who had been the SPC dramaturge when the play was at Spring Festival and had been a strong advocate of and for this play through his work at SPC.

Macdonald's use of Gothic is perhaps most evident in the setting/location of the play, especially when the play is read in reference to Becker's previ-

---

3   In 2002, the SPC Spring Festival of Plays was an intensive eight days wherein four plays were given a three-day workshop and two plays were given a one and one-half day workshop. Months before, the festival dramaturge (during this festival Stephen Heatley) selected the plays in a blind reading and then worked with the selected playwrights and the plays leading up to the festival. During the festival, actors and a dramaturge/director were assigned for each play and the festival dramaturge and the visual dramaturge both worked where they were needed most. The goal of the festival was six public presentations in five days; typically these presentations were no more than staged readings but occasionally plays were "put on their feet."

ously mentioned discussion of small towns and bleak landscape. The Gothic landscape is foregrounded, as is evident when **Marlene** explains why she is confined to walking in circles in the basement:

> ...When I used to walk outside, I'd go around our two main blocks, but I got tired going around in circles and waving to the same four people in one hour:
> [...] And I got tired of seeing nobody in the other houses. All boarded up or on a big truck getting taken away somewhere. And the dirt—or the mud... and two paved roads.... What kind of a place has only two paved roads? [...] Past Starla's, past the cemetery, out towards Herbert's garage and that Quonset, and I saw where the tracks meet the highway, and I just went straight for them. And I got there and stood on the tracks and I looked out. I looked straight down those tracks. All the way down and they ... they just go on forever. There's no bend, no turn, they just .... And the trains that come on them seem to come from someplace so ... so far. And I thought about it. And I thought, I don't want to go for walks outside and see this anymore. And then your father started getting sick and I had to stay close, so I found an excuse not to go out. So I didn't. (38-9)[4]

While most clearly articulated in the preceding passage, the Gothic landscape appears early in the play and references to its unforgiving nature recur repeatedly throughout the text, informing and colouring all of the characters.

While the landscape is a powerful force within the play there are a number of situations that echo well-known Gothic tropes. The most obvious refers back to Derrida's discussion of the "actual and the inactual, the living and the non-living" and talking with ghosts; **Jack** is convinced that **Allabaster Tuckus** has returned from the dead. In an early scene, **Jack** desperately tries to convince **Fred** that **Allabaster** (or his spectral presence) appears in all of the Polaroid pictures that Auntie Arlene took during the wake.[5] Later, as **Jack**

---

4   All quotations from the play, unless otherwise indicated are from Daniel Macdonald, *MacGregor's Hard Ice Cream and Gas* (Toronto: Playwrights Canada Press, 2008).

5   The very fact of Auntie Arlene taking pictures at a wake re-enforces the Gothic nature of the play. **Jack** complains to **Fred** that Arlene not only took pictures of "You, me, and Dad. You, me, Mom, and Dad. Mom and Dad. Auntie Sheilah, Auntie Loretta, Mom and Dad. Uncle Bill, Uncle Bernie, all of Uncle Bernie's kids and Mom ... and Dad", but all sorts of photos of "Dad from above, Dad from straight on, Dad from the doorway. Dad and all of the people who came over in that van from Ardath." While **Fred** is inclined to shrug it off as being "just her way," **Jack** is ultimately less accepting.

brings **Missy** up to date on the happenings of the town he tries to explain **Tuckus**'s existence in two realities:

> **MISSY.** Tuckus isn't dead?
>
> **JACK.** Oh, yeah. He is. Well …. That's the thing isn't it? Dead is such a funny … kind of relative term, isn't it? (*pause*) It's hard to explain. We should go. (32)

Jack is convinced that **Allabaster** is haunting both the MacGregor family and their dying town: "Tuckus has dad in a kind of limbo. He has the whole town in a kind of limbo. Including this family. He's killing people off and then putting them in limbo. Even Mom" (17). He also believes that in order for both the family and the town to prosper **Allabaster** must be defeated in an accordion duel. As a result, he spends much of the play trying to learn how to "master" the accordion in order to defeat the "long dead" district accordion champion. It is important to note that, as the play progresses, **Tuckus** becomes more and more real to **Jack**, transforming from a pictorial image into an actual presence by the end of the first act.

Another Gothic trope is the presence and acceptance of the supernatural (and supernatural events) as part of the reality shared by most members of the MacGregor family. Early in the play, **Missy's** birth is narrated, and yet within minutes of this event (and without either character aging) **Missy** and **Marlene** are conversing about accordions and trains, an event which is both improbable and impossible and yet completely reasonable within the Gothic world that Macdonald has created:

> *The sound of a train is heard in the distance.*
>
> **MISSY.** What's that, Mom?
>
> **MARLENE.** That's a train.
>
> **MISSY.** Where's it go?
>
> *A pause. A small moment of panic passes over MARLENE.*
>
> **MARLENE.** And I looked away as I hoisted you up closer and lied to you. "Nowhere special," I said. (4)

> **JACK.** Polaroids of the dead guy, Fred. Like family pictures. Posing and all smiley. They're all smiling, Fred. Like it's a happy time. Happy. You see Dad smiling in any of these pictures? So, yes. I stole them from her. When she went off to help Mom put away all the puffy cheeses and … and Jell-Os with those mystery chunks in them, I went into her purse and I took them. She can take pictures of somebody else's corpse. Not Dad's. It's like stealing Dad's soul (10–11).

A more obvious use of the supernatural concerns **Missy's** protracted (and therefore unnatural) pregnancy; again improbable, even impossible, yet accepted by the family (and the audience) as if it were completely natural and normal:

> MARLENE. There is no way you're having that baby here.
>
> MISSY. Then I don't know where the hell I'm having it! I tried, Mom. I tried. When I was nine months. In the warmth, near the beaches, where I thought it wanted to be. I tried. I pushed and jumped up and down, I sang to it, I yelled at it. I took hot baths in the ocean and walks in boiling rain. Nothing. So I thought, okay, I'll come home…. Home, Mom. You know how much I dreaded coming home? It was the last…. Doesn't matter. It's worse than ever. It just sits up there swimming and rolling around. What am I supposed to do? Like, suppose it keeps growing in there?
>
> MARLENE. It doesn't want to be born here either. How can you blame it? Look around, Missy. Look at what we are. […] (50–1)

As the play proceeds, its supernatural aspects manifest themselves differently vis-à-vis Macdonald's extensive and unapologetic use of magical realism. Angel Flores writes, "[in] magical realism we find the transformation of the common and the everyday into the awesome and the unreal. It is predominantly an art of surprises. Time exists in a kind of timeless fluidity and the unreal happens as part of reality" (1995, 113). In his discussion of American magical realism, Alejo Carpentier writes: "the marvelous begins to be unmistakably marvelous when it arises from an unexpected alteration of reality" (1995, 86). The use of magical realism not only furthers Castricano's reading of dualism as central to Gothic but, as Lucie Armitt argues, allows for the rethinking of "conventional gothic tropes" (2000, 61). It is, I would argue, Macdonald's extensive use of magical realism—placing various magical moments within what otherwise seems to be a "realistic" play—that makes this play Gothic. It goes without saying that the location, the actions of certain characters, and a strong sense of the supernatural are used to establish a Gothic tone, but it is the ensuing moments of magic that allow the play to cut "through the crud of prairie naturalism" (Nicholls, January 27, 2008, B5), further defining what Prairie Gothic means.

After creating a familiar (if somewhat unusual) prairie ensemble in Act 1 (and just before the house lights come up for intermission), Macdonald begins altering this reality:

Accordion music and lights find **JACK** *riding a three-wheeled ice cream bicycle complete with whistles and horns in the middle of the howling winter wind. He drives with no hands and plays one of those small, round accordions as he shouts over the wind and the accordion music.*

JACK. Ice Cream! Get your ice cream! Prairie Passion! Fancy Berry! Old Tyme Vanilla! Today's special! Half-price because of the cold weather. If it hits minus 35, it's 75 percent off. Come on out! (*Rings bell. Sees someone approaching.*) ... There we go. Hey there old-timer. Come on, now. Don't be shy. A little closer. (*Looks into his containers.*) What flavour would you like? (*He looks up, sees it's* **Allabaster Tuckus**. *Pause.*) ... You. You get outta here, Tuckus. You hear me? I'm not selling ... It's ... store's closed! Run along! Shoo! (**JACK** *starts to go*) ... Ice Cream ... get your ice cream ... (*He stops dead on his bike and turns back*) No! On second thought, Tuckus, stay there! Stay right there! Don't you move till I get back! (41).

What emerges as Act 2 proceeds is the image of a family strangled by a "fantastical kind of inertia" (Nemetz, August 24, 2007). The psychic breakthrough that releases the family from its *stasis* does not actually occur until after an unusually large number of devastating family secrets are disclosed, and when the family *is* finally released from its internal dysfunction, this release does not happen subtly but, rather, in a stunning *coup de théâtre*:

There is a moment where **MARLENE** *gathers herself and slowly, shaking, sits down on the sofa. She looks at it.*

... And I sit in my parlour. On my sofa. Finally. And I look around at the old, stuffy carpet and the red velour and I think, what now? I'm here! Hello! [...] And the walls say nothing, but they know. They watch me, alone, wondering where my children are and why I'm not with them now. And what do I do? I sit. Like the fool I am, unable to move. [...] And the walls know because, like magic, which always works best on cold, prairie nights ... like magic, the walls to my parlour sweep themselves away. And I know they're taking me to where I belong, where I've needed to be ...

[...] **MARLENE** *and her sofa begin to move.* (61–2)

As the walls disappear and **Marlene** and her sofa fly across the snow-covered prairie landscape the play becomes something quite other than what it had first appeared to be. These moments of magical realism (along with the previously discussed tropes) transcend the expected and help identify and create a definition and understanding of Prairie Gothic.

Having discussed the elements of Prairie Gothic within the text, I focus for the rest of this essay on *visualizing* Prairie Gothic, with attention given to my work on the production of *MacGregor's Hard Ice Cream and Gas* at Persephone Theatre. Pamela Howard writes that "working with a new text carries a special responsibility for those who work on its first creation, not the least because it is often unlikely that it will get a second performance" (Howard, 2002, 30)[6]; as such, the primary goal that governed much of the discussion that director Ben Henderson and I had was a desire to respond to the text "as written."

The scenographic challenges of the play's first act involve trying to create a recognizable world that allows for the Gothic tropes and themes to exist alongside the "actual" world of the MacGregor family. The biggest challenge is the fact that the present-day action of the play occurs simultaneously in the attic and the basement of the MacGregor house. Interwoven between these contemporary moments are three scenes between **Missy** and **Marlene** that occur in the distant past (including the early conversation about trains, quoted above), scenes that are textually located in an undefined "memory space." In the premiere production the two specific playing areas were represented as selectively abstract areas of realistic (or at least recognizable) space. The attic (stage right) was nothing more than a small-framed structure that resembled the sloped pitch of a typical, small-town prairie house embellished with visual bits (such as the chimney) that helped to specify the location further. As it was not raised off the floor in any manner, the attic remained very much a part of the deck. The basement area (stage left) was a bit more functional insofar as characters had to be seen physically stepping down (from the kitchen) into this playing area. Again the location was suggested by the open framed structure and, as with the attic, the actors weren't confined to be "in the space" at any given time. These two locations in the house were unified (or at least given some context) by a simple, childlike "drawing" of a frame house that hung centre stage. The house not only connected these two playing spaces as being part of the same house, but provided the nondescript, but necessary, "memory place" for the scenes in the past, a mythic playing place between the realities of the attic and the basement of the present day.

---

6   Howard attributes this sentiment to Howard Bond but provides no citation to support her claim.

Dominating the first half of Act 2 (visually, physically, and metaphorically) is the parlour, the central room in the house. This "special room" is spoken of with great veneration throughout the previous act: **Marlene** refers to it as "[t]he warmest room in a house full of cracks and holes" (3), **Jack** is incredulous when **Missy** says she'll sleep in the parlour, and **Fred** is apoplectic when he indeed finds her sleeping there at the beginning of Act 2. Yet, this room (complete with flocked red wallpaper), central to the mythology of the MacGregor family, must, according to the script, remain unseen until the beginning of Act 2 (when the attic and basement have both disappeared). This in itself can create problems, especially in a theatre ill-equipped to store large scenic pieces. More importantly, as I have described previously, the walls of the parlour also need to "disappear" during the action of the play, creating logistical problems for designer and technical director.

Logistics of set placement and storage aside, the second act is much more challenging insofar as staging the script "as written" puts into sharp focus Macdonald's two oppositional ways of using (and therefore visualizing) the Gothic. As written, the moment that the walls break apart and **Marlene** and her sofa fly into the prairie night, according to the stage directions, actually occurs and is witnessed by the audience:

> *The walls have disappeared and* **MARLENE** *and her sofa begin to move.*
>
> … And I and my sofa sail away … into the snow?
>
> **MARLENE** *looks around. The walls are gone. The air is cold.* **MARLENE** *is on the snow-swept prairie.* (62)

I am unfamiliar with how other productions have handled this moment but, in the Persephone production, the three-sided box set literally broke apart into two large sections of "parlour," and each wall section, propelled by hidden stagehands, disappeared into the wings, leaving **Marlene** on her sofa in the middle of nowhere. Yet, I have become convinced that actualizing this (and other) moments does, in some manner, work against the very nature of magical realism within the play.

The following comparison should make this concern even clearer. Shortly after **Marlene** arrives on the snow-swept prairie with her sofa, she watches **Fred** prepare a grave:

> FRED *enters wearing his welder's mask and holding a blow torch with a large propane tank on wheels following behind.* MARLENE *watches him cross the stage and exit.*
>
> ... And Fred shovels all the snow away from the grave stones in the cemetery and cooks the ground with his blow torch and a tank of propane he borrowed from George Woynarski. And before long he's got a profoundly deep hole for his father. (66)

The hole/grave, as described by **Marlene**, needs to be used, not to bury **John** but, rather, as the final resting place for his ice cream and accordion (which **Marlene** disassembles and tosses bit by bit into the open pit). The action of the play necessitated some sort of physical hole, which couldn't be there for the entire show and so had to "appear" in the stage floor near the end of the play. While the engineering of this effect was not difficult, what perplexed me was (or is) the necessity of a physical reality that works against the magical realism of the text. When the physicality of the grave is compared to the funeral pyre that is built, the conflict of the two stagings within the text again becomes somewhat problematic:

> *Pause. A distant train sounds.* [...]
>
> JACK *crosses through. He is holding as many planks of wood as he can carry and a can of gas.*
>
> MARLENE. ... But down by the tracks I see Jack and Missy pile the wood stripped from boarded-up houses around the coffin, and the train gets closer as Jack lights a fire 10 miles high with town wood that once was nailed to empty windows, and my husband right in the middle of all of it. The coldest night in the history of the world, colder than anywhere else on earth, and a fire, big as a tornado whipping and swirling down at the train tracks. (66)

We created the effect of the pyre by using a rotating gobo and sound; with the help of the narrative, this became a spectacular moment of freedom. As this scene progresses, the moments of magical realism begin to dominate the action and the world of the play until, near the end, it is difficult to know in which reality many of the events are unfolding. After **John's** body has been disposed of and just before **Marlene** catches her train headed "nowhere special," **Missy's** water breaks:

> **MARLENE.** And at that moment, with the train waiting for me and my husband floating away in tiny specs of ash above the tracks, the water that holds your baby up where it plays and swims and lives the day away... (*a look between the two women.*)
>
> **MISSY.** ... It drops to the ground from inside me. And all around us, it melts the snow and turns all that frozen, dead grass into lush, spectacular green.
>
> *The colour green fills the air and the ground.* **MARLENE** *turns and looks at* **MISSY** [...]. (68)

There are a number of motifs in the play: fire, wind, trains, and the accordion have a huge presence in this play. Sometimes the use of these elements is metaphoric, sometimes some of these elements are central (or physical) parts of the story, and sometimes they evoke another place and time; but always there is something fantastical, magical, and Gothic about their use. What needs to be emphasized, not surprisingly, is that many of the fantastical images and moments, including the moment of **Missy's** water breaking, work best when dealt with using sound and light (or even narrated as offstage events), instead of being represented in some "actual reality."

Reviewers have generally commented that Act 2 is somewhat less successful than Act 1,[7] and I think it could be argued that part of the reason for this dissatis-faction is the conflicted nature of staging the Gothic as necessitated by the text. The most successful moments in the play are those moments of magical realism that echo reality but make no attempt to "be" authentic, and this seems to work against the moments of staging spectacle also required from the script. I have, as mentioned, referenced my own design and have been relatively unsuccessful in researching how the three other productions have dealt with these staging and interpretive challenges.[8] I know that of the four professional productions staged,

---

7   While Act 2 does contain less action and is dominated by descriptive monologues of past actions, not everyone sees this as a flaw; Janna Graham writes: "Although the first half is slow at times, the second half has enough quirky and bracing moments to carry the show" (2007).

8   As I have discussed, the Persephone production was quite faithful to the text (building a three-wheeled ice cream bicycle), while the Edmonton production visualized the scene quite differently with **Jack** "hawking ice cream from his sled" (Nicholls, January 27, 2008, B5). This deviation from the text is pragmatic to be sure, but I wonder if the marvelous moment created by the old-time bicycle appearing in the blizzard is reduced by the much more expected images of sled and blizzard ... of

the Prairie Theatre Exchange (PTE) production was the most poorly received (Prokosh, January 27, 2007, C6). However, it also became clear from reading the publicity generated by the theatre that the play was programmed and directed as the "big winter comedy" which, as Macdonald has said, went against his advice (and wishes). The play has, as Nicholls notes, some similarities to Faulkner's *As I Lay Dying* (January 27, 2008, B5) and to deny or play against the Gothic-ness of the play is to invite failure. Decoding and choosing how to stage these many moments of Gothic/magical realism is, I believe, the challenge for both the scenographer and the director of this play. Although I remain a huge fan of this play, I know that the Persephone production was not perfect. I believe that part of the problem with the production was that I didn't fully understand how to represent the Gothic/magical realism/fantastic elements of the text and, as a result, the visual languages chosen did not always commune with each other or with the text itself. Rethinking the text and creating a magical Gothic style that responds to all the fantastical and magical visions of Macdonald in a *relatively* unified manner might provide the visual codes and language necessary to allow this work, like **Marlene's** sofa, to soar beyond the page ... leaving the frozen landscape behind.

Works Cited

Armitt, Lucie. *Contemporary Women's Fiction and the Fantastic.* London: MacMillan Press Ltd., 2000.

Becker, Susan. *Gothic Forms of Feminine Fictions.* Manchester: Manchester University Press, 1999.

Botting, Fred. "Preface: the Gothic." *Essays and Studies Annual* (2001): 1–6.

Boyd, Molly. "Rural Identity in the Southern Gothic Novels of Mark Steadman." *Studies in the Literary Imagination* 27.2 (1994): 41–54.

Carpentier, Alejo. "On the Marvelous Real in America." *Magical Realism: Theory, History, Community.* Eds. Lois P. Zamora and Wendy B. Faris. Durham, NC: Duke University Press, 1995, 75–88.

Castricano, Jodey. "Learning to Talk with Ghosts: Canadian Gothic and the Poetics of

---

course, to the audience, it is the selling of ice cream, not **Allabaster's** ghost, that is the incongruous moment in this scene.

The set for the Ship's Company Production was "eerie and ambitious. Steel railroad tracks run through the middle of the stage. [...] Another section of rail line leaps up into the blue sky [...] Columns of ice and soft snow on the ground bring a chill to the playhouse and frame the interior of the house, which is always too cold" (Graham, 2007). Again, without seeing the production it is difficult to gauge the effectiveness of the scenic interpretation, but such a stylized and non-realistic set may work against the Gothic/magical realism elements of the play.

Haunting in Eden Robinson's *Monkey Beach*." *University of Toronto Quarterly* 75.2 (2006): 801–13.

Flores, Angel. "Magical Realism in Spanish American Fiction." *Magical Realism: Theory, History, Community.* Eds. Lois P. Zamora and Wendy B. Faris. Durham, NC: Duke University Press, 1995, 109–118.

Fuller, Cam. "Persephone scoops up play: Theatre produces world premiere of 'wacky' comedy." *Saskatoon Star Phoenix*, March 3, 2005, final ed.: C1.

———. "Play has charm, substance." Review of *MacGregor's Hard Ice Cream and Gas*, by Dan Macdonald, dir. Ben Henderson. Peresphone Theatre, Saskatoon, SK. *Saskatoon Star Phoenix* March 7, 2005, final ed.: B2.

Graham, Janna. "Hard Ice Cream and Gas aboard the ship." Review of *MacGregor's Hard Ice Cream and Gas*, by Dan Macdonald, dir. Pamela Halstead. Ship's Company Theatre, Parsboro, NS. *Truro Daily News*, August 17, 2007. www.shipscompany.com/news-events/reviews/2007-08-17b.html.

Hammill, Faye. "'Death by Nature': Margaret Atwood and Wilderness Gothic" *Gothic Studies* 52 (2003): 47–63.

Hogle, Jerrold E. "The Gothic at our Turn of the Century: Our Culture of Simulation and the Return of the Body." *Essays and Studies Annual* (2001): 153–59.

Howard, Pamela. *What is Scenography?* London: Routledge, 2002.

Macdonald, Daniel. *MacGregor's Hard Ice Cream and Gas.* Toronto: Playwrights Canada Press, 2008.

Mathieson, Dave. "McGregor's [sic] performance a gas." Review of *MacGregor's Hard Ice Cream and Gas*, by Dan Macdonald, dir. Pamela Halstead. Ship's Company Theatre, Parsboro, NS. *The Springhill Record*, August 17, 2007. www.shipscompany.com/news-events/reviews/2007-08-17.html.

Newman, Judie. "Postcolonial Gothic: Ruth Prawer Jhabvala and the Sobhraj Case" *Modern Fiction Studies* 40.1 (Spring 1994): 85–100.

Nemetz, Andrea. "Worth getting to know the MacGregor family." Review of *MacGregor's Hard Ice Cream and Gas*, by Dan Macdonald dir. Pamela Halstead. Ship's Company Theatre, Parsboro, NS. *Halifax Chronicle Herald*, August 24, 2007. www.shipscompany.com/news-events/reviews/2007-08-24.html.

Nicholls, Liz. "Hard, and very dark, ice cream." *Edmonton Journal*, January 24, 2008: D3.

———. "Absurdist Comedy Embraces the Frozen Prairie Gothic." Review of *MacGregor's Hard Ice Cream and Gas*, by Dan Macdonald, dir. John Hudson. Shadow Theatre, Edmonton AB. *Edmonton Journal*, January 27, 2008: B5.

Prokosh, Kevin. "It's prairie gothic with a sense of humour." *Winnipeg Free Press*, January 25, 2007: D3.

———. "Prairie-set play suffers from dramatic permafrost." Review of *MacGregor's Hard Ice Cream and Gas*, by Dan Macdonald, dir. Robert Metcalfe. Prairie Theatre Exchange, Winnipeg, MB. *Winnipeg Free Press*, January 27, 2007: C6.

Simpson, Lewis P. "Introduction." *3 by 3: Masterworks of the Southern Gothic*. Atlanta: Peachtree, 1985, vii–xiv.

ALBERTA

Overview

No Blood for Oil:
Thirty Years of Playwriting in Alberta

MIEKO OUCHI

W hat does the price of a barrel of oil have to do with playwriting in Alberta?
        Linking playwriting to the vagaries of the oil business could seem like a tenuous premise until you take a closer look at the development of Albertan writing for the stage over the last three decades and the inevitable rises and falls of the theatre community.

Let's start with the 1980s. Alberta's theatre community really came into its own during the first big oil years in the province, the high-flying 1980s. It was during this *Bonfire of the Vanities*-esque boom that many theatres in both Calgary and Edmonton came into being or blossomed with an injection of cash by a province and oil companies flush with money to burn. Happily, this coincided with the theatre movement that had begun in the seventies and was continuing to sweep across Canada: the movement to explore our own Canadian stories. For that decade, the province was a hotbed of new playwrights including John Murrell, Sharon Pollock, Frank Moher, Brad Fraser, Conni Massing, Raymond Storey, Janet Hinton-Mann, Stewart Lemoine, Robert Clinton, Ronnie Burkett, Kenneth Brown, Michael McKinley, Lyle Victor Albert, Blake Brooker and One Yellow Rabbit, and Gordon Pengilly. While their work and eyes strayed to international figures, stories, and history, during this time their plays seemed just as often to reflect and celebrate Canadian and Albertan stories.

Building on the success of breakout plays like John Murrell's *Waiting for the Parade* (1977), and Sharon Pollock's *Walsh* (1973), powerful Canadian stories like Murrell's *Farther West* (1982), *New World* (1984), Pollock's *Blood Relations* (1980), *One Tiger to a Hill* (1980), *Whiskey Six Cadenza* (1983), and *Doc* (1984), Frank Moher's *Odd Jobs* (1985), *The Third Ascent* (1988), and *Prairie Report* (1989), Lyle Victor Albert's *The Prairie Church of Buster Galloway* (1983), Robert Clinton's *The Mail Order Bride* (1988), and Brad Fraser's groundbreaking *Unidentified Human Remains and the True Nature of Love* (1989) began to emerge.[1] Comedic gems like Lyle Victor Albert's *Cut!* and Kenneth Brown's *Life After Hockey* both played the Edmonton Fringe in 1985. Conni Massing's *Gravel Run* premiered at Alberta Theatre Projects in 1988, and even musicals like Raymond Storey and John Roby's 1982 *Country Chorale* featuring k.d. lang and *Haunting Melody* (1988) by Marianne Copithorne and Murray McCune made their debuts at Theatre Network. Some writing and performing ensembles also emerged: in Calgary, most notably One Yellow Rabbit in 1982 with productions like *Changing Bodies* (1986) and *Tears of a Dinosaur* (1988), which featured marionettes by Ronnie Burkett; and in Edmonton, most notably Stewart Lemoine and Teatro La Quindicina, who appeared first at the Edmonton Fringe with *All These Heels* (1982) and continued with plays like *The Vile Governess and other Psychodramas* (1986) and *Damp Fury* (1988).

During this time, we saw an unprecedented number of plays by Albertan playwrights being produced across the province at theatres of all sizes and stripes. Companies focusing almost exclusively on exploring the work of new playwrights in the province included One Yellow Rabbit, Alberta Theatre Projects (ATP) and Lunchbox Theatre in Calgary, and Theatre Network, Northern Light Theatre, and Workshop West Theatre in Edmonton. Even oil got into the new play development movement. ATP's Pan-Canadian (now Enbridge) playRites Festival of New Canadian Plays headed by D. Michael Dobbin made its debut in 1987. Lunchbox Theatre's Petro-Can Stage One Festival debuted in 1988. Both of these aforementioned festivals were funded by oil companies looking to put an artistic and human face on their not-so-sexy oil operations. Regional theatres like the Citadel Theatre in Edmonton and Theatre Calgary in Calgary also produced several Canadian plays in their seasons, as did smaller, significant professional houses such as Edmonton's Phoenix Theatre, a descendent of the even earlier alternative theatre company, Theatre 3 (1970-81).

Collective theatre and popular theatre were represented by three companies in Edmonton: the professional company Catalyst Theatre, headed up by Jan Selman and Ruth Smillie during the 1980s, Azimuth Theatre, headed up by

---

1   All dates refer to first production, not publication.

Deborah Hurford, which began creating issue-based collective plays in 1987 under the wing of the Sherwood Park RCMP Crime Prevention/Police Community Relations Unit, and the tiny upstart Concrete Theatre, which began as a non-professional collective in 1987 founded by Elinor Holt, Jan Selman, Caroline Howarth, Lisa Sokoluk, and myself.

Companies that saw moves into new theatres or centres during this time included Alberta Theatre Projects (ATP) and Theatre Calgary, which moved into the Epcor Centre for the Performing Arts in 1985, followed by One Yellow Rabbit in 1987. Up north, Edmonton's Citadel Theatre, which had moved into its current location on Sir Winston Churchill Square in 1976, saw a massive expansion with the addition of the MacLab Theatre in 1984.

In the 1990s, by the time I graduated from theatre school, a whole new wave of writers was beginning to hit Alberta. These included Vern Thiessen, Marty Chan, Pamela Boyd, Ron Chambers, Eugene Stickland, Ken Cameron, David Belke, Cathleen Rootsaert, Chris Craddock, Stephen Massicotte, Jeff Page and Wes Borg, Darrin Hagen, Clem Martini, Doug Curtis, Floyd Favel Starr, and many others. Some came from the University of Alberta's now defunct and much-lamented MFA playwriting program; others crossed over from professional careers in acting, design, directing, and prose and poetry. Some made use of self-production opportunities like the Fringe Festivals in Edmonton (established in 1982 by Brian Paisley and the Chinook Theatre) and Calgary (first founded in 2001 by Loose Moose Theatre, then restarted in 2005 by Blair Gallant and Jason Rothery after its untimely demise in 2003) and other smaller centres in the province like Fort McMurray (Interplay), Grande Prairie (The Grande Little Fringe), and Athabasca (Athabasca Country Fringe Festival). Still others worked through formalized new play development processes at theatres and festivals, while some playwrights became resident writers at theatre companies.

Plays that first emerged at the Edmonton Fringe in the 1990s included Vern Thiessen's *I Fell in Love with an Eel* (1991), Marty Chan's *Polaroids of Don* (1994) and *The Bone House* (1999), Doug Curtis's 1995 *Paranormal*, Jeff Page and Wes Borg's 1997 *Love Letters from the Unabomber* and 1998 *Granite Man and the Butterfly*, Chris Craddock's *Super Ed* (1995), and Paul Matwychuk's *The Key to Violet's Apartment* (1996). Perhaps the most produced playwright at the Edmonton Fringe during the 1990s was David Belke, who debuted eleven plays at the Festival over those ten years; beginning with *Swordplay* in 1990, his "Fringe hits" have included *The Maltese Bodkin* (1991), *The Reluctant Resurrection of Sherlock Holmes* (1992), *Blackpool and Parrish* (1993), and *Dreamland Saturday Nights* (1998). Darrin Hagen's company Guys in Disguise also had an impressive body of Fringe work in the 1990s that included: *The Edmonton Queen: Not a Riverboat Story* (1996), *Tornado Magnet: A Salute to Trailer Park*

Women (1997), *Tranny, Get Your Gun* (1998) (written by Darrin and Chris Crad-dock), and *Piledriver!* (1999). Other independent company ("indie") hits out of Alberta included Stephen Massicotte's Fringe Jedi Trilogy: *The Boy's Own Jedi Handbook, The Girls Strike Back,* and *The Return of the Jedi Handbook*; One Yellow Rabbit's High Performance Rodeo spawned *The Climate: A Province in deKlein* (1998) and *Stop Thinking!* (1999), both by Ken Cameron.

Plays that emerged from such established playwright-friendly theatres as ATP, Theatre Network, Northern Light Theatre, and Workshop West Theatre spanned the spectrum: *Odd Fish* (1992) by Pamela Boyd; *Metastasis* (1995) by Gordon Pengilly; *Dirt* (1996) and *Marg Szkaluba (Pissy's Wife)* (1994) by Lethbridge playwright Ron Chambers; *Illegal Entry* (1995) and *Selling Mr. Rushdie* (1997) by Clem Martini; *Mom, Dad, I'm Living With a White Girl* (1998) by Marty Chan; *Some Assembly Required* (1994), *Sitting on Paradise* (1996), and *A Guide To Mourning* (1998) from ATP playwright-in-residence (1989-2004) Eugene Stickland.

Ensembles and ensemble-based writing through companies like Catalyst Theatre, under the new artistic direction of Joey Tremblay and Jonathan Christenson, and One Yellow Rabbit's resident company (OYR), which in-cluded Blake Brooker, Michael Green, Denise Clarke, and Andy Curtis, came into their own. OYR saw its flagship festival, The High Performance Rodeo, emerge as an iconoclastic Calgary must-see that merged the vibrant visual and performance art community historically coming out of the Alberta College of Art and Design with the theatre community.

The 1990s was also a period of development and maturing for a number of new, small companies and free-form collectives that encouraged or produced the work of one or several Alberta playwrights. These included Sage Theatre, Ghost River Theatre, and Theatre Junction in Calgary, and the Unconscious Collective, generic theatre, Teatro La Quindicina, the Free Will Players, and Shadow Theatre in Edmonton. My own Edmonton company, Concrete The-atre, moved from a popular theatre mandate to a Theatre for Young Audiences (TYA) company.

Oil came into play again as Syncrude got into the act as the primary sponsor of Theatre Network's NextFest in 1996, a groundbreaking new play festival for young artists under thirty. ATCO Gas similarly became the primary sponsor of the Kid's Series at the Citadel.

The 1990s also saw an exciting new trend in Edmonton, where recent theatre school graduates from both the University of Alberta and Grant MacEwan College began to write and perform their own shows with great success. This wave of new writer/creators included teams like Daniela Vlaskalic and Beth Graham; Daniel Arnold and Medina Hahn; Jared Matsunaga-Turnbull and Chris Bullough, as well as writers working alone or with multiple collaborators like Chris Craddock and myself. Many of these writer/creators honed their skills through the Playwrights Garage at Workshop West Theatre under the leadership of Vern Thiessen, and produced their first productions either at the Fringe Festival or at NextFest, hosted by Theatre Network.

In parallel, in Calgary, a wave of new creation ensembles working in merged mediums began to appear, including the Old Trout Puppet Workshop, the Green Fools, and Le Freak C'est Chic, many of them with skills honed through the OYR Summer Training Intensive. In Red Deer we began to see the emergence of some professional theatrical activity with the birth of Prime Stock Theatre in 1994, which, under the leadership of Thomas Usher, still produces many Alberta plays, including work by playwrights like Gordon Pengilly and Darrin Hagen.

Sadly, during this time we also saw the demise of several professional theatres in Edmonton, including the Phoenix Theatre (1981–1997), Nexus Theatre (1982–1995), a lunchtime theatre company founded by Ben Henderson that hosted the earliest days of the Die-Nasty weekly improvised soap opera among other noteworthy credits, and Stage Polaris (1985–1999), a large TYA company that produced several series, one for families and one for small children.

During the 1990s key festivals for new play development included Workshop West Theatre's Springboards and Kaboom Festivals, Theatre Network's Next-Fest, and Northern Light Theatre's Urban Tales and Erotic Tales in Edmonton; ATP's playRites Festival of New Canadian Plays, OYR's High Performance Rodeo, The Mutton Busting Festival, and Lunchbox Theatre's Stage One in Calgary; and of course the Fringe Festivals in both cities.

In the early 2000s, against all hockey odds, Alberta seemed to open up, and careers that used to exist almost exclusively in one major Alberta city began to become bi-city. Work and plays began travelling between Calgary and Edmonton more and more. Works by OYR, Eugene Stickland, Ron Chambers, Ken Cameron, Doug Curtis and Ghost River Theatre, and Stephen Massicotte were all performed in Edmonton. In Calgary, the plays of Edmontonians Vern Thiessen, Conni Massing, myself, and Rob Moffat were performed.

Building on the successes of some of their 1990s plays at the Fringe and with small independent companies, several playwrights made the leap to the larger stages and national attention. Stephen Massicotte scored with *Mary's Wedding,* a huge hit at ATP's 2002 playRites that became one of the most-produced plays in Canadian history, while Ken Cameron's *My One and Only* (2004) opened off–off Broadway in New York in 2006 as *Making Marilyn*. Vern Thiessen had several hits that brought national attention to his work: *Apple* (2002) at Workshop West, and *Einstein's Gift* (2003), winner of the 2004 Governor General's Award for Drama, *Shakespeare's Will* (2005) and *Vimy* (2007), all for the Citadel Theatre. His plays have gone on to be produced across the country as well as in New York. In 2005 and 2006 Chris Craddock and Aaron Macri's play *Boy Groove* played to sold-out houses at Fringes across Canada and in Toronto and was recognized by the Dora Awards with an Audience Choice Award. In 2008 Chris Craddock and Nathan Cuckow's gay rap opera *Bash'd* enjoyed a four-month run in New York at the Zipper Factory Theater after premiering in Edmonton, earning them a GLAAD Media Award. The Old Trout Puppet Workshop has seen their productions of *Pinocchio,* a commission from ATP and Magnetic North, and *Famous Puppet Death Scenes* tour across the country. Catalyst's hits *Frankenstein* and the Poe-inspired *Nevermore* are currently criss-crossing the country. My two plays *The Red Priest (Eight Ways To Say Goodbye)* and *The Blue Light* have been produced across the country and translated into Japanese, Russian, and French.

In the early years of the new millennium, new writers and voices emerged. In Edmonton, Jeremy Baumung (*Homeless*), Nathan Cuckow (*Bash'd, 3 Different Heavens*), Sheldon Elter (*Métis Mutt*), Collin Doyle (*The Mighty Carlins*), and Tracy Power (*Living Shadows*) all come to mind. In Calgary, Lindsay Burns (*Dough*), Eric Rose (STRUCK), David van Belle (*Dragonfly* with Anita Miotti) and crossover dance/theatre practitioners Glenda Stirling (*Flop*) and Anita Miotti (*Dragonfly* with David van Belle) are oft mentioned.

Today, Alberta is seeing a second oil boom and, with it, a wave of change both positive and negative. On the positive side, for the first time in a decade in Edmonton we have an arts-friendly mayor, Stephen Mandel. He is already making concrete changes such as ensuring more money for the Edmonton Arts Council through municipal arts grants, hosting a newly revamped and high-profile Mayor's Evening for the Arts and Business and, for the first time ever, putting forward a new comprehensive municipal arts and cultural plan, *The Art of Living,* for the city. Additionally, in 2007, Edmonton was named Cultural Capital of Canada, with corresponding money, grants, and events to celebrate this honour. In 2008, Mandel wowed the theatre community by being the first city mayor to attend the Sterling Theatre Awards, alongside city councillor and former artistic director of Theatre Network and dramaturge of the Saskatchewan Playwrights Centre, Ben Henderson, and Liberal MLA Laurie Blakeman, the former general manager of both the Phoenix Theatre and Northern Light Theatre.

Calgary has begun a new Cultural Spaces organization, working with the city on enshrining cultural space into the city's plans over the next few years. The initiative is already paying off: Calgary has seen a renaissance of construction and renovation, resulting in new theatre spaces. These cover the spectrum from the humble Motel at the Epcor Centre, a small space for independent companies, to the very grand, flexible Grand Theatre, home to Theatre Junction as well as a top-notch restaurant. Vertigo Theatre has a beautiful new space with two separate theatre spaces in downtown's iconic Calgary Tower. Calgary also has an exciting new arts-friendly addition at city hall. Alberta Theatre Projects' former technical director and lighting designer, Brian Pincott, is now the city alderman for Ward 11.

Provincially, the Banff Centre continues to be a strong supporter of emerging and advanced playwrights through the playRites Colony and development residencies with the continuance of the Banff Playwrights Colony, artist residencies, and a new Banff/Citadel Professional Theatre Program in partnership with the Citadel Theatre.

Red Deer, long known as the place you stopped to get a much-needed coffee, rest, and a nibble at the midpoint of the highway between Calgary and Edmonton, is finally beginning to reap the rewards of the cohorts of graduates emerging from the Red Deer College Theatre and Motion Picture Arts Programs. Culture Link is a new community-based Red Deer organization that serves as a catalyst to advance and nurture arts and heritage. Small independent theatre companies, such as Ignition Theatre, which started in 2005, are emerging to join established professional companies in town like Prime Stock Theatre. New theatre spaces like the Matchbox Theatre, home to Ignition Theatre, and the Scott Block Cultural Centre have been acquired, and independent programming is happening in both spaces. In central Alberta, long imagined to be the conservative "Bible Belt" of the province, we're beginning to see hit plays by Albertans—such as *Dreamland Saturday Nights* written by Edmontonian David Belke—done side by side with controversial international scripts like American John Cameron Mitchell's *Hedwig and the Angry Inch* and *My Name is Rachel Corrie* by Katherine Viner and Alan Rickman. Scripts At Work, a new play festival hosted at Red Deer College, has brought in dramaturges and directors like Vanessa Porteous, Trevor Schmidt, Eric Rose, Glenda Stirling, and myself to work with new emerging playwrights.

New play festivals have continued to grow and prosper. Calgary has seen the establishment of the new Ignite Festival by Sage Theatre in 2004; based on Edmonton's Nextfest, it also targets emerging artists. Nextfest itself saw the abrupt disappearance of Syncrude as its primary sponsor, as the oil company pulled up all its non-Fort McMurray corporate money, choosing instead to invest all its charitable funds in the far north of the province. Will we see a blossoming of theatre in Fort McMurray as a result? Only time will tell. Speaking of oil, Petro-Can got into the new play development act once again with its sponsorship of the Petro-Can New Play Initiative: FUSE at Theatre Calgary. But not all on the festival front is rosy. Edmonton's sturdiest and most established festival, the Fringe, had a near meltdown in 2007 over a new ticketing system and changes in the administration of the festival. The resulting backlash from Edmonton's professional artists culminated in the venerable Varscona Theatre pulling its venue out of the official Fringe in favour of a self-curated program of professional productions and a rush of long-time Fringe artists eschewing the main lottery to pursue the BYOV (or Bring Your Own Venue) option.

So, yes, we have seen a boom again, fuelling new hope that there will be another renaissance of theatre in Alberta. Yet, paradoxically, that same boom is already ushering in new challenges, concerns, and uncertainties for theatre artists living in the province. And as fast as we could say "boom," we are already seeing a dizzying rollercoaster return to governmental deficits and cutbacks as global markets recover from the financial meltdown that began to impact economies in late 2007.

Despite the current recession, the low cost of living that made it possible for playwrights to make a living almost exclusively from writing seems to be gone. Many are teaching, directing, or doing other things to make ends meet. Many senior theatre artists are returning to school to acquire the advanced MFA degrees required to teach at the post-secondary level. Writing is becoming something very costly to do, or as one person recently articulated to me … an expensive hobby.

Which leads us to the ultimate tragedy … artists are moving away from the province. Many artists can no longer own houses or live in the arts districts like Inglewood, Marda Loop, Old Strathcona, and 124th Street, which, thanks to the artists themselves, are becoming more desirable and gentrified. Some have moved to Saskatchewan. Others have begun to buy houses in former low-income, rough areas like Alberta Avenue in Edmonton. The recent artist-driven Arts on the Ave movement in that area seems to be the beginning of the transformation of the area into a new arts district.

This heated real estate market means that rehearsal space continues to be a hot commodity, and companies are finding themselves progressively rehearsing in less-than-ideal conditions. It also means that theatres looking for space or beginning capital campaigns fear for the success of their searches. Unfortunately, the same boom that is driving the cranes building new theatres in major centres is also financing the bulldozer. Lunchbox Theatre, with a secure home in Bow Valley Square in downtown Calgary since 1975, was ousted by a money-hungry landlord and had to look for a new home, finally securing one in the base of the Calgary Tower. Sadly, in both cities, we saw the beloved and much-used twin theatres named after provincial theatre icons Betty Mitchell and Walter Kaasa—both housed in the basements of the identical Southern and Northern Alberta Jubilee Auditoriums in Calgary and Edmonton—removed during renovations to make room for air-conditioning units for the larger theatres upstairs. Edmonton's Catalyst Theatre has just been given notice that it must leave the space it has been renting within the next three years, and Northern Light Theatre and Workshop West both have been told by the City of Edmonton that The Third Space, the small space in north Edmonton that they have traditionally shared, cannot be used for public performances any more.

Provincially, after the last election, when Conservatives swept the province once again, we were treated to many months of a Culture minister who was a former hog farmer. Culture was merged into a portfolio that includes Sports, Recreation, and Parks. The ray of hope many saw in the 2008 appointment of a new Culture minister who showed early signs of being more genuinely interested in the Arts—Lindsay Blackett—was dashed to the ground at the 2010 Banff Television Festival, where, during a question-and-answer session, Blackett used vulgar language to describe the Alberta film and television industry projects that he funds as minister. Artists and arts advocates across the province were horrified, and the remarks ignited a firestorm of debate.[2]

The lack of female artistic directors at professional companies in both major cities remains an ongoing issue, as does the lack of cultural diversity on- and offstage across the province. The latest StatsCan numbers show that Alberta is quickly becoming more culturally diverse, something that is not reflected in our audiences or onstage. This lack of diversity means that we are not doing a good job at including and welcoming all Albertans, which leads to the danger that we are becoming more and more irrelevant to the community. If the thousands of people flocking to our province are not drawn into the theatre community's waiting arms, we risk losing an important new audience, maybe forever. Over the past few years, small improvements have been made. A new theatre, Alberta Aboriginal Arts, co-founded by Ryan Cunningham and Christine Sokaymoh Frederick, emerged in Edmonton in 2009. Their 2010/11 season of projects included a co-presentation of Native Earth's touring production of Daniel David Moses's *Almighty Voice and His Wife* and second incarnation of their Rubaboo Arts Festival, both with Workshop West Theatre, as well as a dance piece based on Cunningham's nascent play *They Shoot Buffalo Don't They?* (in the Expanse Movement Festival). A third Rubaboo, intended to play in Calgary as part of the Magnetic North Theatre Festival, and at least one production are in the works for 2011.

Finally, in many aspects of our community, it is still too early to say what effect the boom, and the recession that seems to be following it, will have. Over the last few years, we have seen a change in artistic directors at several critical companies and a change of mandate in several companies, which means change... both positive and negative. Theatre Calgary has welcomed Dennis Garnhum, the Free Will Players has welcomed Marianne Copithorne, and

---

2   www.cbc.ca/canada/calgary/story/2010/06/16/calgary-blackett-banff-television-comments-backlash.html.

Workshop West Theatre now has at the helm Michael Clark, the former artistic director of Nakai Theatre in Whitehorse. In a very exciting move, Alberta Theatre Projects has replaced the irreplaceable Bob White with long-time artistic associate Vanessa Porteous.

Despite the uncertainty, Alberta plays continue to be produced. Theatre Calgary has recently produced *The Wars* by Timothy Findlay in an adaptation by Dennis Garnhum and has created a new adaptation of the novel *Lost—A Memoir* by Calgary novelist Cathy Ostlere as co-written by the author and Dennis Garnhum for inclusion in its upcoming 2010–11 season. The Citadel has had recent success with *Vimy* by Vern Thiessen, and Theatre Network did Cathleen Rootsaert's *Choke* and has Chris Craddock's *Public Speaking* on the boards for next season. With Michael Clark as artistic director, Workshop West Theatre now looks beyond just Alberta for plays, but has premiered ten Albertan plays and one by an expatriate Alberta aboriginal writer, Kenneth Williams, in five seasons. Nonetheless, with the occasional exception, Northern Light Theatre has begun to focus almost exclusively on plays from the international canon; Theatre Network is looking more and more towards Canadian playwrights rather than Albertan ones.

In terms of outreach, recently Catalyst Theatre partnered with Keyano Theatre in Fort McMurray as a development partner on their extravaganza *Frankenstein*, which is now touring nationally and internationally. This same development model was used for their newest shows, *Nevermore* and *Hunchback*. Work is travelling to other cities and countries: *Bash'd, Boy Groove, The Red Priest (Eight Ways To Say Goodbye), Mary's Wedding, The Oxford Roof Climber's Rebellion, The Blue Light, Vimy, Apple,* and *Einstein's Gift* are all on the move and are beginning to be translated and staged in other Canadian cities across the country, and in other countries including the United States, Poland, Russia, Japan, and Germany. In fact, in 2005 I had the pleasure of seeing Frank Moher's *Odd Jobs* in Osaka, Japan. Less fortunately for Alberta, perhaps, many playwrights are also on the move to other centres; international success has led to both Thiessen and Massicotte moving to New York, with other senior artists pondering changes of address.

Diversification and striking new alliances within the arts community seem to be crucial to surviving these turbulent times in Alberta. The past decade has seen a number of playwrights beginning to branch out into other mediums. John Murrell is turning his hand to opera along with collaborator/composer John Estacio, their full-length operas, *Filumena* and *Frobisher,* having been recently produced by Calgary Opera. Stewart Lemoine successfully rewrote the book for HMS *Pinafore* for Edmonton Opera. And in film and television, ex-Edmontonian playwright Raymond Storey is the creator of a new series for Global TV, *The Guard,* which I have had the pleasure of acting in. Mark Haroun, another ex-Edmontonian playwright is the senior story editor on the CBC TV series *Heartland*. I, too, have written and directed several documentaries with the National Film Board and recently completed my first made-for-television movie screenplay for Vision TV's Diverse TV Program, a training and mentorship program for culturally diverse writers. After years of poverty, the money is enticing.

So where is Alberta going from here?

That's hard to say, but everyone agrees that something is in the air. We all feel it. We're in the midst of some kind of large-scale change. It's just hard to tell from the inside … What we do know is this: Everyone in the province is trying his or her best to hold onto whatever remains of the dragon's oily tail … where it throws theatre entering the twenty-first century and what fortunes and casualties may occur along the way remain to be seen.

Publish or Perish: Giving Life to the New Play

ANNE NOTHOF

S o who reads new plays anyway? Most often it is actors, directors, and set and lighting designers, but they typically make do with a play script, often hot off the playwright's computer, and often subject to change not only during rehearsal, but up to, and sometimes including, opening night.

New plays are notoriously unstable. Many playwrights consider their text to be only a blueprint, which may change with each production. Many publishers have discovered that a text laboriously edited, designed, and illustrated is past its due date by the second production of the play.

New play scripts are also written in a private code—the dots and dashes have a specific meaning to the playwright, and perhaps to the director and actors if the playwright is on hand for rehearsals, but they are not always placed consistently in the text. For example, three dots may mean a slight pause, and a dash may mean that the words of the next character overlap those of the speaking character, but what does (... ___) mean? Who gets the final word in the publication—the editor or the playwright? One represents the interests of the reader, the other, the interests of the actors. Most presses attempt to standardize their play text format while respecting the wishes of playwrights, and for the most part the relationships are amicable. The script is typically delivered electronically, and the playwright proofs and approves the final version.

What is the target readership for plays? This is rarely discussed at press board meetings, which tend to focus on mundane, monetary matters. There is no expectation that plays will make a profit, but there is some hope that they won't lose too much money. The general consensus is that collections do better than single plays—but collections are expensive to publish, labour-intensive, and a higher risk, so unless the collection is by a recognizable name—like Sharon Pollock, for example—it is approached with extreme caution. However, smaller collections by multiple playwrights may do surprisingly well if they coincide with a fashionable academic interest. *Ethnicities: Plays from the New West* (NeWest Press 1999), for example, has gone into several print runs, probably because it was one of the first "ethnic" collections at a time when multiculturalism was becoming a hot topic in universities.

Do audiences read plays? Rarely. Attempts to flog published plays to loyal subscribers and fans in theatre lobbies where the plays have been produced are good exercises in public relations, but don't result in high numbers of sales, even in the prestigious and well-heeled theatres of the Shaw and Stratford Festivals. The primary target audience for play texts is the university student—that hapless individual who must buy or borrow a text to pass a course. New Canadian playwrights rarely make it to required reading lists. Established ones, like Sharon Pollock, however, are big sellers for English, Drama, and Theatre courses. The NeWest collection of Pollock's plays (*Blood Relations and Other Plays*, 2002), now in a revised edition, has been a bestseller for the press for the past twenty-eight years. Brad Fraser's plays have also done very well, particularly *Unidentified Human Remains and the True Nature of Love*, which has been produced across the country, in the United States, and internationally. For a time, at least, it was also on course lists, despite its predilection for sex and violence.

One of the most important reasons to publish plays is, quite simply, to keep them in existence and available for production. Unpublished scripts have a tendency to disappear over time, even if they are available through the Playwrights Guild of Canada's virtual library. Serendipitous availability in libraries and bookstores is particularly important for the dissemination of Canadian plays across the country and abroad. A director in Canberra produced David French's *Salt-Water Moon* after finding it on the shelves of the Australian National University library among the American plays. Published plays can also function as records of production, since most presses publish only after at least one professional production, and their texts include a history of the premiere: names of actors, director, designer, a description of the set design and music, and, often, production photos. Hence, published plays provide an important historical record of Canadian drama and theatre.

Play publishing in Canada is a relatively recent phenomenon: Talonbooks, based in Vancouver, began publishing plays in 1969 with James Reaney's *Colours in the Dark* and has built up an impressive stable of playwrights since then, including George Ryga, Wendy Lill, Joan MacLeod, Michel Tremblay, and Morris Panych. NeWest Press, based in Edmonton, began publishing new

Canadian plays early in its history—in the late 1970s. Playwrights Canada Press, based in Toronto, published its first six titles in 1984 and now publishes thirty plays on average each year. Other small literary presses, such as Winnipeg's Blizzard and Scirocco, have also contributed important texts. The mandate of NeWest Press was and is to publish new works from Western Canada and the North. Founding board member Diane Bessai was determined to address the dearth of published plays after she initiated a course in Canadian drama at the University of Alberta and found that very few were available in print, particularly plays from the West. With the help of playwright, poet, University of Saskatchewan professor, and NeWest board member Don Kerr, she undertook a "Prairie Play Series" and has been adding to it ever since—at the slow but steady rate of (on average) one play text every year. The rationale for the series is outlined on the NeWest website:

> The Prairie Play Series seeks to acquaint readers with an important aspect of the prairie literary sensibility through the modern drama of the prairie stage. The series includes works by playwrights who showed a healthy western spirit of pioneer determination that was integral to the development of community and school theatre in the Canadian west, such as Gwen Pharis Ringwood, whose plays were produced as early as 1935, and W. O. Mitchell, whose plays were performed on radio in the 1940s and 1950s. Today the Prairie Play Series continues to give voice to the culture of the prairies by publishing new plays by contemporary western Canadian playwrights. (www.newestpress.com)

However, the reasons for publication vary with each play. These include:

1. A talented local playwright with a large and loyal following—unpublished or little known elsewhere in the country; e.g., Edmonton playwrights Stewart Lemoine (*A Teatro Trilogy* 2004 and *At the Zenith of the Empire* 2007), David Belke (*The Minor Keys* 2000), Conni Massing (*The Aberhart Summer* 1999), and Calgary playwright Gordon Pengilly (*Metastasis and Other Plays* 2009).

2. A Western Canadian playwright first published by NeWest who subsequently develops a strong following and whose works are guaranteed production and a strong critical response; e.g., NeWest took a chance on the unknown Brad Fraser by publishing *The Wolf Plays* in 1993. Following the critical acclaim of the Calgary and Edmonton productions of *Unidentified Human Remains and the True Nature of Love*, NeWest invested in Fraser's

subsequent plays, including the text of the play and of the film by Denis Arcand, *Love and Human Remains* (1996), followed by *Poor Super Man* (1995), *Martin Yesterday* (1998), and *Snake in Fridge* (2001), each play selling fewer copies than the preceding one. Fraser has since left NeWest for Playwrights Canada Press, which has reprinted *Human Remains*.

3. An important Canadian playwright whose plays are consistently on reading lists; e.g., Sharon Pollock's *Blood Relations and Other Plays* (1981, rpt. 2002). These playwrights are difficult to identify early in their careers, needless to say. And some are missed, even when the opportunity presents itself; e.g., Stephen Massicotte's *Mary's Wedding*, a memory play set during World War I, was not accepted for publication by NeWest after its first production at Alberta Theatre Projects, and has subsequently been produced thirty-seven times at major regional theatres across the country and abroad.

4. A thematic collection of plays that addresses a topical issue; e.g., *NeWest Plays by Women* (1987) was "a natural reflection of the increasing prominence of women playwrights in the Canadian theatre of the 1980s" (Bessai, "Introduction," vii), two of whom were "well-established" and two just getting established. The volume includes *Whiskey Six Cadenza* by Sharon Pollock, *Play Memory* by Joanna McClelland Glass, *The Occupation of Heather Rose* by Wendy Lill, and *Inside Out* by Pamela Boyd. Bessai's introduction also provides fulsome biocritical information on the playwrights.

    The collection of three plays entitled *Ethnicities: Plays from the New West* (1999) (edited and with an introduction by Anne Nothof) reflects the multicultural diversity of Western Canada: in *House of Sacred Cows* by Padma Viswanathan, ethnicity is performed through the brief occupation by an Indian student of a room in a co-op in a Western Canadian city. In *Mom, Dad, I'm Living with a White Girl* by Marty Chan, the Chinese-Canadian protagonist is caught between two different cultures. *Elephant Wake* by Jonathan Christenson and Joey Tremblay is a lament for a disappearing French culture on the Prairies.

5. A collection of works from a new play festival; e.g., *NeXtFest Anthologies I* and *II* (with funding for the publications provided by Syncrude). Needless to say, private funding is also a determining factor in publication choices since government funding is notoriously sparse, particularly in Alberta.

6. Recommendation of a playwright by a board member who finds a work to be socially, politically, and/or aesthetically engaging; e.g., Chris Craddock's trilogy about teen substance abuse, *Naked at School* (2001); and Lyle Victor Albert's monologues addressing the hazards of shaving and of

life in general encountered by a young man with cerebral palsy, entitled *Scraping the Surface* (2000).

7. Historically important playwrights, such as Wilfred Watson in a collection entitled *Plays of the Iron Bridge or the Autobiography of Tom Horror* (1989); and Elsie Park Gowan, in an extensively annotated collection entitled *The Hungry Spirit* (1992), edited by Moira Day.

8. Unsolicited manuscripts—almost never.

Most of the plays published by NeWest have their origins in Alberta and Saskatchewan, simply because these are typically the ones that board members have seen in the theatre. The first play in the Prairie Play Series was by Rudy Wiebe, not then or even now noted for his plays. Entitled *Far as the Eye Can See* (1977), it was developed with Toronto's Theatre Passe Muraille and was included in Diane Bessai's research into Canadian docudrama. The second play, *Davin the Politician* (1979) by Ken Mitchell, focused on nineteenth-century Saskatchewan politics—a particular interest of board member Don Kerr. It was later included in a collection of three of Mitchell's plays entitled *Rebels in Time* (1991). The remaining two titles in the collection have a more international focus: *Gone the Burning Sun* enacts the life of Norman Bethune (1890-1939), who left Canada to do groundbreaking medical work in the revolutionary struggles of Spain and China during the1930s; and *The Great Cultural Revolution,* set in China during the 1960s, focuses on a playwright who faces persecution because of his political statements. Byrna Barclay's *The Room with Five Walls: The Trials of Victor Hoffman* (2004) is an expressionist account of the 1967 Shell Lake massacre in Saskatchewan, the notorious murder of a family of nine by a schizophrenic young man who relives the event many years later as a nightmare in his cell—not an easy play to read or to publish, but one that examines important issues of guilt and responsibility.

Diane Bessai, now professor emerita at the University of Alberta, continues as series editor for NeWest's Prairie Plays, and other board members, including Anne Nothof and Don Kerr, have proposed and edited play texts for the series. Bessai's original intention was to build a representation of regional plays for university study. These have included NeWest's third play publication, *Prairie Performance* (1980), a collection of one-act plays by Elsie Park Gowan, Frank Moher, Gwen Pharis Ringwood, Joanna M. Glass, W. O. Mitchell, Ken Mitchell, Gordon Pengilly, and Wilfred Watson—all prescient editorial choices; *Showing West: Three Prairie Docu-dramas* (1982), including *Medicare!* by Rex Deverell; and *Prairie Performance II: Eight Plays for Young People* (1984), edited by Joyce Doolittle.

Perhaps because their function was primarily educational, most of these collections included introductions by the editor and bibliographies. Individual play publications may be introduced by the playwright or editor and supplemented with a biography and playography. Brad Fraser has typically introduced his own works with provocative and entertaining accounts of their production history, such as this excerpt from the introduction to *Poor Super Man* (1995):

> At that point, I will start the battle that I've had to fight every time a show is produced. I will charge homophobia. I will threaten legal action. I will enlist the support of my fellow artists. I will pull out reviews and box office reports for all my other plays in order to justify their existence. I will do everything in my power to be granted the same rights and considerations as anyone else. (5–6)

NeWest is loyal to its authors, even contentious ones; however, authors are not always loyal to a press. Opportunities for wider distribution, higher royalties, and better connections inevitably lure some away.

Despite the efforts of more prolific play publishers such as Talonbooks in Vancouver and Playwrights Canada Press in Toronto, and despite the modest efforts of NeWest to represent prairie playwrights, the sad reality is that very few new plays are published, even when they are produced. Not all make for good reading—and this is another consideration when making the hard decisions about where to put very limited financial and production resources. And most play texts go out of print very quickly, once the university library shelves have been stocked and the performance fades from memory—which is, ironically, the very reason why they should be kept alive in print.

Works Cited

Albert, Lyle Victor. *Scraping the Surface*. Edmonton: NeWest Press, 2000.

Belke, David. *The Minor Keys*. Edmonton: NeWest Press, 2000.

Bessai, Diane. "Introduction." *NeWest Plays by Women*. Edmonton: NeWest Press, 1987. vii-xvii.

——, ed. *Prairie Performance: A Collection of Short Plays*. Edmonton: NeWest Press, 1980.

Bessai, Diane, and Don Kerr, eds. *Showing West: Three Prairie Docu-dramas*. Edmonton: NeWest Press, 1982.

Craddock, Chris. *Naked at School: Three Plays for Teens*. Edmonton: NeWest Press, 2001.

Doolittle, Joyce. *Prairie Performance II: Eight Plays for Young People*. Edmonton: NeWest Press, 1984.

Fraser, Brad. "Introduction." *Poor Super Man*. Edmonton: NeWest Press, 1995. 1–6.

——. *The Wolf Plays*. Edmonton: NeWest Press, 1993.

——. *Unidentified Human Remains and the True Nature of Love*. Edmonton: NeWest Press, 1996.

——. *Love and Human Remains*. Edmonton: NeWest Press, 1996.

——. *Martin Yesterday*. Edmonton: NeWest Press, 1998.

——. *Snake in Fridge*. Edmonton: NeWest Press, 2001.

French, David. *Salt-Water Moon*. Toronto: Playwrights Canada Press, 1985.

Gowan, Elsie Park. *The Hungry Spirit*. Ed. Moira Day. Edmonton: NeWest Press, 1992.

Lemoine, Stewart. *A Teatro Trilogy*. Ed. Anne Nothof. Edmonton: NeWest Press, 2004.

——. *At the Zenith of the Empire*. NeWest Press, 2007.

Massing, Conni. *The Aberhart Summer*. Edmonton: NeWest Press, 1999.

Mitchell, Ken. *Davin the Politician*. Edmonton: NeWest Press, 1979.

——. *Rebels in Time*. Edmonton: NeWest Press, 1991.

NeWest Press website: www.newestpress.com

Nothof, Anne. ed. *Ethnicities: Plays from the New West*. Edmonton: NeWest Press, 1999.

Pengilly, Gordon. *Metastasis and Other Plays*. Edmonton, NeWest Press, 2009.

Pirot, Steve, ed. *Nextfest Anthology II: Plays from the Syncrude Next Generation Arts Festival 2001-2005*. Edmonton: NeWest Press, 2006.

Pollock, Sharon. *Blood Relations and Other Plays*. Ed. Anne Nothof. Edmonton: NeWest Press, 2002.

Reaney, James. *Colours in the Dark*. Vancouver: Talonbooks, 1969.

Stirling, Glenda, ed. *NeXtFest Anthology: Plays from the Syncrude NeXt Generation Arts Festival 1996-2000*. Edmonton: NeWest Press, 2000.

Watson, Wilfred. *Plays of the Iron Bridge or the Autobiography of Tom Horror*. Edmonton: NeWest Press, 1989.

Wiebe, Rudy. *Far as the Eye Can See*. Edmonton: NeWest Press, 1977.

Theatres, Theatre Companies and Dramaturgical Centres

Wagonstage in a Park near You!
40 Years of Western Canadian Plays[1]

JOHN POULSEN AND KATHLEEN FOREMAN

> *It is a bright sunny afternoon in a Calgary park. The lumbering,*
> *Ford Econoline Wagonstage van drives across the grass and stops*
> *beneath a large poplar tree. Five young actors burst out and begin*
> *to assemble sets, props, and costumes. Children appear, first in small*
> *groups then in long, boisterous lines trailing lunch bags and swim*
> *towels. The actors settle the crowd. Introductions are quick, and the*
> *show "What Scares Me" transports the audience and actors for the*
> *next 45 minutes. In one scene, a giant child sits on a lumpy couch*
> *that seems to heave and grumble beneath him. The audience begins*
> *to shout warnings while he tries to convince himself that he is not*
> *afraid, that there is nothing to be afraid of. Cries from the audience*
> *build to a crescendo as the giant child is devoured by the ravenous*
> *couch. After the show the children and actors laugh together, sharing*
> *stories about scary things. As the van is packed, children disperse*
> *enacting favourite scenes and echoing memorable lines.*

1   This article is part of a larger work regarding the history and meaning of the Wagon-
    stage Project that is currently under development by co-editors Kathleen Foreman
    and Clem Martini, with contributor John Poulsen. Publication is expected in 2012.

Dedicated to the creation and presentation of new Western Canadian plays, Wagonstage, a Theatre for Young Audiences summer stock touring troupe, has been a joint project of the University of Calgary's Department of Drama and the City of Calgary Department of Arts and Culture (Recreation) for forty years. The partnership that began in 1971 has continued every summer since and is an enduring example of civic programming partnered with post-secondary education. The Wagonstage plays are written and directed by theatre professionals and acted by undergraduate drama students, with production and touring support from the Department of Drama and the City of Calgary. Wagonstage performs in parks, playgrounds, day camps, and public plazas, presenting over seventy performances during a summer season. The majority of the plays produced for Wagonstage have been commissioned from local playwrights and the rest have been collective creations imagined into existence through the collaborative energies of the director and cast. As a result of its long and committed history, Wagonstage has been responsible for the commissioning, creation, workshopping, and first production of dozens of original Theatre for Young Audiences (TYA) playscripts. Many of these scripts have gone on to professional production throughout Western Canada and beyond.

HISTORY

In many ways, Wagonstage grew out of two phenomenally successful and vital theatre movements in Western Canada during the 1960s and 1970s: Theatre for Young Audiences and post-secondary Drama Education. Theatre for Young Audiences (TYA) is a relatively recent phenomenon in the grand scope of theatre history. Doolittle and James (2009) suggest in the *Canadian Encyclopedia* that TYA, in the sense of professional actors creating and performing theatre specifically designed for children, began less than one hundred years ago in Moscow. In Canada, TYA appears to have sprung up as an organic part of the new professional theatre scene developing across Canada after World War II. Toronto became home to many of the first significant English-Canadian theatres devoted to doing new work. The first important professional emergence of TYA in that city was marked by the 1966 debut of the Lorraine Kimsa Theatre for Young People (formerly the Young People's Theatre) to create "professional productions of the highest quality—classic or contemporary—from Canada and around the world, written especially for children and their families" (Lorraine Kimsa, 2009). However, Western Canada had already pioneered professional theatre for children over a decade earlier: the Holiday Theatre of Vancouver, founded in 1953, was the first TYA group in Canada.

Over the 1960s and 1970s, TYA performing troupes continued to flourish on the west coast and across the Prairies either as subsidiaries of regional theatres or as completely distinct companies. Often the links between producing innovative theatre for children and new Canadian and local work that reflected back the concerns, people, and issues of the communities in which the companies were centered were surprisingly close. Again in Vancouver, the Green Thumb Players were founded in 1975 with a mandate to "produce plays for the local community with a focus on entertaining children" (Green Thumb, 2009). In Saskatchewan, the connection between serving the local community while serving its children was even more explicit; the Globe Theatre in Regina, Saskatchewan's oldest and most influential regional theatre, began as a TYA company touring productions of Brian Way scripts in the late 1960s. Way (1923-2006), a British playwright and pioneer of theatre in education, believed his plays "ought to be performed in the round, for specific age groups limited in number, with professional actors capable of interacting with the children. He believed the plays should be entertaining, as well as informative" ("Way, Brian," 2009). His theories and practice helped to revolutionize Canadian approaches towards child and youth drama at a critical stage of growth and expansion in the educational and professional theatre systems.

A similar pattern emerged in both northern and southern Alberta during the 1960s and 1970s. While Edmonton's flagship Citadel Theatre featured much of the standard classical and commercial fare of most regional theatres, its touring educational subsidiary, Citadel on Wheels/Wings, had a more intriguing production history both in terms of community outreach and presenting new or recent Canadian plays. Perkins (2009) writes that between 1968 and 1985, Wheels/Wings "performed 55 plays (65% of them Canadian) in Alberta and the Northwest Territories (making the Citadel the first professional theatre to fly north of the Arctic Circle)." A second TYA company, Chinook Touring Theatre, founded by Brian Paisley and Ti Hallas in Fort St. John, British Columbia, in 1978 "to open an archway to accessible theatre adventures by and for the community" moved to Edmonton in 1980 and changed the face of the summer Canadian theatre scene by founding the Edmonton Fringe Festival in 1982 (Fletcher, 2004). Renamed Fringe Theatre Adventures in 1995, the company still runs the Festival while sponsoring a season of TYA plays for school and family audiences during the winter months (Fringe Theatre Adventures, 2009).

Calgary's record over the same period was equally impressive. Theatre Calgary, the Citadel's regional counterpart, created a TYA company called Caravan Theatre. As "established by Don Shipley in 1970," Caravan "flourished under David Lander (1971 75)" before being transformed in 1977 into the Stage Coach Players under Rick McNair (Doolittle and Day, 2009). The Stage Coach Players, in turn, became the predecessor of Quest Theatre; founded by Rick McNair and Duval Lang in 1984, Quest is still going strong, having performed for over a million young people all across western Canada (Theatre

Calgary, 2009). Alberta Theatre Projects (ATP), now a major theatre in Calgary, traced a similar route to that of Regina's Globe by beginning in 1972 to present "children's theatre, with a mandate to present new Canadian plays emphasizing prairie concerns and bring history alive for children" (Alberta Theatre Projects, 2009). A third company, Keith Johnstone's Loose Moose Theatre, founded in 1977, moved into children's theatre in 1978 as an extension of its original mandate to promote "innovation and excellence in improvisational theatre" (Loose Moose, "About Us," 2009). Based on "classic children's stories that are interpreted and brought to life on stage," their children's plays "start from a basic scenario and are developed through a collective process through to the final new scripted plays" (Loose Moose, "Theatre for Kids," 2009). Most performers at the Loose Moose, "[...] come from [the] volunteer program where individuals help out with various tasks [...] in exchange [for] training and experience in improvisation" (Loose Moose, "Volunteers," 2009).

Wagonstage, then, with its dedication to serving the community with new work that reflected that community's experiences and concerns while creating professional theatre specifically designed for children, was very much part of an explosion of exciting and innovative new theatre across the Western provinces during the 1960s and 1970s that often combined TYA and community mandates.

Where Wagonstage has been unique right from the start, however, has been in its strategic attempt to serve those ends within the context of a pre-professional employment experience for post-secondary students trying to make the difficult transition from an educational to a professional environment. Wagonstage quite consciously grew out of—and continues to grow out of—the recognition that theatre students had to have effective TYA training and experience integrated into their post-secondary education if they were to be properly prepared to seize the emerging professional opportunities in the field, no less in the local community than in the larger national and international scene.

In its pursuit of that mandate, Wagonstage quickly forged dynamic partnerships that have proved uniquely long-term and stable, not only with city recreation but with the new university that was also emerging in Calgary in the mid-1960s, and its dynamic new programming in post-secondary Drama Education.

EARLY YEARS AND SURVIVAL

The University of Calgary first threw open its doors as a university independent from the University of Alberta in Edmonton in 1966, and its new Department of Drama opened at the same time. The department expanded rapidly and by 1967 "students could major in Drama Education taking such courses as Creative Dramatics, Theatre for Young Audiences, Early Childhood Drama Education, and Secondary School Production" (Poulsen and Foreman, 2004, 8). Drama 362: Theatre for Young Audiences, a full-year, full-credit course began to be offered to students in the late 1960s. Like the rest of the curriculum (as originally conceived by Joyce Doolittle), the course was intended to be strongly focused on experiential learning, and the current syllabus continues to reflect that mandate by including an exploration of international and Canadian TYA history, study and performance of published TYA scripts, as well as research, creation, and performance of collectively created scripts. Although it was not a requirement for Wagonstage cast members until 1991, students interested in working with Wagonstage were encouraged to take the TYA course.

The Wagonstage project evolved during this time of professional TYA development and curricular expansion because theatre educators at the drama department realized that there was a need for TYA playwrights, directors, actors, and designers with interests and abilities in this emerging area of theatrical endeavour. The founder of the University of Calgary Department of Drama, Victor Mitchell, recalled:

> Around 1966, when I perceived the need to create jobs for drama students during the summer months, a summer parks program was conceived as one way to create relevant jobs. Engineering students could work on the roads. Drama students should be able to work in theatre. My original idea was to duplicate a settler's wagon and have it towed by a horse into the parks. It grew from its primitive form with the direction of Phil McCoy, who took it over. (Mitchell, 2006)

Starting in the 1960s, Brian Way's plays, theories, and activities, as expressed in his book *Development Through Drama* (1967) and further reinforced through his frequent visits to Canada—he emigrated in 1983 and made Canada his permanent home until his death in 2006—influenced drama curricula in Canada and contributed to the acceptance of theatre-in-education as an exciting new collaborative venture redrawing the traditional boundaries between the educational system and the professional theatre. Another likely influence during this time of TYA growth and the inception of Wagonstage was Richard Courtney (1927-1997), "drama teacher, theatre scholar, leading international expert in children's drama and Professor of Drama from 1971 to 1974 at the University of Calgary. While in Calgary, Courtney also directed theatre and served as President of the Canadian Child and Youth Drama Association as well as being an advisor to the Minister of Culture, Andre Fortier" ("Courtney, Richard," 2009).

However, it was Victor Mitchell (head of Drama), Joyce Doolittle (producer and director), and Philip McCoy (director) who conceptualized and manifested the model of partnership with the City of Calgary Recreation Department that has provided the strong community outreach.

The City of Calgary, like most major centres in Canada, offers summer day camps for children. These week-long recreation programs include a mix of physical and creative activities. When the City wanted to improve Calgary's cultural capital in the early 1970s, the Wagonstage project was an excellent fit for its summer camps. Wagonstage's mobility also enabled the troupe to travel to every community in the city, regardless of social or economic profile. Over the years, Wagonstage has continued to build steadily on both those assets simultaneously to become a regular part of Calgary's roving summer festival scene. Beginning with its traditional opening performance at Canada Day on Prince's Island Park, Wagonstage also offers weekly performances at Olympic Plaza in the city centre, as well as performances at the Folk Festival and Heritage Day Festival. Wagonstage, after four decades of continuous work, has become an important homegrown renewable resource that educates, entertains, and makes theatre accessible to a whole spectrum of the Calgary community beyond the conventional theatre house or subscription season.

Yet despite the success and benefits of the Wagonstage project within the Calgary community, it has always needed champions to ensure its continuation. As the petroleum-driven economy of Calgary has boomed and burst over the years, Wagonstage, as a unique project, has come under threat of budget cuts many, many times. In 1974, the touring troupe had five actors, plus a stage manager, and three plays in its repertoire (Chadbourne, July 24, 1974, 23). Reflecting budget restrictions and rising costs over the years, the 2011 troupe, by contrast, consisted of three actors, one actor/stage manager, and one play.

There is no doubt that the enduring faith of its supporters in Wagonstage's ability—regardless of size—every year to produce quality children's theatre that is entertaining, informative, interactive, and accessible to young (and not-so-young) audiences in every community within the city's boundaries is one of the main reasons it has prevailed for almost forty years. Nor can the inspired and tireless work of individuals from both the University of Calgary and City of Calgary be underestimated. Joyce Doolittle, professor emerita of Drama and Wagonstage director and project coordinator for many years, has suggested that one key to its survival is that it continues to connect people through "live" experiences in a technological age that seems to leave fewer and fewer opportunities for face-to-face encounters of that kind:

> In an age when many children spend untold hours with electronic images, the live human voice and body figure less and

less in their life experiences. Live theatre is unique in that the audience is essential to the experience. It is one of mankind's oldest successful interactive events. (Doolittle, 2003)

Wagonstage has also cultivated a unique relationship with its audience over its long history as audience members have become actors, who have become directors and playwrights, who have become parents who bring their children to Wagonstage every summer. The best advocates to speak about the impact of the Wagonstage experience on behalf of the children of Calgary may be the Wagonstage alumni. Michael Green, artistic director of One Yellow Rabbit Performance Theatre and Wagonstage actor, director, and playwright, explains that "for many children in summer programs and summer camps throughout the city, the Wagonstage performances are their first exposure to the performing arts" (Green, 2003). Duval Lang, artistic director of Quest Theatre and Wagonstage director agrees:

I am one of the many theatre artists that have benefited from participating in a Wagonstage summer experience [...] Prominent Calgary actors, directors, stage managers, designers, playwrights are all proud to list a Wagonstage credit on their resumes. (Lang, 2003)

Numerous reinventions and innovations have also occurred over Wagonstage's long history to encourage renewal and resourcefulness. For example, significant innovation to the program occurred in 1991, when the Department of Drama and Wagonstage teamed up with the Calgary International Children's Festival.

IMMERSION

The Calgary International Children's Festival (CICF) was founded in 1987 and has become the Wagonstage Project's third partner. The CICF is Canada's largest festival of this kind, performing for more than 60,000 young people and their families every year. The festival defines itself as an "arts experience that sparks imagination, inspires creative thought, encourages cultural understanding, and fosters a lifelong passion for the arts" (Calgary International Children's Festival, 2009). Founding producer JoAnne James states:

I was privileged to travel around the world to select and bring to Canada some of the finest work available for young people. I watched hundreds of productions from dozens of countries [...] Writing and directing plays for children tends to be disregarded by theatre professionals and academics, who assume that truly gifted artists will dedicate themselves to creating works for adults. What critics of the genre often fail to realize is the unique talent and perceptiveness necessary for the artists who specialize in Theatre for Young Audiences. These contemporary artists are gifted individuals who have made a deliberate choice to work with young people. (James, 2006, 1)

In 1991, the Department of Drama was invited to collaborate in the Calgary International Children's Festival by offering the TYA course as an intensive 6-week spring session course that included one week of direct participation in the festival. By 2009, this week had evolved into a super-charged international experience for the Wagonstage performers that has had a direct impact on the summer company's process. Through exposing Wagonstage performers to an advanced understanding of TYA and the creation of new work, not to mention some of the best TYA in the world, CICF has enriched and extended new script development in the company.

First, the students see as many performances as they can. Second, they perform at the festival; they have on-site roving performer shifts. Third, the Dean of Fine Arts and the Fine Arts Associates[2] sponsor three workshops with international artists to be attended by the students, as well as being open to public registration. Fourth, students attend "The Colloque," a conversational gathering for the festival artists and facilitated by the festival producer and/ or university faculty. The artists talk about their work and lives in the world of international TYA and the students are encouraged to ask questions. Wagonstage alumnus Braden Griffiths remembers the CICF experience:

> The Children's Festival is the best theatre I have ever seen to this day. Before I attended the Children's Festival I thought kid's theatre was like it is on TV, this 'baby talk garbage.' There was a production of *Moby Dick* [Theatre Triewerk Calgary International Children's Festival Brochure 2003] that a German company did; they had a cello and a black sheet and it was deep, hardcore, almost silent theatre. I was blown away. It was far better than anything I'd seen. It really opened my eyes. (Griffiths, 2007)

2   The Faculty of Fine Arts Associates is a group of patrons and friends of fine arts that makes a yearly donation to help important projects and fund scholarships and research grants for special fine arts activities (email from Ann Calvert to K. Foreman, November 23, 2009).

The CICF festival/course experience enriches the Wagonstage script development process in several ways. It is like walking into an archive of state-of-the-art TYA. The students experience productions from around the globe with a wide variety of content (traditional stories to current issue-based plays) and theatre forms (puppets, storytelling, and mime, to musicals and clowning). For example, the students may see a British production of a classic pantomime or fairy tale, or a contemporary script from a Danish company that focuses on friendship, or a Canadian one-woman show based on the life of Harriet Tubman, written and performed by the playwright.

As young artists, their experiences are enriched through interactions with the international artists. Not only do the students experience TYA as exciting, modern, and relevant theatre, but they also realize that creating TYA requires commitment and training. These theatre professionals become the students' role models and mentors. As playwrights, performers, and producers of original work, the international artists demonstrate their ability to wear the many hats of a TYA professional. They reveal how meaningful narratives, regardless of source (traditional, issue-based, or personal), can be transformed into TYA scripts that have global appeal.

The CICF experience and TYA course work set up the Wagonstage cast for their own process of new script development for the shows that they will tour during the summer.

CREATION

The scripts produced by Wagonstage may be examined from two perspectives: those originating from the playwrights (commissioned plays) and those originating from the director in conjunction with the cast (collective creations). For example, there have been occasions when the Wagonstage project has been approached to develop a new work for a specific purpose (*The Flying Tortoise*, adaptation of a story by Tololwa Mollol, International Children's Literature and the Fin de Siècle Conference, 1999) or has commissioned a new play for a specific celebration (*Gilly Goes West* by Donna Tunney, Alberta's Centennial, 2004).[3] However, the workshop process has been standard practice for all plays.

Playwrights usually value the workshop process because it often gives them the kind of focused feedback they need to generate another draft of the play before the formal rehearsal process gets underway. As an example, several weeks before the rehearsal process begins, the playwright, director, and actors come together for a two-and-one-half-day workshop. The first day begins with a read-through and then a discussion of the play. Questions are asked and answered by the playwright, the actors, and the director. A sec-

---

3   See photograph of a performance of *Gilly Goes* West in the colour insert (photo 16).

tion of the play (usually the part leading to the climax) is examined in depth, memorized, and put on its feet. A discussion following the run of the section examines the "who, what, where, and when" of the play. The actors then study aspects of the characters, such as their motivations, consistency, attitudes to others, and individual throughlines. The group inspects the arc of the story, the humour, the expected impact on the audience, and production requirements for a touring situation. The first day ends with an analysis of another section. Based on the information from the performances and discussions, the next day's schedule is set. Day two begins with putting the new section up on its feet, followed by discussion. Any changes made by the playwright overnight are examined and blended into the work. If possible, a third section is examined in depth, memorized, and put on its feet. The final half-day of the workshop is devoted to a run-through of the entire play. This is usually a mix of reading the sections not previously worked, combined with a performance of the bits that have been workshopped. The workshop gives the playwright an evolving sense of the play in action that includes a sharper awareness of how the play fits this particular cast of actors. The playwright then has a few weeks to mull over the ramifications of the workshop and to create another draft of the play before rehearsals begin.

The director-initiated collective creations often embrace an initial workshop exploration as well. The purpose of the workshop is to generate material that eventually becomes the performance. Collective creation workshops can begin with a variety of material. Some begin with only a concept or a theme. Either way, great things rapidly develop out of small beginnings. Chantelle Lomness, a Wagonstage alumnus, answering a questionnaire for the Wagonstage's thirty-fifth anniversary, reflected on Wagonstage's influence in her life. She credits the strong, creative ensemble work at the CICF as an important influence on the Wagonstage process in this regard:

> Having the chance to meet and train with some amazing people at the Children's Festival. Working in an ensemble to collectively come up with an idea/storyline, come up with a play, work it, perform it, and love it. (Lomness, 2006)

Some summers, the collectively created scripts are developed through the historic *commedia dell'arte* improvisational model that utilizes a list of scene titles (for example: *The Meeting, The Problem,* etc.). In *commedia dell'arte* style, the cast improvises within this plot structure. Rudlin suggests that the scenario for the *commedia* players was "literally 'that which is on the scenery,' i.e. pinned up backstage. All it consisted of is a plot summary, the bare bones of who does what when" (1997, 51).

The Wagonstage director may lay out the structure of a workshop that includes improvisation preceded and followed by discussion. The improvisations are refined to fit the production's vision. The director may have been the initiator of the process, but eventually the play's creation depends on the group's developing vision. After each improvisation the director clarifies what fit with the concept and how the scene could be "tweaked" to be improved. As the process continues, suggestions for improvement or content begin to come from the cast.

Recording of the emerging script is done in a variety of ways. The actors might say the lines they have just improvised while the director writes them down to be revised and put in script form. The script then undergoes a formal rehearsal process where the newly created script is treated as if it were a script from a respected playwright. The original *commedia dell'arte* productions were not formally scripted and, over the years, there have been Wagonstage plays that similarly have never been formally recorded. On one hand this has allowed the Wagonstage cast to keep developing the performance over the summer run, adjusting to audiences and performing conditions. On the other hand, some wonderful new play development and creative work has been lost to the mists of time.

The Wagonstage creation and rehearsal period introduces the student performers to professional practices of script development in an intensive, interactive, and immersive process. This experience is designed to encourage their investment and ownership of the new play that will be premiered, tested, evolved, and refined throughout the seventy-performance tour engaging young audiences in every community in the city of Calgary.

REFINEMENT

Continual refinement of the new scripts is integral to the Wagonstage experience. The opportunity to perform a new work two or three times a day encourages conversations about "what worked" and "what didn't" as a daily occurrence. When the tour begins the actors are charged with the responsibility for maintaining the quality of the performance and encouraged to refine as they work. Periodic visits by the director occur throughout the summer, so adjustments are continual. Whether the play is written or created, the actors have a sense of ownership of the material and continue to discuss the ideas and refine the style and skills that make the play better over the course of the summer tour. One undeniable catalyst of script refinement is the audience. Wagonstage's audiences are as honest as any artist could hope for … children. If the play is boring they will wander off or announce loudly to family and friends that they'd really rather go play on the swings. If the story captivates them and the performances are energetic, they will participate fully, at times requiring restraint from parents.

This demanding audience encourages refinement of the new work, as well as continual skill building as the play is tested in a wide variety of environments. Wagonstagers improve their vocal clarity and volume in response to the challenges of working in outdoor settings, such as traffic noise (sometimes the only place to set up is beside a busy intersection), lawn mowers (parks workers are often on tight schedules and cannot hold off mowing for forty-five minutes), audiences coming in late or audiences leaving early, and the ever-present prairie wind. They discover the realities of the life of a TYA performer. The adage "the show must go on" encapsulates the Wagonstage experience. Rarely is a show cancelled as the performers' sense of commitment to their audiences and responsibility to the quality of the show continues to deepen. In response to challenges, the performers simply improve.[4]

IMPACT ON PLAYWRITING

Believing in their own effectiveness as theatre makers and performers is an important aspect of the Wagonstage experience that has had significant long-term ramifications for the theatre careers of many of its alumni. Wagonstage alumni Katie Sanders comments:

> I was telling a friend out here [Toronto], you know, you do these
> things like Wagonstage, and then you move on and you never
> really stop to think about them. But when I did, I realized that
> I really owe almost every single aspect of my career, in one way
> or another, to Wagonstage. (Sanders, 2007)

The troupe undeniably develops a deep understanding of how a theatre ensemble creates, develops, and refines new work. This, in turn, has led some Wagonstage alumni to become the founding members of professional theatre companies (One Yellow Rabbit, Quest Theatre, Monster Theatre) that have excelled in the creation of new Canadian scripts. Jeff Gladstone of Monster Theatre[5] suggests that as a result of his and his brother's experience with Wagonstage, their "first professional theatre gig," they both "continue to write and tour Children's shows and other shows to this day!" (Gladstone, 2006).

It is the vital combination of plays commissioned from local playwrights and plays created by these young performers out of their experiences growing up

4   See photographs of Wagonstage performances from 2006 and 2008 in the colour insert (photos 15, 17, and 18).

5   Founded in 2000, "Monster Theatre is one of the Canadian Fringe Circuits premiere acts, proving themselves year after year with sold-out performances, 5 star reviews and hit shows. (5 Star reviews; Winnipeg, Saskatoon, Edmonton, Vancouver Fringe Festivals)" www.monstertheatre.com/11356.html.

in Calgary, mixed with imagination and refined by professional direction, that ensures that the experiences of Calgarians are valued and raised in celebration of the community. Not every Wagonstage alumnus becomes a playwright or creator of original work, but those who have gained vital experience through the workshop process and refining the play over a summer of performance. The benefits of the Wagonstage experience ripple through the creative development of the playwrights, directors, designers, and casts of the project, but perhaps do not stop there. Wagonstage alumnus and award-winning playwright Clem Martini comments that

> Wagonstage is absolutely unique in that it offers superb enter-tainment and an introduction to theatre for this city's young audiences, as well as a bit of a hands-on clinic in how to create theatre. Young people can, and often do, talk to the cast about the process of developing a new work. For youngsters who are on the verge of making their own career and vocational choices, the knowledge that theatre doesn't have to be something created elsewhere, by someone else, but can be created here by local artists, can be of vital importance. (Martini, 2003)

Wagonstage alumni that have gone on to work and publish as professional playwrights include Clem Martini, JoAnne James, Alexandria Patience, Lana Skauge, Michael Green, Trevor Schmidt, and Rebecca Northan. New works by non-alumni playwrights Sandy Paddick, Rose Scollard, Zina Barnieh, and Rob Moffat have also been developed as part of the project in recent years.

The number of professional and student participants over four decades is significant and has enabled Wagonstage to build a profile that extends beyond the city of Calgary while remaining true to its original community and TYA mandate. Heather Inglis, artistic director of Theatre Yes in Alberta and dramaturge for the Saskatchewan Playwrights' Centre, comments, "I have worked in theatre for young audiences for the past ten years and I have rarely encountered a program with as much integrity as Wagonstage [...] By investing in Wagonstage the city has created a unique opportunity for youth and adults to come together in a common forum, which celebrates healthy minds, hearts and families. Calgary is to be commended for investing in its young people" (Inglis, 2003).

Wagonstage brings theatre to communities and helps to create commu-nities in which the arts are promoted and valued. It allows children to see high-calibre theatre created and performed by artists who are part of their community. Wagonstage has flourished for forty years, dedicated to the creation of new plays for young audiences. So, next time you are wandering through a Calgary park on a hot summer day, be warned, a new Canadian play may be coming your way.

Works Cited

Alberta Theatre Projects (ATP). "ATP History." www.atplive.com/AboutATP/atp_history.html (accessed November 5, 2009).

The Calgary International Children's Theatre Festival. "Vision, Mission and Values." www.calgarychildfest.org/info/mission.php (accessed November 5, 2009).

Calvert, Ann. Letter to Kathleen Foreman. November 23, 2009. Email.

Chadbourne, Eugene. "Hoots, howls screams galore at playground." *Calgary Herald*, July 24, 1974: 23.

"Courtney, Richard." www.en.wikipedia.org/wiki/Richard_Courtney (accessed December 30, 2009).

Doolittle, Joyce (Revised Moira Day). "Theatre Calgary." *Canadian Encyclopedia*. Historica-Dominion Institute, 2009. www.thecanadianencyclopedia.com/index.cfm?PgNm=TCE&Params=A1ARTA0011600 (accessed November 5, 2009).

Dolittle, Joyce, with Joanne James. "Theatre for Young Audiences." *Canadian Encyclopedia*. Historica-Dominion Institute, 2009. www.thecanadianencyclopedia.com/index.cfm?PgNm=TCE&Params=A1ARTA0007947 (accessed November 5, 2009).

Doolittle, Joyce. Letter of support for Wagonstage to City of Calgary Parks and Recreation, September 15, 2003. Typescript, Kathleen Foreman Papers. University of Calgary AB.

Fletcher, Jennifer Lind. "History of Chinook Theatre/Fringe Theatre Adventures." *Chinook Theatre/Fringe Theatre Fonds 1978-1997*, University of Alberta, June 21, 2004. www.archive1.macs.ualberta.ca/Findingaids/ChinookFringe/Chinook_Fringe.html (accessed November 5, 2009).

Fringe Theatre Adventures. "2009/2010 Transalta Family Theatre Series." www.fringetheatreadventures.ca/family_theatre_series.php (accessed November 5, 2009).

Gladstone, Jeff. Alumni Questionaire. June, 2006. Typescript. Wagonstage 35th Anniversary file. Wagonstage Papers. Kathleen Foreman, University of Calgary AB.

Green, Michael. Letter of support for Wagonstage to City of Calgary Parks and Recreation, October 16, 2003. Typescript. Kathleen Foreman Papers. University of Calgary AB.

Green Thumb Theatre. "A History of Green Thumb Theatre." www.greenthumb.bc.ca/who.asp?pageid=696 (accessed November 5, 2009).

Griffiths, Braden. Personal interview by Kathleen Foreman, Brian Dorscht, and Clem Martini. April 13, 2007. Typescript. Wagonstage Papers. Kathleen Foreman, University of Calgary AB.

Inglis, Heather. Letter of support for Wagonstage to City of Calgary Parks and Recreation, September 14, 2003. Typescript. Kathleen Foreman Papers. University of Calgary AB.

James, JoAnne. "Unmapped: Exploring the Landscape of Creation in Theatre for Young Audiences." MFA thesis, University of Calgary, 2006.

Lang, Duval. Letter of support for Wagonstage to City of Calgary Parks and Recreation, September 15, 2003. Typescript. Kathleen Foreman Papers. University of Calgary AB.

Lorraine Kimsa Theatre for Young People. "History." www.lktyp.ca/en/about/index. cfm (accessed November 5, 2009).

Lonness, Chantelle. Alumni Questionaire. June, 2006. Typescript. Wagonstage 35th Anniversary file. Wagonstage Papers. Kathleen Foreman, University of Calgary.

Loose Moose Theatre Company. "About Us." www.loosemoose.com/contact.htm (accessed November 5, 2009).

———. "Theatre for Kids." www.loosemoose.com/kids.htm (accessed November 5, 2009).

———. "Volunteers." www.loosemoose.com/volunteers.htm (accessed November 5, 2009).

Martini, Clem. Letter of support for Wagonstage to City of Calgary Parks and Recreation, October 26 2004. Typescript. Kathleen Foreman Papers. University of Calgary AB.

Mitchell, Victor, Personal interview by Kathleen Foreman. May 1, 2006. Typescript. Wagonstage 35th Anniversary file. Wagonstage Papers. Kathleen Foreman, University of Calgary AB.

Monster Theatre. www.monstertheatre.com/11356.html (accessed November 20, 2009).

Perkins, Don. "The Citadel Theatre." *Canadian Encyclopedia.* Historica-Dominion Institute, 2009. www.thecanadianencyclopedia.com/index.cfm?PgNm=TCE&Params=A1AR TA0001631 (accessed November 5, 2009).

Poulsen, J., and K. Foreman. "Alberta: Theatrical Wildfires." *Canadian Drama Mosaic Summer 2004: A Historical Perspective of Canada's Theatre-in-Education.* Ed. Margaret Burke. Vancouver: Calamus Publishing and Theatre/Théâtre Canada, 2004, 7-10.

Rudlin, John. *Commedia dell'Arte, An Actors Handbook.* London: Routledge, 1997.

Sanders, Katherine. Personal interview by Kathleen Foreman. April 25, 2007. Typescript. Wagonstage Papers. Kathleen Foreman, University of Calgary AB.

Theatre Calgary. "Theatre Calgary—History." www.theatrecalgary.com/about/history/ (accessed November 5, 2009).

"Way, Brian." www.en.wikipedia.org/wiki/Brian_Way (accessed November 20, 2009).

Alberta Report vs. *Prairie Report*: The City of God vs. The City of Man on the Canadian Prairies, 1973-2003

MOIRA DAY

I n 1988, award-winning Alberta playwright Frank Moher[1] wrote a contemporary comedy, *Prairie Report*. Premiered at Workshop West Theatre in Edmonton in October of that year,[2] it dealt with a weekly newsmagazine

....

1 Born in Edmonton in 1955, Frank Moher is a prolific editor, playwright, director, actor and teacher/lecturer, arts reviewer, and commentator. His arts writing has been featured nationally in the *Globe and Mail, Saturday Night, National Post,* and *backofthebook.ca,* as well as in *Alberta Report.* He also writes musicals, children's drama, and work for film, television, and radio. Two of his plays, *The Third Ascent* and *Prairie Report,* won Sterling awards in 1988 and 1989 respectively. His most popular play, *Odd Jobs,* first produced at Theatre Network in Edmonton in 1985, was nominated for a Governor General's award and Chalmers award and won the Los Angeles Drama-Logue Award in 1993. It has been produced across Canada and the United States, and internationally in Ireland, New Zealand, and Japan. While Moher has made Gabriola Island in British Columbia his permanent home since the 1980s, many of his stage plays continue to be premiered in Alberta, most recently at Alberta Theatre Projects in Calgary. (See entry on Frank Moher in the *Canadian Theatre Encyclopedia.*)

2 *Prairie Report* was first produced by Workshop West Theatre at the Kaasa Theatre in Edmonton on October 21, 1988, with the following cast: Leona Brausen (**Lois Fawcett**), Jacqueline Dandeneau (**Maria Semchuk**), Tony Eyamie (**Stuart McFadden**), Steven Hilton (**William Coolen**), David Mann (**Dick Bennington**), Wendell Smith (**Simon Kael**), Susan Sneath (**Pauline Brett**), and Michael Spencer-Davis (**Otis Bennington**). It subsequently won the 1989 Sterling award for best new play

A provocative comedy about journalism

PRAIRIE REPORT

Workshop West Theatre

By Frank Moher

October 21 - 30 8 PM

Kaasa Theatre, Jubilee Auditorium

Coarse language warning

Benefactor Sponsor (**ESSO**) IMPERIAL OIL LIMITED

Media Sponsor CBC Radio Edmonton 740

Poster for 1988 production of *Prairie Report*. WORKSHOP WEST ARCHIVES.

that not only focused exclusively on the Canadian Prairies, but was exclusively owned, managed, and published by prairie entrepreneurs. Further, while the magazine is outspokenly conservative in its mandate, the founding editor/publisher, **Dick Bennington**, a hot-tempered newspaperman of the old school, has insisted on hiring and training anyone—regardless of gender, ethnic origin, political stripe, or sexual orientation—who is prepared to work hard, think hard, and commit his or her whole passion and being to the enterprise. As the play opens, the magazine's odd, combustible mix of a news team is facing yet another chronic financial crisis. But this time, to the shock and dismay of everyone, **Bennington**, for all his passion and eloquence, is unable to dissuade the board from selling the magazine to large Eastern Canadian business interests with agendas of their own. One by one, each of the characters, including **Bennington**, is forced to confront the ramifications of "selling out," and what that means in both the larger and more personal senses of that word.

As was customary, Mr. Moher claimed that *Prairie Report* was a work of fiction, and as such was not intended to be a literal depiction of any real-life newsmagazine or person (Moher, *Prairie*, 1990, 13; Morrow, "Soft Spot", October 26, 1989, C1). No one in Alberta believed him, least of all, Ted Byfield,[3] the longtime editor/publisher of the *Alberta Report*, who wrote on November 7, 1988:

---

produced in Edmonton over the 1988/89 season and was later produced at Alberta Theatre Projects in Calgary in October 1989. According to Moher, revised versions of the play were also staged "at Douglas College, New Westminster in 1997 under the title *The Funny Pages*, and at Theatre North West, Prince George, BC in 2000 under the title *Western Edition*" (Moher, 2008). See photographs of the 1988 production of *Prairie Report* in the colour insert (photos 19 and 20).

3   Edward Bartlett "Ted" Byfield was born in Toronto in 1929. After working on newspapers in Washington D.C. and Ontario, he moved to Winnipeg to work for the *Free Press* in 1952. In 1962, he abandoned journalism for teaching in the wake of a radical religious conversion. Moving to Stony Plain near Edmonton in 1968 to found a second school for the Company of Saint John, an Anglican lay order, Byfield returned

One of the penalties you pay as proprietor of the last domesti-
cally owned general news publication in western Canada, is the
necessity of being recurrently 'explained' by the CBC. Twice in
the last couple of years I have been featured on CBC programs
[...] (dangerous ideologue) [...] (religious fanatic). Now I
notice the CBC is prominent among the sponsors [...] of yet
another explanation, this one a stage play about this magazine
called *Prairie Report* where I am once again featured (peevishly
pompous bore.) [...]

   Anyway, there I was the other night, right in front of myself
so to speak at Edmonton's Kaasa Theatre where I appeared at
centre stage as **Dick Bennington**, a man of cultured tones (true
enough), impeccable language (absolutely), and constricted
views (now how can they say that?) [...] At issue is the sale of
this priceless treasure, i.e.: the magazine, to a vicious horror figure, i.e. an eastern businessman [...] In the end, the bag man gets
it and runs it under the nominal direction of my semi-moronic
son [**Otis Bennington**] who has been rendered clueless, oafish,
inarticulate and dazed by the two insurmountable disabilities
that have wrecked his life, they being (a) farming and (b) me.
[...] Both the right and the left are pounded in this play, say
its promoters, an assertion that is exactly half-true. (Byfield,
November 7, 1988, 52)

And those, as Moher was to comment in his own lengthy critique of the
Byfield column two years later, were the *good* things his former employer had
to say about the play. Yet Moher, who had served first as writer, then book editor for the magazine between 1983 and 1986, and been positively reviewed by
the magazine as a playwright, had clearly been perceived by Byfield himself as
one of the magazine's protégés. If Byfield quickly recognized himself as **Bennington** in *Prairie Report*, he also recognized Moher in the sympathetic, leftist

---

to journalism in 1973 with the founding of the *Saint John's Edmonton Report*, intended
by the Company to cover Edmonton news from a religious, conservative perspective. The Byfield family took over the management of the magazine, now renamed
Alberta Report in 1977, and Byfield, as its editor/publisher between 1977-1985, reached
national notice as a powerful conservative voice for Western alienation. Between 1985
and 2003, he remained active with the magazine as a columnist under the editorship
of his sons, Link and Mike Byfield, but his energies went increasingly into writing
and editing a series of books on Alberta history for its centennial year of 2005. He
is currently working as a writer and editor on a series of books documenting the
history of Christianity. He continues to live in Edmonton. (See appendix.)

spokesperson of the play, editor **Pauline Brett**—"(left-wing, and therefore caring, noble, perceptive, honest and courageously outspoken)" (52)—whose relationship with both **Bennington** and the magazine is portrayed in the play as being simultaneously affectionate and critical.

Two reviewers in two cities had seen *Prairie Report*, and its relationships between **Bennington** and the rest of his newsroom staff, including **Brett**, as infused with "genuine affection for journalism as it was practiced in a [*sic*] era gone by" (Nicholls, October 22, 1988, F1) and something of a "wistful valentine to an old-time, grassroots style of journalism" (Morrow, October 27, 1989, F6). Yet, Byfield himself was, if anything, even more scathing in his attack on Moher, and the ideological perspective that **Brett** embodied as Moher's presumed spokesperson, than he was of his own portrayal as **Bennington**. Clearly, to judge by Moher's equally acerbic response in the 1990 preface to the published play, Byfield's suggestion that Moher had little business writing "plays 'to explain' the West to Toronto" from his new home "among the retired millionaires and aging hippies on Gabriola Island in the Georgia Strait" (Byfield, November 7, 1988, 52) was an accusation that still rankled almost two years later. What underlay this final public outburst and parting of ways between former colleagues who each ultimately accused the other of "selling out" the magazine and the hope it represented for the future of the arts in Western Canada?

In some ways, the dispute reflects an older Augustinian conflict between the City of God and the City of Man going back to at least the nineteenth century in Western Canada. Riel was only the first of a stream of populist visionaries eager to find a way to build the Kingdom of God on earth in the new human institutions rising out of the Western Canadian frontier. While both of his Rebellions were short-lived and Riel himself was hanged as a traitor, the early-twentieth-century heirs of his restive Western utopianism—the various farmers' parties and most notably the United Farmers of Alberta (UFA), the socialist CCF, and the right-wing Social Credit—were more long lived and successful as political movements. All these early revolutions and reform movements, with their underlying currents of Christian mysticism or social gospel activism, had profoundly shaped the social, political, and psychic landscapes of the Western provinces by the time a young newspaperman from Ontario, Ted Byfield, arrived in Winnipeg in 1952 to join the *Free Press*.[4]

Though he won a national journalism award in 1957, Byfield had already embarked on an intensive reading of the works of G. K. Chesterton and C. S. Lewis that was to deepen his early formal affiliation with Anglicanism into a radical, life-transforming commitment to Christian service.

---

4   For more on the history of these movements see Friesen (1990).

Subsequently, he became one of the founding members of the Anglican lay order, the Company of the Cross, associated with Saint John's Cathedral in Winnipeg, and left journalism in 1962 to become a teacher of History and French, with a specialization in Canadian history, at the Company's private school for boys. In 1968, he moved to Alberta to help the Order establish a second school near Stony Plain, about an hour's travel from Edmonton. The acquiring of a printing plant in connection with the school's work led to an opportunity for the Company, and Byfield in particular, to combine a love for journalism, religion, and the prairie region into a unique institution: a weekly newsmagazine loosely modelled along the lines of *"Time Magazine,* [...] *Newsweek* and *U.S. News"*(Bennett et al., November 7, 1973, 1a) that (1) would supply readers with more concise, accurate, reflective reportage of the people, events, and issues of the region than a daily newspaper could and (2) would ask readers consciously to consider the everyday world around them through an informed religious, conservative, and regional lens.

Thus, on November 7, 1973, *Saint John's Edmonton Report* was born: publisher and spokesman, Keith Bennett; senior editors and founders, Gordon Dewar and Ted Byfield. *Saint John's Edmonton Report* was consciously designed to be a subversive force right from the start: one that questioned not only centralist assumptions about the regions, but also modern and postmodern assumptions about life. Week after week it would point out to its readers the absurdities in the liberal, centralist, and modern lens through which they were usually being asked to view both their spiritual and geopolitical region. And it could do so, subtly, regularly, and accessibly, precisely because it was using the popular media form. As Byfield commented in an address to the Company of the Cross in 1976:

> Effective propaganda in the print media must be subtle. It's the implied life-style, the inferable values, the unsubstantiated moral assumption, that gets through. That's how the media works in any cause, Christian or anti-Christian. No, we do not have a cross on the cover. What we put on the cover is designed to entice people into the magazine. What matters is not that we look Christian, but that we are Christian. (quoted in Paquin, 1991)

If the full life of the city was what enticed people to read the magazine, then the full life of the city was what it had to mirror. By June 1974 the *Report* had made two important decisions in that regard: firstly, to move the publishing plant into Edmonton from the rural reaches of Stony Plain with the declared intent of seeing if its ascetic, communal brand of Christianity could still flourish in a bustling urban environment (Bennett, June 10, 1974, 1a); secondly, to expand its initial sections on People, Economy, Government, Schools, and the Faith to include Sports, Law, Science and, significantly, the Arts:

> The necessity of what will be called *The Arts* section is obvi-
> ous. Edmonton has an unusually fertile interest in the theatre,
> a good tradition in music, a fair range of authors, active art and
> photo clubs, and even a fledgling movie business. (Bennett,
> March 7, 1974, 1a)

The magazine's unique regional/religious focus gave its arts coverage a distinct "house brand" tone that steadily developed over the Bennett years from 1973 to 1977 and reached its most expansive under Ted Byfield's editorship from 1977 to 1985. "What is to be the attitude," Bennett inquired, "of a Christian publication covering, say, the X-rated films being shown on television, or sex shops operating in the downtown area, or the sale of dirty magazines, or the prosecution of night clubs for less than legal floor shows?" Reasoning that moral outrage would serve no purpose with a secular audience, Bennett declared that the magazine would instead subvert and reform through the use of ironic humour. "'The Devil,' said Martin Luther, 'cannot bear scorn.' The person who laughs proves without knowing it that he has resisted the permeation of the modern myth" (Bennett, January 11, 1974, 1a).

Heedful of the spiritual welfare of its audience, the magazine's reviewers, at least during the Bennett years, were never wholly comfortable with nudity, violence, the avant-garde, or alternative sexualities in public art. They deplored the "glorification of homosexuality" in contemporary drama ("Fag Fad," March 22, 1976, 28), and archly asked how many marriages had collapsed as a result of the continuing popularity of *A Doll's House* in contemporary performance (Byfield, November 17, 1975, 30–32). Nonetheless, acknowledging with "critic Father M. Owen Lee" that "'some decadent art has cast an almost theological light on the mysteries of suffering and sin'" (Slay, February 14, 1977, 36), the reviewers continued earnestly to interrogate the world and the flesh as they found them in public art and culture, often combining philosophical speculation, journalistic investigation, and a saving grace of wry, ironical humor in the same piece.

While the magazine's moralistic approach to culture grated with some, its regional justification for covering the arts tended to strike a chord with its more liberal, arts-oriented readership, including Frank Moher. In covering the 1974 federal election, Bennett had deplored the apparent decision by the Trudeau Liberals to write off the West in favour of strengthening their hold in Ontario by "defending the interests of the industrially rich East against the struggling efforts to create industry in the West." He freely acknowledged the concern that "a Canada divided ever more powerfully by regional interests" may have difficulty surviving as a nation. Nonetheless, he also expressed his concern that Canada could survive as country only "if the depopulation of the Maritimes and the West" due to "industrial under-development" and lower living standards could be checked:

> If our regional disparities are not corrected it will rapidly dawn upon the survivors in these remote places that if they are going to live in a state of abandonment anyway, then they might as well live that way as an independent state and have a greater freedom, or as part of the American union and have a greater income. [...] After all, Houston pays more. Toronto has never been very good at paying. (June 3, 1974, 1a)

At the same time, Bennett argued in another editorial that while it was "simple insanity" to fear industry and to try to create a suspect "moral stature" by "demanding we bite the hand that feeds us" it was equally wrong to revere industry "as a god." That was to succumb to the ancient heresy of materialism. If the Greeks were right about "beauty, truth and goodness" being the end of all human endeavour, then the beauty of the natural landscape and the lives of those who depended on it—human, animal, and plant—needed to be preserved in a way they had not been in the heavily industrialized East (February 14, 1974, 1). Byfield, in a much later 1985 editorial, similarly reiterated:

> we stand closer than any of the other regions to our pioneer roots. For most of us the farm is but one generation behind. We are therefore closer than they to the beliefs and traditions of the past, and we have the advantage of seeing what happens when those values are too hurriedly cast aside in favour of a state-centred secularism of glittering promise and baleful result. It is a view not well represented in the contemporary media of the West, an omission we propose to correct. (December 9, 1985, 52)

Both views were to underlay the best of the magazine's arts reportage under first Bennett, then Byfield, and to draw a wider range of liberal writers and readers to the magazine than its religious mandate may have suggested. The conservative bias of the reportage did not go uncriticized by the arts community, but the spirited rebuttals in the letters to the editor section suggested that the magazine was being read and taken quite seriously. In fact, in 1976, Frank Moher, speaking as a publicist on behalf of artistic director Mark

Schoenberg and Theatre 3, one of Edmonton's most important "art theatres," thanked the *Report*, for its "intelligent, considered coverage" and "invaluable support" (Moher, September 13, 1976, 2).

Heading into the late 1970s, the magazine, which had steadily grown in size and subscription base to a comfortable, sustainable level of 20,000 readers by 1976 (Byfield, December 6, 1976, 3), seemed to have established a comfortable niche for itself on the Edmonton scene. Its expansion into the full spectrum of the city's secular life reflected the growing material prosperity and optimism of the times. At the same time, the magazine managed to maintain its underlying regional and religious mandates in a delicate balance.

Much was to change after 1977, when Ted Byfield replaced Keith Bennett as both publisher and editor.[5] The very success of the magazine was forcing it to move further and further from its origins as a religious, communal project paying its workers a dollar a day and living expenses to live and work together communally. Between 1977 and 1979, the magazine began to hire salaried workers and to incorporate more provincial news; in 1977 it also expanded to include a Calgary bureau. Finally, in 1979, the magazine amalgamated its Calgary and Edmonton papers into the *Alberta Report* published by Alberta Report Limited, under editor/publisher Ted Byfield. Significantly, the *Saint John* had vanished from the title. While the Company of the Cross continued to own the magazine, explained Byfield, the order had come to the conclusion that the magazine's commercial nature was out of keeping with the Company's original charitable and educational mandate and had decided to withdraw from the publishing business as soon as feasible (Byfield, September 7, 1979, 1). A year later, the ownership was firmly in Byfield hands, and a new era had begun.

While the religious mandate remained implicit under the new regime, it was clear that the paper intended to embark on a more muscular and militant regional mandate as defined in its initial number:

> More and more [... Edmonton and Calgary's] interests have been merged through the intensity of the province's economic development. This change has made the whole country highly conscious of Alberta, and as a consequence made Albertans highly conscious of their own identity with their province.

5   In an article written on September 26, 1977 ["Publisher to Reporter"], the magazine explained that while Bennett had served as publisher and spokesman for the sjer in his capacity as head of the school and minister of the Company of the Cross he took no active part in the management of the magazine, and that its editor, Ted Byfield, was the general manager of its operations.

It will be the purpose of *Alberta Report* to describe that identity in all the various ways it develops, whether through government, law, the arts, agriculture, sports, business, education, science, or of course, religion. [...]

We feel at this time, more than any time in her history, Alberta needs its own voice. We will presume to provide it. (1)

For many readers, the years between 1979 and 1985—when the implementation of the hated National Energy Program under the strongly centralist Trudeau Liberals threatened the region's burgeoning postwar economic and political growth—constituted *Alberta Report*'s finest hour. Never had the twin halves of its stated mandate both to confirm and consolidate an identity for a region while challenging the full range of spiritual and physical conditions limiting its growth manifested themselves more fully than under the threat of economic war with the centralist imperialists. A similar wave of evangelical fervor and Western alienation from the "Old Boy" social, political, and economic structures of the East had brought the fledgling Social Credit movement to power in 1935 in a stunning upset victory over the established parties in the province.[6] Now, fifty years later, *Alberta Report* rode a similar wave to popular power and influence. As in the case of Aberhart, the "we" presuming to provide Alberta's voice became increasingly centred in that of an intelligent, strongly religious, and educationally minded ex-Easterner who had fallen deeply and passionately in love with his adopted land. At the height of his popularity in the mid-thirties Aberhart had reached nearly 300,000 people, or nearly half the province, with his radio broadcasts. At the height of *Alberta Report*'s popularity in the mid-1980s, Moher suggests in the preface to *Prairie Report*, it was estimated that the magazine had over 50,000 subscribers and that Byfield's columns were read by some 250,000 people a week—or one in every four Albertans (12).[7]

The similarity in the writing styles of Aberhart and Byfield is also striking. Both were highly entertaining writers with a folksy, down-to-earth charm that punctured bureaucratic and political pretentiousness with a combination of sharp observation and acidic wit. In their more serious moods, they

6   Many of Aberhart's speeches, both as recordings and as typescripts, can be found in the Glenbow Museum and Archives in Calgary and the Provincial Archives of Alberta in Edmonton. For more on Aberhart's life and career see Elliott and Miller (1987).

7   In an appeal for subscriptions entitled *"Alberta Report is* Alberta," the magazine claimed, by June 7, 1982, to have 55,000 paid subscribers and more than 215,000 weekly readers. By January 12, 1987 ("A special," 45), it claimed to have an overall readership of over 300,000.

were by turns angry, passionate, lyrical, and persuasive, appealing to a heady combination of myth, history, philosophy, logic, poetry, and religion often intermingled in the same form.

The mythic visions of Alberta that each man constructed were also strikingly similar in many respects. Byfield's more rational, platonic, Anglican universe eschewed the grand thundering Old Testament and apocalyptic imagery of Aberhart's fundamentalist evangelism and drew more from the sweep of Western philosophy and history than from the sweep of biblical history. However, the same great morality play between the centralist forces of cultural, economic, and political oppression—the decadent, urban aristocrats at Versailles-cum-Ottawa—and the simple, rural, hard-working regional peasants was very much in evidence.[8] "Without justice," stormed the *Report*, quoting St. Augustine against the latter-day emperors of Ottawa, "what are kingdoms but great robberies?" ("Fire," November 14, 1980, 2).

Both also shared a complex understanding of what "land" meant. On one level, it was a source of economic power and self-development—now in the form of oil resources rather than wheat; on another, it functioned as an expression of personal and political hegemony to be defended against the ravages of the invader; on a third level, it was the tough teacher of the classical, manly virtues of resourcefulness, self-sufficiency, and hard work to the emerging republic; and finally, it served as the source of divine inspiration to the individual soul: the site of an ineffable platonic grace that drew kindred spirits together in a higher communion beyond gender, race, ethnicity, class, and time and space. Byfield was certain that "the new pioneers," centralist-born, foreign-born, and urban as many of them were, would "acquit themselves as well as had the old" in the face of adversity (May 31, 1982, 60).

The artist had a role to play in the new Republic precisely because of his or her affinity with the ancient Greek virtues of truth, beauty, and goodness. While acknowledging, like Bennett, the greatness of the Greeks at the height of their philosophy, Byfield then proceeded to draw a telling contrast between the decadence of a morally decayed and over-legislated—read "socialist"—Hellenic state, and the simple moral and civic virtues of the young Roman Republic that had conquered them (October 15, 1984, 60). Like Plato and Aristotle before him, Byfield did not dismiss the importance of genius or inspiration in

8   Byfield did not hesitate to draw parallels between situations faced by current epic figures in the Alberta scene and iconic Western figures such as Riel, Social Credit, and the UFA and CCF parties. In two particularly controversial editorials he compared Lougheed's situation as regards the National Energy Program to Riel's earlier struggles with Ottawa. See "Buffcan" (May 4, 1979, 2) and "The Riel-Lougheed Parallel" (May 18, 1979, 2).

creating art, or of the power of the aesthetic form to shape human conscious-ness profoundly. Nonetheless, the focus of Byfield's own poetics is curiously Horatian. The emphasis is less on the artist as poet-genius communicating or inspiring the ecstasy of the spiritual and the divine in his work, than on the artist as a good craftsman/citizen employing the harmony of the aesthetic form, as studied in the great masterpieces of the past, to help educate and produce the future virtuous citizens of a virtuous republic. Byfield stated:

> we very much need artists. They are more indispensable than the plumber and the accountant, possibly even the beer waiter, and as a phenomenon of society infinitely older [...] Because he is an artist his eye can discern beauty and truth in what he beholds. Because we are not artists, the rest of us cannot dis-cern it. But once the artist has discerned it, it is no longer his alone. It belongs to us all, and it is his particular responsibility to convey what he has discerned to as many of the rest of us as he can. (December 4, 1981, 60)

The artist's obligation not just to delight but also to teach was particularly important in the formal education of the young, the heirs of a classical human-ist tradition devoted to the teaching of virtue.

> For the purpose of education, surely, is not broadmindedness; it is goodness. And it needs to be advanced, not with clever little exercises on moral dilemmas, but with sure focus and exhortation using the best literature, the best poetry, the best art, the best music human nature has created. The central moral lesson, after all, did not conclude on a blackboard but on a cross. (March 6, 1981, 52)

Towards the mature citizenry, the artist had the equally grave responsibility to promulgate the best of what was thought, experienced, or envisioned by a "province verged on its finest era [...] a shining decade" (March 15, 1982, 60):

> in such things as the return of melody and meter to music, and in the gradual reappearance of recognizability in western Canadian art, perhaps all these things are evidence of a revolution in the hinterland, a return to high principle, a renaissance of sanity. To describe it in music and art I used the terms discipline and precision. Better words are forms and structures [...] We could have the best schools, the best theatre, the best music, the best

art, the best poetry, even the best lives to be lived in this, the best of lands. All we need are courage to follow where conscience and mind direct, and guts enough to spit in the face of fad and fashion. (March 27, 1981, 60)

Spit in the face of fad and fashion *Alberta Report* most certainly did, often to the dismay of its more liberal readership. This about Martin Sherman's *Bent*: "Pansy panning: A storm over 'deviants' makes *Bent* a hit" (Brunanski, April 17, 1981, 49). This about *Not a Love Story*: "A failing feminist diatribe" (Dolphin, January 18, 1982, 50). Performance art?—"Performance art and pecan pie: Junk is junk, said the janitor and trashed it" (May 16, 1980, 46–47). Abstract art?—"Progressing by drips and bands; Abstract expressionism: a new age, or showing off?" (June 20, 1980, 40–41).

Positively, the *Report's* focus on aspects of rural community and culture that it felt were frequently overlooked or undervalued by the more heavily industrialized and urbanized East led it to cover the arts unusually well in a rural as well as an urban context. Expanding its "beat" to cover art forms that it felt sprang directly out of an uncorrupted "conscience and mind," especially outside of the major cities, the magazine could at times wax almost Tolstoyvian in its praise of such small-town phenomena as the Rosebud School of the Arts (Weatherbe, August 6, 1984, 33), a "weird 320-acre art happening" at Rocky Mountain ranch near Calgary (Weatherbe, April 11, 1983, 44–45), and folk art and painting by rural women, First Nations, and ethnic minorities. It drew its readers' attention to the vivid "primitive" paintings of Doris Zaharichuk ("Little lady," December 29, 1978, 25) and moving devotional church art of Julian Bucmaniuk (Herchak, November 21, 1983, 45).

In the same spirit, it also gave regular and positive coverage almost from the start to Aboriginal art and culture intended to reflect a distinctive Aboriginal voice and to self-run Aboriginal organizations, such as CANUE, intent on developing that voice ("Native culture," September 2, 1974, 7–8). It also wrote sympathetically about the attempts of the short-lived Atchemowin Native Theatre to move into greater public production and become Edmonton's first all-native professional theatre company (Houle, March 15, 1976, 29):

> If Atchemowin continues to grow and improve, Alberta audiences will be provided with something that's still lacking in local drama—true-to-life productions featuring native casts who've been trained in their own home-grown theatre.

"At its best," noted *Toronto Star* writer Dave Olive in an otherwise critical 2003 article, the magazine "told stories of local heroes and regional artists, academics and scientists that eluded the sometimes slow-footed *Edmonton Journal* and *Calgary Herald*" (July 12, 2003, F3) . Even when the magazine covered the more established or mainstream aspects of the arts in Alberta, it consistently wrote best and most sympathetically about those writers, poets, performers, and painters whose work—and often lives—reflected a pastoral idealism at work, with its warmest reviews being reserved for prairie landscape painters, such as Kurelek, where the link between land, art, and transcendence was most clearly and concretely seen ("William Kurelek," November 14, 1977, 47–48). The work of novelist Aritha van Herk was also praised as having a transcendent mystical quality unappreciated by too many central Canadians (Bergman, March 13, 1981, 46–48). Award-winning writer Rudy Wiebe, who was described as an Albertan version of Tolstoy, also received regular positive attention (Bergman, August 25, 1981, 39).

While it covered the full spectrum of theatre in Edmonton, the magazine again gave particular attention to playwrights who, in its estimation, captured a genuine folk or spiritual sensibility deriving from close contact with the land. George Ryga's *Seven Hours to Sundown* (Weatherbe, June 7, 1976, 30–31), Ken Mitchell's *This Train* (Demmon, April 26, 1976, 27), Frank Moher's *The Broken Globe* (Weatherbe, March 1, 1976, 24), and W. O. Mitchell's *The Black Bonspiel of Wullie McCrimmon* (Weatherbe, July 11, 1980, 39) were praised for their sensitive rural nuances, as was the work of Theatre Network, a new collective theatre dedicated to creating new Alberta plays on Alberta themes for local audiences (Weatherbe, September 13, 1976, 27).

Equally significantly, to the extent that art was not only an expression of the lives of the people, but also a reflection of the growing economic, cultural, and political power of the prairies, the magazine, over the 1970s and early 1980s, documented the rise of a growing regional literature, art, dance, film, television, and publishing scene with genuine passion and insight. In 1965, there had been only one professional theatre in Edmonton, the Citadel, which was largely focused on producing works from the British and American repertoire. By 1980, reflecting the rapid development of the University of Alberta Department of Drama, there were six professional companies, most of them focused on doing new, experimental, avant-garde, and social action work with preference given to Canadian and Albertan artists.[9] The magazine wrote enthusiastically of the growing number of theatre companies and artists who were staying and thriving in Edmonton ("Stage," September 29, 1975, 24–28) and gloried in the carnivalesque exuberance of Edmonton's new Fringe Festival (Dolphin, September 2, 1985, 32–36). It documented the warm

9   For a more comprehensive study of Edmonton's theatre scene over these decades, see Bessai.

reception of Alberta dancers ("ABC," January 5, 1979, 25–27), artists ("Art form," November 8, 1976, 38), and filmmakers ("Movies," April 7, 1975, 26) abroad. While the magazine had ambivalent feelings about patronage of the arts, it still optimistically reported that "the diverse film men and women of Alberta are flexing their newly developed muscles, hoping to find a place in the economy alongside cattle and crude as something which will be known for being from this province" ("Motion Pictures," September 30, 1974, 21).

It was this Byfield and this *Alberta Report* that Frank Moher—like his leftist spokesperson in the play, Pauline Brett—had loved and served over the late 1970s and early 1980s, despite his growing unease with its conservative mandate. A similar view of the magazine was expressed by Paula Simons, a self-described "feminist, pro-choice, gay-positive demi-Jewish agnostic" who worked as a copy editor, reporter, and senior editor at the paper over 1987-1989:

> In its heyday, *Alberta Report* [...] did more than rail against abortion, sodomy and Ottawa. It championed Alberta culture— our playwrights, our artists, our writers, our sports heroes, our festivals, our history. It told Albertans, rural and urban, their own stories. (June 24, 2003, B1)

Beyond the 1980s, however, she felt that the magazine she "loved to hate and hated to love" became a stranger to her; increasingly, a magazine that had, at its best, seemed to catch the pulse of the province as a profoundly human "place" seemed to be losing its way (B1). And, as he portrayed it in *Prairie Report*, it was a substantial change in the leadership of the magazine and the directions it began to move beyond 1985 that forced Moher to take stock of his own situation at the magazine and reach the reluctant decision to leave because of what he regarded as a deepening incompatibility between the conservative mandate of the paper and his own regional vision.

In real life, there was no takeover of the magazine by central Canadian "big-business" interests; the magazine remained proudly Western owned, published, and edited until the end. Nonetheless, a combination of severe financial setbacks and the temptation to expand the magazine to a wider readership were to significantly change its character, especially under Link Byfield, who replaced his father as editor/publisher in 1985 and ran the magazine until its demise in 2003.

Between 1986 and 1990, the magazine, convinced that its rising tide of regional conservatism would sweep it into Saskatchewan, Manitoba, and British Columbia as well, had attempted to publish first a *Western Report* magazine, then, when the subscriber base didn't rise above 3,500, a *BC Report* as a sister magazine to *Alberta Report*. Unfortunately, the departure of Pierre Trudeau and the defeat of the Liberal party by the Mulroney conservatives in 1984 removed one of the magazine's most popular rallying points of Western grievance, just as recessionary times struck the publishing industry a devastating blow. By 1990 the magazine was in receivership and had to be rescued by a massive infusion of cash by two Calgary businessmen who took over the financial affairs of the paper. While it was understood that the Byfields would maintain editorial control over the content of the magazine, it was a substantially different magazine for the remaining thirteen years of its existence. In an editorial on the Western Canadian Concept (WCC), once one of the most promising of the Western separatist parties, the older Byfield wrote:

> But will we turn in our desperation to the WCC? [...] Does the WCC offer solutions worth trying? And even more, are its leaders so committed to it that they will sacrifice their own interest to its success? [...] The public will forgive much in a populist movement. Crass opportunism it will not forgive. It was the saints and the martyrs of the farmer movement in the '20s and Social Credit in the '30s that gave them their greatest credibility. Whether the same virtues exist in the WCC we will soon know. (March 4, 1985, 52)

The same, Moher suggested, could have been said of *Alberta Report* after 1985; it ultimately failed the test, at least with the regional arts community it had originally served so well. In his 1990 preface to the published version of *Prairie Report*, in which he dealt point by point with Byfield's 1988 criticism, Moher first of all disputed Byfield's assertion that "to accomplish a western Canadian school of anything [...] the very first thing we must do is forget about being western Canadians," and aim for universals instead (November 7, 1988, 52). This, Moher argued, would have been poor advice for such "regional" playwrights as Sophocles, Molière, Shakespeare, O'Casey, Lillian Hellman, Tennessee Williams, David Hare, and a string of others up to David French (18). Even sharper was Moher's response to Byfield's criticism that in embracing the same kind of "pinko" leftist creed as central Canada, and the arts policies that logically arose from it, *Prairie Report* was asking that the West simply duplicate the same kind of "pampered ghetto of 'Canadianism'" (Byfield, "Why," November 7, 1988, 52) that the East had already imposed on unwilling taxpayers.

> I had often wondered, if in a pinch the magazine was somehow forced to choose between its two major proclivities, its regionalism and its conservatism, which would be held supreme—which was the dog, and which the tail? I suppose I had held on there for those many months hoping that, in the

final analysis, both were equally important. But I was wrong. Here, at last, was the answer: in the Byfield world-view, western Canada is not important because it is western Canada, a nation needing artists, journalists, and politicians to speak for it; western Canada is important only in so far as conservatism may be writ upon it. (18–19)

Whether it was true or not, the magazine, under the more dogmatic, reactionary regime of Link Byfield, was perceived as taking on more and more of the agendas favourable to the new owners' business interests and to explicitly conservative regional parties such as Reform. While the older Byfield continued to write a column for the magazine, by the early 1990s his energies were increasingly diverted into writing first a twelve-volume Time-Life–style history of Alberta to be completed for the province's centennial year, 2005, then a new multi-volume popular history of Christianity to be entitled *The Christians: Their First Two Thousand Years*. The *Report*, over the same post-1990 period, abandoned its arts and sports sections, and increasingly concentrated on business, government, and more ideologically driven pieces on social trends and the family. When it dealt with the arts at all, especially during recessionary times, it tended to deal with them harshly, measuring them against an increasingly hardline conservative social and fiscal platform, and the measure of their commercial marketability at home and abroad.

The *Report*'s aggressive late-1980s attack on a central Canadian cultural elite using the peasants' tax dollars to impose a subsidized form of socialist-liberal State art—CBC and CanLit—on the rest of the country in the name of "nationalism" may have scored well with a general readership inclined to blame its own recession-pinched pockets on the skewed priorities and fiscal irresponsibility of the centralist Canadian power elite. However, the attack did not sit entirely comfortably with arts lobbyists increasingly worried about the impact of free trade and globalization on local arts, culture, and the economy alike. Like Moher, they may have wondered when plays like *Prairie Report* had stopped being considered part of an enlightened new Alberta—where "our artists flourished" no less than "our technology [...], our cities [...] and [...] our farmers" (Byfield, March 15, 1982, 60) in defiance of oppressive federal policies—and had started to be viewed instead as simply one more part of that larger, ongoing, Central Canadian plot to undermine the West.

That discomfort tended to sharpen into alarm as the magazine's growing dedication to free enterprise eventually escalated into attacks on *all* forms of government subsidization for the arts, even at the provincial level, as a form of pernicious socialism in action. Gone was the *Report*'s earlier affirmative view of a vibrant regional arts scene as an indispensable part of a vibrant regional culture; gone was its sympathetic coverage of the Alberta theatre's struggle to remain viable in the face of increasing recessionary pressures within and beyond the province. Instead, at a time when many established theatres were fighting to adapt and survive in a hostile economic environment, the magazine increasingly argued that if entertainment was an industry like any other, then it should be left to live or die by the rules of supply and demand like any other industry. If art purported to reflect the values and standards of a given community, then let that particular community support and pay for it, itself. In contrast to the earlier years, when the magazine urged industry to remember that men "did not live by bread alone," the later magazine supported industrial expansion with few such reservations.

At the same time, the magazine's attack on moral "deviance" in any form became sharper and more hostile in an apparent attempt to retain its original strong core of conservative religious believers in rural areas, while aiming at a wider conservative audience outside the province. Yet ironically, the very industrial expansion that the magazine was promoting as being good for the economic and political health of the province was continuing to erode that constituency and the traditional lifestyles associated with it. Both Byfield and Aberhart had appealed to a mythic vision of Alberta that had bestowed heroic dimensions on its human community by situating it within the great, sweeping Judeo-Christian saga of salvation and redemption on one side and the eternally sustaining and regenerative powers of the land on the other. Yet, even by 1971, the crushing defeat of Social Credit signalled that the religious, rural-based Alberta of Aberhart and E. C. Manning was sliding irretrievably into the past.[10] As Edmonton and Calgary exploded into increasingly large, diverse cosmopolitan centres heading into the new century, the *Report* could no longer rely on appealing to a conservatism that was automatically grounded in a classical humanism shaped by traditional morality and religion. It could no longer draw on a shared perception of the land as simultaneously a source of divine inspiration that bonded all the diverse elements of its population in a human sense and an exploitable natural resource yielding limitless gain, profit, and prosperity to all involved. Perhaps even more significantly, the magazine could no longer safely appeal to a heterogeneous human community bound by a common history and experience of land and region or by an older understanding of ethnicity, culture, and religious tradition shaped largely by

10   In a rather poignant note, former Social Credit premier, E. C. Manning, the father of Preston Manning, the founding leader of the Reform Party, wrote to the magazine on June 5, 1981, requesting the support, interest, and prayers of its readership in getting CFCN Calgary to reverse its decision to discontinue the "Back to the Bible Hour" program that had been running in the Sunday morning slot since 1925.

British and European influences. By 1998, the *Report*'s subscription base had fallen by thirty-four percent from its 1985 height. In June 2003, the magazine went out of existence after almost thirty years of publication.[11]

Still, the original question remains. Was it possible to negotiate a reconciliation of Byfield's prairie City of God, in the Augustinian sense of that word, with Moher's prairie City of Man in the modern and postmodern sense? The lay order of Anglicans who left their retreat at Stony Plain to descend into the real world in 1973 optimistically believed there was, especially in the bright, new regional world that seemed to be unfolding in the late 1970s. So, in their own ways, did the fiery old crusader and the young book editor of the 1980s who saw that bright, new regional world being threatened by the policies of a misguided centralist government that seemed to encompass all the philosophical, historical, and socio-economic ills that could possibly afflict that bright new world. But by the late 1980s that hope had started to fade. On some level, one suspects Moher and Byfield's mutual disenchantment with each other symptomatic of a deeper anger and pain over the loss of an earlier wholeness of vision going back to the early decades of the province and the fear that those rapidly fragmenting and diverging regionalities of the modern West might never be made whole or complete again.

Viewed from the distance of 2008 ("Telephone interview"), Byfield confessed that *Prairie Report* had disappointed him because he actually *had* expected it to be a sharp, spirited, "fun" send-up, in Morrow's words, of an "old-fashioned, grassroots style of journalism"(October 27, 1989, F6). Measured against that expectation, the play had certainly failed, he thought, to capture the creative human, financial, and organizational chaos of the newsroom with its constant bustle, energy, and work. He had gone into the theatre expecting to see an Albertan version of Ben Hecht's *The Front Page* and was taken aback to find himself in what he regarded as a rather heavy, dreary, philosophical universe as divorced from the frantic dynamics of a real newroom as one could imagine. Given the fact that Moher had at one time been part of that newsroom himself, Byfield had been all the more disappointed that the play had not got that critical aspect of the magazine right.[12]

....

11   While the majority of this article's information is drawn from the complete 1973-2003 run of the magazine itself, which was usually frank with its readership about its changes in management and its financial and subscription statistics, the *Report* was also the focus of many articles, interviews, and documentaries. For overviews of the magazine in its later years and assessments of its influence at the time of its demise, see Paquin (1991), "A Magazine Mourned" (2003), Gunter (2003), Olive (2003), Walton (2003), and Woodard (2003).

12   Inevitably perhaps, the demise of the magazine spurred a number of memory pieces by former newsroom veterans like Paula Simons (2003), Lorne Gunter (2003), and

Yet, on a deeper level, one suspects that *Prairie Report* struck a nerve not because it had purportedly missed the mark, but because it had all too accurately nailed the dilemma of the magazine at a watershed moment of its existence when it could no longer be all things to all people nor even pretend to be. The time was gone when, in **Bennington's** words, "you could argue with the CCFers at a town hall meeting, and still go out for a beer with them after. When sometimes you could hardly tell Tommy Douglas from Bill Aberhart. When conservatives looked like human beings—and not like something out of a department store window" (97). If the changing dynamics of the Alberta theatre in the closing decades of the twentieth century made Byfield's neoclassical poetics seem dated, then the idealistic, celebratory regionalism of the 1970s expressed in the early collective work of Theatre Network and some of Moher's first plays also seemed to have become a more muted theme in an increasingly postmodern Albertan theatre intent on delving into international themes, styles, and subject matter.

Sadly, it is the brightest, best, and most idealistic members of the original news team—**Dick Bennington** and **Pauline Brett**—who choose to go down with the older ship and have disappeared from the world of the play by the final scene. In real life, by 1988, Moher had left not only the magazine but Alberta itself to pursue his writing career in British Columbia. Byfield, by contrast, remained in Alberta but increasingly withdrew from the magazine to return to his earlier passions for historical and religious writing. Ominously, the final moments of the play focus on the image of the beleaguered new publisher, **Otis Bennington**, preparing to launch the new version of the magazine into uncertain, treacherous waters with suspect associates and a new agenda. Not long after that, *Alberta Report* dropped the curtain on its own regular arts coverage, and finally exited from the Alberta scene altogether.

Ultimately, neither Moher nor Byfield was right about *Prairie Report* being a fictional representation of *Alberta Report* whose darker undertones could either be dismissed as inappropriate for what should have been a spirited spoof of the magazine's old-style journalism, or defended as an appropriate element of a lively, engaging "comedy of ideas." Fifteen years later it was clear that, to an extent not realized by either Moher or Byfield himself in 1988, *Prairie Report*, far from" getting it wrong," had got the essence of *Alberta Report* and its particular tragedy hauntingly and terrifyingly right.[13]

Shawn McCarthy (2003), who remembered both Byfield and their time with the paper as delightfully creative, chaotic learning experiences. McCarthy in particular cites *Prairie Report* as an accurate portrayal of the frenetic energy and dynamics of the *Report's* newsroom as he and others remembered it in the 1970s and 1980s.

13   I am enormously indebted to both Frank Moher and Ted Byfield for reading over an

Works Cited

"The ABC [Alberta Ballet Company]: 'one of the best little companies in Canada.'" *Saint John's Edmonton Report* [SJER] 6.5 (January 5, 1979): 25–27.

"*Alberta Report is* Alberta." *Alberta Report* [AR] 9.25 (June 7, 1982): 35.

"'An art form distinctly Western Canadian': 75 Alberta art works back from a year's tour." SJER 3.49 (November 8, 1976): 38.

Bennett, Keith et al. [Saint John's Company of the Cross]. "Why a News Magazine For Edmonton?" SJER 1.1 (November 7, 1973): 1a.

Bennett, Keith. "Letter from the Company." SJER 1.8 (January 11, 1974): 1a.

——. "Letter from the Publisher." SJER 1.12 (February 14, 1974): 1a.

——. "Letter from the Publisher." SJER 1.15 (March 7, 1974): 1a.

——. "Letter from the Publisher." SJER 1.27 (June 3, 1974): 1a.

——. "Letter from the Publisher." SJER 1.28 (June 10, 1974): 1a.

Bergman, Brian. "A penetrating exchange: When the *Globe*'s French knocks van Herk, Rudy comes up swinging." AR 8.14 (March 13, 1981): 46–8.

——. "Understanding Rudy Wiebe. Alberta's Tolstoy: Much admired, rarely read." AR 8.38 (August 25, 1981): 39.

Bessai, Diane. "Canada's Citadel and the alternatives." *Theatre in Alberta*. Ed. Anne Nothof. Toronto: Playwrights Canada Press, 2008. 144–68.

Brunanski, Craig, and Stephen Weatherbe. "Pansy panning: A storm over 'deviants' makes *Bent* a hit." Review of *Bent* by Martin Sherman, dir. Raymond Clarke. Theatre 3, Edmonton AB. AR 8.19 (April 17, 1981): 49.

Byfield, Ted. "Theatre Three: How many more marriages were helped to cave in?" Review of *A Doll's House* by Henrik Ibsen, dir. Mark Schoenberg. Theatre 3, Edmonton, AB. SJER 2.50 (November 17, 1975): 30–2.

——. "Letter from the Editor." SJER 4.1 (December 6, 1976): 3.

——. "Buffcan and the Louis Riel tradition." SJER 6.22 (May 4, 1979): 2.

——. "The Riel-Lougheed Parallel: How Absurd." SJER 6.24 (May 18, 1979): 2.

——. "*Alberta Report*." AR 6.40 (September 7, 1979): 1.

——. "The great 'values' flap - It failed, thank goodness." AR 8.13 (March 6, 1981): 52.

——. "The unrecognized heroes of an Alberta revolution." AR 8.16 (March 27, 1981): 60.

——. "Art is not for art's sake; that is why the crowd matters." AR 8.52 (December 4, 1981): 60.

——. "Ottawa's bells are screaming the rising defiance of the West." AR 9.13 (March 15, 1982): 60.

——. "The great test is now upon us, but the contestants look ready." AR 9.24 (May 31, 1982): 60.

earlier draft of this paper and the accompanying appendix. Their comments, corrections, and suggestions did a great deal to improve both the article and the appendix in their final form.

———. "The Greek model and why it will kill us." AR 11.43 (October 15, 1984): 60.

———. "The NDP won, but the real Tory nemesis is the WCC." AR 12.11 (March 4, 1985): 52.

———. "Introducing *Western Report*, an idea whose time has come." AR 12.51 (December 9, 1985): 52.

———. "Why can't the CBC leave a nice guy like me alone?" AR 15.47 (November 7, 1988): 52.

———. Telephone interview with Moira Day. Notes. August 18, 2008.

"Byfield's magazines provided a unique Western voice," [editorial]. *Vancouver Sun*, June 26, 2003: A10.

Demmon, Calvin. "A ghost town repeopled through memory." Review of *This Train* by Ken Mitchell, dir. Scott Swann. Northern Light Theatre. SJER 3.18 (April 26, 1976): 27.

Dolphin, Ric. "A failing feminist diatribe." Review of *Not a Love Story* (NFB film), dir. Bonnie Klein. AR 9.5 (January 18, 1982): 50.

———. "The Fringe is on top: How Brian Paisley created an institution." AR 12.37 (September 2, 1985): 32–6.

Elliott, David R., and Iris Miller. *Bible Bill: A Biography of William Aberhart*. Edmonton: Reidmore, 1987.

"Fag fad gathers in city's culture clutch: Journal, the Citadel and Stage West." Review of *Norman, Is That You?* by Ron Clark and Sam Bobrick dir. William Fisher. Stage West. SJER 3.16 (March 22, 1976): 28.

"Fire on the prairie: The dream of a free West is luring thousands to its promise." AR 7.50 (November 14, 1980): 12–13.

"Frank Moher". *Canadian Theatre Encyclopedia*. www.canadiantheatre.com/dict.pl?term=Moher%2C%20Frank. Last updated 2006-10-24.

Friesen, Gerald. *The Canadian Prairies, A History*. Toronto: University of Toronto Press, 1990.

Gunter, Lorne. "*Alberta Report* once had an impact." *Edmonton Journal*, June 25, 2003: A18.

Herchak, Gayle. "Saving stunning church art: At St. Josaphat's Cathedral, rye bread is the miracle cleaner." Review of murals by Julian Bucmaniuk, Edmonton, AB. AR 10.48 (November 21, 1983): 45.

Houle, Ann. "All-native theatre group's first big play." Review of *Twin Sinks of Allan Sammy* by Cam Hubert, dir. Bryce Missal. Atchemowin Native Theatre, Edmonton, AB. SJER 3.15 (March 15, 1976): 29.

"The little lady from Willingdon gets a showing at the Art Gallery." Review of exhibit of paintings by Lois Zaharichuk, Edmonton Art Gallery. Edmonton, AB. SJER 6.4 (December 29, 1978): 25.

"A Magazine Mourned." *Globe and Mail* [Toronto]. June 25, 2003: A16.

Manning, E. C. Letter to the editor, ["Back to the Bible silenced"]. AR 8.21 (June 5, 1981): 38.

McCarthy, Shawn. "A eulogy for the cranky *Alberta Report*." *Globe and Mail* [Toronto], June 28, 2003: R14.

Moher, Frank. *Prairie Report*. Winnipeg: Blizzard, 1990.

———. Letter to the editor. ["Support for Theatre 3"]. SJER 3.41 (September 13, 1976): 2.

———. Letter to Moira Day. September 18, 2008. Email.

Morrow, Martin. "Soft spot for press: Magazine inspired play." *Calgary Herald*, October 26, 1989: C1.

———. "ATP's play shrewd, funny: Press has to take its lumps." Review of *Prairie Report* by Frank Moher, dir. Brian Deedrick. ATP, Calgary, AB. *Calgary Herald*, October 27, 1989: F6.

"Motion Pictures: Cinema group focuses on becoming major industry." *SJER* 1.44 (September 30, 1974): 21.

"The Movies: Polish gesture latest honor in Filmwest 12-award career." *SJER* 2.18 (April 7, 1975): 26.

"Native culture buffs are paddling their own CANUE." *SJER* 1.40 (September 2, 1974): 7–8.

Nicholls, Liz. "Literate play whacks right, left with gusto". Review of *Prairie Report* by Frank Moher, dir. Gerry Potter. Workshop West Theatre, Edmonton, AB. *Edmonton Journal*, October 22, 1988: F1.

Olive, Dave. "Shelved Reports gave voice to right; stories of local heroes and artists. At its worst, it veered close to the rhetoric of hate literature." *Toronto Star*, July 12, 2003: F3.

Paquin, Carole. "How the West was Won." *Ryerson Review of Journalism* (Spring 1991). www.rrj.ca/issue/1991/ spring/112/ (accessed December 17, 2009).

"Performance art and pecan pie: Junk is junk, said the janitor and trashed it." *AR* 7.24 (May 16, 1980): 46–7.

"Progressing by drips and bands: Abstract expressionism: a new age, or showing off?" Review of Abstract Expressionism exhibit. Glenbow Museum, Calgary, AB. *AR* 7.29 (June 20, 1980): 40–1.

"Publisher to reporter in a single week, but now he really works for the magazine." *SJER* 4.42 (September 26, 1977): 24–5.

Simons, Paula. "Love it or hate it, *Alberta Report* never dull." *Edmonton Journal*, June 24, 2003: B1.

Slay, Joe. "Decadence: Sensual violence served in heaping proportions." Review of *Salome* by Richard Strauss. Edmonton Opera Association. Edmonton, AB. *SJER* 4.10 (February 14, 1977): 35–6.

"A special subscription offer from *Alberta Report*." *AR* 14. 4 (January 12, 1987): 45.

"Stage activities making Edmonton known as live theatre centre of Western Canada: City developing pool of competent actors who find opportunities here to stay busy." *SJER* 2.43 (September 29, 1975): 24–8.

Walton, Dawn. "Bible of the Prairie right is silenced after 30 years." *Globe and Mail* [Toronto], June 24, 2003: A1.

Weatherbe, Stephen. "*The Broken Globe* is powerful theatre." Review of *The Broken Globe* by Frank Moher, dir. Randy Maertz. Theatre 3, Edmonton, AB. *SJER* 3.13 (March 1, 1976): 24.

———. "Grassroots troupe gives premiere of Ryga's slow-moving Western drama." Review of *Seven Hours to Sundown* by George Ryga, dir. Mark Manson. Studio Theatre and Theatre Network, Edmonton, AB. *SJER* 3.27 (June 7, 1976): 30–1.

———. "Original play *Two Miles Off* hangs together with vignettes." Review of *Two Miles Off* by Theatre Network [collective creation], Edmonton, AB. SJER 3.41 (September 13, 1976): 27.

———. "Satan meets his match: Presbyterians can outcurl Old Nick any day." Review of *The Black Bonspiel of Wullie McCrimmon* by W. O. Mitchell, dir. Guy Sprung. Citadel Theatre, Edmonton, AB. AR 7.31 (July 11, 1980): 39.

———. "Strange, strange on the range: Maurice Strong's ranch is turning into a weird 320-acre happening." Review of "Ranch" [site-specific art] by Alan Wood. 24 miles southwest of Calgary, AB. AR 10.16 (April 11, 1983): 44–5.

———. Rosebud's arts school: A very special program thrives on Main Street." AR 11.33 (August 6, 1984): 33.

"William Kurelek, 1927-1977: Overcoming despair to paint prairies and the faith." SJER 4.50 (November 14, 1977): 47–8.

Appendix.

ALBERTA REPORT AND ITS TIMES—A TIMELINE

1905   Provinces of Alberta and Saskatchewan formed. Join older provinces of Manitoba (1870) and British Columbia (BC) (1871) to form Western Canada. Manitoba the result of the First Riel Rebellion (1869-70). Second Rebellion in Saskatchewan (1885) sees Louis Riel, Métis leader of the Rebellions, hanged as a traitor to the Canadian Government amidst widespread controversy and dissent.

1921   United Farmers of Alberta (UFA), a farmers' co-operative movement, becomes government of Alberta. Under Herbert Greenfield (1921-1925), John Brownlee (1925-1934), and Richard Reid (1934-1935), dominates provincial politics until 1935.

1928   **Edward Bartlett (Ted) Byfield (TB)** born in Toronto, Ontario. Son of Vern Byfield, a reporter for the *Toronto Star* and *Toronto Telegram* in the 1920s and 1930s and later an editor for the *Ottawa Journal* and the *Washington Star*.

1932   CCF (Co-operative Commonwealth Federation), a democratic, socialist party, founded. First leader, J.S. Woodsworth, a former Methodist minister. Becomes the NDP in 1961.

1935   **August.** Social Credit Party of Alberta wins surprise landslide victory in Alberta under right-wing evangelist, William "Bible Bill" Aberhart. Under Aberhart (1935-1943), Ernest Manning (1943-1968), and Harry Strom (1968-1971) the Socreds dominate politics in Alberta for 36 years.

1944   T. C. ("Tommy") Douglas, former Baptist minister, forms first socialist government (CCF) in North America in Saskatchewan (1944-1961). Serves as first leader of first federal socialist party, the NDP (1961-1971).

1945   **Byfield** family moves to Washington, DC, USA. **TB** drops out of George Washington University to get first newspaper job as a copy boy with the *Washington Post* at age 17.

1947   Oil struck in Alberta. Alberta starts to move from one of poorest to one of richest provinces.

1948   **TB** moves back to Canada. Works as reporter with *Ottawa Journal* and as an editor for the *Timmins Daily Press* and *Sudbury Star.*

1949   **TB** marries fellow reporter, **Virginia Nairn**. Family grows to 6 children, including one adopted son.

1952   **TB** moves to Winnipeg. Joins the *Winnipeg Free Press.* Begins to read deeply into Christianity and the works of C.S. Lewis and G.K. Chesterton in particular. Son of a nominally Anglican mother and atheist father, he becomes devout Anglican.

1957   **TB** wins National Newspaper award for spot news on political story.

John George Diefenbaker, charismatic politician from Saskatchewan, scores stunning upset victory over the federal Liberals. First Prime Minister from Saskatchewan. Holds power until 1963 when defeated by Lester Pearson's Liberals.

1962   **TB** helps found, along with other parishioners of St. John's Cathedral, an Anglican lay order, the Company of the Cross, and a private school for boys. Leaves journalism to become a teacher of History and French with a specialization in Canadian history.

1968   **TB** moves to Alberta to help found a second St. John's School for boys 24 miles southwest of Stony Plain, Alberta, near Edmonton.

Liberal Party led by Pierre Elliot Trudeau sweeps into power, succeeding the Pearson Liberals (1963–1968), and moves Canada in socialist directions. Dominates federal government from 1968–1984.

1971   Socred Party, still overly reliant on conservative agrarian, rural base even as the province is becoming more urban and industrialized, decimated. Conservative Party of Alberta elected. Dominates Alberta politics under Peter Lougheed (1971–1985), Don Getty (1985–1992), Ralph Klein (1992–2006) and Ed Stelmach (2006–2011) for over 35 years.

St John's Edmonton Report 1973-1979

1973   **November.** *Saint John's Edmonton Report* founded as a weekly regional magazine along the lines of *Newsweek* or *Time*, though with a religious, conservative mandate. Publisher and spokesman, **Keith Bennett.** Senior editors and founders, Gordon Dewar and **TB**. Initially run, like the schools, by an Anglican lay order. Staff earn a dollar a day, plus living expenses, are housed in a communal apartment block, and attend morning and evening chapel services. **Vern Byfield**, Ted's father, serves as assistant editor. **Mike Byfield**, Ted's son, serves as one of the apprentices. By 1990, 5 of Byfield's 6 children—**Mike, Link, Vincent, Philippa**, and **Mary Frances**—have served in some capacity on the magazine.

1977   **TB** replaces **Keith Bennett** as editor/publisher. Magazine begins to move away from religious commune system because of high staff burnout and turnover.

Calgary Bureau established. *Saint John's Calgary Report* founded.

Alberta Report 1979-1985

1979   **June.** Federal Conservative Party led by Joe Clark, an Albertan, defeats Trudeau Liberals and forms a minority government. Falls after only 9 months in March, 1980.

August. *Saint John's Edmonton Report* and *Saint John's Calgary Report* merge to become *Alberta Report* under editorship of **TB**. Paper moves to a more commercial basis, hiring and paying real wages. Now published by Alberta Report Limited.

1980   Edmonton entrepreneur, Allan Hardy, passes away barely a year after bailing magazine out of trouble. **John Byfield**, Ted's brother and a California physician, comes up with $125,000 Canadian to put ownership of the *Report* in **Byfield** hands as Interwest Publications Inc.

October. Trudeau government institutes NEP.

Western Canada Concept Party (WCC) formed by Doug Christie to promote separation of the provinces of Manitoba, Saskatchewan,

Alberta, and BC, and the territories of the Yukon and the North West Territories, to form a new nation. First of a wave of small, radical, conservative—and generally unsuccessful—parties advocating Western Separatism.

1982   First and only MLA of WCC Party, Gordon Kessler, elected in by-election in rural Alberta. Loses seat in regular provincial election held later that year.

1983   **Byfield, Ted**. *"The Deplorable Unrest in the Colonies:" Letters From the Publisher Published in Alberta Report between 1979 and 1982.* Edmonton: Alberta Report, 1983.

1984   *Atlas of Alberta.* A special project by *Alberta Report.* Editor: **Ted Byfield**.

June. Trudeau retires and is replaced by John Turner.

September. Conservative Party under Brian Mulroney elected in a massive landslide.

1985   **April. Link Byfield** takes over as publisher after year of transition. **TB** begins slowly to relinquish editing and publishing duties to **Link** over next decade, though he continues writing a column for the magazine until its end.

Alberta Report hits the height of its subscription base, 52,277, in early 1985. Estimated that it reaches 250,000 readers a week or almost one of every four Albertans.

Western Report, Alberta Report, BC Report 1986-1990

1986   *Western Report,* meant to serve all four Western provinces, begins.

Spring. Drop in oil prices sends Alberta economy into sharp recession. Circulation of both AR and WR suffers. Only 3,500 WR subscribers.

1987   **October**. Reform Party of Canada founded under Preston Manning, son of former Social Credit premier of Alberta, Ernest Manning. **TB** gives keynote address at founding convention of the Reform Party. First significant federal party with a specifically conservative, regional mandate. Reform champions balanced budgets, preservation of family, back to basics teaching, and tougher sentences for young criminals. **Byfields** play strong role in creating and promoting the Reform Party, which eventually becomes the Opposition, and, then— reorganized into Alliance and amalgamated with the old Progressive Conservative party—the government of Canada in 2006.

1988   **October.** *Prairie Report* by **Frank Moher**, a full-length play based on Moher's experiences as first a book reviewer (from 1981) then an editor for *Alberta Report* (1983-86), produced at Workshop West Theatre, Edmonton. TB sees and responds critically to play in *Alberta Report* column.

Mulroney Conservatives returned to power with much reduced majority.

1989   *Prairie Report* by Frank Moher wins 1989 Sterling award for best new play performed in Edmonton over the 1988-89 season. Play also produced at ATP in Calgary.

BC *Report* begins; **Virginia Byfield** becomes senior writer on paper. *Western Report* discontinued.

March. Deborah Grey, first M.P. for the Reform Party, elected.

October. Stan Waters, first elected senator, wins election in Alberta. Appointed to Senate by Brian Mulroney in June 1990.

Alberta Report, BC *Report 1990-1998*

1990   Founding of BC *Report* drives magazine into financial crisis. Interwest Publications goes into receivership, then bankruptcy. Calgary oilmen John Scrymgeour and Donald Graves bail out magazine with $1.8 million and run it under continued **Byfield** editorial control as United Western Communications Ltd.

Prairie Report by **Frank Moher** published by Blizzard.

1991   **Summer.** TB begins multi-volume history of Alberta in the 20th century, based on Time-Life formula for producing and marketing history books. To be "journalistic" in focus and based on newspaper archives. Also writes a column for the *Edmonton Sun* and for the *Financial Post* over the 1990s.

September. Stan Waters, first elected Canadian senator to hold office, dies.

1992   Mulroney resigns, government massively unpopular because of its inability to solve constitutional crises or recession. Replaced by Kim Campbell, the first woman prime minister of Canada. Progressive Conservative Party decimated in 1992 election. Jean Chrétien's Liberals form majority government. Reform Party replaces the Conservatives as the major right-wing Party in Canada.

1997   Chrétien Liberals win by a majority. Reform Party forms official Opposition for the first time, but only wins 8 new seats, and is unable to spread appeal beyond its Western base.

1998   Last volume of *Alberta Report* under that name. Circulation drops to 34,903 in first 6 months of year, down 34% from 1985. TB blames recession of late 1980s for decision to drop mainstream sections on the Arts and Sports and concentrate on more ideologically driven pieces on social trends and the family. Acknowledges that decision to write for "true believers" prepared to pay for the magazine regularly may have led them "to preach to the converted."

Byfield, Ted. *The Book of Ted: Epistles from an Unrepentant Redneck.* Edmonton: Keystone Press, 1998. Collection of columns from the back pages of the magazine.

The Report, Citizens Centre Report 1999-2003

1999   *Alberta Report, BC Report, Western Report* collapsed back into *The Report.*

2000   **March**. Reform Party becomes the Canadian Reform Conservative Alliance Party.

2001   TB completes Volume 9 of the History of Alberta, *Manning and the Age of Prosperity*. Asks Paul Bunner, a long-time member of *Report,* to assume the editorship of the last three volumes in the series. TB embarks on a new multi-volume book project, a popular history of Christianity entitled *The Christians: Their First Two Thousand Years.*

2003   **Feb 3.** Last publication of *The Report.*

Feb 17. Becomes the *Citizens Centre Report* in conjunction with **Link Byfield's** Citizen's Centre for Freedom and Democracy.

June. *Citizens Centre Report* shuts down in state of bankruptcy after 10 issues.

November. Volume 12, *Alberta takes the Lead,* is published, completing the Alberta History set for the centennial year. Book sales approaching 225,000.

December. Canadian Alliance merged with old Progressive Conservative Party to form the modern Conservative Party.

Jean Chrétien resigns. Paul Martin takes over Liberal Government.

2004   Ownership of *History of Alberta* transferred to *Alberta Business Report.* **Link Byfield** continues to work as a columnist for the *Calgary* and *Edmonton Sun.* Elected, along with Tom Sindlinger, as first independent senator-in-waiting in September 27th election. First independent elected in an Alberta election since 1982. Remains Chair of Citizens Centre for Freedom and Democracy, a lobby group.

2005   **Link** and **Ted Byfield** receive Alberta Centennial Medals.

2006   **February.** Conservative Party of Canada under Stephen Harper, a founding member of the Reform Party, forms minority government, defeating the Martin Liberals. Wins second term as minority government in 2008.

2007   **July.** Bert Brown, the only candidate to run in all three of Alberta's senatorial elections (1989, 1998, and 2004) and to be re-elected as a senator-in-waiting (2004), is appointed to the Canadian Senate by Stephen Harper, becoming second elected Alberta senator to sit in the Canadian Senate.

2011   **May.** Conservative Party of Canada under Stephen Harper forms a majority government.

PHOTO 1. The Grain Exchange Building, Winnipeg, home of the Manitoba Theatre Workshop, later Prairie Theatre Exchange, from 1973 until 1987. PHOTO COURTESY OF THE WINNIPEG BUILDING INDEX, ARCHITECTURE/FINE ARTS LIBRARY, UNIVERSITY OF MANITOBA.

PHOTO 2. In the Prairie Theatre Exchange mainstage theatre, the set of *The December Man (L'homme de décembre)* by Colleen Murphy, January 26–February 8, 2011. Set design by Carole Klemm. PHOTO BY BRUCE MONK.

PHOTO 3. Jessica Burleson, Lisa Lorteaux, and Danielle Savage in *Absolute Perfection* by Cairn Moore at FemFest 2006. PHOTO BY LYNNE KOLLER.

PHOTO 4. Jessica Burleson in *Absolute Perfection* by Cairn Moore at Fem-Fest 2006. PHOTO BY LYNNE KOLLER.

PHOTO 5. Raoul Granger, Frédérique Baudemont, and Karène Paquin in La Troupe du Jour's 2003 performance of *Du vent dans les brances de sassafras* by René de Obaldia. PHOTO BY DANY ROUSSEAU.

PHOTO 6. Gilles Poulin-Denis in La Troupe du Jour's performance of *Rearview* (2009) by Gilles Poulin-Denis. PHOTO BY YVAN LEBEL.

PHOTO 7. Benoit Lortie, Geneviève Messier, Yvette Forcier, Roger Gauthier, and Julian Thibeault in La Troupe du Jour's 2005 performance of *Le mariage d'la fille Gareau* by Raoul Granger. PHOTO BY DANY ROUSSEAU.

PHOTO 8. Saskatchewan Native Theatre Company's performance of *Life is Wonderful* by Curtis Peeteetuce. Part of the Rez Christmas Story series, it was directed by Alan Long and played in Saskatoon and Saskatchewan First Nations communities in December 2008. Seated (left to right): Waylon Machiskinic and Curtis Peeteetuce. Standing (left to right): Jennifer Bishop and Arron Naytowhow. Much of the delightful humour in these plays comes from young men playing the role of female elders. The characters are based on the playwright's and actors' own grandmothers (kokohms). PHOTO BY ALAN LONG.

PHOTOS 9–14. *MacGregor's Hard Ice Cream and Gas* by Daniel Macdonald, Persephone Theatre, 2005. PHOTOS BY TIBOR FEHERGHAZI.

PHOTO 9. Sharon Bakker as Marlene; Cheryl Jack as Missy.

PHOTO 10. Sharon Bakker as Marlene.

PHOTO 11. Skye Brandon as Jack.

PHOTO 12. Skye Brandon as Jack; Cavan Cunningham as Fred.

PHOTO 13. Sharon Bakker as Marlene; Cheryl Jack as Missy.

PHOTO 14. Sharon Bakker as Marlene.

PHOTO 15. *Sempleton Marvelous* by Michael Green. Wagonstage 2006. Left to right: Mike Tan and Kristen Eveleigh. PHOTO BY JEFF YEE.

PHOTO 16. *Gilly Goes West* by Donna Tunney (commissioned for the 100th anniversary of Alberta), Wagonstage 2005. Left to right: Genevieve Bourdon, Bradley Alto, Andrew Oberhoffer, and Amanda Fox. PHOTO BY KATHLEEN FOREMAN.

PHOTOS 17 AND 18. *Home Made Play Too*, Wagonstage 2008. Left to right, in top photo: Charlotte Wyvill, Jeremy Verkley, Mark Ikeda, and Kara Sturk. PHOTOS BY JOHN POULSEN.

PHOTO 19. 1988 production of *Prairie Report*. Left to right: David Mann as Dick Bennington and Jacqueline Dandeneau as Maria Semchuk. WORKSHOP WEST ARCHIVES.

PHOTO 20. 1988 production of *Prairie Report*. Left to right: Michael Spencer-Davis as Otis Bennington, Susan Sneath as Pauline Brett, Wendell Smith (back) as Simon Kael, Tony Eyamie (forward) as Stuart McFadden, Steven Hilton as William Coolen, Jacqueline Dandeneau (front) as Maria Semchuk, and David Mann as Dick Bennington. WORKSHOP WEST ARCHIVES.

crossing
REGIONAL BORDERS

Fertile Minds in a Barren Season: Western Canadian Women Playwrights and the Great Depression

ARND BOHM

The politics of the Canadian West look quite different depending where one is standing. From the perspective of central Canada, the West is often stereotyped as a zone of conservative values and policies, always slightly behind the times. Prairie dwellers, however, are justifiably proud of their progressivist heritage. They point to figures such as Emily Murphy, who led the fight to get women recognized as "persons." They recall the radicalism of the Winnipeg railway strikers. They know that Canada's health care program emerged out of Saskatchewan and the convictions of Tommy Douglas. Not least, Westerners are keenly aware of their innovative cultural institutions, especially the theatre. Social issues have often been at the forefront of plays written and performed in the West, as they are in Minnie Evans Bicknell's *Relief* (1937), Elsie Park Gowan's *Homestead* (1933), and Gwen Pharis Ringwood's *Still Stands the House* (1939), three short works by Western Canadian women playwrights who witnessed the Depression and who showed how global forces intruded upon the most intimate spheres and destroyed ordinary lives.

After the hitherto unimagined horrors of the First World War, the decade that followed would linger in memory as the "Golden Twenties," when jobs were plentiful and times were good. But the optimism was shattered with the crash of the American stock market in 1929 and subsequently of the global economy (Johnson, 1979, 231–60). Everywhere people attempted to make sense of an event whose causes were only vaguely understood but whose consequences were all too apparent: massive unemployment, poverty and hunger, intense social conflicts, and the appeal of totalitarianism. Although its reach was universal, the Depression's effects were borne unequally (Neatby, 1972, 21–36). In Canada, the western provinces, whose wealth was based on wheat, were devastated once the markets collapsed.[1] There were also disparities between urban and rural sectors, as farmers found themselves bound by debt to land that was often commercially worthless and that retained little more than symbolic value. Within families, men and women faced gender-specific challenges according to their respective resources. This historical background, sketched in a few broad strokes, only becomes meaningful when it is fleshed out with individual experiences and narratives. Many Americans derive their knowledge of rural life during the Depression from John Steinbeck's *The Grapes of Wrath* (1939; film version 1940) or from James Agee and Walker Evans's *Let Us Now Praise Famous Men* (1941).[2] Canadian readers are familiar with Sinclair Ross's *As for Me and My House* (1941), or have learned about the Depression from family chronicles,[3] and yet the study of Depression-era writing still has gaps. In this context, three short plays by women who were witnesses to the Depression's impact on the Prairies deserve attention.

In March 1937 Minnie Evans Bicknell's one-act play *Relief* won the Cameron McIntosh trophy at the Saskatchewan Drama Festival in Regina. It went on to win honourable mention in the Dominion Drama Festival the following month and was cited as "best topical play for 1937" by the *University of Toronto Quarterly*.[4] The themes of the play were very much on the minds of Canadian audiences. With stark realism Bicknell captured the despair and the physical, emotional, and spiritual exhaustion of a farm family worn out by years of struggle. The cruel irony of the title would have been quite evident to

1   For a succinct overview, see Holland.
2   The fieldwork was done in 1936 in rural Alabama.
3   See, for example, Bye. Bye's study gives an excellent entry point into the relevant historical literature, as well as a moving personal account. For a critical review of relevant studies, see also McPherson.
4   Milne, 372. Print copies of the play are rare, but the text is readily available on microfiche in the collection *Peel Bibliography on Microfiche / Bibliographie Peel sur Microfiche* (Ottawa: National Library of Canada, 1975–), Nr. 3598. Virtually nothing is known about Bicknell. Apparently there is in the Macmillan archive at McMaster University some correspondence relating to Macmillan's publishing of *Relief*, filed under F. W. Bicknell (First Accrual, Box 74, F14). A positive reception has not been encouraged by the remark at the end of a paragraph in which Michael Tait mentioned *Relief* in one sentence: "The chief drawback of almost all these depression plays is a confusion in their authors' minds between the impact of emotion recollected in excitement and the effects of art" (151).

contemporary audiences: there was no relief in sight, no solution to the overwhelming crisis. The concept of "relief" was itself controversial and summed up the confused efforts of governments to cope with the situation.[5] For most Canadians, the idea that unemployed, destitute people should be given public charity violated the stern work ethic inherited from the nineteenth century. To receive relief marked the recipients as lazy and as incompetent managers of their own finances. Merchants in small towns worried that if people were given things then the already limited local demand for goods would dry up (Hande, 1991, 23–24). Rather amazingly, some governments, apparently unaware of rural conditions, thought that settling the unemployed on the land would provide "relief": for the people from want and for the government from political pressure to do something (Bowen, 1995; Danysk, 1994). In reality public relief was shameful to apply for, was difficult to get, and soon exhausted federal and provincial treasuries. **John**, the farmer in Bicknell's play, sums up the frustration evinced by the mention of relief: "Relief! Relief! Hell! A fine name for this system of slow starvation!" (8) However, there was no better alternative to propose. On the contrary, like the government planners who looked to the land as a reservoir with which to replenish the economy, **John's** son **Ralph** intends to try homesteading, even though he knows that conditions are just as bad everywhere: "I had a letter from Jim: he says there is a quarter I can get, close to their homesteads, and if I come now, they will help me build a shack, and I can work with them and put up hay this summer" (18). He envisions a return to the land, to the imaginary wilderness of plenty with which the settlement of the Canadian West had been advertised: "I'll take my gun, and I can shoot, and you and Winnie can pick berries. Dad can cut wood and we'll manage to get a garden ploughed before it is too late, so we can raise some vegetables" (19).[6] Neither an abundant wilderness nor a beneficent government brings relief, and when it does come through private means, it is too late. The other son, **Bob**, who studied to become a doctor, has managed to raise some money and has written that the family should "get ready to come at once. Have option on farm" (26), but **John** never hears the good news since he has committed suicide.

Bicknell was not the only woman playwright at the time to wrestle with the bleakest decade in Canadian history. Already in March 1933 Elsie Park Gowan's *Homestead*, under the title *The Man Who Wouldn't Fight Back*, had been performed by the Edmonton Little Theatre and was presented in Febru-

---

5   Although it is not focused on the Prairies, see the informative article by MacKinnon on Canadian attitudes and policies on relief. See also Bye (153) on the hesitation to accept pensions.
6   On the idyllic vision of life on the prairies, see Jones.

ary 1937 by the University of Alberta Dramatic Club at the Alberta Regional of the Dominion Drama Festival in a revised version as *God Made the Country* (Gowan, 1992, 44).[7] Then, in 1939 Gwen Pharis Ringwood's *Still Stands the House*, which had had its premiere in 1938 in Chapel Hill, North Carolina, received first prize among Canadian plays at the Dominion Drama Festival.[8] Ringwood followed up this one-act play, amplifying the theme and plot while retaining the subject matter, with *Dark Harvest: A Tragedy of the Canadian Prairie*, published in 1945 and first produced in January 1945 by the University of Manitoba Dramatic Society (Anthony, 1981, 63).

In all of these works the impenetrable workings, or rather malfunctions, of the world economy are literally brought home to the audience, as the effects of inflation, drastic overproduction of basic agricultural commodities, the growing social gap between urban and rural dwellers, and unresolved gender inequities reveal the incapacity of nuclear families to serve as bastions of comfort and security, as "havens in a heartless world" (Lasch, 1979, xix). These plays shattered the illusion that rural life was a placid realm where families had been spared the social devastations already visible in nineteenth-century cities and presented by realist literature. Gowan acknowledged the influence of Thomas Hardy's realism on *Homestead*: "I was going through at that time, a Hardy fad—reading all of Hardy's books—and the theme of the cruel environment, the pitiless environment that stretches humanity right to the edge was what I was really trying to express" (Gowan, 1992, 39). While it is likely that these Canadian playwrights had become aware of the intense scrutiny of sexual and emotional conflicts in the family sphere by dramatists such as Ibsen, their personal experiences and observations were also sources of raw material and gave insights into the actual conditions of rural Canada. Again, Gowan was explicit:

> Well, *Homestead* was taken almost literally from the place that
> I stayed at Rocky Mountain House. I was living with a family
> who were barely on the edge of survival. My hostess was a
> charming woman [...] And I saw the struggle they were having,
> the struggle *she* was having to keep her children fed and have
> something on the table when I got home from school. (38–39)

7   On Gowan, see the introduction by Day. Gowan's papers are held at the University of Alberta Archives.

8   "Still Stands the House," *Canadian Theatre Encyclopedia*, online at www. canadiantheatre.com/ (accessed August 12, 2007). On Ringwood, see Anthony's essay (1987) and the monograph (1981), as well as the entry by Day online in *The Literary Encyclopedia*, www.litencyc.com/php/speople.php?rec=true&UID=3796. Ringwood's papers are held at the University of Calgary Archives.

Similarly, both Bicknell and Ringwood had been able to observe first-hand the hardships that they drew upon for their plays. The evidence from these texts opposes Yvonne Hodkinson's speculation that "[p]erhaps the economic Depression which tempted people to evade social reflection also prevented women from questioning their position in Canadian society" (10). Such a view represents the expectations of critics rather than the works that were actually being written.

The determination of these women playwrights to examine lived reality was less surprising in Western Canada than back in Ontario. For one thing, there was a lively public discourse about political and economic issues on the Prairies, which ultimately gave rise to the most radical social experiments in Canada. For another, the direct involvement of women as workers in agriculture instilled in them a sense of their worth and at the same time confronted them with their powerlessness under patriarchy (Scowby, 1996; Rollings-Magnusson, 1999). As the Depression wrecked the global economy, the burden on women as workers in the family intensified. In *Relief,* the opening stage directions signal the fundamental issues. The wind is blowing, both a cause of and emblem for the environmental catastrophe, and we see **Martha Weatherby** alone, *"patching or darning some article of man's clothing."* She is *"a kindly woman of 45 or 50 years. There is an unmistakable expression of anxiety about her once happy countenance. […] She carefully examines the article she is mending, as if looking for more holes […]."* (7) The action of trying to patch and mend represents the woman's determined attempt to use her skills and resources to repair both the material substratum as well as to keep the social fabric intact. There is no money for new clothing; the growing debts continue to open up new holes in the tattered remnants of the family's aspirations. Darning was considered women's work (Bye, 2005, 146), which might be denigrated as contributing little economic value, yet the woman continues to be productive at a time when the man has no work to do in the masculine domains of the farm. She also continues to do the psychological work of keeping her husband's spirits up:

> I know, John, things do look bad now, but maybe they won't turn out so bad after all. We did raise a little last year, and we have managed to keep some horses, and our cows are living, even if they don't give milk. Something will happen, I am sure. (9)

After he brusquely rebuffs her efforts, **John** turns upon her viciously, attacking her competence in managing family affairs:

> We had money in the Bank, and should have set tight and held on to it. (*Turns to* **MARTHA** *and with louder voice*): I knew it at

the time. But no, Bob must finish his course in medicine. The children must have their chance. They could work and pay back later, you said. (9–10)

As the dialogue of recriminations spirals out of control, **John** asserts his patriarchal authority, based on his position as the one who brings cash into the family: "Trouble is with you, Martha, your ideas are always bigger than my pocket-book" (11). Goaded to an extreme, she responds *"in low, deadly tone"*: "Look here, John Weatherby, you are not the only one around this place who has worked. I have worked, and so have the children, and they deserve—" (11). Looming over this exchange is the legal context of the time, whereby rural women were deemed by the law to have no financial share in their husband's farms and land, no matter how much labour they had contributed. Rather than accepting his wife's counsel as well as all her other efforts, he retreats even more into patriarchy, assuming familiar postures: "I have been a darned jelly-fish, that's what I've been. From now on, I'm boss. I say where the money goes—if we ever have any" (14). Because he is unwilling to accept that the family is a space of co-operative ventures, **John** has no faith that their son **Bob** will ever come to their aid, and so takes his own life. The logic of patriarchal authority triumphs in the abstract over the feminine alternative, but at the price of self-annihilation.

The death of a man at the end of Elsie Park Gowan's *Homestead* also signals the continuing dominance of the patriarchal order. **Freda Neilson** is a younger woman expecting her first child with **Brandt Neilson**, a homesteader who *"speaks with his mouth full, in a way that permits no argument"* (46). **Brandt** has no time or sympathy for a wife whose dream of life in the woods "pretty [...] like on a calendar" (54) has evaporated in the presence of reality. She, too, has learned that the lure of the West had been exaggerated in advertising: "Yes I came. *Fiercely*. And I got *fooled*. I can't see the mountains. They're just as far away as ever. And the trees aren't beautiful any more" (54). Her husband cannot understand her distress because he reduces everything to hard economic facts:

Sorry for yourself, ain't you? My God, don't I work hard enough? I work from the time the sun comes up over them trees, 'til it goes down over there. Can I help it if the dam' lumber company don't pay? Can I help it if the hail got that patch of wheat? Can I help it [...]. (48)

Defining himself as the economic motor in the family, **Brandt** disregards his wife's work in the garden, dismisses her anxieties about the upcoming childbirth, and cannot imagine why **Freda** recoils at the thought of falling into a traditional maternal role: "Say, what's the matter with you? All women want to have young ones, don't they?" (48) **Brandt** is confident that the old order is a correct one and bars any alternatives. He believes in self-reliance and has no patience with suggestions that the homesteaders need to co-operate if they want to gain more control over their economic situation: "Stick to-gether. I'd like to see the bunch of horse-thieves in these woods stick to-gether. *Spits*" (50).[9]

Trapped by custom and circumstance, **Freda** has limited possibilities for becoming independent. From her "turkey money" she is expected to pay for staples: "Matches [...] and salt—a big sack; and baking powder, and coffee; and brown shoe polish" (51–2). Only after those basic necessities are covered does she get to articulate her personal desires for "nice smelling soap, like in the advertisements" and a poetic book (52). She expresses these wishes to the neighbour **Hugh Forbes**; **Brandt** would almost certainly have refused to let her buy anything for herself. As Rollings-Magnusson observes, the husband's control over the wife's money was integral to the workings of the patriarchal economy: "In some cases this was carried to the extreme and some wives who worked all year on the farm producing goods for sale would not receive any money at all for their own use" (1999, 176). She quotes from a 1913 letter written to *The Grain Growers' Guide*:

> I never see one cent the whole year round. He does all the shopping himself, and then keeps an account of every five cents that is spent. Eggs and butter that I send up to town in summer go for groceries, I never see it. If I do happen to get to the town once in a while, I get what I want in the store, my husband comes in after me and pays the bill and asks for the receipt for goods got. (176)

It is small wonder that women often felt trapped in a system of endless work. Their husbands might talk about how everyone had to contribute for the common good, but legally women were barred from claiming their share of the farm's value, so they were in effect working for mere subsistence (McPherson, 2000, 78; Bye, 2005, 149).

Without money, **Freda** cannot even afford to give simple gifts unless she can make them herself, as when she knits a pair of socks (59). The frontier has become a prison, rather than a space where individual freedom can flourish: "I'm crying because I'm so tired, and I hate this place so, and I'm caught here [...] I'm caught here in these awful trees, and I guess I'll stay here 'til I die" (57–58). Out of desperation in such circumstances, **Freda** even dallies with

9   The difficulties in getting primary producers organized were plain to see in the case of wheat, where voluntary co-operation failed (Irwin).

the thought of running off with **Hugh**. However, the implacable wilderness prevents that escape, as **Hugh** is killed in a storm by a falling tree. The play ends on a note of muted despair as **Freda** prepares a symbolic nuptial bed for the corpse: "Yes, bring him in to me—for to-night" (63). The gestures are those of ordinary domestic chores: "*She unfolds a rug, spreads it carefully, smoothes the pillow where his head will lie*" (63). The work is futile, an expenditure without any further possibility of improving her condition because it is used up privately; there is no market for broken dreams or figments of love.

In Gwen Pharis Ringwood's *Still Stands the House: A Drama of the Canadian Frontier*, the tensions between husband and wife are complicated by the introduction of a third figure. **Hester Warren** is **Bruce Warren**'s sister and hence precluded from engaging in overt sexual relations with him, but she is strongly attached to her brother. Her internalized, repressed patriarchalism leads to the fatal tragedy. As **Bruce** and his wife **Ruth** disappear off stage into the fierce January blizzard, **Hester** remains behind to guard the dead father's legacy:

> Everything will be the same now, Father. (*She opens the Bible*). I'll read to you, Father. (*She reads with quiet contentment*.) 'And the winds blew, and beat upon that house; and it fell not: for it was founded upon a rock.' (43)

Patriarchalism triumphs in **Hester** because **Bruce** refuses to let go of the farm, even though he has not "had a crop, a good crop in five years" (37). Like **Freda Neilson**, **Ruth Warren** feels betrayed by the harsh reality of life on the land, recognizing that the barrenness of the farm has seeped into their marriage: "You two and your father lived so long in this dark house that you forgot there's a world beating outside, forgot that people laugh and play sometimes" (38–9). **Bruce** has stubbornly refused to sell the farm even though he knows that the land is poor and that the soil is blowing away. Whereas **Ruth** must think about the future because she is pregnant, he remains captivated by memories and loyalties. Everywhere the farm reminds him of the labour his parents and he had invested:

> Those rocks along the fence out there, I picked up every one of them with my own hands and carried them there. I've plowed that southern slope along the coulee every year since I was twelve. (*His voice is torn with a kind of shame for his emotion*). (38)

Like **John Weatherby** in *Relief* and **Brandt Neilson** in *Homestead*, this man will be destroyed because he clings too tightly to the habits and attitudes that once made men strong and gave them authority but which cannot cope with the massive challenges from the climate and the economic conditions. What they need to learn is how to be flexible, how to accept reality, how to adapt to changed circumstances, how to move on. As **Ruth** says, new attachments are possible: "You'd feel the same about another place after a little while" (38). But **Bruce** identifies with his property despite the evident odds against him: "When I saw the wind last spring blowing the dirt away, the dirt I'd plowed and harrowed and sowed to grain, I felt as though a part of myself was blowing away in the dust" (38).

It is not hard to locate the origin of the wives' willingness to leave the land and the rigid patriarchalism that dominates the farm economy. Unlike their husbands, the women concentrate upon their children and want better opportunities for them. The men short-sightedly invest their efforts and hopes in the land, which they have long controlled. Through the land they also control their wives and families. When the wives construe the family in personal, individual terms rather than as an economic unit, the men perceive this as something unnatural. When the women are troubled by the idea of having to bear and raise children in an isolated rural setting, the men are baffled. For **Brandt Neilson** it is utterly expected that women should want to be mothers: "Say what's the matter with you? All women want to have young ones, don't they?" (48). His sentiments are echoed closely by **Bruce Warren**: "What kind of a woman are you that you don't want your child?" (37).

The bafflement of these men when confronted with alternative theories of what a good family is and what a family owes to all the members corresponds to their inability to understand what has gone awry in their world. For them the functions of families, of fathers and husbands, of mothers and wives, have always reflected an unquestioned and functioning natural order. When factors such as drought and the Depression disrupt that order, they feel personally attacked and respond with stubbornness or with anger. Unable to rage against the land, they vent their emotions on their spouses, holding them somehow responsible for the way things have turned out.

The extremes to which patriarchy will go to maintain the status quo, even when things are in disarray, is represented by **Hester Warren**. One critic has described her as a force of nature: "the madness of nature's blizzard is reflected in **Hester**'s derangement. All blend into the land and become one with it" (Anthony, 1987). However, **Hester**'s actions are logical under the circumstances. As a woman she had not inherited the land—even though she was the older child—because of the prevailing social attitudes.[10] Without property and with only the training that prepared her to be a farm housewife, she is completely

10   On the legal and social constraints on women as landowners see: McPherson, 78; Rollings-Magnusson, 173–6; Bye, 149, 155.

dependent on her brother. Any change, particularly selling the farm, is a direct threat to her well-being, since he has no other way to make a living. For the same reason she sees in **Ruth** a competitor for scarce resources. What she cannot transcend are the values of possessive individualism. When **Ruth** proposes that they co-operate, **Hester** reacts coldly to protect what she owns:

> **HESTER.** (*rising and facing* **RUTH** *with a sudden and terrible anger*)
> Don't touch that picture. It's mine.
>
> **RUTH.** (*startled, she faces* **HESTER**) Why, Hester—
>
> **HESTER.** Can't I have anything of my own? Must you put your fingers on everything I have? (32)

For **Hester**, life has always been about productive labour; she cannot be idle and "*gives all her attention to her knitting*" (32). Her work ethic has no capacity for accepting **Ruth**'s efforts to introduce a spot of beauty into their environment. She finds **Ruth**'s care for the hyacinths disproportionate: "You've gone to as much trouble for that plant as if it were a child" (31). It is a small step from disparagement to sabotage; she furtively breaks one of the stems (35). To the uninformed bystander the episode demonstrates irrational pettiness, but at stake are fundamental issues about the utility of beauty when resources are scarce. Growing flowers was one of the few opportunities for rural women to express their creativity, but doing so was a cost to the farm economy.[11] The point is made explicit in Ringwood's later play, *Dark Harvest: A Tragedy of the Canadian Prairie*. **Lisa Hansen** wants to grow some lilacs, but her husband **Gerth** insists he cannot spare the water or the time: "I haven't time to stand here and argue. I need the water for the flax. If you've got to set those things out, you'll have to carry water for them. You've more time than I have" (72).

Hester's destruction of the hyacinth is a reminder that producing beauty is a waste of effort. The cruel little gesture anticipates her utterly ruthless defence of herself and the prevailing order when she sets the stage for her brother and sister-in-law to die in the blizzard. The means of murder are consistent with the logic of the domestic economy: by not doing the chore of filling the lantern, by consciously withholding her labour, she destroys the other family members. At the same time she deploys precious energy to get rid of the hyacinth, putting it outside to freeze. What is remarkable is the efficiency with which **Hester** acts, harnessing the winter to do the work of destroying. In the process she also economizes by not filling the lanterns

---

11 See Scowby, 11. The role of ornamental plants in the rural domestic economy is examined in detail by Lyon-Jenness.

and by extinguishing the lamp at the window. After all, kerosene had to be paid for with cash, something rural farms were always lacking. The curtain falls on a household, on an economy, that is **Hester**'s desperate attempt to hold all flux at bay.

Unlike the playwrights, who were alert to the social and economic factors in the Depression, critics have been somewhat reluctant to see the plays in their historical contexts. Judith Hinchcliffe, for example, read *Still Stands the House* for its universal symbols:

> The symbols are not arbitrarily attached to the Warrens' situation then, but are naturally found in it. The hard, dangerous life on an Alberta farm is linked to all similar moments in the history of the human race as the common nouns 'lamp,' 'storm,' 'wind,' 'cold,' etc., bring with them a sense of how they have functioned in other times and other places. (184)

However, one needs to add other common nouns to the list, such as "money" and "property," in order to comprehend the play, which opens with the real estate agent trying to persuade **Ruth** that they should sell: "Five thousand dollars and an irrigated quarter is a good price for a dry-land farm these days" (29). Why **Manning** wants to close the deal so urgently and where the capital is coming from are not explained. The air of mystery reflects how the activities of capital, directed from urban business centres far away, were invisible until they touched rural families with palpable blows such as foreclosures, offers to buy, or fluctuations in interest rates.

Reading these plays in terms of universal symbols and abstracted myths filters out their specific historical meaning. It also undermines the playwrights' determination to show that rural women have to be seen for what they were: intelligent, hard-working people conscious of their status and their interests. This revises traditional gendered images of women and the land as "essentially feminine—that is not simply the land as mother, but the land as woman, the total female principle of gratification" (Kolodny, 1975, 4). Here the women are active. They think for themselves, come to their own conclusions, and speak back to their husbands, challenging the simplistic assumption that all wives want to be mothers above everything else:

> **BRUCE.** (*going blindly on*) What makes you feel the way you do then? Other women have children without so much fuss. Other women are glad.

> **RUTH.** (*intensely angry*) Don't speak to me like that. Keep your land. Eat and sleep and dream land, I don't care! (37)

Not incidentally, **Hester Warren** applies to herself the metaphorical language used by men, equating women with the passivity of land: "My hair fell to my knees, and it was black as a furrow turned in spring" (41). But even she rejects the notion that like the land she can be compelled to bear, stating that she can choose: "I can have a husband any time I want, but my duty is here with Father" (41). Thus she turns the authority of patriarchy against itself. In the same vein **Freda Neilson** in *Relief* mocks the clichés of "Mother Nature":

> **FORBES.** Do you know, I had a sort of picture in my mind, of nature, like a kind motherly old lady, like old Mrs. Ryan.
>
> **FREDA.** Mrs. Ryan! Kind! Motherly! That's a good joke, that is.
>
> **FORBES.** *Not seeing it.* Well, ain't she?
>
> **FREDA.** Oh, she's motherly all right. She gets fifteen dollars for every baby born in this settlement, and the more there is, the better she's pleased. She doesn't care if there's no money to bring them up, or what happens to us. (55)

Talk of "Mother Nature" is quaint, hardly relevant to a world where crops of wheat and of children are measured in dollars.

If the content of these plays was radical and new, what of their form? Sherrill Grace found little that was innovative: "Resources were scarce, and Canadian taste was decidedly conservative. No truly experimental Canadian play won in the Dominion Drama Festivals, which began in 1932, and by the 1940s attention had turned to the war" (80). According to Grace, even *Still Stands the House* lagged behind, although it "exploits slight expressionistic touches" (80). Such an assessment is consistent with contemporary views of the one-act play as a genre of predictability. W. S. Milne (1936–37) attributed the popularity of one-act plays to their marketability for the amateur theatre:

> As long, then, as Canadian authors find that they have more chance of having one-act plays presented than full-length efforts, they will very naturally confine themselves to the shorter form. In some respects this is a pity, because the one-act play has practically no place in the professional theatre to-day. (369)

Practical considerations doubtless were a significant impetus for the production of one-act plays, but that should not completely obscure ways in which the genre was a sophisticated response to the challenge of representing the Depression on stage. Every dramatist writing historical and documentary plays has to find ways to bring complex events to the stage. The comprehensive approach, exemplified by Friedrich Schiller's *Wallenstein* trilogy, presents history as a complex tapestry involving many actors, many micro-events, and many brief interactions that together convey the totality of an overarching event such as a war. But how can the nebulous workings of the global economy be made visible? Bertolt Brecht developed his complex theory of epic theatre in order to explain and critique capitalism.[12] Bicknell, Gowan, and Ringwood opt for the intensive approach, concentrating on the moment when the conjunction of forces explodes within the domestic sphere. The one-act play is powerful theatre, akin to classical tragedy in the unity of time, place, and action. The reduction to just the climax of the tragedy is effective in the modern period because history has come to be understood as a series of crises.[13] The crash of the stock market in 1929 was an example of such a spectacular crisis. In a sense, each of these one-act plays re-enacts the crash. Just as the whole world was shocked by the economic catastrophe, so each family rehearses again locally the global rupture in time and the mundane world. In miniature, and using that utmost frugality women had learned from coping in hard times, these plays are stark visions of crisis, bared for all to see. After the shock of the Depression nothing could ever be the same again for the **Weatherbys**, the **Neilsons**, the **Warrens**, and thousands of other Canadian families.

It would be risky to venture more than tentative conclusions about the future reception of these plays. Certainly *Still Stands the House* has become established in the Canadian canon and is regularly performed here and abroad. Whether the analysis of the political and economic situation really concerns today's audiences may be a moot point. After a performance in Toronto, one reviewer saw the theme of the play as follows:

> Discrimination isn't a situation reserved just for women; every person on this planet has been subjected to discrimination in one form or another at some point in their life. Discrimination arises when we fail to take into consideration the feelings and opinions of an individual and use stereotyping to assume an individual's

12 On Brecht and the "representability of capitalism," see Jameson 149–60.
13 On the crisis as a basic structure for historical events, see Koselleck. A succinct overview of the topic is provided by Starn.

> personality, judging them based on the common stereotype of
> gender, ethnicity, social status, etc. (Jackson, 2007)[14]

The problems of the Depression have faded into the background for the reviewer. But then again the continued interest in *Still Stands the House* means that the issues it presents, including the economic and social ones, remain visible and alive. This could arouse renewed interest as well in Gowan's and Bicknell's treatments of similar themes with different emphases. The conjunction of these three plays invites further analysis and consideration. For example, the impact of technology in the process of modernizing agriculture altered the nature and status of traditional knowledge about farming and home economics. The need to innovate was counterbalanced by the responsibility to preserve and reproduce knowledge and values not available elsewhere in society. The tension between innovation and preservation continues to be critical for farmers, as Katherine Koller's recent play *The Seed Savers* presents, which brings the impact of genetic plant manipulation to the stage brilliantly.[15] Once again, global forces impinge on the most intimate spheres of the farm family, pitting economic gain against life-sustaining values. Like her predecessors, Koller has found a way to bring complex issues home and, like them, she makes clear that the distant prairie is close to us all. Why women playwrights have been drawn to the topics in these plays is worth pondering, more now than ever.

---

14 Performed February 4, 2007, at The Graduate Centre for Study of Drama at the University of Toronto.

15 A world premiere reading was performed at the "West-words into the 21st Century" conference in May 2007. The play subsequently received its first professional production at Workshop West Theatre (Edmonton), October 30–November 8, 2009. The play was produced again at the Station Arts Centre in Rosthern, Saskatchewan, July 1–August 1, 2010.

Works Cited

Agee, James, and Walker Evans. *Let Us Now Praise Famous Men*. New York: Ballantine, 1974.

Anthony, Geraldine. *Gwen Pharis Ringwood*. Boston: Twayne, 1981.

——. "Gwen Pharis Ringwood: Biocritical Essay [1987]." Online at University of Calgary Library, Special Collections. http://www.ucalgary.ca/lib-old/SpecColl/ringbioc.htm (accessed August 16, 2007).

Bicknell, Minnie Evans. *Relief*. Toronto: Macmillan, 1938.

Bowen, Dawn S. "'Forward to a Farm': Land Settlement as Unemployment Relief in the 1930s." *Prairie Forum* 20.2 (1995): 207–29.

Bye, Christine Georgina. "'I like to hoe my own row': A Saskatchewan Farm Woman's Notions about Work and Womanhood during the Great Depression." *Frontiers* 26.3 (2005): 135–67.

Danysk, Cecilia. "No Help for the Farm Help: The Farm Employment Plans of the 1930s in Prairie Canada." *Prairie Forum* 19.2 (1994): 231–51.

Day, Moira. "Elsie Park Gowan: A Hungry Spirit." In Gowan, *The Hungry Spirit*. 5–35.

——. "Gwen Pharis Ringwood." *The Literary Encyclopedia*. www.litencyc.com/php/speople.php?rec=true&UID=3796 (accessed December 8, 2009).

Gowan, Elsie Park. *The Hungry Spirit: Selected Plays and Prose*. Ed. Moira Day. Edmonton: NeWest Press, 1992.

Grace, Sherrill E. *Regression and Apocalypse: Studies in North American Literary Expressionism*. Toronto and London: University of Toronto Press, 1989.

Hande, D'Arcy. "Saskatchewan Merchants in the Great Depression: Regionalism and the Crusade against Big Business." *Saskatchewan History* 43.1 (1991): 21–33.

Hedley, Max. "Relations of Production of the 'Family Farm': Canadian Prairies." *Journal of Peasant Studies* 9.1 (1981): 71–85.

Hinchcliffe, Judith. "*Still Stands the House*: The Failure of the Pastoral Dream." *Canadian Drama* 3 (1977): 183–91.

Hodkinson, Yvonne. *Female Parts*. Montreal: Black Rose Books, 1991.

Holland, Robert. "Imperial Collaboration and Great Depression: Britain, Canada and the World Wheat Crisis, 1929–35." *Journal of Imperial and Commonwealth History* 16.3 (1988): 107–27.

Irwin, Robert. "Farmers and 'Orderly Marketing': The Making of the Canadian Wheat Board." *Prairie Forum* 26.1 (2001): 85–105.

Jackson, Stephanie. "Not Just Trifles, but Rather Discrimination." *The Window* (March 22, 2007). www.thewindow.net/arts/0307_plays.html (accessed December 8, 2009).

Jameson, Fredric. *Fables of Aggression: Wyndham Lewis, The Modernist as Fascist*. Berkeley: University of California Press, 1979.

Johnson, Paul. *A History of the Modern World: From 1917 to the 1980s*. London: Weidenfeld and Nicolson, 1984.

Jones, David C. "'There Is Some Power About the Land'—The Western Agrarian Press and Country Life Ideology." *Journal of Canadian Studies* 17 (1982–1983): 96–108.

Kolodny, Annette. *The Lay of the Land: Metaphor as Experience and History in American Life and Letters*. Chapel Hill: University of North Carolina Press, 1975.

Koselleck, Reinhart. *Kritik und Krise: Eine Studie zur Pathogenese der bürgerlichen Welt*. Frankfurt a.M.: Suhrkamp, 1959.

Lasch, Christopher. *Haven in a Heartless World: The Family Besieged*. New York: Basic Books, 1979.

Lyon-Jenness, Cheryl. "Bergamot Balm and Verbena: The Public and Private Meaning of Ornamental Plants in the Mid-Nineteenth Century Midwest." *Agricultural History* 73.2 (1999): 201–21.

MacKinnon, Mary. "Relief Not Insurance: Canadian Unemployment Relief in the 1930s." *Explorations in Economic History* 27 (1990): 46–83.

McPherson, Kathryn. "Was the 'Frontier' Good for Women? Historical Approaches to Women and Agricultural Settlement in the Prairie West, 1870–1925." *Atlantis* 25.1 (Fall-Winter 2000): 75–86.

Milne, W. S. "Letters in Canada: 1936. III. Drama." *The University of Toronto Quarterly* 6 (1936–1937): 369–77.

Neatby, H. Blair. *The Politics of Chaos: Canada in the Thirties*. Toronto: Macmillan, 1972.

Ringwood, Gwen Pharis. *The Collected Plays of Gwen Pharis Ringwood*. Ed. Enid Delgatty Rutland. Ottawa: Borealis Press, 1982.

Rollings-Magnusson, Sandra. "Hidden Homesteaders: Women, the State and Patriarchy in the Saskatchewan Wheat Economy, 1870–1930." *Prairie Forum* 24.2 (Fall 1999): 185–209.

Scowby, Christa. "'I Am A Worker, Not A Drone': Farm Women, Reproductive Work and the *Western Producer*, 1930–1939." *Saskatchewan History* 48.2 (1996): 3–13.

Starn, Randolph. "Historians and 'Crisis.'" *Past and Present* 52 (August 1971): 3–22.

Tait, Michael. "Drama and Theatre." *Literary History of Canada: Canadian Literature in English*. Vol. 2. General ed. Carl F. Klinck. Toronto and Buffalo: University of Toronto Press, 1977, 143–67.

Finding Regina, Third Wave Feminism, and Regional Identity

SHELLEY SCOTT

I teach in Lethbridge, Alberta, a prairie city with a population of just over 80,000, and I taught the play *Finding Regina* by Shoshana Sperling in my third-year undergraduate Canadian Theatre course in the spring of 2007. This paper is grounded in the response of my forty-four students to the play, and in the power of *Finding Regina* to speak to my student demographic. The manner in which the play deals with regionalism is an especially effective representation of colonialism and its continuing effect on Canadian identity; regionalism also manages to intertwine with the play's feminism in an intriguing and contemporary way.

The students were assigned a weekly written report on the plays we studied, and for *Finding Regina* I asked them to write about whether or not they could relate their own high school experiences to those of the three characters in the play. As I had anticipated, most of them related very strongly, and, in most cases, the students cited the characteristics common to growing up in a small city or town. Their hometowns in Alberta ranged from small cities like Lethbridge and Fort MacMurray (51,000), to very small places like Brooks (12,500), Drumheller (6,500), and Coaldale (6,000). Hometowns outside of Alberta ranged from Langley, British Columbia (117,000), Summerland, British Columbia (11,000), Weyburn, Saskatchewan (9,000), and Blind River, Ontario (4,000), down to Ste. Anne, Manitoba, with a population of 1,500. Students from cities the actual size of Regina (population 200,000) or larger, such as Vancouver, Calgary, and Saskatoon, had a harder time relating to the play, but those students were in the minority.

The majority of my students are from places much smaller than Regina, and yet these were the students who spoke repeatedly of how well the play depicted life in a small city or town just like their own. One student wrote: "It was uncanny: the similarities in everything from the weather to the people to the cars to the stereotypes."[1] Beyond the expected points of recognition around things like blizzards and hockey, there were two main topics of intersection: first, the realities of substance abuse and suicide in their communities; and second, the love-hate relationship they have with their hometowns, and their profound sense that where they come from informs who they believe themselves to be. One student referred to the experience of reading the play as "a forced review of my life thus far."[2] Identifying with where you live is a kind of kinship bond. Many of my students wrote about the experience of coming from a place where they know everyone and everyone knows them; as one student put it, "One mistake and you'll never live it down."[3]

In *Land Sliding: Imagining Space, Presence, and Power in Canadian Writing* (1997), W. H. New asks what constitutes a city in Canadian literature and concludes that it is size and economic advantage: "But relative size, along with location and local influence and reputation, also determines the image that any urban area projects" (157). He cites Vancouver, Calgary, Winnipeg and Halifax as cities struggling between a desire to be recognized as "world class" and a desire to remain neighbourly, and then asks: "What, then, of 'small cities': Kelowna, Regina, Saint John, Trois-Rivières? As far as power is concerned—"at least, *felt* power"—they are all equally remote from the centres of real power, which New identifies as Toronto and Montreal (157–58). New concludes that this sense of being remote from the centres of power leads, in small cities, to a sense of political injustice: "people attach multiple resonances of meaning to place when they claim 'place' for an identity" (131). In other words, to identify with one's geographic location is a "claim upon significance" resulting from a desire for influence that comes from this "felt *lack* of power" (131). In the introduction to *A Sense of Place: Re-evaluating Regionalism in Canadian and American Writing* (1998), Herb Wyile et al. write that "[t]he use of the term regionalism, indeed, has always been a conflicted one, bringing into view tensions between the centre and the periphery, the rural and urban, the local and cosmopolitan, the regional and the national" (xi). My students identified with the experience of marginalization through the belief that their hometown does not really count in the larger identity of the nation. This marginalization from

---

1   Whitney Exelby. All student quotations are from students enrolled in Drama 3130: Canadian Theatre, University of Lethbridge, Spring 2007. Used with permission.
2   Nic Barker.
3   Megan Tolsdorf.

power is further compounded by virtue of their age and status as students, in some cases by their race, and—because the majority of my drama students are female—also by their gender.[4]

Finding Regina was published in Winnipeg by Scirocco Drama in 2003. The play began as *The Regina Monologues* in Toronto at the Buddies in Bad Times Rhubarb Festival in 2001, and was then produced as *Finding Regina* by the Globe Theatre in Regina, in association with Nightwood Theatre and Theatre Passe Muraille. It premiered at the Globe on October 8, 2002, directed by Nightwood's artistic director, Kelly Thornton, and then went on to a run at Passe Muraille in Toronto (February 18 to March 9, 2003).

The cast featured Shoshana Sperling herself as **Annabel**, with Jeremy Harris as **Josh** and Teresa Pavlinek as **Rae**. Shoshana Sperling had been better known as a stand-up comedian than as a playwright, often performing character-based comedy at Toronto venues and on television.[5] Sperling describes *Finding Regina* as a love letter: "this play is really an homage to Regina because I have this love for the place that I just can't quite shake" (quoted in *Nightwood* 2003, 1). In fact, the published play is prefaced with a list of acknowledgements written in the form of a letter to Regina, which begins, "I miss you so much when I'm away from you." Further along, she writes, "This play is for me and also those still finding Regina way out in Toronto, Vancouver, Calgary, Montreal" (5).[6] Sperling has received many comments that "the play could be set anywhere in Canada as it is such an honest depiction of going home" (*Nightwood* 2003, 1). As Sperling implies, to "find one's Regina" is a metaphor, meaning to reconnect with where you come from and who you are.

In his *NOW* article, the theatre critic Glenn Sumi offers a brief summary of the play: "In Sperling's deceptively simple piece, three former high school friends meet up in the local ICU when another friend attempts suicide. They reconnect, throw their weight around, smoke up, then bemoan their current lives and chip away at the past and each other with emotional ice picks" (2003, 58). The situation does not immediately read as explicitly feminist, yet feminist concerns underline all the themes of the play. The focus is on the fortunes of a generation that grew up together in Regina, and the disproportionate

---

4   All but two of the students I quote in this paper are female.

5   Other plays by Sperling include the one-person shows *The Rise and Fall of Vella Dean,* *The Golden Mile,* and *Sheboobie.* Most recently, she wrote *The Guilty Play Room* with Teresa Pavlinek and premiered it at the 2004 Hysteria Festival in Toronto. Most of her work has been done at a Fringe or other festival context. *Finding Regina* is Sperling's only published work. After leaving Regina, she attended York and Concordia universities.

6   All quotations from the play are taken from Shoshana Sperling, *Finding Regina* (Winnipeg: Scirocco Drama, 2003).

number of them who have committed suicide. Old high school pals **Annabel**, **Rae**, and **Josh** have gathered at the hospital in Regina to wait for news about their friend **Clarky**, who has attempted to kill himself. **Annabel**, the character played by Sperling, has moved to Toronto and is doing a master's degree in Women's Studies, "with a specialization in concepts of male and female archetypes in Western Civilization" (Sperling, 22). This allows **Annabel** to deliver a mini-lecture on how classics written by women have been "misinterpreted by patriarchal society" (22). She tries to explain her thesis but the other characters are unable to follow her argument, which is dense with academic jargon, especially after they share a joint or two in **Josh's** car. Thus, **Annabel's** feminism is positioned as something that is vital to her new life in Toronto, but irrelevant once she comes back home to Regina.

The character **Rae**, a pretty and popular girl in high school, has moved to Vancouver and become a wife and mother. She is now thirty and, like **Annabel**, she has been back to Regina a few times—often for the funerals of friends— but this is the first time in ten years that all three have been together. At first **Rae** seems shallow, bragging about her status as a "permi parent" volunteer at her daughters' private school and her husband's skill as a provider (17). **Rae** is a proponent of popular psychology and self-help books to explain her marriage, but **Annabel** cynically rejects all such theorizing about personality and identity. **Annabel** declares: "It's all about looks. We're conditioned to believe that if we find a mate with ideal physical beauty, then we'll fall in love" (27). She argues that marriages based on looks alone will end up being empty and devoid of intimacy, concluding that, "most people who grow up being splendidly beautiful might find themselves in a relationship that might be splendidly empty" (28). She is obviously referring to **Rae**, and the roots of her hostility become apparent later in the play.

Josh is the character who stayed in Regina. In recounting his extensive sexual exploits, past and present, **Josh** inadvertently reveals that he does not remember having sex with **Annabel** in high school. This prompts an angry **Annabel** to reveal that she was, in fact, very promiscuous throughout her high school years: "But not looking as girls should look, it was kept a secret. Boys tell their adventures. Unless they're embarrassed" (38). Unlike popular and sought-after girls like **Rae**, whom **Annabel** describes as "tall, thin and perfect" (38), **Annabel** never had a "public" boyfriend, but she did have sex with many guys in secret simply because she made herself available. She explains: "Girls wanted to have sex but they were so worried for their reputations. I never worried about any of that because … No one ever told. They just came back for more. I practised this behaviour into my university years until I finally moved out of Regina" (38). For **Annabel**, **Rae** is the centre and she is at the margins.

This focus on a complex and unequal relationship, and the differences between the two women, mark the play as third wave in its feminism. While the suffrage movement is considered to have been the first wave of feminism, and the 1960s through the early 1980s was the second wave, we are currently in the third wave. Individual (rather than collective, gendered) identity, personal choice, and sexual freedom are issues pertinent to the third wave, which has been particularly willing to address the differences and antagonisms between women as topics for feminist inquiry. **Annabel** and **Rae** were the best of friends, but their shared gender was not enough to unite them in the face of sexual competition and a culturally determined beauty standard. To watch a play that addresses honestly a painful dynamic in female relationships is exciting for the audience, especially for young female spectators who recognize and have grappled with similar issues themselves, but may not have seen them dealt with onstage before. By the end of the play, the two friends are able to clear the air and admit they miss each other, but their physical and economic circumstances will continue to have a major impact on their very different female identities.

The issue of sexual choice also relates to the repressive atmosphere of secrecy that has prevented their friend **Clarky** from revealing his homosexuality. **Annabel** discloses that **Clarky** came out to her in high school, but that there was no one else he could tell, including his homophobic best friend **Josh** (40). She claims that **Josh's** extreme promiscuity with women was subconsciously an attempt to distance himself from **Clarky**. **Annabel** criticizes **Josh** for downplaying his friendship with **Clarky**, characterizing it only as that of casual drinking buddies. She accuses **Josh**: "He's the only real relationship you've ever had outside of your family. The most important relationship in your life is with a gay man. He didn't try to kill himself because he was gay. It's because he was alone. With you every day and totally alone" (49).

In retaliation, **Josh** confronts **Annabel** with the fact that she, too, once attempted suicide, the summer after high school, and that it was **Clarky** who found and saved her. **Annabel** admits how much she hated her life at that time: "I just had nothing to look forward to. I was always comparing myself to others. What they had, that they were loved, the way they looked and I was never as good" (52). There are fascinating parallels here with the classic colonial belief that life is better elsewhere, some*where* more glamorous. The same dynamic is echoed in the experience of the young woman who believes that life is better for some*one* else, some*one* more glamorous. **Annabel** remembers that **Clarky** drove her home from the hospital "and helped me pack my stuff and got me out of Regina cause he knew it was killing me to stay. And not the city, the place" (53). When **Clarky** called her unexpectedly years later she did not return his call because his voice brought it all back to her: "I'm not the same person I was… his voice is this place to me and the way he sounded…

is...me. The old me and ...I didn't call him back" (53). Like so many others, **Annabel** tries to disavow the margins of geography and to distance herself from the experience of where she is from in an attempt to build a new, more cosmopolitan identity for herself at the centre.

One could argue that **Annabel** and her friends blame Regina for their distress, even though their problems have clearly followed them to their new cities. Frank Davey has argued that geography seems more important to the concept of regionalism than to the concept of the nation-state as a whole, and because of this, regionalism can seem more concrete and less abstract, more inevitable:

> What is often obscured in these various constructions are the politically oppositional aspects of regionalism: that regionalism is cultural rather than geographic, and represents not geography itself but a strategically resistant mapping of geography in which historic and economic factors play large but unacknowledged parts (1998, 4).

New suggests that representations of land "illustrate many of the sociocultural and socioeconomic issues raised by post-colonial theory: the issues of colony and empire, wealth and power, centre and margin, the opportunity to speak and the likelihood of being heard" (1997, 11).

Other theorists have also speculated on the cultural nature of regionalism. Marjorie Pryse suggests that "[a]s a preliminary definition, we might agree that regionalism represents the deep structure of local knowledge, where geographical and literary landscape become imbued and interwoven with features of culture" (1998, 19). David Martin says that "[a] local colour story [...] tries to render the inner logic of these places—what the people are like, how they live, and why" (1998, 37).

One of the things my students found most compelling about the play is the recognizable way the characters talk; the students appreciated the way the dialogue is layered with local expressions and references. Geography is deeply resonant with shared associations—in this case, with particular locations in Regina. This is evident in *Finding Regina* in the characters' humorous nicknames for Regina, which include Red China; Reggie; and Vagina, Saskratchyerbum (31). (My own students could cite "Deathbridge" as our near equivalent.) Another geographically related topic of humour in the play is the intense cold. The play begins with the iconic song by Foreigner—"Cold as Ice"—and the references continue with jokes about wind chill, how quickly exposed skin can freeze, and an elaborate classification system for degrees of winter coldness, culminating with the very coldest—"Humongatory Frozanation" (42). New writes that

> [t]hose whose sense of land (and self, and the language of ex-pressing this connection) reinforces and is reinforced by their dominant position within the culture at large will differ from those whose sense of land, self, and language (however acute and locally fulfilling) still divides them from the dominant forms of social power (1997, 117).

There is an irony in the fact that the use of local language binds the characters in a shared sense of belonging, history, nostalgia, and comradeship, and yet all of this is predicated on disenfranchisement. As Linda Hutcheon has noted, irony, like other forms of doubleness, paradox, and self-reflexivity, is a technique for "resisting yet acknowledging the power of the dominant" (2004, 82). As one of my students wrote:

> Every word that came out of the characters' mouths made me want to keep reading. I felt as though I knew the characters, and as I read the play I assigned images of people I know to the roles. This play is intensely Canadian in its words, characters, loca-tions, and actions. Shoshana Sperling has done an impeccable job of not creating a world, but recreating a world. A very real world which exists not only in Regina, but in all marginalized Canadian cities struggling to find identity.[7]

Post-colonial plays draw attention to cultural differences and one clear example is the authenticity of language, the celebration of local (not proper) usages. New concludes that those writers who are "the most forceful challeng-ers of the normative presumptions of anglophone Ontario male history" are writing from regionalism and marginality—whether of geography, ethnicity, or gender (152). As a Jewish woman growing up in Regina, Shoshana Sperling would certainly qualify. At one point, her character **Annabel** asks after an old friend, sarcastically identifying him as "another member of the massive Jewish population in Regina" (30).

Finding Regina also touches on racism towards the Aboriginal population. There are references to police abuse of Natives, stories about violent crime, and the recounting of an urban legend: a gang of Native girls who allegedly disfigure pretty white girls at the mall (34). This was an aspect that resonated

---

7   Michelle Thorne.

with some of my students; one wrote about moving to Portage la Prairie, Manitoba (7,000) to go to high school and the attitude she encountered there:

> The one thing I noticed when I was in high school was that everyone was extremely racist toward Aboriginals in the community. Since I grew up in a northern community with both Caucasian and Aboriginal people who lived happy together, I literally had no clue what racism was. It hurt my heart hearing these two groups of people fist fight and call each other horrible racist names. It was a definite eye-opener for me.[8]

Other negative aspects of the characters' experiences, and those of my students', are the abuse of drugs and alcohol and the prevalence of suicide and untimely death. In reference to the widespread use of cocaine in her hometown of Brooks, one student wrote:

> This is in part due to the large amount of money generated by the oil industry and partly due to the fact that there is officially nothing to do there. The summer after high school, I worked in a local bar and one of my jobs was to regularly go into the bathrooms and wipe my hand across the top of the toilet tank and do a 'coke check'.[9]

In *Finding Regina*, **Josh** recounts the fate of one of their classmates who died in a "[d]rinking and driving accident near Prince Albert. Froze to death. They found her sitting straight up 100 feet from the car. She mighta lived if anyone had driven by" (36). New says that when writers place their works on the prairies, "*distance* is one of the chief attributes of description. [...] distance is an image affiliated with time as much as with space, and with pressure as much as with comfort" (1997, 126). Most often, my students attributed the death of their peers to drinking and driving:

> Probably because there wasn't much to keep us occupied, and we couldn't always go to Calgary, people turned to substance abuse instead [...] The high school isn't known for any significant suicide rate [...] but only because people tended to kill themselves with overdose and reckless driving.[10]

---

8   Pattie Dwyer.
9   Jenna Erlandson.
10 Karin Atkinson.

Yet another student wrote:

> Within this past year I have had to unfortunately bury two of my
> friends from high school. Each of the funerals became largely
> high school reunions and we would all spend hours catching
> up and re-connecting with each other. I haven't spoken to any
> of them since the last funeral, but I know that we all still share
> a special bond. We survived the most awkward years of our
> lives together.[11]

And in one further example, "I have been out of high school for three years,
and since then, three people I went to school with have committed suicide."[12]

Finding Regina is not the official story, not the "Chamber of Commerce"
narrative, but is, instead, postmodern: of the margins. It is not a metanarrative
but a fragmented and subjective piecing together to create a story of a place,
according to these characters. The negative interpretation of **Josh** is that he is
still acting like he is in high school and is in denial about **Clarky's** pain (49).
But **Josh** did leave at one point and chose to come back. His biggest fear is
that he will be the last one of his generation who does stay; at the end he
recounts a nightmare: "I look around and I'm the only one who's my age. You
know? Anywhere. The city is totally cleaned out of people from 19 to I don't
know…40. They're all gone" (59). In the dream **Josh** realizes that everyone
from his yearbook is dead and "I know that I'm the only one left to say anything
over the coffins" (60). **Josh** tells the stories, recounts the lives, of everyone
they went to school with. His narrative is multiple, spiralling, unravelling, and
defies any coherent, centralizing interpretation. **Josh** claims: "Everyone knows
me and I know all of them. Most of them intimately" (31) and urges the two
women to test him: any name they call out, **Josh** knows what happened to
that person. He is the keeper of community.

W. H. New believes that "Canadian writing recurrently takes characters on
journeys home; far from the standard American model of eternal progress—
'you can't go home again'—Canadian writing advises that you must return, in
order to place the past apart, to read its other-centred rules in a fresh way, and
to make the present and future home, whatever its relationship with a distant
childhood, your own." New quotes a character from Margaret Atwood's *Sur-
facing* who declares "sardonically and self-deprecatingly" that she is "on home
ground, foreign territory" (1997, 159–160). Many of my students expressed

---

11   Jenn Campbell.
12   Amy Davey.

ambivalent attitudes towards the places they went to high school and, not surprisingly, related most with **Annabel**, who escaped through education.

One female student wrote:

> Like **Annabel**, I feel like my life is more worthwhile now that I am away getting an education. I hope I never have to go back to where I am from for any extended period of time because it is a draining place to be and one that is very unhealthy to my growth as a person.[13]

In a similar vein, one student wrote, "Looking at my graduating class of 2004, it is apparent that the people who left as soon as humanly possible are the ones that will end up making something of themselves."[14]

On the other hand, some students became nostalgic for what their hometowns had meant to them: "It really made me miss my back home friends. Reading this play made me remember what a double-edged sword going back home can be. Your friends are the people who know where you've come from, but they are also the ones who have the hardest time accepting who you want to become."[15] Many expressed gratitude for having grown up in a close-knit community that they feel they can always go back to. As one Aboriginal student said, "I always find [...] that when someone dies, like so many people do on the rez [...] that's when your true family and friends come back into your life."[16]

Another student pointed out that the three characters had better stories about their lives in Regina than about their new lives in Vancouver or Toronto; she reflected:

> Those stories made them who they are and growing up in a small town made me who I am ... I still have a little **Josh** inside me that wants to just stay in Brooks and party with my old friends and know everyone I see in Safeway and raise my kids the way I was raised: catching gophers with my bare hands. There is also a little **Annabel** in me who wants to be free and live in a place where no one knows me and can appreciate things like art and theatre and music that isn't by Garth Brooks ... Also there is some **Rae** in me who wants a family in a big city where I can put my kids through private school and buy them designer diapers. This

13   Cathie Brown.
14   Jenna Erlandson.
15   Michelle Thorne.
16   Murray Pruden.

play was basically a blueprint of my life and it made me realize a little more that I would not trade growing up in a small town for anything in the world.[17]

As Sperling has commented, "Where we are from is who we are. I'm still friends with so many people from Regina. When I meet people from the prairies, even from Winnipeg, there's a bond. Maybe it's the weather that makes you reach out. If you see a car on the side of the road you pull over, because there's not going to be another for a long time and that person might freeze to death" (quoted in Sumi 2003, 58).

Sperling's equation of weather-related peril to a sense of responsibility is an excellent illustration of the link between geography and identity. It is a clear example of how shared hardships help to forge lifelong bonds. **Annabel** (and Shoshana Sperling herself) would not feel the pull to return if she did not take an almost perverse pride in having survived a difficult adolescence in a place she hated, but with people she loved. **Annabel** owes it to **Clarky**, and to Regina, to come back and help. It is interesting to note that the Saskatchewan government plays on a similar sense of responsibility in their print advertisement campaign, which runs in Alberta newspapers and invites those who have moved away to come back. The message is that, even for those who have left, Saskatchewan will always remain "home" in a way that no other place can become. *Finding Regina* captures the contradiction between a lingering colonial sense of disenfranchisement, and an experience of regionalism that profoundly shapes one's sense of identity and belonging.

Works Cited

Davey, Frank. "Toward the Ends of Regionalism." *A Sense of Place: Re-evaluating Regionalism in Canadian and American Writing.* Ed. Christian Riegel and Herb Wyile. Edmonton: University of Alberta Press, 1998, 1–17.

Edwards, Justin D., and Douglas Ivison. "Introduction: Writing Canadian Cities," and "Epilogue." *Downtown Canada: Writing Canadian Cities.* Ed. Justin D. Edwards and Douglas Ivison. Toronto: University of Toronto Press, 2005, 3–13 and 197–208.

Hutcheon, Linda. "'Circling the Downspout of Empire': Post-Colonialism and Postmodernism." *Unhomely States: Theorizing English-Canadian Postcolonialism.* Ed. Cynthia Sugars. Mississauga: Broadview Press, 2004, 71–93.

17   Jill Oberg.

Martin, David. "'Regionalist' Fiction and the Problem of Cultural Knowledge." *A Sense of Place: Re-evaluating Regionalism in Canadian and American Writing*. Ed. Christian Riegel and Herb Wyile. Edmonton: University of Alberta Press, 1998, 35–50.

New, W. H. *Land Sliding: Imagining Space, Presence, and Power in Canadian Writing*. Toronto: University of Toronto Press, 1997.

Nightwood Theatre: Excellent Theatre by Women (Spring 2003 Newsletter). [Distributed to its membership, three to four times yearly, by Nightwood Theatre.]

Pryse, Marjorie. "Writing Out of the Gap: Regionalism, Resistance, and Relational Reading." *A Sense of Place: Re-evaluating Regionalism in Canadian and American Writing*. Ed. Christian Riegel and Herb Wyile. Edmonton: University of Alberta Press, 1998, 19–34.

Sperling, Shoshana. *Finding Regina*. Winnipeg: Scirocco Drama, 2003.

Sumi, Glenn. "Shoshana Sperling: Funny Girl Plays with her Regina." *NOW* 22.25 (February 20–26 2003): 58.

Wyile, Herb, Christian Riegel, Karen Overbye, and Don Perkins. "Introduction: Regionalism Revisited." *A Sense of Place: Re-evaluating Regionalism in Canadian and American Writing*. Ed. Christian Riegel and Herb Wyile, Edmonton: University of Alberta Press, 1998, ix-xiv.

Confidently Canadian:
Questioning Canadian Regionalism

MARTIN PŠENIČKA

I. SENSE OF PLACE

Canada, this "magnificent abstraction" of a nation, as Vincent Massey puts it in his seminal 1922 essay "The Prospects of a Canadian Drama" (2004, 59), has always lacked (and in principle has refused) a defining historical breaking point or distinctive "proto-national conditions" (i.e., language, race, religion) (Hobsbawm quoted in Filewod, 1992, 5–9), which would assert once and for all its own national identity. Consequently, the urge for the staging or, better to say, re-staging of a nation and re-writing of its national ideology has always played a crucial and necessary role in order to make "the abstraction" a concrete and unified socio-political entity.

Having been situated since its early years between "contradicting 'primals'" (Grant, 1994, 17) of colonial tradition and neo-imperial modernity, of national interests and seductive capitalist internationalism, Canada as a national entity *sui generis* has embodied, as Alan Filewod argues, a site for production(s) of "changing national ideologies of nationhood" (Filewod, 1992, 4) and "conflicting readings of the nation" (3). As a territorially, rather than ethnically, linguistically, or religiously delineated "Noah's ark of a nation" (Verdecchia, 1997, 74), it cannot be easily perceived, even by itself, as a traditional nation-state shaped by a clear sense of manifest divine or cultural identity. Thus, Canada's search for a unifying national principle and firmly anchored identity has never embodied a simple solution. That is why any attempt to achieve a stable modus vivendi represents, in the case of Canada, an unfinished project, or "continued failure" (Filewod, 1992, 3), and that is why Canada was classified by some as "an uncertain nation" (Grant, 1994, 37). However incomplete or abstract, Canada's pursuit of "true Canadianism" has taken place within cultivated and peaceful intellectual debates, thus evoking language games rather than the battlefield. As such, that pursuit has represented a cultural process of unceasing reinterpretation and self-deconstructing re-evaluation. Canada could therefore be considered a prototype of the post-nation-state constructed by means of discourse (rather than ideology)—a place of constant renewal, re-creation, and recontextualization. By embracing discourse as the centre of identity, Canada might well merit its description in some critiques as "a poststructuralist paradise" (Flamengo, 2004, 147).

Regionalism is one of the significant concepts/discourses that have made a substantial contribution to the perpetual language game over the nature of the Canadian nation. Over the past four decades, regionalism as a term denoting a form of cultural as well as political critique has undergone many shifts and turns. For some regional essentialists, regionalism embodied a missing substance of "the Canadian nation as it historically and geographically exists and as it is likely to exist in any foreseeable future" (Woodcock, 1987, 23). As George Woodcock argues: "Region making and nation making are aspects of the same process, since the special character of Canada as a nation is that of a symbiotic union of regions, as organic as a coral reef" (31). For others involved in the national fervour of the 1970s, regionalism carried "a negative force of fragmentation" (Flamengo, 2004, 241) or even a "frostbite" (Frye, 1971, 134), restraining and disintegrating the construction of one unified Canada. Positively, regionalism has served as a critical counterdiscourse to the politics of homogeneity by decentralizing and dismantling "wrong-headed histories written by Eastern historians" (Kroetsch quoted in Moss, 2003, 9) and providing an alternative means by which "Canadians sometimes write back to other Canadians" (9).

Since the mid-1980s, in the era of accelerated globalization paving the way for the post-national Canada as Northrop Frye foresaw it (1982, 15), regionalism turned into a last hope for sustaining local (that is, Canadian national) distinctiveness vis-à-vis swamping multinational corporationalism. Ironically enough, a post-national present as "a social universe in constant motion, a moving cartography with a floating culture and a fluctuating sense of self" (Fuentes quoted in Verdecchia, 1997, 70) exposed regionalism as a rather limited and unsuitable binary model. As with the concept of nation, the concept of region as an entity "distinguished by a dominant geographical feature and an associated industry or way of life" (Flamengo, 2004, 244) as distinct from that of other regions or centres has been rendered obsolete by globalization and the electronic age. Similarly, a time-honoured concept of region as defined by a close sense of human bonding with a particular land or place, or as Woodcock expresses it, "the geographical feeling of locality, the historical feeling of a living community, the personal ties to a place where one has been born or which one has passionately adopted" (1987, 23), fatally errs in lumping together and homogenizing a huge chunk of increasingly diverse individuals, identities, and formations existing within a shifting flux of time and space.

Region—or, better to say, the boundaries and means by which regions are mapped out—has been radically transformed and blurred. In his 1993 "Introduction" to *The* CTR *Anthology*, Alan Filewod employed a now famous term—"region of experience" (xv-xvi)—that is profoundly detached from any geographical determination. However essentialist that concept might also be, it brought forward a new perspective on a region as a socio-political space. Ongoing investigations in regional and border issues influenced by post-structuralist and post-colonial theories extended this view, envisaging a region in a far more complex and ambivalent light as "a space [...] created in language" (Flamengo, 2004, 245). Hence, region is neither a naturally given quality pre-existing human activity, nor a stable shared experience that is self-referential. Instead, it is a human construct—an imagined, changeable, and discursively created entity—only suggesting (if not ideologically prescribing) what region or shared experience could or should be rather than what it actually is. It is language as a powerful human weapon with its mighty ability to conquer reality by the force of naming that brings things, animals, and continents into existence. In other words, a region becomes a region discursively at the very moment of language invasion, at the moment of utterance that captures, dominates, and essentially forms a reality.

II. SENSE OF PLAYS

What is, then, the West and its possible "words," the words of the twenty-first-century Canadian Prairies we are supposed to assess here? First off, in accordance with Craig S. Walker, author of the brilliant work *The Buried Astrolabe*, for whom "universally ascribe[d] identity [...] is not only illiberal and dehumanizing but demonstrably inaccurate" (2001, 18), I am convinced that any generalization, however politically or socially empowering it might be, is a sterile—and misleading—approach that depersonalizes the individual and unrepeatable act of human creation. For the purposes of this paper, I have selected three plays written by three contemporary Prairie playwrights— Brad Fraser's *Unidentified Human Remains and the True Nature of Love* (1989, published 1990), Brian Drader's *Prok* (2003), and Vern Thiessen's *Einstein's Gift* (2003)—whose work could be linked together in two above-mentioned regional modes: geographical and experiential. Brad Fraser and Brian Drader can be associated with each other on the grounds of their gender, while Drader and Thiessen, both originally coming from Winnipeg,[1] could be related by means of their shared geographical experience.

Fraser's *Unidentified Human Remains and the True Nature of Love* and Drader's *Prok* could be certainly easily distinguished, as it were, as gay plays deconstructing the ideology of heteronormativity. Nevertheless, Fraser's human tragicomedy, enwrapped in the horror atmosphere of the contemporary city of Edmonton as haunted by a serial killer, embodies an anarchistic portrayal of a sick world on the verge of collapse and deterioration. Composed of a cobweb of people and relations, Fraser's play focuses on a literal unmasking of regimes of normality ideologically constructing and eliminating the inappropriate/abnormal other. Explicitly displayed homosexuality, heterosexuality, love, sex, sensuality, infidelity, and violence are not only natural parts of Fraser's "queer-planet"[2] ("queer" in both senses of the word), but constitute this universe by means of their mutual coexistence and interaction.

Unlike Fraser's spectacular and shocking tour de force, Drader's structurally spare memory play, *Prok,* could be considered a dramatic philosophical essay. Based on the life story of controversial American sexologist Alfred Kinsey ("Prok") (1894–1956), whose monumental studies *Sexual Behaviour in the Human Male* (1948) and *Sexual Behaviour in the Human Female* (1953) were accused of "destroying morals of Western civilization" (Drader, 2003, 65), the central theme of the play represents a concept of normality in relation to sexual behaviour of humans per se. Kinsey's work is well known for its subversion of fixed sexual behaviour categories, that is, heterosexuality, homosexuality, and bisexuality. Convinced of the versatility and fluidity of sexual preferences, Kinsey replaced these three simplifying categories with what is known as Kinsey's scale; this consists of seven, or more precisely eight, ranks that reflect various forms of male and female sexual activities (a rank eight called "X" regarding humans without any sexual desire was not included in the scale). According to Kinsey, "Males do not represent two discrete populations, heterosexual and homosexual. The world is not to be divided into sheep and goats. It is a fundamental of taxonomy that nature rarely deals with discrete categories [...] The living world is a continuum in each and every one of its aspects" (Kinsey, 1948[3]). Publication of Kinsey's research achievements that became "more

1 Actually, Thiessen spent his formative "theatre" years in Edmonton, studying Drama at the University of Alberta, and, hence, could be also, from this perspective, related to Fraser.

2 Here I freely paraphrase a term used in the title of the anthology, *Fear of A Queer Planet: Queer Politics and Social Theory,* Ed. Michael Warner (Minneapolis: University of Minnesota Press, 1993).

3 Alfred Kinsey, *Sexual Behavior in the Human Male* (1948). Quoted in "What is 'The Kinsey Scale'?" www.kinseyinstitute.org/research/ak-hhscale.html#what

powerful than an atomic bomb, than an entire army" (Drader, 65) turned the existing heterocentric regime of normality/oddity upside down and "Prok" grew into a popular icon symbolizing the beginning of sexual revolution.

To interpret both plays within the narrow terms of sexuality would, however, violate their structural as well as thematic richness. Fraser's *Unidentified Human Remains*, ushering in the wave of "in yer face" theatre of the 1990s, is mainly about desperate loneliness and estrangement in the nuclear age of growing consumerism and technological development. Despite its ideological affinity with Drader's *Prok*, it shares more, both structurally and thematically, with plays such as Mark Ravenhill's blatant inquiry into the modern world's shallowness and superficiality, *Shopping and Fucking*, or Roland Schimmelpfennig's rather poetic condominium story, *Arabian Night*. A play about human beings' never-ending fairy tale of desire to reach out for human contact in the face of the inexorable separateness of human beings, Schimmelpfennig's work formally intensifies the conflict by the employment of introspective and highly descriptive monologues that, at times, spring forth into dialogues.

Drader's *Prok*, then, is by no means a simplifying interpretation of Kinsey's theory, but a complex work elaborating on issues that go far beyond the scope of the conventional "gay play." These include women's position in society, scientific ethics, and the interconnection between private and public life. Of particular interest is the feminist-like approach of the play, whose major protagonist and storyteller is a woman—Kinsey's wife, **Clara**, who gave up her promising scholarly career after falling in love with **Prok**. At one point, **Clara** commemorates a work by Dr. Mary Stopes who, in 1918, wrote a sexual manual, *Married Love*: "It was an excellent, straightforward guide, largely ignored because it was written by a woman, and in 1918 women were not considered sexual beings. They were considered receptacles for penises. Prok knew about her work. He thought the manual was quite good. He never addressed it in public though. He was afraid people wouldn't take him seriously" (Drader, 55).

The character of **Clara** could serve as a bridging element between Drader's *Prok* and Vern Thiessen's *Einstein's Gift*, wherein a character of the same name and profession sacrifices her career and eventually her life for a beloved husband. Nevertheless, the two plays are linked by more than a similarity in the main female characters. Defying any simple categorization or placement, *Einstein's Gift* is a complex drama based on the lives of two German-Jewish scientists, one a chemist, Fritz Haber (1868–1934), and the other a physicist, Albert Einstein (1879–1955), whose scientific accomplishments became directly responsible for thousands of people being killed in WWI and WWII. Like Michael Frayn's retrospective *Prok*-like play, *Copenhagen*, which elaborates on the lives of German physicist Werner Heisenberg (1901–1976) and his Danish colleague, Nils Bohr (1885–1962), Thiessen's play poses poignant questions closely related to regional identity: in this case, the extent to which a Euro-American region is a direct descendant and carrier of the project of modernity and an Enlightenment rationality that places the human brain and scientific knowledge in a dangerous closeness to God's Providence. As Thiessen's **Haber** asserts: "We don't want to be God, but we all try to be more *like* God" (Thiessen, 2003, 9). From this perspective, both *Einstein's Gift* and *Copenhagen* could be deemed tragic parables of modernity that "enthroned man at the centre of epistemology" (Gandhi, 1998, 34) and, as such, made him an "all-knowing subject of consciousness—an entity which insists that our knowledge of the world is nothing other than the narcissism of self-consciousness" (35).

Thiessen's wartime play, however, is not a mere dispute over moral accountability for human action, but a modern morality play of medieval proportions, with its essential structure consisting of sin, failure, penitence, and redemption. The moral crucible of the play lies in **Haber's** rejection of his spiritual (that is, religious) home in favour of an earthly home (the German nation); its fickleness and volatility soon teach him a cruel lesson. Stripped of his citizenship and exiled from his country on account of his Jewish origin, **Haber** finds himself dying in Switzerland, a kind of purgatory, where he waits for the day of reckoning. This eventually comes with **Einstein** and his gifts—a new *Kippa*[4] and a beautiful *Tallis*.[5] As **Einstein** gives **Haber** his present, he concludes his act, which is eventually an act of retrieval, with the following words: "Welcome home Haber" (101). Home in Thiessen's world is not a physical place, but the universe articulated by means of language, of signs conventionally accepted as ours.

To conclude this brief survey: I believe that the only home, the only region as defined by the individual acts of creation I have discussed here, is represented, as in Thiessen's play, by the action of language conquering creatively and imaginatively the surrounding chaos; an act that ascribes to the world the necessary meaning that allows us to dwell in this world. Relying fully on language as a source of creative energy, all three playwrights, whose "region" is a cosmopolitan region of the world, speak confidently from their Canadian milieu, creating their own cosmos that crosses the cultures and the continents.

---

4   The *Kippa* is a skullcap worn by orthodox male Jews at all times and by others for prayers.

5   The *Tallis* is a fringed shawl worn by Jewish men during morning prayers.

Works Cited

Drader, Brian. *Prok*. Winnipeg: Scirocco Drama, 2003.

Filewod, Alan. "Between Empires: Post-Imperialism and Canadian Theatre." *Essays in Theatre / Études theâtrales* 11.1(1992): 3–15.

——. "Introduction." *The CTR Anthology: Fifteen Plays from the Canadian Theatre Review*. Ed. Alan Filewod. Toronto: University of Toronto Press, 1993, xi–xx.

Flamengo, Janice. "Regionalism and Urbanism." *The Cambridge Companion to Canadian Literature*. Ed. Eva-Marie Kröller. Cambridge, UK; New York: Cambridge University Press, 2004, 241–62.

Fraser, Brad. *Unidentified Human Remains and the True Nature of Love*. Winnipeg: Blizzard, 1990.

Frye, Northrop. *Bush Garden*. Toronto: Anansi, 1971.

——. *Divisions on a Ground: Essays on Canadian Culture*. Toronto: Anansi, 1982.

Gandhi, Leela. *Postcolonial Theory: A Critical Introduction*. Edinburgh: Edinburgh University Press, 1998.

Grant, George. *Lament for a Nation: The Defeat of Canadian Nationalism*. Ottawa: Carleton University Press, 1994; first published 1965.

Kinsey, Alfred C., Wardell B. Pomeroy, and Clyde E. Martin. *Sexual Behavior in the Human Male*. Philadelphia: W.B. Saunders Co., 1948.

Massey, Vincent. "The Prospects of a Canadian Drama." *Canadian Theatre History: Selected Readings*. Ed. Don Rubin. Toronto: Playwrights Canada Press, 2004, 50–62; first published 1922.

Moss, Laura. "Is Canada Postcolonial? Introducing the Question." *Is Canada Postcolonial?: Unsettling Canadian Literature*. Ed. Laura Moss. Waterloo, Ontario: Wilfrid Laurier University Press, 2003,1–26.

Ravenhill, Mark. *Shopping and Fucking*. London: Methuen Drama in association with the Royal Court Theatre and Out of Joint, 1997.

Schimmelpfennig, Roland. *Arabian Night*. Trans. David Tushingham. London: Oberon Books, 2002.

Thiessen, Vern. *Einstein's Gift*. *The West of All Possible Worlds: Six Contemporary Canadian plays*. Ed. Moira Day. Toronto: Playwrights Canada Press, 2004; first published 2003.

Verdecchia, Guillermo. *Fronteras Americanas (American Borders)*. Vancouver: Talon, 1997.

Walker, Craig S. *The Buried Astrolabe: Canadian Dramatic Imagination and Western Tradition*. Montréal and Kingston: McGill's-Queen's University Press, 2001.

Warner, Michael, ed. *Fear of A Queer Planet: Queer Politics and Social Theory*. Minneapolis: University of Minnesota Press, 1993.

"What is 'The Kinsey Scale'?: Kinsey's Heterosexual-Homosexual Rating Scale." The Kinsey Institute for Research in Sex, Gender and Reproduction. www.kinseyinstitute. org/research/ak-hhscale.html#what (accessed December 8, 2009).

Woodcock, George. "The Meeting of Time and Space: Regionalism in Canadian Literature." *Northern Spring: The Flowering of Canadian Literature.* Vancouver: Douglas & McIntyre, 1987; first published 1981.

Wyile, Herb. "Regionalism, Postcolonialism, and (Canadian) Writing: A Comparative Approach for Postnational Times." *Essays on Canadian Writing* 63 (1998): 139–62.

The Future of Audio Drama

ALLAN BOSS AND KELLEY JO BURKE

I n the spring of 2007 at the Congress of the Humanities at the University of Saskatchewan, Canadian Broadcasting Corporation Arts and Entertainment producers Kelley Jo Burke (Saskatchewan) and Allan Boss (Alberta) were invited, in conjunction with the "West-words" conference, to give a talk on radio drama production. Boss ran into difficulties while travelling from Calgary to Saskatoon during a late-May snowstorm (shades of "Still Stands the House") and couldn't make the session. Kelley Jo Burke presented the lecture solo.

After the event was over, Moira Day asked Burke and Boss if they would provide a written article detailing the discussion they were to give. Neither producer had prepared a formal lecture, hoping their session about radio drama would be a discussion, a question-and-answer. But seeing as Day was interested in what they had to say, they agreed to provide a document.

After some discussion Burke and Boss agreed on their format. In order to retain some of the spontaneity of the original planned session, and because they were a province apart, they began a conversation by e-mail. The article that follows (without the sound cues) is that discussion.

MUSIC.   1930S MUSIC. LIGHT, HAPPY. RECORD PLAYER POPS AND SKIPS WITH
AGE. ESTABLISH. CONTINUE UNDER.

BIZ   OVERLAPPING DIALOGUE FROM OLD RADIO PLAYS: *WAR OF THE
WORLDS, THE INVESTIGATOR, WAYNE & SCHUSTER*, ETC.

MUSIC   CRACKLES & FADE OUT.

SOUND.   SILENCE FOR A BEAT.[1]

Boss: Do you think radio plays are a dying, nearly dead, art form?

Burke: Yes. Traditional long-form radio dramas, in standard broadcast form, are dying.

Tom Stoppard was asked a few years ago when he thought the best time was to air radio drama. "1936," he answered.

The time when radio was an evocative enough medium to regularly hold the attention of a large, demographically diverse slice of the population is gone—I think. Hell, I produce 'em, and unless I'm on a long-distance drive, I don't listen to them.

However, that doesn't mean the form is worthless, just that the medium and its delivery are no longer appropriate.

The minute we [CBC] can contractually podcast[2] dramas, a whole new audience is available to us. An audience that lives with their iPods in their pockets, and loves to listen to documentaries, interview shows, and talking books will listen to plays. But *when they choose to listen*—not on a radio station's schedule.

A television viewer who has tried TiVo[3] never goes back. Why wait on the program schedule when you can watch what you like when you want it? The audio audience is the same—they are increasingly

1   The Standard format for radioplay scripts indicate SOUND, BIZ (background business), MUSIC cues in all caps and underlined, so actors can immediately distinguish between lines of dialogue and technical cues.
2   Podcasts refer to a series of digital media files, either audio or visual, which are released episodically, usually as part of an ongoing program or series, and downloaded and accessed through web syndication.
3   TiVo was developed in the late 1990s as a digital recording device that recorded material directly on to a hard drive rather than a videocassette or disc. A variety of movies, videos, television programs, photos, and music are made available to consumers on a paid subscription basis. TiVo service has been available in Canada since 2007.

content to have radio as background noise, with news updates and weather reports interspersed, but why sit around at 10 PM waiting to hear the end of a play that you walked in on halfway through, especially if you're not sure what's going on and you've got to put in another load of laundry so you're gonna miss the end anyway?

For a population accustomed to mass data access—what is called Pull Technology, in that the users pull what they want, and reject broadcasters' attempts to Push media at them—it makes no sense.

But once we can make these shows available as podcasts—I think we'll see a renaissance. Our technology for making these plays is as good as it has ever been. We have a critical mass of fine writers in the country who know how to write this stuff. We also have contemporary European models of experimentation in audio art, like the work being done in Germany, France, and the Netherlands with pure audio art creations that are essentially compositions of sound.

Canadian practitioners like Chantal Dumas[4] of Montréal, who works in pure audio art, and Chris Brookes[5] of Newfoundland, who uses audio art in the creation of radio documentary, are taking broadcast audio in exciting places that I think should inform our expansion and experimentation with the form in the performance area.

I think the opportunities for creating new forms of audio drama art are endless. We just have to find the right platform to deliver it.

In the meantime, short-form drama and comedy that represent different approaches to telling news and current affairs stories can have a place with the audience receiving their audio in real time. News editors are constantly looking for a new way to tell the story. Short comic performance pieces or dramatic audio vignettes can often expand the understanding of an issue in a way that hard-core journalism with its emphasis on objectivity cannot.

4 Chantal Dumas has produced more than twenty-five pieces broadcast on public radio in Canada and abroad (Europe, the United States, Australia). She has won two awards at the International radio competition *Phonurgia Nova* (www.phonurgia.org/ association_Us.htm) in Arles, France: the first documentary prize for *Le Petit Homme Dans La Reille* (2001) and the fiction prize for *Le Parfum Des Femmes* (1997).

5 Chris Brookes is a Canadian feature maker whose work has won numerous international awards for radio documentary. His work has been broadcast on public radio in the United States, Ireland, the Netherlands, Australia and England as well as on the CBC. His work for the latter broadcaster as a producer for a number of years in both Newfoundland and Toronto included a long stint on *Sunday Morning.*

I'm thinking of some of Rick Mercer's sketches for TV, when he was still with *This Hour Has 22 Minutes,* where he would go through a complicated news story with a pointer and a series of images on a screen, and comically haul the audience through the connections in the story that indicated idiocy, corruption, collusion, and criminality on the part of newsmakers. It was comedy. And he was performing. However, there was an educative aspect to the performance. It helped the listeners understand the actual events of the day.

I think Jason Sherman[6] was my favourite practitioner of that particular kind of radio comic drama, with David S. Craig[7] coming in a close second, though Craig is a far gentler satirist.

And I think for radio audiences geared towards listening for daily updates, there is an appetite and engagement with that sort of comedy.

I also think this generation of constant current affairs monitors do have some appetite for the issues-based radio drama that writer Emil Sher[8] has specialized in. I'm thinking of *Mourning Dove,* which was inspired by the story of Robert Latimer, or *Sibling Rivalry,* which is a speculative fiction piece about people living in a society where, like China, parents are only allowed one live birth. Because, at the time of broadcast for each of those pieces, the issues that prompted the writing of the play were still very much in the news, I think the

6   Jason Sherman's plays include *Remnants (A Fable); It's All True; Patience; Reading Hebron; The Retreat; The League of Nathans;* and *Three in the Back, Two in the Head,* which won the Governor General's Award for Drama. He has also written a number of radio dramas for CBC, including *National Affairs,* and CBC radio's most notorious radio series, *The PMO,* and is one of the founding creators of *Afghanada,* a gritty radio series about Canadians serving in Afghanistan, currently (as of 2009) airing on CBC Radio 1.

7   Playwright David S. Craig is responsible for one of CBC's most popular radio serials, *Booster McCrane,* a Capra-esque story of a small-town Western Canadian who becomes prime minister.

8   Emil Sher has written a series of highly successful and topical radio plays for the CBC, beginning with *Benefit of the Doubt,* his first long-form radio play, which was broadcast in March 1993. He is currently a contributor to the radio serial, *Afghanada.* Working in a variety of genres, including stage plays, radio dramas, short fiction, essays, and children's television, he is particularly drawn to character-driven stories, narratives fuelled by individuals struggling to navigate their way through a world rarely of their own making. His radio plays have been broadcast around the world, and three have been published in the collection, *Making Waves: Three Radio Plays* (Toronto: Simon & Pierre, 1998).

work felt relevant and engaging for an audience hungry for current news. I suspect such dramas would be serialized in shorter forms in the current broadcast climate at CBC.

But I am afraid that the true radio drama as a pure art form—which I love and believe in—will be less and less a part of the live broadcast cycle in the next ten years.

What do you think? Are there other forms of radio literature that you think have a greater chance of survival?

Boss: Other forms of literature? I think it's all been done before in one way or another. For god's sake, the award-winning CBC radio series *Afghanada*, about Canadian soldiers in Afghanistan, is traditional in form, using techniques similar to the plays in Andrew Allan's[9] *Stage* series, which began in 1942. There aren't any new literary forms. (Watch, someone will prove me wrong tomorrow and invent some new literary form!) We are in a moment of renaissance, but this renaissance is not about art; rather it is about content delivery and methods of consumption.

It's intriguing that you only listen to long-form audio dramas in your car on the way to someplace. It's the same with me. I never tune in to the radio to hear dramas unless they are my own and then it's only for a minute or two to make sure everything is up and running. But I listen in my car. I listen in the studio. I listen on my computer. I listen when and how I want to listen.

I agree with you that things will change if the CBC and the writers' union can agree on some way to make audio dramas available on the Internet. Only when listeners can decide where, when, and how to listen to whatever program they desire will the form become popular again.

I also agree with you about the accessibility of radio dramas. The audience is consuming entertainment in vastly different ways than they once were. Families aren't gathering around their radios on

---

9   Scottish-born Andrew Allan (1907-1974) was head of CBC Radio Drama from 1943 to 1955 during the Golden Age of radio drama, so named because CBC radio drama productions during this period won multiple awards, many of which were gold in colour. Allan worked with some of Canada's top actors and cultural innovators, including Mavor Moore, Lister Sinclair, Jane Mallett, William Shatner, and many others. Allan's torn office chair sits on a pedestal outside of the Toronto drama-recording studio and its ownership is metaphorically passed from one head of drama to the next.

dark winter nights, fireplace crackling in the background, in order to tune in the only form of electronic entertainment. Gone are the days of Andrew Allan. Today's audience consumes on demand.

But it's interesting and appropriate to consider the legendary radio drama producer Andrew Allan. He found himself out of a job when television started to become popular. At that time some "experts" predicted television was going to kill radio, but that didn't happen ... completely.

But we are in a period of transition, just as he was in the 1950s. For example, a film can be released one day and be accessible on the Internet the next—if you don't believe me check out one of the many bittorrent apps available on the Internet, like uTorrent, Deluge, or Vuze. The manner of consumption has changed, leaving radio drama behind and barely breathing. Nonetheless, it's still alive and still revivable, but not (it seems to me) as traditionally delivered "radio drama."

I agree with Stoppard's assertion that radio drama peaked in 1936. But we aren't talking about radio drama any more. Really, what is "radio drama?" Literally, drama delivered on the radio. But conceptually it's something else: theatre of the mind, sound and silence and mood. It's auditory storytelling.

The only way audio drama (time to quit using radio drama) could die, I think, is if people lost the ability to hear and quit loving stories. This is why audio drama remains on the radio, be it ever so humble an existence.

What elements do you look for in a great script/proposal; have those requirements changed over time?

Burke: Actually, in some ways, what I look for in a script or script proposal *has* changed radically.

I agree with you—I think I am working on audio drama, not radio plays, and what I look for in audio drama is quite different than what I was taught to look for in a radio play.

For starters, I am not very interested in physical space in audio pieces anymore—though I was trained in classical, realistic direction and production. I have pretty much given up on door opens/closes, footsteps, and cars pulling away—I mean you have to do that sometimes to convey a change in time or place without a lot of exposition, but I don't think realistic production uses the medium to its full potential.

What's the use of having a theatre of the mind, with no time/space limits, and then sticking to a rigid, natural time/space structure?

You know those sound machines that make wave noises, supposed to calm you down? Ever notice how completely unsatisfying those waves are? Like the tea Arthur Dent asks the computer to make on the Heart of Gold in *Hitchhiker's Guide to the Galaxy*? He receives a hot, brown liquid that is molecularly nearly identical to, and in no way resembles in taste—tea. That's what audio ocean waves are like—there's no thud under your feet, no salt taste on your tongue, no grumble of gulls settling. It sounds not even third best.

That's how I feel about my earlier naturalistic work—like I was making not even third-best waves. I would have been so much better off using the magic of language, and music, and impressionistic sound to create a feeling of wonder that was like the wonder I feel when I hear waves. I should have worked *in* my experiential medium, rather than using it to approximate another.

I know that if you use sub-woofers, and good sampled sound, and all kinds of wonderful tricks, you can make a naturalist soundscape that is very satisfying—but in a broadcast environment in which spoken word work is only heard in mono (CBC Radio 1 is a mono broadcast; CBC Radio 2 is the stereo broadcast and does not typically broadcast any original audio literary productions)—what's the point? You have to move into impressionism or expressionism or something that can come straight up the mono audio middle and have an effect over the car noise, or dishwasher sound, or just the hum of modern life, over which radio is listened, if you are going to serve the writing.

So rather than classic, well-made play structure, I now look for writing that seeks to explore the medium, not just make theatre for the blind.

I also have given up trying to teach prose writers how to work in spoken dialect. If a prose writer wants to be on the radio, and I think his or her work is audiophonic—that is: very concrete, with sense-based images ... with an evocative visual language ... with alliteration ... sometimes humour ... often musicality ... with narrative tension ... a strong sense of personality with which the listener can make a personal connection ... lush ... sometimes ... emotionally direct and unavoidable ... with strong sound, and musical references ... and so, primarily for the ear ... and able to carry its story in a single telling ... I just produce the prose. I don't say—hey, this would make a great radio play. Great prose writers, I have learned, are not necessarily great dialogue writers, just like many playwrights can't write a short story to save their lives. It's a different talent.

Finally, I don't shy away from one-person pieces any more, though I was taught they were death on radio. On the contrary—with an evocative and interpretive approach to the sound bed, I find single-voice pieces, especially where the focus is on the relationship between the voice and music, very compelling, and I love producing them.

One thing remains the same. I get very excited when I see something genuinely funny come across my desk. I think real humour is the rarest and most precious thing in the world, and wit is something that always works incredibly well in an audio context. If someone is genuinely witty, I will find a way to make the presentation of the writing really exploit the medium. So, ultimately, I work with traditional stage playwrights less, and comedians, screenwriters, and performance artists more, because I find them less wedded to the naturalist model than this generation of stage dramatists.

How do you find directing for radio differs from your stage directing work?

Boss: Stage play vs. radio play directing ... hmmm ... I believe directing, in whatever genre, is affected by the process every production goes through.

To begin, the script: why does one (at the CBC) choose to produce a particular script? Often these choices are made after a committee scrutinizes many proposals or scripts. One must factor the committee's voice—its focus, desires, expected outcomes, and its biases—into the producer/director's own decisions. Since the producer/director will inevitably want to fulfill those desires to ensure the possibility of future projects and continuing work, that committee voice undoubtedly influences both the creation and outcome of the project.

There are other options for production that exist at the CBC. An individual producer can be assigned a project. Again, there are influencing factors. It could be that an executive producer chose one producer over another because one had more extensive or specialized experience with a particular genre. It could be that a producer is chosen because of a regional connection to the writer or a star actor. (For example, CBC Producer Kathleen Flaherty gets the call when Thomas King is involved because of their long history working together on *Dead Dog Café Comedy Hour*.) And even if the individual producer is choosing his or her own project without a committee's influence, that producer will desire to fulfill CBC expectations. All those factors influence directing.

Burke: And I want to give a little shout out here to Western writers. I think that when they do get produced by CBC it's often because of their isolation from the eastern theatrical community. A lot of writers in Western Canada come to radio plays as a way to make a living in their profession. Because main-stage theatre productions are thin on the ground in Western Canada, especially for alternative theatre playwrights, many of the writers are coming into radio with alternative backgrounds. So they're coming far more often from alternative theatre backgrounds, including film writing, or performance theatre, and actually bring fewer of the conventional theatrical assumptions to their audio writing. I think there's a freshness to Western work, and writers' willingness to simply tell the story without any reference to any theatrical tradition can be a real positive for radio writing. Sorry to interrupt. What happens next, Allan?

Boss: That's okay, Kelley Jo. I'm totally interested in Western Canadian writers and radio plays; in fact, I wrote an article for *Canadian Theatre Review* a couple of years back called "CBC Radio Drama in Alberta: Featuring Wild Rose Writers"[10] about many Western radio dramatists including Sharon Pollock, Frank Moher, and Blake Brooker. So I understand your passion.

Back to stage vs. radio directing. In radio the producer either has a script or a proposal for the creation/writing of a script. If the script already exists, the producer skips a developmental step and moves on to casting, a process I will address in a moment.

Developing a script is another process that is part of the bigger process; it involves meetings and emails and phone calls with the writer in order to shape the script. This is one place that audio drama

10   Boss, Allan. "CBC Radio Drama in Alberta: Featuring Wild Rose Writers." *Canadian Theatre Review* 136 (Fall 2008): 34.

development differs from that of the stage play; (in my experience) radio scripts are not workshopped; a group of actors does not come in to read the play to help the writer develop his or her new script. I've seen that process happen with radio programs, but not individual dramas; that being said, collectively written dramas like *Afghanada*— projects that are not one-offs, and that have a number of writers and an ensemble cast—inevitably undergo a developmental process. Either way, individual radio producer/directors will be motivated by the work and how it develops; they will make discoveries about the script that will influence their directorial choices.

Of course, the next step is casting. This is the moment, I believe, that "decides" the fate of the play; for it is in this moment—the choosing of the play's "voice"—that each producer makes an ultimate directorial decision. Personally, I look for acting talent and ability, experience and enthusiasm, and the manner in which the actor takes direction.

But here is another significant difference between stage and audio: where on stage a director might be concerned with casting actors who can make a certain visual impression for the audience, with audio drama the "look" is about voice. I make sure the cast has varied vocal tones and timbres. (If there's one thing I hate it's an audio drama where different characters have similar voices and I can't figure out who is talking!)

Additionally, while stage directors need actors capable of projecting their voices "live" in theatre spaces of varying sizes, in audio drama projection is not an issue as recorded sound is intimate; a high-quality microphone centimetres from an actor's face can pick up the slightest breath or waver or shake of a word. For audio drama the actor is speaking to one person: the audience is usually alone, driving a car or baking a cake or changing spark plugs. The actors are not projecting to five hundred people in a conventional theatre.

Adding dimensionality to sound, however, does become a priority for me in audio drama: having actors slowly turn into a microphone in order to imitate an approach, using different microphones and spaces to create different settings. A concrete jail cell will sound different than a stadium, which again will sound different from the inside of a stomach. I use the tools I have to create whatever environment I desire. This can be realistic, surrealistic, unrealistic, musical, wet, dry, silent, noisy, or anything one might want. I can record in an actual location if that's desirable.

My hope as a director is to make every audio drama I work on the best it can be by using (or not using) every method at my disposal. I believe realism works, as does expressionism, impressionism, surrealism, or whatever "ism" one suggests. I would not negate any method. The only thing I would negate is the forcing of method. Every piece has a life of its own, and I believe that life arises organically out of the process through which it develops. I believe simple is better.

That's part of how my audio directing process differs from stage, but in many ways it is similar. All I desire is to make the piece the best I can.

And I haven't even begun to discuss post-production, which is a huge part of creating audio drama. It's in post-production that the producer decides which "takes" to use, which to cut according to time, how to affect voice with any of many studio techniques like reverb (so useful to indicate interior monologues), and this is the time to add extra sound, to provide the layers. For example, a scene I remember from the production of Clem Martini's *Conversations with my Neighbour's Pitbull* took place on the front porch of a house during a summer afternoon. I'd recorded the scene with actors in the studio. And as we both know, studios do not scream summer afternoon. So after I'd edited the scene I added sounds that included, as a base, a summer day in the suburbs. Now, you and I both know that outdoor summer audio tracks are most often indicated by maybe a soft breeze through tree leaves and typically the sound of birds. But it's important to choose a bird that will place the listener where you want them: a mountain raven puts a listener in a far different place than a jungle parrot. But for this I chose robins, or something like that. Then, I added a layer of distant traffic, and to instantaneously make this a summer day in the suburbs, I added that immediately identifiable sound of … a distant lawn mower. Boom. The listeners know where they are and the time of day. In this way, audio drama is similar to film, and oh so different from theatre. With audio drama the piece is given life in post-production, in the studio, long after the actors are home sipping a glass of red wine. It is not simultaneous. But that's another discussion.

I often find myself adding to, or deleting, sounds the writer put into the script because they just don't fit, or they really do fit. When you're in post-production, how closely do you follow the sound cues suggested in the script?

Burke: Like most questions worth asking, the answer is "depends." If the writer is someone with a very clear aural sense, I would ignore the sound cues at my peril. Many aren't. And if they do put in sound cues, they are often of the "we hear a red dress rustle" category. ... How exactly does a dress *sound* red?

Often the best production clues come from the kind of music the writer hears with the piece. Because many, many writers reference film when writing radio scripts, they hear film scores in their imaginations more than sound cues.

One of my jobs, before a script goes to studio, is to take all the lines the playwright has included as exposition (to help with the visual to auditory translation) and figure out how many can simply be done with sound. And then cut, cut, cut the talk.

Audio drama really is its own art form. There are only a handful of people who tell their stories through sound initially, and without translation. Many writers come to radio writing with a visual imagination that I try to translate to the auditory. When radio drama was a more commonly accessed form, I suspect there were more people who did that naturally. It is not common; many writers come to audio drama without even having heard a real radio play. And so the translation into sound art is often and essentially my job.

Boss: This is all interesting to me, Kelley Jo. There is one final point I'd like to make, and it is an offshoot of a comment you just made. I've so often heard that audio drama sounds "old." As in old-fashioned. As in affected. As in ... bad. But when I ask *What was the last audio drama you listened to?*, the same person will pause, the silence pregnant with meaning, and will nudge the conversation in another direction. So I'm thinking: the reason people say audio drama sounds "old" is that the only ones they've heard are from the 1940s. And even though these same people might have heard a short play on *Sounds Like Canada* or a half-hour drama on a Friday morning, they wouldn't recognize these as audio dramas. Why? Because audio dramas sound old and these don't.

Audio drama is a wonderful medium. It is malleable, far quicker to make than film, far more controllable than stage, and can elicit responses that the other mediums cannot. Why? Because it involves the audience's mind. Listeners build images using words and sounds. So in that way they must be willing participants—and not in a "suspension of disbelief" way, but actively. Perhaps that is why some people love audio drama, and others would rather lick the posts on a nine-volt battery.

But for those who love it, the investment is similar to reading. I contend that audio drama is the most literary of the dramatic genres; it is the one where poetry works best, where description and fluidity are paramount, where words and harmony and sound work together as music. Ethereal, effervescent, cerebral—complex, yet simple—an inviting and compelling investment.

Burke: Absolutely. My pitch to writers is that audio drama is the most intimate of performance arts. It enters the consumer's consciousness like a lover's whisper in the ear and, done right, establishes a very personal place in the consciousness. I look forward to its next phase of evolution.

MUSIC.   MODERN MOOD MUSIC—ARVO PÄRT OR PHILLIP GLASS—SNEAKS IN UNDER FINAL SPEECH. FADE UP, THEN OUT AS THE MUSIC MOVES TOWARDS SOMETHING, THEN FINALLY HANGS IN TIME.

—end—

Works Cited

Boss, Allan. "CBC Radio Drama in Alberta: Featuring Wild Rose Writers." *Canadian Theatre Review* 136 (Fall 2008): 34.

Contributors

Arnd Bohm received his PhD in German from The Johns Hopkins University in 1984. He now teaches in the Department of English at Carleton University as a Professor of English. He has also been an adjunct professor in the Department of German at Queen's University (Kingston, Ontario). His areas of research interest include German and English literary history from 1700 to the present, Anglo-German literary relations, and the history of ideas. He has published on German women writers (Luise Gottsched; Charlotte von Stein; Sidonie Hedwig von Zäunemann) and on gender and style. Recent publications include "Wordsworth's 'Nutting' and the Ovidian 'Nux'" (*Studies in Romanticism*) and "Increasing Suspicion about Browning's Grammarian" *Victorian Poetry*); *Goethe and European Epic: Forgetting the Future* (Camden House); "Naming Goethe's Faust" (*Deutsche Vierteljahrsschrift*); and "Just Beauty: Ovid and the Argument of Keats's 'Ode on a Grecian Urn'" (*Modern Language Quarterly*).

Claire Borody is an Associate Professor in the Department of Theatre and Film at the University of Winnipeg where she teaches studio and theory courses in theatre and performance. Her research interests include 20th–21st century acting and performance theory, devised and collectively conceived performance work and the documentation of original process, inter-disciplinary performance, cross-cultural performance, and contemporary Canadian theatre. She is the former Artistic Director of Avera Theatre, a devised theatre company, which she founded in 2003. She has also worked extensively with devised theatre companies, out of line theatre, and theatre fix, since 2003. She has extensive experience as a freelance director, dramaturge, and creative consultant on various independent theatre and dance projects and has published articles and reviews in *Canadian Theatre Review, Canadian Literature, The University of Toronto Quarterly* and *Prairie Fire*. With colleague Per Brask she is the co-founder of the online journal *Canadian Journal for Practice-based Research in Theatre* on which she serves as co-editor with Monica Prendergast.

Allan Boss is Cultural and Historical Services Team Leader in Okotoks. There he programs, curates, and directs gallery and museum exhibits, while producing music and theatrical productions in the Rotary Performing Arts Centre. Before Okotoks, he worked for CBC as Drama Producer.

His successes included producing and hosting *Alberta Anthology* and editing two book anthologies. He also wrote/narrated a docudrama called *Updrafts,* which won nominations for the Peabody, New York Festivals, Gabriel, and Prix Italia awards. Other projects he produced and/or directed for the CBC include: *Conversations with my Neighbor's Pitbull* by Clem Martini; *Andrew Allan's Chair* by Blake Brooker; and *An Eye For An Eye* by Ghost River Theatre. *An Eye For An Eye* represented CBC at the world festival of radiodrama, *Worldplay 2007.* A regular contributor to *Canadian Theatre Review* and *Blue Skies Poetry,* he has a BFA in Writing from the University of Victoria, an MFA in Film Production from the Mel Hoppenhein School of Cinema at Concordia University, and a PhD in Drama from the University of Calgary. *Identifying Mavor Moore* and *Discovering Mavor Moore* (Playwrights Canada Press), two new books by Boss, hit store shelves in 2011.

Kelley Jo Burke is an award-winning playwright and poet, a director, storyteller, documentarian, and broadcaster. Her plays have been produced and published in Canada and around the world, including her stage plays, *Ducks on the Moon, The Selkie Wife, Jane's Thumb,* and *Charming and Rose: True Love,* and her most recent radio play *Big Ocean,* which was heard in seven countries in 2000. She is the 2009 recipient of the Saskatchewan Lieutenant-Governor's Award for Leadership in the Arts, the 2009 recipient of the City of Regina Writing Award, the 2008 recipient of a Saskatoon and Area Theatre Award for playwriting, and was a nominee for the 2009 City of Regina Mayor's Award for Innovation in the Arts. She dramaturges, directs, and produces for stage and radio, is still the host/producer of CBC Saskatchewan's radio art performance hour *SoundXchange,* and has written and produced a number of documentaries for CBC Radio's *Ideas.*

Pam Bustin was born in Regina, Saskatchewan, and raised in a host of small towns across the Prairies. She currently lives *mostly* in Saskatoon with a lovely man and 1001 books—though she still tends to wander. Pam's play *Saddles in the Rain* had its world premiere at 25th Street Theatre in Saskatoon, won the John V. Hicks Manuscript Award, and is published in the anthology *The West of all Possible Worlds.* Her other stage plays include *barefoot* and *The Passage of Georgia O'Keeffe,* which have travelled to Fringe Theatre Festivals across Canada. Three of her radio dramas (*Coffee in Lloyd, The White Car Project,* and *Talking with the Dead*) have aired nationally on the CBC and her fiction and non-fiction work has appeared in *The New Quarterly, Cahoots Magazine, Spring!,* and *Transitions.* Her novel, *Mostly Happy,* won the First Book and Fiction awards at the Saskatchewan Book Awards (2008), made the Pennsylvania School Librarians Association's YA Top Forty Fiction List, and won the Ontario Library Association's White Pine Award (2010).

Moira Day is an Associate Professor of Drama and Adjunct Professor in the Women's and Gender Studies Department at the University of Saskatchewan. She has published and edited extensively in the area of Canadian theatre. A former co-editor of *Theatre Research in Canada* (1998–2001) she has also edited two scholarly play anthologies featuring the work of pioneering and contemporary Western Canadian playwrights. She has also co-edited two special issues of *Theatre Research in Canada*: Canadian Theatre Within the Context of World Theatre (with Don Perkins, University of Alberta), and Theatre and Religion in Canada (with Mary Ann Beavis of St. Thomas More College, University of Saskatchewan).

Kathleen Foreman is a performing artist and teacher specializing in actor training, improvisation, performance creation, mask creation and performance, Forum theatre, theatre for young audiences, creative pedagogy, and educational drama. She is an original member of the Loose Moose Theatre Company and masQuirx: a company of masks and mask performance. She is a Professor in the Department of Drama at the University of Calgary.

Louise H. Forsyth is Professor Emerita and Adjunct Professor, University of Saskatchewan, in Women's and Gender Studies, Languages and Linguistics. Her research is on women playwrights and poets of Québec, feminist theories of theatricality, theatre translation, and professional francophone theatre in Saskatchewan. She is a founding member of CATR/ARTC, from which she received an award of lifetime achievement. Administrative positions include: Chair, Department of French (UWO), Dean, Graduate Studies and Research (Saskatchewan), President, Humanities and Social Sciences Federation of Canada. She has published articles and books in her areas of research. Her three-volume anthology of Québec women's plays in English translation (twenty-eight plays covering the period of 1966–2009) is published by Playwrights Canada Press.

Katherine Foster Grajewski is a doctoral student at the Graduate Centre for Study of Drama, University of Toronto. She holds an MA in drama from the University of Toronto and a BA in English from the University of Manitoba. Katherine's current research interests are in intercultural theatre practice with an emphasis on the dissemination of practical and training methodologies across cultural boundaries. Recently Katherine worked as the Co-Artistic Director for the "Festival of Original Theatre: Dissolving Borders," a student-run conference and performance festival that took place at the Graduate Centre for Study of Drama at the University of Toronto in February 2009.

Don Kerr is the author of nine books of poetry, seven plays, a short fiction collection, a teen fiction novel, and non-fiction books on politics and the history of the city of Saskatoon. He served on the Saskatoon Public Library Board for eleven years, and as chair for five of those years. He was the first chair of the Saskatoon Heritage Society and the first chair of the Saskatoon Municipal Heritage Committee. He was elected Saskatchewan Governor for the Heritage Canada Foundation. He is the Poet Laureate for Saskatchewan.

Alan Long is a theatre artist and writer who lives and works in Saskatoon. Completed in October 2007, his interdisciplinary MA thesis, titled *George Mann was not a Cowboy: Rationalizing Western versus Aboriginal Versions of Life and Death "Dramatic" History*, was an analysis of the competing narratives of the short historical event 'The Escape to Fort Pitt,' that took place on April 2, 1885. Part of the thesis was a play titled *Friends or Friendlies?*, which engages multiple voices from Aboriginal and non-Aboriginal cultures, past and present, to reveal the complexity of Canadian colonial history. Recent publications include "Emory Creek: The Environmental Legacy of Gold Mining on the Fraser River," *British Columbia History* 39.3 (Spring 2007). Alan has worked as an acting teacher at the University of Saskatchewan and in several capacities at Saskatchewan Native Theatre Company including teacher, director, and production manager. He recently accepted the position of general manager with the company.

Hope McIntyre has a BFA in theatre performance from the University of Saskatchewan, an MFA in directing from the University of Victoria, and completed a performance apprenticeship in England. Hope is in her tenth year as Artistic Director of Sarasvàti Productions. She is a published playwright and has received awards and productions for her scripts across Canada, the U.S., and Australia. Her directing credits include: *Grace and After* (Alumnae Theatre), *Drama At Inish* (Toronto Irish Players), *A Streetcar Named Desire* (Rubber Gun Productions), *Risk Everything* (venus.calm), *Revisioning* (Short Pencil Productions) and numerous productions for Sarasvàti Productions. In 2006 Hope was awarded the YWCA Women of Distinction Award for Arts and Culture. She has taught theatre at Mount Allison University, Brandon University, and the University of Manitoba. She currently teaches at the University of Winnipeg's Department of Theatre and Film and is Past President of the Playwrights Guild of Canada (Dec 20, 2009).

Bruce McManus has written twenty plays, including *The Chinese Man Said Goodbye, Ordinary Days, Schedules, Calenture,* and *Selkirk Avenue,* which was nominated for a Governor General's Award for Drama in 1998 and has been produced in both Canada and the United States. Adaptations for the stage include *Three Sisters* and *A Doll's House* produced at Prairie Theatre Exchange in 1998 and *A Christmas Carol* produced at Manitoba Theatre Centre in 2005. His newest work, *All Restaurant Fires Are Arson,* was produced at Prairie Theatre Exchange in the 2007–08 season. He has also written for radio and film. He served as Artistic Director of Theatre Projects Manitoba, a professional company devoted to developing and producing new work by Manitoba playwrights (1995–2000), was a founding member of the Manitoba Association of Playwrights, regularly works as a dramaturge and mentor to many established and developing playwrights, and continues to work closely with the school, community, university, and professional theatre communities in Winnipeg. He has been playwright-in-residence at various times at Manitoba Theatre Centre, Prairie Theatre Exchange, the University of Winnipeg, and the Manitoba Association of Playwrights. He was writer-in-residence at the Winnipeg Public Library from October 2008 until August 2009.

Glen Nichols is Director of Drama at Mount Allison University in Sackville, NB. He has published articles on theatre history, theatre translation, and Acadian theatre. He translated a collection of five contemporary Acadian plays published by Playwrights Canada Press in 2003 under the collective title *Angels and Anger: Five Contemporary Acadian Plays in Translation.* One of his translations, Laval Goupil's *Le Djibou* (*Dark Owl*) was selected for production at the National Theatre School in

Montréal and was also presented in June 2003 at the Magnetic North Theatre Festival in Ottawa. Glen Nichols served as president of the Association of Theatre Research in Canada from 2004 to 2008 and is currently editor of *Theatre Research in Canada*.

Anne Nothof is Professor Emerita of English at Athabasca University in Alberta, Canada, where she has developed and taught undergraduate and postgraduate distance education courses in literature and drama. She has published critical essays in journals such as *Theatre Research in Canada, Modern Drama, Mosaic,* and the *International Journal of Canadian Studies,* and in two texts on postmodern theatre: *Siting the Other* and *Crucible of Cultures.* She has contributed essays on Canadian theatre for Camden House's *History of Literature in Canada* and the *Cambridge History of Canadian Literature.* She has edited a collection of essays on Canadian playwright Sharon Pollock for Guernica Press, a collection of essays on Alberta theatre for Playwrights Canada Press, and an issue of *Canadian Theatre Review* on Alberta theatre. For NeWest, she has edited collections of Alberta plays, novels, and creative non-fiction; and for Playwrights, a collection of Alberta plays entitled *The Alberta Advantage.* Her most recent publication, "No Cowpersons on this Range: The Cultural Complexity of Alberta Theatre," in *Wild Words: Essays on Alberta Literature,* published by AU Press in 2009 is available online. She is a board member and editor for NeWest Press and AU Press, and past president of the Canadian Association for Theatre Research. She is also editor for the *Canadian Theatre Encyclopedia* (www. canadiantheatre.com).

Mieko Ouchi is an Edmonton-based actor, writer, director, and filmmaker and a graduate of the University of Alberta BFA Acting Program. Her full-length plays *The Red Priest (Eight Ways To Say Goodbye), The Blue Light,* and *The Dada Play* have been produced across the country and in the United States and have been shortlisted for the 4 Play Series at The Old Vic in London, the Governor General's Literary Award for Drama, and the City of Edmonton Book Prize, winning the Canadian Authors Association's Carol Bolt Prize. Her plays are published by Playwrights Canada Press and are translated into French, Japanese, Russian, and Czech. They have been read and/ or produced by Alberta Theatre Projects, Chekhov International Theatre Festival, Centre des Auteurs Dramatiques in Montreal, Citadel Theatre, Concrete Theatre, DMV Theatre Collective, Firehall

Arts Centre, Globe Theatre, Keyano Theatre, NAC On The Verge Festival, NYU hotINK International Reading Series, Red Deer College, St. Mary's University College, Tarragon Theatre, Thousand Island Playhouse, Workshop West Theatre, and the University of Oklahoma. Her essays have been published in CTR, *Swerve Magazine* and in *Reel Asian: Asian Canada on Screen* for Coach House Press. Mieko is a co-founder and artistic co-director of Concrete Theatre and was the inaugural Faith Broome playwright-in-residence in 2009 at the University of Oklahoma. Her new play, *Nisei Blue*, is premiering at Alberta Theatre Projects in 2011.

Wes D. Pearce is currently Associate Dean (Undergraduate) for the Faculty of Fine Arts (University of Regina) where he teaches design and general interest theatre courses. His research focuses on three distinct areas: contemporary Canadian scenography (and its practice), issues of homophobia and queer identity in theatre, and issues of pedagogy, ethics, and community. He sits on the board of the Associated Designers of Canada and has designed dozens of productions for many theatres including: Globe Theatre, Persephone Theatre, Alberta Theatre Projects, Western Canada Theatre, and Prairie Theatre Exchange. He is an active member of a number of theatre associations/societies and currently sits on the executive of the Association for Canadian Theatre Research and the Saskatchewan Drama Association.

John Poulsen is an Associate Professor at the University of Lethbridge in the Faculty of Education. His main focus is Drama Education—both Drama as a distinct subject and Drama integrated with other areas. He also instructs in the area of Evaluation and Curriculum. He directed "Rockies Revealed" for Parks Canada, which received a Silver Award for Excellence. He is a founding member of "masQuirx," a mask creation and performance company.

Martin Pšenička completed a PhD on contemporary Canadian playwrights in the Theatre Department at Masaryk University in the Czech Republic and is now an Assistant Professor at The Department of Theatre Studies of Faculty of Arts and Philosophy, Charles University, Prague. Over 2004–08, he received several scholarships to study Canadian, and particularly Western-Canadian, theatre and drama at the University of Saskatchewan. His current research focuses on contemporary theatre and performance theories. Martin Pšenička is a member of a Czech-Japanese theatre company, The Little Theatre of Kyogen.

Shelley Scott is Chair and Associate Professor in the Department of Theatre and Dramatic Arts at the University of Lethbridge, where she teaches Theatre History, Canadian Theatre, and special topics courses in Dramatic Literature and Theory, and occasionally directs department productions. Shelley has published in *Modern Drama, Canadian Theatre Review, Theatre Research in Canada, Resources for Feminist Research,* and the *British Journal of Canadian Studies.* In 2007 her book *The Violent Woman as a New Theatrical Character Type: Cases from Canadian Drama* was published by The Edwin Mellen Press, and in 2010 *Nightwood Theatre: A Woman's Work is Always Done* was published by Athabasca University Press. Shelley is the current president of the Canadian Association for Theatre Research.

Index

A

A Kingdom of My Own, 124

Aberhart, William, 222–23, 222n6, 230, 232, 237

The Aberhart Summer, 194

Aboriginal Peoples Television Network (APTN), 155

Aboriginals/Aboriginal theatre: across Canada, 142–44; in Alberta, 189, 225; and Circle of Voices program, 150–54; in Finding Regina, 269–70; future of, 156–57; historical relationship with Saskatchewan francophone community; 128, 131; and K. Williams, 154–55; and Len Borgerson, 149–50; marginalization of, 140–41; and Maria Campbell, 145–49; Saskatchewan productions of, 82, 160–61; training for, 142–43, 150–52. see also Saskatchewan Native Theatre Company

Above the Line (Chicago), 119

Absolute Perfection, 24–27, colour insert photos 3, 4

Adams, Philip, 118

Adhere and Deny, 42–43, 42n5

Afghanada, 286n6, 286n8, 287, 292. see also CBC

The Afternoon Edition, 120. see also CBC

Agassiz Theatre, 4, 6

Agee, James, 248

Albert, Lyle Victor, 181, 182, 195–96

Alberta Aboriginal Arts, 189

Alberta Book Award for Drama, 123

Alberta College of Art and Design, 184

Alberta Playwrights Network (APN), xiii, 118

Alberta Report: arts coverage as Saint John's Edmonton Report, 218–221, as Alberta Report, xviii, 221–22, 225–27, 229–30; downfall of, 227–28, 230–32;

rise of, 216n3, 221–22, 222n7; timeline, 237–43

Alberta Theatre Projects (ATP) (Calgary), xiii, xvii, 103n11, 103n12, 106n17, 111n22, 117, 118, 119, 121, 122, 124, 165n1, 182, 183, 184, 185, 186, 187, 189, 195, 202, 214n1, 215n2

Alexander the Great, 110, 118

Alkoremmi, 32

Almost Home, 117

All Restaurant Fires Are Arson, 18

All These Heels, 182

Allan, Andrew, 287, 287n9, 288

Allen, Kent, 126

Allen, Lauren, 138

The Alley, 151, 152, 160

Allison, Kathy, 124

Almighty Voice and His Wife, 189

alternative theatre: criticism of, 36–37, 41–42, 45; funding bias against, 37–38; lack of documentation on, 46–48; marginalization of, 37–43; struggle for survival in Winnipeg, 42–46

Alto, Bradley, colour insert photo 16

Alumnae Theatre (Toronto), 29

Amateur theatre, xii, 77, 78, 258

Amos, Janet, 121

Anderson, Alan B., 142n6, 145n14

Anderson, Wendy, 126

Andy and Annie, 109, 119

ANDPAVA. see Assocation for Native Development in the Performing and Visual Arts

Angel Claire, 126

Angels Are Us, 111, 117

Angelstad, Sheila, 127

Annabelle, 161

Annie Mae's Movement, 161

Anniversary, 51, 53, 55–57, 60, 65, 69

H

ENVIRONMENTAL BENEFITS STATEMENT

CPRC Press, University of Regina saved the following resources by printing the pages of this book on chlorine free paper made with 100% post-consumer waste.

TREES	WATER	SOLID WASTE	GREENHOUSE GASES
13	5,734	348	1,191
FULLY GROWN	GALLONS	POUNDS	POUNDS

Environmental impact estimates were made using the Environmental Paper Network Paper Calculator. For more information visit www.papercalculator.org.